Women and Employment in Public Policy

Women and Employment in Public Policy

Learning from the UK Women and Work Commission (2004–2009)

Susan Milner

OXFORD
UNIVERSITY PRESS

OXFORD
UNIVERSITY PRESS

Great Clarendon Street, Oxford, OX2 6DP,

United Kingdom

Oxford University Press is a department of the University of Oxford.
It furthers the University's objective of excellence in research, scholarship,
and education by publishing worldwide. Oxford is a registered trade mark of
Oxford University Press in the UK and in certain other countries

Published in the United States of America by Oxford University Press

198 Madison Avenue, New York, NY 10016, United States of America

British Library Cataloguing in Publication Data
Data available

Library of Congress Control Number: 2023951853

ISBN 9780198875437

DOI: 10.1093/9780191987359.001.0001

Printed and bound by
CPI Group (UK) Ltd, Croydon, CR0 4YY

Foreword by Mary-Ann Stephenson

An event on the gender pay gap in early 2000s organized by the Women and Equality Unit. In the room, government ministers, civil servants, trade unionists, feminist campaigners, and academics. We have just finished listening to a presentation on the various elements contributing to the gender pay gap. The Minister thanks the speaker, smiles, and says, 'as you academics often say, "further work needs to be done in this area"'. 'We don't need more research,' responds the speaker; 'we know what needs to be done, we need the government to do it.'

The scene sums up so much from the experience of feminist campaigners during the New Labour years—the doors of government are open, ministers engage and express support, and evidence is collected and presented. But the action needed to see real change does not materialize.

As we read this account of a 'stalled revolution' for women in the workplace, the frustrations of many of the interviewees are all too familiar. Despite the committed efforts of feminists in key positions in trade unions, in the civil service, and on the back benches, the tireless work of ministers like Harriet Harman, and the research and lobbying of academics and campaigners, women's policy demands have often been marginalized by the men at the centre of government.

Some victories were possible, but only where women could link their demands to the priorities of the men in charge. The Women's Budget Group (WBG) succeeded in ensuring that child tax credits were paid to the 'main carer' (usually a woman), rather than the 'main earner' (usually a man), by showing that this was the best way to ensure that money was spent on children. The WBG, the Fawcett Society, and others have argued successfully that Gordon Brown's ambition to end child poverty could only be achieved by tackling women's poverty. This got the issue on the political agenda, but we knew it framed women's incomes as a priority only in relation to their role as mothers. A wider focus on the gendered nature of poverty was far harder to achieve.

At times this strategy of reframing demands to fit the government's priorities worked for some groups of women but not for others. Campaigners for greater flexibility in working hours were repeatedly told by supportive ministers and officials that we needed to make a 'business case' for flexible working. This largely rested on the recruitment costs incurred if women left the workplace because they could not fit their paid work around caring responsibilities. But this argument was always more powerful when applied to well-paid, more senior staff, in whom companies might have invested a great deal in training and who were more expensive to replace. For companies whose business model was based on low pay and which already factored in relatively high turnover, these 'business-case' arguments were less likely to resonate.

As Professor Milner shows, the New Labour years were marked by considerable activity around women's economic position. The Women and Work Commission, around whose work this book is framed, was part of a wider series of reviews, consultations, and round-table meetings to address equal pay and low pay, flexible work, women in senior management, and maternity, paternity, and parental leave. Some of these were a response to EU legislation, and some the result of feminist campaigns inside and outside government. But all too often high ambition led to watered-down policy. As is pointed out in this book, 'commissions and ad hoc committees ... have generally been seen as a way of deferring action', and it is difficult to disagree with that view.

Many of the advances that were seen, such as the increasing number of women in senior positions in the public sector, were quickly undermined following the 2010 election and the formation of the Coalition Government. The austerity policies introduced by the Coalition hit women hardest. As the WBG and others argued, women were hit by a 'triple whammy', as those most likely to rely on public services and social security, those most likely to work in the public sector, and those most likely to have to increase their unpaid work to fill the gaps when public services were cut.

Austerity also undermined key elements of the legislative framework for equality introduced by Labour. One of the last acts of the Labour Government had been the Public Sector Equality Duty (PSED), contained in the 2010 Equality Act. Many had hoped the PSED would deliver a transformative approach to equality by refocusing attention from outlawing discrimination to placing a positive duty on public bodies to promote equality. But the incoming Coalition Government weakened the specific duties proposed by Labour and argued that equality impact assessments (a key tool for public bodies to meet their obligations under the PSED) were unnecessary red tape. In this context, equality initiatives were easily cut by public bodies trying to protect 'front-line services' in the face of major reductions to their budgets from central government.

At the same time, the opportunities for the women's sector to organize were reduced by the closure of the Women's National Commission (WNC), which had been the voice of the women's voluntary sector to government since the 1960s. The WNC was closed in the 'bonfire of the quangos' shortly after the election, removing a vital element of the 'women's policy machinery'.

This book provides an important review of the frustrations and compromises of the 'stalled revolution' and shows how easily many of the changes that were achieved could be unpicked by a change of government. But it also reminds us that, despite the problems and barriers detailed by the interviewees, women still achieved change, some of which has remained. Although the pay gap remains, it was reduced by the National Minimum Wage, which had a significant impact on the lowest paid women. Women's participation in the labour market has continued to increase. The PSED may not have delivered on a vision of transformation, but it was a useful tool for unions and others in some legal challenge to austerity policies. Attempts to undermine the Equality Act using the 'red-tape challenge' did not succeed. And the legal protection for all-women shortlists and other positive action measures delivered an increase in women's political representation, which has been sustained since 1997.

This history provides important lessons for future policy development. It shows that high aspirations do not always translate into transformative policy, preparing us for struggles ahead. And it reminds us that hard-won changes can be lost again with a change of government. But it also shows that change is possible where women inside and outside government work together.

Dr Mary-Ann Stephenson

Director, Women's Budget Group
June 2023

Preface

The research that forms the basis of this book began in the shadow of the Covid-19 pandemic. Of course, I had not anticipated this when I first thought of the project, in early 2019. The questions I sought to answer had been raised in an earlier investigation, conducted under the auspices of the Institute for Policy Research at the University of Bath in 2018. Triggered by the outcome of the referendum in May 2016 on the UK's membership of the European Union (EU), the earlier project sought to understand the likely impact of withdrawal on women's employment rights. The discussions I had with a range of policy actors in 2018 convinced me of the need to look back at the earlier period when, under a Labour administration, the UK had signed up to the Amsterdam Treaty, including what had previously been a social chapter of the treaty with a British opt-out, and transposed the European directives on parental leave and part-time working. Several respondents also drew attention to the difficulties faced by the voluntary sector in a tougher funding environment (exacerbated by the loss of EU support) and expressed regret at the loss in 2010 of the Women's National Commission, which had raised the voice of women's campaign organizations.

I decided to focus on the Women and Work Commission (WWC), which in 2006 had produced a report widely regarded (and still referred to) as an authoritative set of evidence and recommendations on women's situation in the labour market, and to investigate what had changed in the intervening period. In January 2020, I met Baroness Prosser (who had chaired the WWC) for the first time in the House of Lords. The meeting reassured me that the project was feasible and that it had something to contribute to current concerns: Baroness Prosser spoke of her plans to introduce a private member's bill to strengthen gender pay gap reporting, which she presented several days later.[1]

By early 2020, when I started to plan interviews for my Leverhulme Major Research Fellowship, conditions for research were about to change unexpectedly. Meanwhile, the labour market was on the verge of drastic upheaval, with many female-dominated occupations in health and social care subjected to intensification of working conditions and exposure to serious illness, while other female-dominated occupations such as retail shut down, sometimes resulting in long-term job losses.

In March, I had arranged to meet Kay Carberry (former assistant general secretary of the Trades Union Congress, and a member of the WWC) in London, when disquiet about the Covid-19 virus was starting to spread. We decided to speak remotely, and I carried out my first online interview. It was a time of shock and anxiety, with the labour market in collapse at the start of lockdown. In such times, did it make sense to talk about debates on women and work from nearly two decades ago?

Even before the pandemic ripped into our lives, weakened entire sectors of the economy, and set women's fragile rights back, so much had changed since 2006: women were present in the labour market in greater numbers than ever, but still concentrated in low-paid jobs and sectors, while progress at the top was painfully slow. More than ever, women were trapped in part-time work with low pay and little control over hours, and their labour-market status had if anything become more precarious.

As evidence grew in 2020 of women's continued vulnerability to job losses, insecure work contracts, and low pay, as well as unsafe working conditions,[2] I became even more convinced that learning about the past can still help us to understand what is happening now. Indeed, in many ways the pandemic has highlighted how important and undervalued women's work is, and how much policy needs to address its vulnerability. Yet governments in recent years have done little to tackle these problems: a long-awaited employment bill based on Matthew Taylor's 2016 proposals on 'good work'[3] was repeatedly shelved (although, as discussed in the first chapter of this book, plans to make it easier to access the right to request flexible working were announced in December 2022), and the parenting and care strategy promised in 2019 following a national consultation was not presented.[4] At time of writing this book, calls to build a 'caring economy'[5] to support the country out of the pandemic and build a stronger society remain unanswered.

My original interest in this project was based on a conviction that solutions to social problems require attention from a range of actors, not just a group of political leaders and civil servants drawn from a narrow social pool. The WWC's composition reflected a belief that the world of work needs to be represented in policy. As we live with the economic consequences of the pandemic, there is growing evidence that this approach works best to support fragile economies into recovery.

Another reason for my long-term interest in the commission lies in its broad-based approach to understanding women's situation in the British labour market. Several, although not all, of the commissioners were associated with the wider Labour project, which saw women's labour-market disadvantage as part of a wider set of social inequalities. Understanding women's employment was not just about the choices and constraints they faced as women, but about those they faced as women coping with other structural factors such as living in areas of socio-economic disadvantage, or a poor start in life owing to inadequate access to educational opportunities, as well as discrimination on grounds of disability, nationality, or the colour of their skin. The title of the commission's report, *Shaping a Fairer Future*, indicated this wider concern with social justice.

The interviews I carried out for this project gave me fascinating insights into the way authoritative figures in the New Labour years approached the question of women and employment, and their reflections shaped the way I developed my thinking about the commission and its relevance today. Written in the shadow of Covid-19, and in a tough economic climate, the book will, I hope, appear at a more optimistic time of recovery and renewal, although at time of writing forecasts are gloomy. But the pandemic laid bare the inequalities that continue to divide society, undermine political trust, and result in loss of human potential for current and future generations. As the United Nations and other international organizations argue, unless the question of women's employment is taken seriously by policymakers, in all its dimensions, recovery may falter and will not be sustainable.

Notes

1. The Equal Pay (Information and Claims) (EPIC) Bill (HL Bill 65) was presented by Baroness Prosser in the House of Lords on 28 January 2020. The same bill was presented in the House of Commons by Stella Creasy MP on 4 May 2021. It sought to make provision for a right for employees to obtain information relating to the pay of a comparator and to require certain employers to publish information about pay differences between male and female employees and between employees of different ethnic origins. The bill failed at second reading.
2. See Women and Equalities Committee, *Unequal Impact? Coronavirus and the Gendered Economic Impact* (London: House of Commons, 2021).
3. M. Taylor, *Good Work: The Taylor Review of Modern Working Practices* (London: Department for Business, Energy and Industrial Strategy, 2017).
4. The consultation response was finally published on 29 June 2023: Department for Business and Trade, *Parental Leave and Pay. Good Work Plan: Proposals to Support Families* (London: HM Government, 2023). In its response, government proposed only limited reform to existing rights, which it acknowledged would disappoint many of those who had contributed to the consultation: the proposals aim to make current entitlements more flexible in terms of timing of fathers' share of leave.
5. Women's Budget Group, *Creating a Caring Economy: A Call to Action* (London: Women's Budget Group, 2020).

Acknowledgements

The research on which the book is based was funded by a Major Research Fellowship from the Leverhulme Trust (MRF-2019-160). I would like to express my thanks to the Leverhulme Trust for their generous support, and the freedom it gave me to follow the trail set by the material I found.

As stated in the Preface, the idea for the book originated in an earlier sabbatical with the University of Bath's Institute for Policy Research, and I would like to thank Professor Nick Pearce and IPR colleagues for their continued intellectual support.

In preparing this book, I have been grateful throughout to Oxford University Press editor Dominic Byatt, who showed interest in my initial proposal and guided it through multiple reviews, as well as to the various anonymous reviewers who helped me to make sense of what I wanted to say about the mass of data I had gathered, and to Phoebe Aldridge-Turner for her patience and responsiveness.

My main debt of gratitude—and it is huge—is to the people who took part in the research. Without the time and trouble that participants took to speak to me about policy on women and employment in the Labour years, I would have had no project. I am immensely grateful to all of them for the insights they gave me.

Baroness Prosser spoke to me at an early stage in the research and helped me to work out whom I needed to approach. Tracy Vegro OBE helped me to locate several of these essential participants.

Several participants not only gave time to speak to me but hunted out materials, and in some cases offered follow-up interviews to give further reflections. Some participants read early drafts of chapters and significantly advanced my thinking about key events.

I would like to thank in particular Matilda Quiney and Jenny Watson CBE for the time and trouble they took to read and comment on draft chapters, at more than one stage in the process.

At a late stage in the preparation of the book script, Oxford University Press asked me to contact interviewees to request permission to use the material. This renewal of contact proved invaluable to me, as it helped me to correct errors of interpretation and often provided new insights. I have greatly enjoyed the conversation with everyone who contributed to this book.

I would like to extend special thanks to the Right Honourable Patricia Hewitt and the Honourable Meg Munn, both of whom provided careful and constructive reading of chapters at the final stage, and were patient in correcting mistakes that had crept in. I also owe particular gratitude to Dame Stella Manzie and to Janet Veitch OBE for their thoughtful comments on chapters.

Of course, any errors or misinterpretations that remain are entirely my doing, but through sustained engagement with the project the participants helped me to identify and reduce the most egregious of these, I hope.

In addition to interviewees named in the book, I owe thanks to Professor Hazel Conley for comments on Chapter 13.

David Perfect gave valuable comments on an early draft of Chapter 4 and pointed me towards important reports from the Equal Opportunities Commission, to which David Sparrow kindly gave me access at the EOC's office in Manchester.

I would also like to extend thanks to the archivists (at the People's History Museum in Manchester, The National Archives at Kew, the Modern Records Centre at the University of Warwick, and the Joanna Foster archive at Oxford Brookes University) whose work supported my research, as well as library staff at the University of Bath.

The people who contributed their recollections and material to this book have a distinguished career of public service, and I reiterate my gratitude to them for responding to my requests. Not everyone I interviewed is cited directly in the book, but all interviewees gave invaluable information and insights. Nor was I able to name everyone who gave help along the way. The time and attention given by all my research participants to the questions I raise in the book attest to their extraordinary interest in and commitment to the cause of women's rights in the workplace.

In my research, I uncovered decades of work by women (and men) to make women's experience in the world of work visible, and to try to find solutions to problems that are too easily dismissed as 'intractable'—that is, too difficult to resolve. That we as a society are still talking about the gender pay gap is a reminder of the scale of the challenges. It is also in itself a reflection of the efforts of many persistent people not to give up at each setback, but to keep on pushing to work for a fairer future. This book is dedicated to all of them.

Contents

List of Abbreviations

ACAS	Advisory, Conciliation and Arbitration Service
AEEU	Amalgamated Engineering and Electrical Union
APL	Additional Paternity Leave
APPG	All-Party Parliamentary Group
BERR	Business, Enterprise, and Regulatory Reform Committee
BIS	Business, Innovation, and Skills
BitC	Business in the Community
CBI	Confederation of British Industry
CC4G	Computer Clubs for Girls
CCRU	Central Community Relations Unit
CIPD	Chartered Institute of Personnel and Development
Cohse	Confederation of Health Service Employees
DCLG	Department of Communities and Local Government
DCSF	Department for Children, Schools, and Families
DfE	Department for Employment
DfES	Department for Education and Skills
DLR	Discrimination Law Review
DPO	Dipartimento per le Pare Opportunità
DTI	Department of Trade and Industry
DWP	Department for Work and Pensions
EEC	European Economic Community
EHRC	Equality and Human Rights Commission
EIGE	European Institute for Gender Equality
EOC	Equal Opportunities Commission
EPA	Equal Pay Act
EPIC	Equal Pay (Information and Claims)
GED	gender equality duty
GEO	Government Equalities Office
GMB	General, Municipal, and Boilermakers' Union
HR	human resources
ILO	International Labour Organization
IoD	Institute of Directors
IPR	Institute for Policy Research
LPC	Low Pay Commission
LSC	Learning and Skills Council
MSC	Manpower Services Commission
NALGO	National and Local Government Officers Association
NAO	National Audit Office
NAWO	National Alliance of Women's Organizations

NEC	National Executive Committee
NEET	not in education, employment, or trianing
NGO	non-governmental organization
NHS	National Health Service
NPF	National Policy Forum
NUPE	National Union of Public Employees
OECD	Organization for Economic Cooperation and Development
ONS	Office for National Statistics
PAFT	Policy Appraisal and Fair Treatment
PCS	Public and Commercial Services Union
PSED	public-sector equality duty
RMT	Rail and Maritime Transport Union
SDA	Sex Discrimination Act
SMEs	small and medium-sized enterprises
SMP	statutory maternity pay
SOCPO	Society of Personnel Officers in Local Government
SPL	Shared Parental Leave
STEM	science, technology, engineering, and mathematics
TEC	Training and Enterprise Council
TGWU	Transport and General Workers' Union
TSSA	Transport Salaried Staffs Association
TVEI	Technical and Vocational Education Initiative
TUC	Trades Union Congress
UMF	Union Modernization Fund
UN	United Nations
USDAW	Union of Shop, Distributive and Allied Workers
WAC	Women's Action Committee
WAVE	Women Adding Value to the Economy
WBG	Women's Budget Group
WEC	Women and Equalities Committee
WEF	World Economic Forum
WES	Women in Engineering and Science
WEU	Women and Equality Unit
WISE	Women in Science and Engineering
WNC	Women's National Commission
WPTF	Work and Parents Task Force
WWC	Women and Work Commission

List of Interviews

All interviews conducted during 2020–2, with follow-up correspondence in 2023.

Sarah Anderson (former Women and Work Commissioner, then director of Mayday Group Limited)
Dr Ed Blissett (former senior organizer, GMB)
Kay Carberry (former Women and Work Commissioner, then deputy general secretary of the Trades Union Congress)
Nita Clarke (former adviser on trade unions, prime minister's office)
David Coats (former head of economic affairs, Trades Union Congress)
Dan Corry (former policy adviser, Department of Trade and Industry)
John Cridland (former Women and Work Commissioner, then deputy director of the Confederation of British Industry)
John Hannett (former Women and Work Commissioner, then general secretary of USDAW)
Patricia Hewitt (former MP, former Minister for Women and Equalities and Secretary of State for Business and Industry)
Professor Susan Himmelweit (economist; founder director of Women's Budget Group)
Sally Hopson (former Women and Work Commissioner, then human resources manager at Asda)
Professor Diane Houston (former policy adviser, Department of Trade and Industry)
Adeeba Malik OBE (former Women and Work Commissioner, then chief executive officer of QED)
Meg Munn (former MP, former Minister for Women and Equalities)
Dame Stella Manzie (former Women and Work Commissioner, then chief executive of Coventry council)
Geoffrey Norris (former policy adviser on business, prime minister's office)
Carey Oppenheim (former policy adviser on family and care, prime minister's office)
Baroness Margaret Prosser (former chair, Women and Work Commission)

Matilda Quiney (former civil servant at the Department of Trade and Industry)
Professor Jill Rubery (professor of comparative employment systems, Manchester Business School)
Dame Ruth Silver (former Women and Work Commissioner, then principal of Lewisham College of Further Education)
Sarah Veale (former head of equality and employment rights department, Trades Union Congress)

1

Women and Employment

A 'Stalled' Revolution

Introduction

A remarkable change has taken place in the British economy and society: from around 1985 until the Covid-19 pandemic in 2020, there was an almost continual rise in women's employment, much of this increase taking place in full-time employment.[1] Even after the pandemic, women's full-time employment continued to grow, although the number of women in part time employment decreased owing to labour-market withdrawal. The number of households where both parents work full-time rose sharply in the years of Margaret Thatcher's governments (from 1980 to 1990) and then more steadily in the Labour years (especially between 1997 and 2002). This change resulted from both supply-side and demand-side changes, in women's labour-market behaviour, and in the labour market itself.

However, women's economic position relative to men's has been slow to change. Women remain less likely than men to be in top decision-making positions and other types of jobs that are well paid, such as technical roles, and they are concentrated in a few occupations that are associated with low pay, contractual insecurity, and little control over working hours: in caring, cleaning, catering, and clerical work. They are still much more likely than men to work part-time. These imbalances are reflected in the aggregate gender pay gap (the difference between women's and men's average pay), which is high in international comparison: for example, the International Labour Organization (ILO) placed the UK's gender pay gap in 2018–19 at 23.6 per cent (based on median hourly pay), compared to an international average of around 15 per cent, and 20.6 per cent based on mean hourly pay, compared to 16%.[2]

Over their lifetime, women continue to earn substantially less than men, particularly if they work in lower-skilled or mid-skilled jobs. In 2019, on average, women earned about 59 per cent of men over a lifetime, up from 56 per

Women and Employment in Public Policy. Susan Milner, Oxford University Press. © Susan Milner (2024).
DOI: 10.1093/9780191987359.003.0001

cent in 2004. Even adjusting for hours worked, women were paid about a fifth less than men over their lifetime.[3]

The British situation may be regarded as a 'stalled revolution', where women's labour-market participation has not been matched by supportive measures such as childcare provision, generous and flexible leave for parents, and women-friendly workplace cultures, as well as by a more egalitarian division of labour at home.[4] The Labour years (1997–2010) introduced several important changes, but opportunities to equalize gender roles and make the workplace a better place for women were not systematically followed up. For the decade 1999–2009, the ILO's analysis showed the UK at the bottom of a league table of forty-eight countries, with only the Netherlands showing a larger gender pay gap throughout.[5] This is perhaps surprising given the record number of women MPs returned in 1997, half of them owing to Labour's adoption of an all-women shortlists policy.[6]

The Labour years also saw record numbers of women ministers, and the establishment of a policy machinery (minister and civil service unit) within government. Undoubtedly, feminization of parliament and government had an impact on policy affecting women. However, policy often failed to make much difference to women's economic situation relative to men's,[7] particularly in the context of countervailing economic policy and political choices, which resulted in the outsourcing of women's jobs, downward pressure on wages, and the extension of employer-driven flexibility, which eroded women's ability to demand better conditions.[8] For example, the introduction of a national minimum wage benefited women, because they make up the majority of low-paid workers, and, according to most scholars, it has had the largest impact on the gender pay gap of any policy measure.[9] However, it was fixed at a low rate from the beginning, and progression in low pay failed to keep pace with much bigger rises for male-dominated top earners.[10] New rights for working parents were adopted, such as paid paternity leave, longer maternity leave, and a new additional paternity leave to encourage parents to share parental leave. But these new rights were too limited in scope and payment to affect parents' choices.[11] The Labour period saw a more expansive approach to equalities, with the adoption of the Equality Act 2010 and the creation of a new Equality and Human Rights Commission, but the timing of its adoption late in the Labour period meant that parts of its substance were eroded in the context of the financial crisis and the impact of austerity on public services.

A sense of missed opportunities characterizes the treatment of equal pay during the Labour period, despite the creation of a ministerial post dedicated to women. It was a time of unprecedented data-gathering, giving policymakers robust evidence on which to base proposals. It was also a time when the conditions for a more consensual form of policymaking could potentially develop: Tony Blair's leadership of the party rested on a break with trade unions' grip on policy through the annual conference, and new forms of policy development had been established in order to widen the social base for ideas and proposals.[12] However, new forms of policy formulation were contained by centralized leadership;[13] they did not necessarily given women's rights campaigners a stronger voice, and, while work–family policy became an area ripe for political exchange between party and unions, it did so in ways that continued to limit the impact of new measures.[14]

Recommendations for authoritative instruments—notably mandatory gender pay audits (or pay review), rights for mothers to reduce their working hours, and paid parental leave with a dedicated allocation for fathers—were widely discussed but adopted in minimalist form. The Task Force on Equal Pay, set up by the Equal Opportunities Commission (EOC) in 2000 (the thirtieth anniversary of the Equal Pay Act 1970), made a strong case for mandatory gender pay reviews within a broader multi-level approach aimed at encouraging and supporting employers, but the government gave only minimal backing to its recommendations. The Women and Work Commission (WWC), convened in 2004 to examine causes of the gender pay gap and make recommendations to address them, had a broad remit but worked within a circumscribed policy space. Established by the prime minister in response to growing trade union pressure, the WWC issued a wide range of recommendations aimed at building employer capacity, supporting workplace equality actors, and funding initiatives to enhance women's career progression through training and 'quality' part-time roles, but the pilot projects did not lead to longer-term initiatives.

Tensions around the regulation of pay had not lessened with the adoption of the Equal Pay Act in 1970, but rather intensified in the following two decades. In such a context, policymakers spent time 'retro-fitting' rights that had already existed in neighbouring countries for decades.[15] Arguably, in such conditions, change could not take place overnight but rather had to be underpinned by wider cultural change ensuring that regulatory interventions would lead to the desired outcomes rather than 'tick-box' compliance.[16] During the Labour years, it is also true that governments had a dauntingly large agenda to address, owing to the legacy of keeping equal-pay claims at bay and the lack of a strong legal and enforcement machinery on which to develop progressive policy.[17]

Two decades after the establishment of the WWC (and over fifty years since the Equal Pay Act 1970), the question of how to address the UK's gender pay gap is as pertinent as ever, and the missed opportunities of the Labour years can be acknowledged as such, while also being viewed in a different light as lessons for the potential of policy renewal today. The last major review of the UK's gender pay gap was undertaken by the parliamentary Women and Equalities Committee (WEC) in 2016. The committee's inquiry noted the government's stated intention to eliminate the gender pay gap within a generation and called upon ministers to 'match the scope of their ambition ... with effective action'.[18] Like the WWC a decade earlier, it called for all jobs to be made flexible by default; the introduction of a non-transferable period of leave for fathers and second carers; an industrial strategy for low-paid, highly feminized sectors; and the creation of a National Pathways to Work scheme to support women on their return to employment. In other words, parliament acknowledged that a lost decade had taken place since the WWC reported in 2006.[19] Five years later, in February 2021, the same parliamentary committee found that the Covid pandemic and its economic consequences had worsened the situation to the extent not just of stagnation but of potential regression of women's position.[20]

This book, based on interviews with leading policy advocates and practitioners from the Labour period, starts from the premise that we can learn important lessons about the way policy operates, and what kind of policies are effective, by looking at the missed opportunities as well as the successful initiatives of the past. It focuses on the WWC, which set out to examine the situation of women's labour-market advantage, in all its complexity, and therefore remains the most comprehensive inquiry on the subject undertaken in the UK. The questions posed at that time, about what businesses can do to tackle gender disparities in the workplace, and what governments can do to improve conditions for women in employment, remain not just valid but pressing today.

Defining the Policy Space: Actors and Institutions

This book is about gender politics. It is concerned with actors—who acts within the policy space, and in whose interests—and the power relations between those actors. It understands policy as being shaped by the power relations within formal and informal institutions, which are intersectionally gendered—that is, are structured by the way gender intersects and overlaps with other characteristics, in particular race and ethnicity, but also age and indicators of social class such as educational background and family wealth, as well as disability.[21]

Feminist political analysis explains politics and policy through a focus on 'ideas, interests, and institutions, which are intertwined'.[22] Institutions are not only formal bodies and the formal and informal rules and practices that underpin them, but also wider rules about the conduct of politics and policy (the 'rules of the game' and what is expected of participants), and the place of those bodies within those rules and expectations. These institutions are of interest to feminist scholars because they shape the possibilities for transformative policy and social justice. Feminist analysis is activist in wishing to contribute to an equalization of gender relations; in this sense it is normative. A central question is how to achieve change within the capitalist state. The state can liberate and transform, but it can also reproduce oppression and even create new divisions and exclusions—for example, around race and nationality.[23]

State institutions are not monolithic but offer arenas or spaces in which demands are expressed and brokered, including from groups that have traditionally been marginalized or minoritized, and responses formulated and enacted. Such spaces are opened up particularly at times of far-reaching change such as economic or other upheavals, major political change (such as can occur in the British context when one major party has been in power for a decade or more and is succeeded by its opponent) leading to institutional as well as policy innovation, or constitutional change.[24] Devolution of powers to territorial assemblies and governments is an example of constitutional change that can open up spaces for new forms and content of decision-making.[25]

In the British case, power was devolved to varying degrees in Scotland, Wales and Northern Ireland in 1998 and has been seen as a process during which new legislatures and executives have learnt to exercise power independently in areas where they have authority, favouring the feminization of representation and new approaches to policy. In less direct ways, the influence of the European Union was at its strongest during the period of the Labour years, creating opportunities for campaigners to push the boundaries of state–market regulation and strengthening the hand of some aspects of the equality machinery associated with anti-discrimination enforcement, as discussed in Chapter 4.

Opportunities also arise when new trends and innovations seek to change the way politics is done, including ways of reforming old institutions through new practices, such as quotas for representation of specific groups of people, or methods such as social-impact assessments (used in gender mainstreaming).[26] Feminist institutionalists have focused on how women achieve office through party selection and election procedures, what they do in legislatures and the political executive when they get there, and how the equality machinery within the state and in arm's-length relationships with the state (such as quasi-non-governmental bodies or enforcement bodies) operate, as I discuss further in Chapter 2. They have also highlighted non-decision-making in the form of stalling or dilution of feminist demands.[27]

Reviewing the progress made by 'femocrats' (feminist activists working within the structures of the state) in Sweden and Australia from the 1960s and 1970s respectively, Jessica Lindvert emphasized the importance of existing and dynamic institutional 'rules of the game' which shaped policy outcomes. Under changing conditions, equality activists adapted their discourse (in Sweden) to suit the shift from social-democratic to liberal frames, or found new ways of organizing, by working in new arenas and building coalitions.[28] Swedish femocrats learned to link their demands to other political concerns (such as child development), whilst Australian activists used networking strategies in the context of a federal state which offered different opportunities for alliances at different levels. In liberal market economies such as the UK, feminists learned to frame their demands within the 'business case' for equality and diversity.[29] These examples highlight the dilemmas around how best to achieve transformative change within the opportunity structure afforded by institutional politics on the one hand and the dominance of neoliberal policy frames on the other, whereby gendered social norms about the private and public spheres structure economic life.[30]

Regulation and the Regulatory Space: The Role of Organized Business

The idea of a 'stalled revolution' reflects a failure of women's movements to sustain momentum, but this failure is unsurprising, given the cultural and political obstacles they face. In the British case, legislative victories have often proved disappointing owing to weak enforcement, reflecting an established policy preference for voluntary or symbolic measures over strong authority instruments.[31] The dominant approach to policymaking is explained, in institutionalist analysis, by the way in which gendered institutions shape the flow of ideas, values, and priorities.[32]

Within the specific context of western economies, particularly in Anglo-American countries, Leigh Hancher and Michael Moran argue that states seek to regulate economic activity in a way which combines 'organization on market principles, domination of many sectors by giant firms, and political rules according to formally democratic principles', creating tensions in the policy sphere. In the British case, a deferential political culture meant a regulatory culture of business self-regulation (rather than statutory intervention), from which a wider range of organized interests were excluded. As this culture came under challenge due to 'a combination of government policy failures, changes in social structure, and wider alterations in the character of popular values', newer groups sought to enter the public space of decision-making.[33]

In the British social and employment policy context, the role of organized business is important, despite its formal weakness (in terms of its constitutional mandate). The Confederation of British Industry (CBI) was the main employer organization for the period studied here (1997-2023).[34] It was formed in 1965 as a membership organization focused mainly on lobbying government, and with no bargaining mandate. Constitutionally, it has no formal links with political parties and no formal consultative role in government. It was long seen as a relatively weak body with little influence over policy. However, its policy influence grew in the 1990s and 2000s. In the area of women and employment, the CBI's position changed after the mid-1980s owing to labour-market changes, focusing on women with childcare responsibilities. The CBI called for the state to act as a facilitator for women returning from maternity leave—for example by introducing tax credits and exemptions for nursery care.[35]

At the same time, organized business strongly resisted any moves to regulate employment by giving individual employment rights, owing to a fear of litigation, as well as to collective rights that could help to enforce them. The shift to a greater political role for the CBI reflected changes within the industrial systems away from collective bargaining, from which local employers increasingly withdrew, and towards legal regulation, which the organized employers' lobby saw a strong interest in resisting.[36] The CBI's lobbying power was deployed to resist the push towards individual rights. Meanwhile, Labour's commitment to global competition reframed the parameters of social and employment policy to make them 'compatible with contemporary capitalism'.[37] The CBI, which under the Thatcher governments had been sidelined in favour of the more explicitly ideologically right-wing Institute of Directors (IoD), was consulted more frequently by Labour than in previous years, and was drawn into a nexus of partnerships with government: in training policy through the Learning Skills Council, in regional health partnerships, and routinely through the formation of reference groups within key departments such as those dealing with business, trade, and employment. The CBI therefore became an institutional entrepreneur lobbying for business interests in opposition to legislation, and steering 'good practice' through voluntary business initiatives in areas of interest to the government.

Outside organized business lobbies, the influence of large employers also grew, as they became partners and sponsors of government initiatives, in the context of economic globalization and increasing fragmentation of public-service provision by the state.[38] This growing influence has been seen in the policy area of women and employment, where large US-based companies such as McKinsey, Deloitte, and Catalyst have effectively driven policy on women on corporate boards, through publication of annual data, benchmarking, and research reports. As well as large individual businesses, new networks also appeared to promote 'good practice' and to involve the corporate world in society, reflecting (at least in part) a conscious quid pro quo on the part of businesses keen to support privatization and a smaller role for the state.[39] Business in the Community (BitC) was established in 1982 as a response to the Brixton riots, and reflected awareness by some senior business leaders that, as they continued to make large numbers of people redundant, they had a wider social responsibility to take action to mitigate the impact of business changes, through participation in urban regeneration and employment training agencies.[40] Later, when Labour came to power, BitC proved a useful a way of coordinating frequent calls by government for partnership initiatives with large companies.[41]

BitC made its first foray into diversity management with the Opportunity 2000 (later Opportunity Now) initiative led by Baroness Howe[42] and supported by Prime Minister John Major. Originally with sixty-one (soon over a hundred) members, it expanded to become the leading membership organization dealing with gender equality and diversity. It promoted the business case for equality and diversity through publications and events, as well as awards and benchmarking, and developed links with Cranfield University's School of Management to provide annual benchmarking data, as well as with the EOC, the IoD, and national charities.[43] In the context of British governments' preference for 'light-touch' regulatory solutions, BitC pioneered and championed the 'what gets measured gets managed' approach to equality and diversity in the workplace, encouraging businesses to lead the way in socially progressive practices through public reporting and benchmarking. As Joni Lovenduski observed, the basis for this business-led approach was set during the long period of Conservative government between 1979 and 1997, especially during the early 1990s under John Major.

The role of organized business and leading businesses and their networks in setting the agenda on women and employment has been very little studied,[44] and yet it is crucial to understanding the Labour years. Nita Clarke,

Tony Blair's adviser on trade unions between 2001 and 2007, emphasized that 'politics is the art of the possible', with policy in the Labour years essentially defined by the need to translate European legislation into British law in as flexible a way as possible, so as to work with employers rather than against their opposition to statutory regulation.[45] As Linda Dickens argued in 1994,[46] the overwhelming predominance in the British case of 'business-case' arguments shaped the trajectory of policy on gender equality, leaving substantial gaps. By their nature, such actions generate only a partial, selective approach, and they are highly contingent on economic circumstances. Instead, Dickens argued, a more effective approach required both incentives to encourage employer behaviour, and regulatory action to encourage consistency and long-term behavioural change: the carrot and the stick.

In 2011, BitC published an overview of changes over two decades in women's empowerment, recording only modest changes. Women's political representation had changed more substantially, but women remained in a minority of decision-makers: 6 per cent of MPs were women in 1990, and 22 per cent in 2010; 13 per cent of peers in the House of Lords were women in 1990, and 20 per cent in 2010; 5 per cent of senior civil servants were women in 1990, and 36 per cent in 2010.[47] This pattern of relatively slow change is also seen in the UK's position in the European Institute for Gender Equality's annual index, published annually after 2005. After 2005, the UK showed improved scores for all aspects of gender equality, but at a slower pace of progress than other member states. Although its 'power' score (measuring women's share of top jobs and positions of political power) increased over the period, inequalities remained pronounced, with a score of only 56.5 per cent in 2017.[48]

Regarding women's progression into top roles, the public sector has done better than the private sector, owing to stronger duties (discussed in Chapter 13), but here too there are gaps and weaknesses, and overall an uneven approach to regulation. The Athena SWAN Charter in British higher education is a good example of an employer-led equality initiative that relies on voluntary actions, but also on a highly prescriptive reporting template and on strong incentives for compliance (for science and engineering subjects, access to research grants has been conditional on accreditation since 2011). It originated in an informal voluntary initiative in the early 2000s, in the form of a web resource and a network of participants, which was formalized in 2005 with the creation of the Equality Challenge Unit to administer accreditation. Formalization and conditionality ensure a high level of engagement, which in turn enables institutional change within organizations and has resulted in an increased number of women in higher-level posts (professors, deans, vice-chancellors, and pro-vice-chancellors), but women are still under-represented in such posts relative to workforce composition. The gender pay gap has likewise decreased but remains higher for universities than for the national median average.[49] Evaluation studies of the Athena SWAN initiative indicates that real organizational cultural change has proved elusive, and that recognition of the barriers women face in career progression in the form of specific supports is rare.[50]

The business-led voluntary approach is also seen in the series of initiatives taken since 2011 to promote women in the boardroom. Eschewing formal quotas, government gave high-level support to an informal voluntary initiative, with targets set over a five-year period and monitored annually. Pressure for change came from the publication of benchmarking data and reputational costs of non-compliance. The result was a high level of formal compliance and achievement of targets for the appointment of women directors, supported by a myriad of new organizations aimed at training and coaching women, and widespread awareness of the business case for more gender-balanced decision-making. The initiative, which started with the top hundred publicly listed companies (FTSE 100) and extended to the top 350, also helped to establish similar processes for increasing the ethnic diversity of boards.

However, these sustained, data-driven efforts have made little impact on the gendered nature of the top tier of executive decision-making.[51] A decade after the launch of the first review, the number of women at chief executive level 'remains flat and stubbornly low',[52] increasing from 6 to 8 per cent, and only 14 per cent of board chairs were women in 2022. In the business world as in political decision-making, change is slow, and, at the current rate of progress, men will continue to dominate top roles for years to come.[53]

Defining the Policy Space: What Is on the Agenda?

Substantively, the policy space on women and employment includes direct provision (such as the provision of healthcare, or childcare); distribution, such as through the tax and welfare system; and regulation, through individual and collective rights of employees and the laws governing women's specific rights as a disadvantaged group.[54] How this policy space is regulated and mediated, and by whom, has an impact on the working lives of individual women. This question concerns the actors and institutions responsible for making policy, and the range of voices involved in decision-making.

The application of a gender lens to the study of the policy process draws attention to the question of whose interests are promoted and whose rights protected. Discursive institutionalism highlights the impact of ideas and the way in which policy is framed, including the question of whose claims are included in that framing. While this book does not adopt a discursive–analytical approach, it nevertheless acknowledges the importance of such approaches in drawing attention to 'the non-innocence of how "problems" get framed within policy proposals, how the frames will affect what can be thought about, and how this affects possibilities for action'.[55] Probably the most influential exponent of this approach in gender politics,[56] Carol Bacchi, reminds us to consider not only how the problem is framed, but what is excluded from this framing, and why (for example, because of the costs involved in solutions responding to alternative framings).

The way in which the policy problem of women and employment was presented in the New Labour years is a good example. During the New Labour years, the gender pay gap made its appearance onto the parliamentary agenda, and onto the government agenda, as the main focus of policy attention to the situation of women in paid employment. In 2001, the Labour manifesto committed the future government to addressing it. Prior to discussion of the gender pay gap, parliamentary debates had referred to equal pay, or more generally to women's situation in the labour market.

The gender pay gap is a multidimensional and complex problem, which opens up many different ways of resolving women's labour-market disadvantage relative to men.[57] Proposed solutions may be complementary or competing—that is, they may have a mutually strengthening effect or alternatively close off alternative ways of approaching the problem. How the gender pay gap is discussed in the public space, and how solutions to the gap are presented, are therefore important questions for policy analysis, as discussed further in Chapter 3, and will be an important theme of this book.

Commissions in the Policy Process

As noted above, the reports produced by the WWC in 2006 (and its follow up in 2009) and the WEC in 2016, both focusing on the gender pay gap, may be seen as markers or milestones setting out the available evidence on women in the labour market and providing an insight into the regulatory tensions within the policy space.

Commissions of inquiry are particularly important in (Anglophone) countries characterized by the Westminster model, and in Scandinavian countries, where they form part of a broader neo-corporatist approach that involves organized interests in policymaking, although their role has declined in importance in all these settings.[58] Given the resources devoted to policy commissions, it is widely thought that their principal function is to solve problems for government, where problems are seen as either new or requiring a new approach (for example, because of sudden external or societal change), or particularly complex, divisive, and/or intractable. Commissioners bring experience and expertise to the problem, as well as networks that enable a wide range of perspectives.[59]

Expert information-gathering and collation of as full a range as possible of differing opinions form the backbone of commissions' work. Their value is enhanced by the expectation of impartiality; this is usually intended to be achieved by balance in the composition of commissioners. They therefore help government to defuse controversial questions and may also be used to 'buy time' or defer decision-making. They may also be used to give expert backing to decisions that the government wanted to take anyway but wanted to test first.[60] Although often influential in the field of criminal law and procedures, they have been seen as mostly ineffectual in the broad field of social and employment policy, with governments ignoring recommendations in many cases.[61] Consequently, commissions are frequently criticized as time-wasting exercises. Nor have they always succeeded in damping down controversy; on the contrary, they have sometimes sparked further protest.

Commissions and ad hoc committees, as well as scientific reports commissioned by government or statutory bodies (such as the Equal Opportunities Commission, and its successor the Equality and Human Rights Commission), have been a striking feature of government responses to demands from women's organizations and trade unions for equal pay, and have generally been seen as a way of deferring action.[62] In this, as for the use of commissions more generally, it is difficult to disagree with a cynical view about why they are established. Indeed, the word 'cynical' was used by several of my interviewees to describe their general attitude towards this type of exercise. However, both for commissioners and for campaigners, the commission itself was viewed as a landmark event and an opportunity to achieve change, mainly because of the broad remit, which was seen as allowing for a range of strong recommendations and a clear overall vision, and because of the credibility of the participants.

Durability is one way of defining a problem as intractable,[63] and this feature certainly applies to the case of gender equality.[64] Another key reason for apparent policy insolubility (and therefore government reluctance to intervene directly) relates to the specific context of equal pay claims in the British context. At the time the WWC sat, a small number of historic pay claims in the public sector had made their way successfully through the judicial system, with others pending, making the question of pay equality potentially very costly for employers and increasing the political sensitivity of the problem. This situation sharpened the potential for conflicting opinions in the context of the situation outlined above, where employers' preferences were framed as both politically salient and normatively 'good', reducing the chances of intervention on behalf of a relatively weaker target group of women (especially low-paid women).[65]

In assessing the effectiveness of a commission or similar body, several features have been found to influence outcomes. The first is composition: the chair should be actively engaged throughout the life of the commission and possess interpersonal skills usually associated with those of a business executive. Smaller committees can work in a focused way and more easily attain consensus, while larger groupings are useful in capturing a range of perspectives and later presenting the work to a broad public, but are usually divided into smaller working groups to achieve cohesiveness.[66] Feminist institutionalist literature also emphasizes the networking capacity of a given body and its individual members, and their access to the centre of political power, as well as to wider society through civil society groups and networks.[67]

Sources

The research on which this book is based relies on original sources and participants' recollection of events. Contemporary history can be understood as the study of the immediate past, when participants are still able to give their version of events, and when their oral testimony, provided with the benefit of hindsight, gives a powerful insight into what happened and why.[68] It is particularly useful in bringing to light features of the policy institutions that may not be apparent from reading documentary sources, such as the informal relations between participants, and unwritten norms and assumptions about the way things are done. Memory of events that took place fifteen to twenty years previously is patchy and unreliable, however, and needs to be triangulated against other accounts (published and unpublished) and contemporary written sources.

The study of contemporary history requires a 'wide-ranging and inventive' approach to sources,[69] not least because the official record may be incomplete owing to government confidentiality rules or archiving policy. In principle, the full government record of the WWC was due for release in the National

Archives in 2024 under the twenty-year rule (reduced from thirty years in stages after 2010). The archive would in theory include minutes of the commission meetings and proposal papers prepared by civil servants in advance of meetings, written communications from commissioners, as well as drafts of the report, synthesis papers on the available research evidence, and a summary of submissions. However, my investigation indicates that the commission papers were lost in the many moves of the responsible government department (the Government Equalities Office).

To some extent, I was able to fill in some of the gaps through independently held papers, although not as much as I had anticipated. Archiving of online reports and government publications such as green papers and consultation records cannot be expected to be comprehensive; on the contrary, much of this 'grey' material is now widely unavailable. Submissions that are routinely published online by associations and campaign groups quickly disappear, as they are taken down and replaced, and such groups do not always have the resources to archive material systematically. Nor could I rely on commissioners' own records to fill in the gaps. Very few of the people I contacted had kept copies of correspondence or papers, although some were found when I contacted individuals or consulted public archives (such as Women's Budget Group notes, and an EOC position paper that formed part of a file available at the National Archives). Archiving of web-based material of government agencies, available in the National Archives, often consists of ad hoc collections of web pages, with links that may have been discontinued. As a result of these gaps, there is a risk of losing collective memory of activism in an important area of policy and of women's lives, from a period when this activism was fundamental to the construction of a policy machinery. This book sets out to fill at least some of the gaps.

Structure of the Book

The first section of this book sets out an analytical framework and provides context, tracking the history of women's demands in the contemporary period and showing how these demands made their way into the political mainstream, largely through female agency.

Chapter 2 sets out the theoretical framework that informs this book, based on comparative gender politics scholarship, which seeks to explain advances in the field of women and employment with reference to women's representation in political decision-making and the importance of the women's policy machinery and equality machinery.

Chapter 3 examines evidence from cross-national research on different types of 'woman-friendly' policy, in particular claims that policy on women and employment is a class-based policy, which is more likely to be adopted when left-of-centre parties are in power and may also be associated with participation of trade unions in the policy process. Equal-pay policies straddle regulatory and redistributive instruments and may therefore be particularly difficult to adopt, unless a strong combination of women's organizations, trade unions, significant women's presence in parliament, and women's policy machinery is achieved.

Chapter 4 provides an overview of the legal framework for pay equality, starting with the Equal Pay Act 1970, and shows how the way in which the Act was formulated and implemented created a relatively weak legislative framework, which was subsequently, but not comprehensively, developed. It uses the concept of regulatory space to show how, at various points, the gender equality machinery sought a proactive role in supporting individual claims and lobbying for changes in the law, creating tensions in the relationship with government but keeping equality demands in the public policy space.

Chapters 5 and 6 track the context of the Labour years, looking first at changes in the mode of policymaking and the evolution of the relationship between the party and trade unions, and next at the women's policy machinery. Chapter 5 shows how the WWC resulted from a political exchange between party and unions, but also existed within a wider political opportunity structure based on feminist activism within and outside government, in the regulatory space for equal pay.

Chapter 6 analyses the development of the women's policy machinery during the Labour years and subsequently. The women's policy machinery consisted of a women's unit within government and a minister for women. However, it has never been fully independent and has frequently moved around government departments, with responsibilities often split between departments, resulting in a failure to embed women's policy in the core of executive decision-making. Moreover, governments have resisted moves to mainstream gender in policy through consistent formal practices, despite the development of a public-sector equality duty as outlined in Chapter 13.

Chapter 7 presents the process through which the WWC operated (in its initial mandate and the 2009 follow-up report) and considers the impact of the way the formal and informal 'rules of the game' influenced outcomes. The remit and form of the WWC is compared to those of the Low Pay Commission, on which several WWC members also sat.

Chapter 8 examines the follow-up to the Commission's report and the political factors which caused its recommendations to be short-lived and largely swept away by the financial crisis.[70] The political factors refer mainly to the women's policy agency, as well as changes in the regulatory space which effectively crowded out demands relating specifically to women's situation, and they also include the long, conflictual interregnum at the top of government.

The remainder of the book examines the principal areas of policy on which the WWC focused and made recommendations, shifting from process to potential policy instruments. In each chapter, the problems identified by the commission are tracked through to the present day in order to evaluate the extent to which they have been remedied or alleviated by policy subsequently. By looking in more detail at specific areas of policy concerning women and employment, the idea of 'unfinished business' or a 'stalled revolution' is expanded and explained.

Chapter 9 discusses pay-equality legislation, the most contentious area. The chapter focuses on the main reforms advocated by the EOC and equality campaigners, including trade unions: reform of the tribunal system, generic or representative (or 'class') actions, intersectional claims, and full equal-pay audits. After 2010, although trade unions maintained their advocacy of pay audits, attention shifted to transparency through reporting, with largely symbolic (but still important) results.

Chapter 10 focuses on part-time employment (the second most contentious area). Although the WWC's solution was to find ways of innovating in partnership with business, opportunities were subsequently missed to embed and take forward this work. Policy attention to women's part-time work has waned, but it remains a major structural feature of the gendered British labour market.

Chapter 11 examines family and care, an area where the Labour governments introduced innovations that found widespread support and opened the way to more equal sharing of care. Labour's failure to extend its early innovations led to a pattern of unequal access to supportive measures for working parents, although the flexible working agenda continued to be pursued to varying degrees under subsequent governments.

Chapter 12 deals with education and training. Following a series of investigations by the EOC, the WWC set out a broad-ranging agenda for change through opening up opportunities for girls and women, starting in schools, and focusing on training to enable older women trapped in low-paid jobs to progress. Training, an apparently consensual policy area, is in practice under-resourced and conflictual.

Chapter 13 focuses on the public sector. The WWC followed closely preparations for the equality duty that was introduced in 2007 and later integrated into the Equality Act 2010. Like the Kingsmill review before it, the commission placed high hopes in the government's stated plans to enact strong equality duties for all public services, and to bring the private sector with it through conditionality in procurement of goods and services. The public-sector equality duty is a potentially powerful tool to achieve transformative change across a range of areas that affect everyone's lives (particularly women, who are disproportionately affected as service users), but, owing to weak implementation, its impact has been uneven, and it risks being counterproductive in some cases, by encouraging 'tick-box' compliance behaviours. Meanwhile, the potential of public procurement clauses has still to be realized in Britain.

In the book's Conclusion (Chapter 14), I acknowledge the extraordinary gender equality activism of the years before and after Labour's 1997 election victory, as second-wave feminism accessed political power. The chapter sets out the unfinished agenda for change those activists sought to enact and examines its significance for women in today's labour market. A commission on women and work today would need to take an explicitly intersectional approach, and to examine the ways in which the landscape of employment has changed for many women, especially those entering the labour market now: the Covid-19 pandemic exacerbated trends in many female-dominated sectors towards extreme job insecurity and narrowing of employment choices. The consequences are already being felt in terms of falling birth rates, while the consequences of impoverishment over the life course are likely in later years. Meanwhile, the unfinished policy revolution of care is still waiting for a receptive government: as countless British and international reports have shown since 2006, it would boost the economy and help to rebuild a better and healthier society.

Notes

1. B. Roantree and K. Vira, *The Rise and Rise of Women's Employment in the UK* (London: Institute for Fiscal Studies, 2018).
2. ILO, *Global Wage Report 2018–2019* (Geneva: ILO, 2018), 24. A gap of 23%, for example, means that women are paid on average 77 pence for every pound paid to men, taking all hourly pay into account. The UK's gender pay gap narrowed in the pandemic owing to the decrease in part-time employment but remains above the international average.
3. P. Collinson, 'Women Paid £2600,00 Less than Men over their Careers—Report', *Guardian*, 28 October 2019.

4. The idea of a 'stalled revolution' has often been used to describe the state of play in gender politics in advanced capitalist economies. As Paula England argues, it is particularly apposite in anglophone liberal countries, where strong women's movements encountered the dominance of male norms in the world of paid employment: P. England, 'The Gender Revolution: Uneven and Stalled', *Gender & Society*, 24 (2010), https://doi:/10.1177/0891243210361475.
5. M. Oelz, S. Olney, and M. Tomei, *Equal Pay: An Introductory Guide* (Geneva: ILO, 2013), 14.
6. See D. Cutts, S. Childs, and H. Fieldhouse, '"This is what Happens when you Don't Listen": All-Women Shortlists at the 2008 General Election', *Party Politics*, 14 (2008), https://doi:10.1177/1354068808093391.
7. D. Grimshaw, 'New Labour Policy and the Gender Pay Gap', in C. Annesley, F. Gains, and K. Rummery (eds), *Women and New Labour: Engendering Politics and Policy?* (Bristol: Policy Press, 2007), 133–54.
8. D. Coates and S. Oettinger, 'Two Steps Forward, One Step Back: The Gender Dimensions of Treasury Policy under New Labour', in Annesley et al. (eds), *Women and New Labour*, 117–31.
9. See A. Bryson, H. Joshi, B. Wielgoszewska, and D. Wilkinson, *A Short History of the Gender Wage Gap in Britain*, Institute of Labour Economics (IZA) Discussion Paper 13,289 (Bonn: IZA, 2020).
10. D. Grimshaw and J. Rubery, *Undervaluing Women's Work* (Manchester: EOC, 2007).
11. S. Milner, '"Choice" and "Flexibility" in Reconciling Work and Family: Towards a Convergence in Policy Discourse on Work and Family in France and the UK', *Policy and Politics*, 38 (2010), https://doi.org/10.1332/030557309X445591.
12. J. Lovecy, 'Framing Claims for Women: From "Old" to "New" Labour', in Annesley et al. (eds), *Women and New Labour*, 63–92.
13. See M. Russell, *Building New Labour: The Politics of Party Organisation* (London: Palgrave Macmillan, 2005); see also Ch. 5.
14. S. Milner, 'Employment Regulation and the Problem of the Gender Pay Gap under New Labour', *Historical Studies in Industrial Relations*, 43 (2022), https://doi.org/10.3828/hsir.2022.43.5.
15. Interview, Nick Pearce.
16. Interview, Nita Clarke.
17. See G. Kelly and N. Pearce, '"Riders on the Storm": What Would an incoming Labour Government Face?', *Renewal*, 31 (2023). https://renewal.org.uk/riders-on-the-storm-what-would-a-labour-government-face.
18. WEC, *Gender Pay Gap: Second Report of Session 2015–16* (London: House of Commons, 2016), 6.
19. The TUC referred to this situation in its evidence to the 2013 inquiry by the WEC, noting that its evidence to the committee was 'as relevant today as it was in 2005' (WEC, *Women in Work*, https://publications.parliament.uk/pa/cm201213/cmselect/cmbis/writev/womeninworkplace/m20.htm (accessed 13 November 2020)).
20. WEC, *Unequal Impact? Coronavirus and the Gendered Economic Impact: Fifth Report of Session 2019–2021* (London: House of Commons, 2021).
21. See K. W. Crenshaw, 'Mapping at the Margins: Intersectionality, Identity Politics, and Violence against Women of Color', *Stanford Law Review*, 43 (1991), 1241–99;

P. Hill Collins, 'Intersectionality's Definitional Dilemmas', *Annual Review of Sociology*, 41 (2015), https://doi:10.1146/annurev-soc-073014-112142. The political actors who are the focus of this book are overwhelmingly white, able-bodied, middle class, and highly educated; almost by definition, they belong to the political elite. It is nevertheless important to be attentive to intersectionality in the policies discussed.

22. J. Lovenduski, 'Foreword', in M. L. Krook and F. Mackay (eds), *Gender, Politics and Institutions: Towards a Feminist Institutionalism* (Basingstoke: Macmillan, 2011), pp. vi–x, at p. ix.
23. See E. Lombardo and J. Kantola, *Gender and Political Analysis* (Basingstoke: Macmillan, 2017).
24. F. Mackay, M. Kenny, and L. Chappell, 'New Institutionalism through a Gender Lens: Towards a Feminist Institutionalism', *International Political Science Review*, 31 (2010), https://doi.org/10.1177/0192512110388788.
25. See M. Kenny and F. Mackay, 'Gender and Devolution in Spain and the United Kingdom', *Politics & Gender*, 7 (2011), https://doi.org/10.1017/S1743923X11000122; J. Morrison and E. Gibbs, 'Feminist Institutionalism and Women's Political Leadership in Devolution Era Scotland', *British Politics*, 18 (2021), https://doi.org/10.1057/s41293-021-00197-1.
26. F. Mackay and G. Waylen, 'Introduction: Gendering "New" Institutions', *Politics & Gender*, 10 (2014), https://doi.org/10.1017/S1743923X14000385.
27. See C. Bergqvist, E. Bjarnegård, and P. Zetterberg, 'When Class Trumps Sex: The Social Democratic Intra-Party Struggle over Extending Parental Leave Quotas in Sweden', *Social Politics*, 23 (2016), https://doi:10.1093/sp/jxv017; M. Saari, J. Kantola, and P. Koskinen Sandberg, 'Implementing Equal Pay Policy: Clash between Gender Equality and Corporatism', *Social Politics*, 28 (2021), https://doi:10.1093/sp/jxz020.
28. J. Lindvert, 'The Rules of the Game: Organizing Gender Policies in Australia and Sweden', *Social Politics*, 14 (2007), https://doi:10.1093/sp/jxz020.
29. See J. Kantola and J. A. Squires, 'From State Feminism to Market Feminism?', *International Political Science Review*, 33 (2012), https://doi:/10.1177/0192512111432513.
30. W. Waller and M. V. Wrenn, 'Feminist Institutionalism and Neoliberalism', *Feminist Economics*, 27 (2021), https://doi.org/10.1080/13545701.2021.1883194.
31. See E. Tutchell and J. Edmonds, *The Stalled Revolution: Is Equality for Women an Impossible Dream?* (Bingley: Emerald, 2018), especially pp. 248–52.
32. See, e.g., V. D. Burau, H. Theobold, and R. H. Blank, *Governing Home Care: A Cross-National Comparison* (Cheltenham: Edward Elgar, 2007).
33. L. Hancher and M. Moran, 'Organizing Regulatory Space', in L. Hancher and M. Moran (eds), *Capitalism, Culture, and Economic Regulation* (Oxford: Clarendon Press, 1989), 271–299, at 273.
34. In 2023, the future of the CBI was thrown into question following a series of allegations of serious sexual misconduct. It reformed under new leadership but relations with employer members were undermined by the allegations.
35. K. Farnsworth, 'Minding the Business Interest: The CBI and Social Policy', *Policy Studies*, 19 (1998), 19–38. Lack of affordable childcare provision continues to be a matter of concern for the CBI: see CBI, 'Spring Budget Submission', Submission to HM Government, February 2023, https://www.cbi.org.uk/media/utccayj5/cbi-budget-submission-2023.pdf (accessed 10 February 2023).

36. L. Gooberman, M. Hauptmeier, and E. Heery, 'The Evolution of Employers' Organisations in the UK: Extending Countervailing Power', *Human Resource Management Journal*, 29 (2019), https://doi.org/10.1111/1748-8583.12193.
37. Gooberman et al., 'The Evolution of Employers' Organisations', 481.
38. K. Farnsworth and C. Holden, 'The Business–Social Policy Nexus: Corporate Power and Corporate Inputs into Social Policy', *Journal of Social Policy*, 35 (2006), https://doi:10.1017/S0047279406009883.
39. D. Grayson, 'Business-Led Corporate Responsibility Coalitions: Learning from the Example of Business in the Community in the UK: An Insider's Perspective' (Harvard University and Cranfield School of Management, 2007), 14.
40. Grayson, 'Business-Led Corporate Responsibility Coalitions', 20–1.
41. Grayson, 'Business-Led Corporate Responsibility Coalitions', 27.
42. Elspeth Howe was deputy chair of the EOC from 1972 to 1979. In 1990 she chaired the first report of the Hansard Society on women in public life ('Women at the Top') and, having been made a life peer in 1991, launched Opportunity Now with Major's support. She subsequently sat on the Department of Employment's Working Group on Women's Issues (1992–7). See E. Howe, 'Women and the State: Re-Gendering our Institutions', in R. Campbell and S. Childs (eds), *Deeds and Words: Gendering Politics after Joni Lovenduski* (Colchester: ECPR Press), 133–5.
43. Grayson, 'Business-Led Corporate Responsibility Coalitions', 31. The development of national charities alongside that of business campaigns has recently been charted by Sarah E. Stoller: *Inventing the Working Parent: Work, Gender, and Feminism in Neoliberal Britain* (Cambridge, MA: MIT Press, 2023). Grassroots campaigns for childcare and job-sharing respectively led to the formation in 1980 of the Working Women's Association, which in 1994 became Parents at Work, and the creation in 1979 of the Job Share Project, later New Ways to Work; in 2003, Parents at Work and New Ways to Work merged to form Working Families: see also Working Families, *Changing the Way we Work: 40th Anniversary Brochure* (London: Working Families, 2019). These charities worked closely with Opportunity 2000/Opportunity Now, the EOC, and at various points with government departments, as discussed in Ch. 11.
44. One reason may be lack of access to 'insiders' within the CBI and lack of archival material, in contrast to the TUC, which has substantial archival records. Grayson in his overview of BitC also notes a tendency towards reactiveness and its corollaries, poor institutional memory and patchy record-keeping: Grayson, 'Business-Led Corporate Responsibility Coalitions', 50.
45. Interview, Clarke.
46. L. Dickens, 'The Business Case for Women's Equality: Is the Carrot Better than the Stick?' *Employee Relations*, 16 (1994), 5–18; also L. Dickens, 'Beyond the Business Case: A Three-Pronged Approach to Equality Action', *Human Resource Management Journal*, 9 (1999), 9–19; L. Dickens, 'The Road Is Long: Thirty Years of Equality Legislation in Britain', *British Journal of Industrial Relations*, 45 (2007), 463–94. https://doi.org/10.1111/j.1467-8543.2007.00624.x.
47. BiTC, *Opportunity Now: 20th Anniversary Review* (London: BitC), 5.
48. European Institute for Gender Equality, *Gender Equality Index 2017: Measuring Gender Equality in the European Union, 2005–2015. Report* (Luxembourg: EU Publications, 2017).

49. C. Guiberg, 'Big University Gender Pay Gap Revealed', BBC News, 29 March 2019, https://bbc.co.uk/news/business-47723950 (accessed 4 May 2021).
50. See, e.g., K. Bhopal and H. Henderson, 'Advancing Equality in Higher Education: An Exploratory Study of the Athena SWAN and Race Equality Charters' (University of Birmingham, 2019).
51. See S. Milner, 'Self-Regulation Comes at a Cost: Closing off Authoritative Policy for Gender Equality on Corporate Boards in the UK', in I. Engeli and A. G. Mazur (eds), *Gender Equality and Policy Implementation in the Corporate World: Making Democracy Work for Business* (Oxford: Oxford University Press, 2022), 59–85.
52. FTSE Women Leaders, *Achieving Gender Balance* (London: FTSE Women Leaders/KPMG, 2022), 8.
53. C. Marren and A. Bazeley, *Sex and Power 2022* (London: Fawcett Society, 2022), 16.
54. See F. Vibert, *The New Regulatory Space: Reframing Democratic Governance* (Cheltenham: Edward Elgar, 2014), 13–14.
55. C. Bacchi, 'Policy as Discourse: What Can It Mean? Where Does It Get Us?', *Discourse: Studies in the Cultural Politics of Education* (2000), https://doi.org/10.1080/1350176042000164334.
56. C. Bacchi, *Women, Policy and Politics: The Construction of Policy Problems* (London: Sage, 1999).
57. See J. Rubery and D. Grimshaw, 'The Forty-Year Pursuit of Equal Pay: A Case of Constantly Moving Goalposts', *Cambridge Journal of Economics* (2015), https://doi.org/10.1093/cje/beu053.
58. C. Dahltström, E. Lundberg, and K. Promin, 'No More Political Compromise? Swedish Commissions of Inquiry 1990–2016, *Scandinavian Political Studies* (2021), https://doi:10.1111/1467-9477.12205.
59. A. Hunter and C. Boswell, 'Comparing the Political Functions of Independent Commissions: The Case of Migrant Integration Policy', *Journal of Comparative Policy Analysis: Research and Practice* (2015), https://doi:10.1080/13876988.2014.896117.
60. M. Bulmer, 'Increasing the Effectiveness of Royal Commissions: A Comment', *Public Administration*, 61 (1983), 436–42, at 436. See also M. Rowe and L. McAllister, 'The Role of Commissions of Inquiry in the Policy Process', *Public Policy and Administration* (2006), https://doi:10.1177/095207670602100408; M. Bulmer, 'Introduction', in M. Bulmer (ed.), *Social Research and Royal Commissions* (London: Routledge, 1980), 1–7.
61. B. Lauriat, '"The Examination of Everything": Royal Commissions in British Legal History', *Statute Law Review*, 31 (2010), https://doi:10.1093/slr/hmq001.
62. See, e.g., K. M. Fraser, *Same or Different: Gender Politics in the Workplace* (London: Routledge, 2018), 148.
63. See G. Peters, 'The Problem of Policy Problems', *Journal of Comparative Policy Analysis* (2005), https://doi:10.1080/13876980500319204.
64. See S. L. Weldon, 'Power, Exclusion and Empowerment: Feminist Innovation in Political Science', *Women's Studies International Forum* (2019), https://doi.org/10.1016/j.wsif.2018.05.014; L. Raymond, S. L. Weldon, D. Kelly, X. B. Arriaga, and A. M. Clark, 'Making Change: Norm-Based Strategies to Address Intractable Problems', *Political Research Quarterly* (2013), https://doi:10.1177/1065912913510786.

65. See A. L. Schneider and H. M. Ingram, 'Social Constructions, Anticipatory Feedback Strategies, and Deceptive Public Policy', *Policy Studies Journal*, 47 (2019), https://doi:10.1111/psj.12281.
66. Bulmer, 'Increasing the Effectiveness of Royal Commissions', 433.
67. On the latter, see also (on the Australian case) M. Mintrom, D. O'Neill, and R. O'Connor, 'Royal Commissions and Policy Influence', *Australian Journal of Public Administration*, 80 (2021), https://doi:10.1111/psj.12281.
68. See P. Thane, 'Contemporary History', in *International Encyclopaedia of the Social & Behavioural Sciences*, 4 (London: Elsevier, 2015), 762–8.
69. Thane, 'Contemporary History', 767.
70. See R. Ward, 'The Women and Work Commission Legacy in the Age of Austerity', *Local Economy*, 27 (2012), https://doi.10.1177/0269094212455303.

2

Feminizing British Politics?

Women in the Legislature and the Executive

Introduction

'Woman-friendly' policy strives towards equal representation in public and private life, and promotes measures which benefit women and girls. These two goals are inter-related because comparative scholarship finds incontrovertibly that policy aimed at improving the life chances of women is driven by women's access to political decision-making.[1] However, feminizing politics as a political agenda is about more than numbers of women in decision-making spaces. It is, in Joni Lovenduski's words, about 'how institutions, processes and procedures are affected by the changing numbers of women, about what else happens when the numbers of women change'.[2] The UK falls behind countries with similar levels of income per capita when it comes to the proportion of women elected to parliament (28.9 per cent in 2019, compared to 47.3 per cent in Sweden or 36.6 per cent in Australia). In 2022, it was placed joint forty-fifth in the Inter-Parliamentary Union for Democracy's ranking of national parliaments, based on the proportion of women representatives.[3] While the number and proportion of women in the House of Commons has increased (reaching 34 per cent after the 2019 general election), female presence at ministerial level remains low.[4] The UK stands in seventy-ninth place in the United Nations (UN) rankings for the proportion of women in ministerial positions, with 23.8 per cent in 2021, compared to 35 per cent for Europe as a whole (including the Nordic countries, and 29.1 per cent without them).[5]

The UK also performs less well than might be expected, given both its economic power and strong female educational attainment, in terms of women's economic empowerment. The World Economic Forum (WEF) ranks it twenty-third, well below the Nordic states, and below its close neighbours France, Germany, and Ireland (thirteenth out of twenty-two West European and North American countries).[6] Thus, in the British case, a low level of economic empowerment mirrors a low level of political empowerment of women.

Women and Employment in Public Policy. Susan Milner, Oxford University Press. © Susan Milner (2024).
DOI: 10.1093/9780191987359.003.0002

Theoretically, feminists have drawn on Hannah Pitkin's work to ask whether descriptive representation leads to substantive representation of women's interests: do women representatives identify as women, and do they act on behalf of women? The four main dimensions of representation (formal, descriptive, substantive, and symbolic) set out by Pitkin[7] are interrelated, although the precise nature of the relationship is difficult to pin down and measure. Formal rules about representation (the number of seats in an electoral district, and the electoral system) primarily affect descriptive representation (who stands for election as a person with certain identifying characteristics), which in turn has a bearing on substantive representation (acting as an elected representative on behalf of the population with those identifying characteristics).[8] In other words, in very general terms we can expect that rules governing the electoral system and process will influence how many women feel able and willing to stand as candidates, and their likelihood of being selected; that women who are elected representatives identify broadly with women's interests, however they choose to define them; and that they will therefore be more likely to promote a 'woman-friendly' policy agenda.

Empirically, however, the relationship between descriptive and substantive representation is problematic. Feminist scholars have cast doubt on any assumption that there is an automatic link between descriptive and substantive representation. One reason for this is that legislative representation forms only one—albeit central—aspect of the process of policy development, which may also be influenced by bodies and networks outside parliament such as interest groups (in this case, the strength and influence of the women's movement), as well as policy networks outside parliament and the civil service, such as business or practitioner groupings. Another question is methodological, concerning the question of how to investigate women's presence in parliament. It is relatively straightforward to map contributions of male and female MPs onto the outcome of bills in parliament, but less easy to document the more informal discussions held outside debates in the parliamentary chamber.

Despite these methodological caveats, comparative research finds that women are more likely than their male counterparts to participate in debates about and to vote for bills that further women's rights to education, healthcare, and other aspects of care.[9] This raises the general expectation that women's increased parliamentary representation will lead to greater attention to policy issues that further women's rights and interests. However, while women are indeed more likely than men to act in this way, it does not mean that they will always do so.[10] Parliamentary behaviour is also strongly mediated by party ideology, individual positioning and preferences (which may apply particularly to doctrinal issues such as abortion), and individuals' perception of their constituency preferences. Women MPs are not a homogenous group; nor do they as individuals represent all the different experiences of what it is to live as a woman in British society.[11]

Moreover, the question of whether women 'act for women' also depends on discussions of their capacity to do so. Numbers of women representatives seem to be important, but 'critical mass' is difficult to measure: at what point do women representatives feel that they have the capacity within a given political institution to advance or support claims made on behalf of women? As discussed further below, the election of 120 women MPs in 1997 (double the numbers in the previous parliament) marked a 'sea change', as Harriet Harman MP asserted, particularly as a record number of women from that intake also went on to become ministers.[12] This change was symbolic, she later argued in her memoirs: women throughout the country recognized it as meaning that politics more accurately represented them.

Increased descriptive representation also marked a change in substantive representation: Harman claimed that she and her parliamentary colleagues represented a critical mass of women who together could not just act for women but change the way politics was done in the UK.[13] Nevertheless, moves towards the enactment of a woman-friendly policy agenda could not be taken for granted after 1997, and in practice were the focus of continued conflict. As Sarah Childs shows in her analysis of the 1997 intake of 'New Labour women', rather than marking a definitive break from old to new practices, this incomplete feminization ushered in uncertainty, with the potential for transformative action but also the persistence of traditional expectations. Childs also found scepticism among women MPs about the extent of change and their own capacity to effect it.[14]

Altogether, as Fiona Mackay observes, the links between descriptive and substantive representation of women are 'theoretically bothersome and empirically contingent'.[15] In this chapter, I set out first to review academic literature on women's descriptive representation in order to understand under what conditions it is increased, and conversely why it is so difficult to achieve in the 'particularly tough case' of Westminster politics.[16] The proportion of women in legislatures is a useful starting point that allows for comparison between states. From there, I go on to look at women in the core executive (government) and consider the women's policy machinery or dedicated agencies within government to further women's interests. Consideration of the core executive is important, because the British Westminster model is highly centralized, the executive dominates the policymaking process, and government initiates almost all legislation.[17]

In considering women's political representation, I refer here to explanations based on cultural attitudes as well as structural–institutional features of politics in a given country, such as electoral systems, the presence or absence of mechanisms for representation of minorities, or time expectations that clash with women's unpaid care work. The argument that differences in female representation in state legislatures could be attributed largely to variations in the relative strength of beliefs and expectations underpinning political life, notably traditionalism (which results in preferences to keep women out of public life) or 'moralistic' cultures (which focus on social-justice arguments and can encourage recruitment of women, as well as Black and minoritized people[18]), has long been confirmed by quantitative comparative analysis.[19] Moreover, such cultures are self-reinforcing: those 'early-adopter' states characterized by 'moralistic' or social-justice attitudes continue to increase numbers of women in legislatures.

Manon Tremblay, in seeking to explain cross-national differences in women's representation in national parliaments, has observed that, in longer-established democracies, cultural attitudes have a more important impact on outcomes than formal rules such as the existence of quotas.[20] Quotas can have a powerful impact, resulting in rapid increases in the number of elected female representatives.[21] However, institutions, including those in liberal democracies, are underpinned by gendered norms about 'acceptable' behaviours within them, and outside them in wider society.[22] These informal 'rules of the game' are taken into account within an institutionalist perspective.

Women and Political Representation in the UK: The House of Commons

The UK is viewed as a 'laggard, not a leader' in women's descriptive representation, although progress has been made since 1997.[23] In the British case, cultural attitudes reinforce the effect of strong institutional inhibitors, in particular the highly exclusive functioning of the single member (first-past-the-post) electoral system for general (UK parliamentary) elections, which has preserved the stranglehold of majoritarian political parties and their leadership traditions. Compared to other old democracies, especially those in western Europe, women's representation has therefore remained 'exceptionally low' at Westminster.[24] The electoral system is shared by other Anglophone countries that imported the Westminster model of liberal democracy, but it exhibits specific features such as highly centralized government not shared by those other states, which tends to exclude outsider groups.[25]

On the other hand, the strength of the main parties within the system means that top-down change can result in swift and potentially transformative action. This gives an opportunity for action by women within party organizations to bring about change through manifesto commitments to the adoption of new candidate-selection rules.[26] Change is contingent on positive attitudes of party leaders, which may be affected by instrumental concerns such as wider party reorganization or attractiveness to women voters.[27] Instrumental rationality shown by party leaders has been seen as the main reason why women activists within the Labour Party were able after many years of campaigning to secure the adoption of all-women shortlists.[28] When institutional changes occurred after 1997, in the specific context of proportional voting systems at subnational level, of devolved legislatures, and of the adoption of positive action (all-female shortlists) by political parties, the result was increased numbers of women in legislatures, and some moves towards greater presence of women in government.[29] However, such changes have proved inconsistent, and have consequently made little impact on underlying cultural attitudes.[30] Despite modifying the formal 'rules of the game', they did not address entrenched attitudes and were not necessarily accompanied by the strong and consistent messaging from the party leadership that could have helped to encourage cultural change.

In seeking to explain the under-representation of women in British political life, scholars emphasize three interrelated factors: first, the incomplete modernization of the main political parties and resistance to the adoption of pro-active measures such as quotas or seat allocation; second, the barriers facing women at selection stage in local constituencies; and, third, the masculine norms and practices of the Westminster institutions themselves.[31] At local level, a study of local constituency selection before the 2010 general election found that women had less access to the conventional pathways to selection, other than trade-union activism, which is an increasingly narrow route in the context of membership decline; local activists often held traditionalist views, even where party leadership had adopted a more egalitarian policy.[32]

Within the main three parties, leaders have been reluctant to adopt specific measures aimed at overcoming local resistance, although they have all established training and other support programmes to encourage women and Black and minoritized candidates to stand. However, under pressure from activists, the Labour Party initially introduced all-women shortlists in 1993, to be used in all vacant seats in winnable constituencies. The measure was withdrawn in 1996, following a court ruling that it contravened the Sex Discrimination Act, but it had already led to feminization of the party's candidates for the 1997 general election, and resulted in a doubling of the number of women elected. The all-women shortlists policy was reinstated for the 2005 general election after a change in the law in 2002 to allow positive action.[33] Compared to the Conservatives and Liberal Democrats, Labour selects significantly more women and those from Black and minoritized backgrounds, and it places such candidates in a greater number of winnable and marginal seats than the other two parties.[34] This change showed that positive measures can result in increased female representation in political life, whereas informal measures aimed at boosting the supply of candidates have much weaker impact as candidates encounter local resistance rooted in masculinist values.[35]

The practices of Westminster parliament reflect and perpetuate the masculinist bias of political parties.[36] Indeed, concern about the sexist culture of the House of Commons as a peculiar institution exempt from the rules of workplace behaviour has grown owing to a series of scandals since 2010.[37] As a famously long-established legislature, the practices of both houses are rooted in deeply entrenched informal conventions that serve to exclude outsiders: initially those from lower social classes, and more recently women and Black and minoritized people.

Since 2008, following an initiative by the Speaker, the House of Commons has seen a series of initiatives to address under-representation of women, minoritized groups, and disabled people.[38] An All-Party Parliamentary Group (APPG) on Women in Parliament established in 2010 recommended in particular the creation of a parliamentary select committee on women and equalities (achieved in 2015), a more predictable parliamentary calendar, and the introduction of parental leave for MPs.[39] Sarah Childs, who had assisted the APPG in its inquiry, conducted further research within the House of Commons leading to the publication of the *Good Parliament* report in 2016.[40] Childs focused on the need for changes in four main areas: first, mandatory monitoring data by political parties, in line with the requirements of Section 106 of the Equality Act 2010, and further actions by parties to improve their selection procedures; second, the strengthening of the new Women and Equalities Committee; third, formal requirements for parliamentary committees and other institutions to take account of equality and diversity; and, fourth, the alignment of parliamentary working practices with those in the outside world, including rights for working parents. These reports and the institutional processes they established began a slow and difficult process of change within the British political system.[41]

The Scottish case following devolution sheds light on the relationship between institutional and cultural factors in encouraging or inhibiting women's representation. The first elections to the Scottish parliament resulted in a rise in the number of women selected as candidates and elected as MSPs, owing to the novelty of the institutional setting, the adoption of proportional representation (a combination of constituency voting and regional lists), and the 'gender guarantees' adopted by the main parties. The measures taken by the parties were largely informal and rested in principles of equality in nominations and training for women, rather than formal targets or quotas, but they appear to have raised awareness and encouraged more women to stand. However, such gains proved fragile, and the number of women elected fell in 2007. Meryl Kenny's study of a local selection process highlighted the way in which 'traditional' and 'local' identities worked in favour of male candidates, and were reinforced by unspoken, informal ways of organizing the selection process.[42] In 2011 and 2016, the situation appeared to stall, with forty-five female MSPs elected each time.

However, in 2021, the number of women elected to the Scottish parliament reached a record high of fifty-eight (including two women from Black or minoritized backgrounds), or 45 per cent of the total. Political parties had come under intense pressure to introduce new measures, given the lack of progress after 2007. The Labour Party was the first to adopt a policy of 'zipping' lists, where male and female candidates are alternated, and twinning, where constituencies are matched to achieve gender balance overall.[43] The Scottish Green Party and the Scottish National Party (the biggest party) subsequently adopted gender quotas. The Scottish case therefore indicates that institutional change can make a positive impact over time, when changes in formal rules are combined with pro-active policies by party leaders aimed at combating hidden obstacles to women's selection.

In post-devolution Wales, too, the transformation of women's representation has been striking. Thanks to positive action measures by the three left-of-centre parties (all-women shortlists in the Labour Party, twinned seats and 'zipped' lists, and Plaid Cymru's prioritization of women on regional lists), which together form a relatively stable majority in Wales, women accounted for 41.7 per cent of those elected to the first National Assembly in 1999. The proportion of women members rose to 50 per cent in 2003, then dropped slightly to 47 per cent in 2007.[44] In 2011, the proportion slipped further to 42 per cent, then recovered to stand at 47 per cent in 2021.[45] The positive action measures introduced in 1999 had an immediate effect and were supported by the electoral system (additional member system, with one vote for the constituency and another for the wider region). The Welsh experience also suggests that institutional changes in parliamentary recruitment affect the number of women in the core executive, by increasing the supply of ministerial candidates and by contributing to wider cultural change. Although parity in government was achieved in 2000–3, men outnumbered women in government by two to one after 2011,[46] but women's appointments subsequently increased, and in 2021 women ministers formed a slight majority.

The combination of formal and informal rules gives institutions the capacity to endure over time and 'locks in' disadvantage.[47] Measures that address both formal and informal rules, such as the move towards all-women shortlists accompanied by strong messaging from party leadership and supportive measures for women in the form of training and material resources, can help to shift the existing combination of rules. Over successive electoral cycles such changes have the effect of not just increasing women's numerical presence but culturally normalizing it.[48] Similarly, measures that address the parliamentary space as a gendered workplace help to challenge masculinized norms—for example, by finding ways of limiting working hours, proxy voting rules for parents, or provision of childcare facilities.[49] The success of such initiatives cannot be taken for granted, because they need sustained efforts at all levels (including party leadership) in order to embed them within day-to-day practices. Otherwise, there is a high risk of inertia or backsliding.

Women in the Upper House

The Westminster parliament contains a distinctive feature: an unelected second chamber originally composed of hereditary peers and religious leaders, which in 1999 was reformed by the Labour government and became mostly made up of life peers appointed by the government of the day.[50] The controversial 1999 reform had the effect of politicizing the upper house and strengthening it in relation to the elected lower chamber, although its formal authority remains secondary, and it has no formal veto powers. Whereas in the past the House of Lords lacked legitimacy and did not use its formal powers to the full, the largely appointed chamber showed more readiness to use them and to inflict defeat on government bills in some cases. The government can overturn defeats in the Lords when the bill returns to the House of Commons, but most bills must be passed in identical terms by both chambers, meaning that the Lords are sometimes able to secure significant amendments in the process of reaching agreement.

The introduction of appointed life peers, initially in 1958, was justified at least in part by the need to reflect more accurately the make-up of British society, including by gender. The 1999 reform gave political leaders the opportunity to nominate and secure appointment of women in equal numbers. This 'correctional' or compensatory mechanism, aimed at balancing the gender composition of parliament in response to women's under-representation in the elected chamber, appears to have been used by leaders of the main parties, particularly the Conservative and Liberal Democrat parties, which have lower proportions of female MPs than Labour, but it has occurred only to a limited degree.[51] After 1999, the proportion of women in the upper house rose from 8.8 per cent to 15.9 per cent. However, it subsequently grew more slowly, to 19.9 per cent in 2008 and 28 per cent in 2021.[52] Since a common route for elevation to the peerage is service in the House of Commons, the most obvious reason for continued under-representation of women peers is that the supply of candidates is constrained by low numbers of women MPs. In addition, there are multiple reasons for political patronage through appointments, and correctional measures to achieve gender balance compete with other priorities of party leaders.

Partial feminization of the upper house thus forms part of the wider pattern of feminization of British politics, and, although the formal rules of the game differ from those of parliamentary candidates, the informal barriers to equal representation are similar.

Women in the Core Executive

Even more than women's presence in parliament, their appointment to ministerial posts is likely to increase women's and girls' sense of empowerment as citizens,[53] and it is also likely to lead to the adoption of policies for women, particularly those concerned with reproductive rights, gender-based violence, and same-sex couple rights.[54] While women's representation in legislatures has increased, their presence in ministerial posts has been slower to approach anything like parity, but some countries have made greater strides towards gender-equal government. Mona Krook and Lena O'Brien advance three explanations for cross-national variation in women's access to ministerial power: political institutions, social indicators of gender equality, and trends in political recruitment (women's access to public appointments that might form a supply line to political power).[55] While all three explanations have some validity, they found that political factors (form of government, the electoral system, party system and ideology, and the system of government and degree of legislative control) have the strongest explanatory power. This finding was more significant and consistent for some countries, including the UK, than for others.[56]

Building on this and other work,[57] Claire Annesley, Karen Beckwith, and Susan Franceschet show how informal and formal rules are configured to make access to ministerial power more difficult for women than for men.[58] They note that, while formal rules are relatively few in number, informal rules about selection and who is seen as 'best for the job' proliferate and are highly gendered. In the British case, the need to self-nominate for posts (which tends to favour male over female candidates) is accompanied by the need to lobby through established party networks, which are mainly male dominated.[59] Criteria for proving merit as candidates—such as what make a 'good leader'—are established with reference to the norms of the dominant (male) group. Conversely, women's experiences are often downplayed.

Women's shorter parliamentary careers, on average, also reduce opportunities for advancement into ministerial careers.[60] Women MPs leaving parliament in 2010 were found to have had much shorter tenures than their male colleagues (irrespective of age), and those surveyed reported concerns about long working hours and being the target of abusive behaviour as reasons for leaving, which suggests that the factors deterring women from parliamentary careers also tend to shorten them.[61]

There is often disproportionate attention—to extreme levels, at times—to women parliamentarians' and ministers' physical appearance and apparel rather than their abilities.[62] Meanwhile women who are seen to be ambitious and have a strong agenda of their own can be cast as un-collegial, strident, or 'difficult' (to use a word that was famously used of Theresa May by her Conservative party colleagues). These gender norms apply across political parties: in the Labour Party, even a political powerhouse like Barbara Castle, who deliberately downplayed her support for feminist causes, was seen by male colleagues as self-serving simply for behaving as men did,[63] and Harman was often described, as she later said, as 'loud and aggressive when you are just doing your job'.[64] These gendered practices are widespread and serve to 'police' women's behaviour as well as to restrict the opportunity to compete for ministerial posts on the same level as male MPs, in an intensely competitive environment driven by male norms.[65]

Women's Policy Machinery

Another change in formal rules that has the capacity to usher in wider change is the introduction of women's policy agencies, or government departments or units with responsibility for promoting a 'woman-friendly' agenda across all aspects of government work. Theoretically, feminist scholars have drawn on different strands of thought in their focus either on representation (starting with Pitkin, as outlined above) or policy machineries, which originated in feminist thinking about the nature of the state, rather than combining these approaches, but both sets of scholars share a concern with understanding how women's presence within decision-making bodies affect women's policy outcomes, and the institutional constraints that shape this relationship.[66]

A key demand of second-wave feminism, taken up by the UN in the early 1980s,[67] women's policy machinery comprises a range of agencies that vary across countries but that meet common criteria of having formal (government-established or commissioned) responsibility for furthering women's status or promoting sex-based equality.[68] Women's policy machinery is seen in feminist institutionalist literature as important for bringing women's perspectives and interests into the policy realm (agenda-setting and the politics of attention), preparing legislation and other government interventions, and ensuring effective implementation.[69] Giving a visible presence to women's interests as a specific group, these agencies have the potential to strengthen women's voice within the legislature and the executive. They may also provide women's campaign groups with access to political power.

However, although countries responded to the UN's call by setting up women's policy agencies, the embarrassment of being seen as a laggard did not necessarily encourage governments to go beyond tokenistic initiatives, lacking resources and support from top-level political leaders.[70] Scholars assessing women's policy machineries in practice identified a number of factors determining their effectiveness in achieving change: clarity of mandates, formal powers of initiative and enforcement, formal channels of access, financial and other material resources creating administrative capacity, leadership, and independence, as well as relations with social movements.[71]

As the 'daughter' of the women's movement, the women's policy machinery encountered both opportunities to influence policy and severe constraints in the operation of government. Marian Sawer's research on the development of the women's policy machinery in Canada, New Zealand, and especially Australia showed that it successfully challenged the idea that policy is 'gender-neutral' and encouraged policymakers to consider the gender impact of proposals. It also provided activists with the opportunity to influence policy on childcare and family-friendly policy by exploiting political expediency arguments. Labour leaders could be persuaded to adopt such policies on the grounds that it helped the party to appeal to women voters, resulting in electoral competition that mainstreamed their advocacy.[72] However, Sawer also found that 'femocrats'—women activists working inside the state—struggled to sustain political attention for their policies, in the context of neoliberal economic priorities. Worse, Sawer found evidence of male politicians using a backlash discourse in which they claimed that women's policy machinery was 'feminism gone too far'.[73]

As discussed further in Chapter 5, the development of a strong women's policy machinery became a central demand of women activists within the Labour Party in the 1980s, alongside calls for positive action to increase the number of women selected as parliamentary candidates. With reference to the French ministry of women's rights (the first in the world) established by the Socialist Party's Yvette Roudy in 1981, Labour women campaigners argued that a dedicated minister with cabinet responsibility would raise the profile of woman-friendly policy and enable its mainstreaming into all areas of government work.[74]

The French experience demonstrated the potential for rapid transformative change, as Roudy (who had the personal backing of the French president, and a well-resourced stand-alone government department) introduced significant and durable measures across the range of women's rights: reproductive (abortion and contraception) rights, anti-discrimination laws which challenged the traditional gender culture, and a positive duty on employers to address the gender pay gap. Yet the French case also highlighted the limits of the institutional innovation of a ministry for women's rights. In later interviews Roudy referred to the backlash and the lack of institutional embeddedness, which entailed 'constant combat'.[75] Even when the ministry was at its most powerful in the period 1981–5, Roudy was obliged to compromise in the face of lack of top-level political support on some issues, such as women's political representation.[76]

Although Roudy's reforms were to have a lasting impact on policy, successors enjoyed neither the resources nor the status she had attained. At the 1986 elections, the conservative right won the parliamentary majority; Roudy kept her seat but lost the ministry, which was swept away. Roudy later called removal of the ministry 'an act of vandalism' caused by partisan opposition.[77] Subsequent departments (variously named 'delegation' or 'secretariat of state') all had subordinate status within host ministries, reflecting the 'relative unimportance' in the policy agendas of governments of any ideological hue.[78]

The comparative literature on women's policy machinery highlights two main sets of concerns. The first relates to the formal resources of the agencies, including access to formal institutions of power such as cabinet and government departments, and the way these resources are mediated by informal networks and behaviours of political leaders. The second relates to the mechanisms of gender mainstreaming as an approach to policy, based on templates for gender impact assessment and more generally a recognition of the need to take the interests of women as a group with specific needs into account in all aspects of policymaking. Several obstacles—material, contextual, and conceptual—limit the potential of gender mainstreaming in practice: the knowledge capacity of civil servants tasked with evaluation, the wider culture of evaluation practices, material resources in the context of public expenditure cuts, and the wider lack of attention to female-dominated activities such as care in liberal economies.[79]

Conclusion

The different approaches to women's representation in parliament and government discussed in this chapter have in common a concern with understanding political decision-making as gendered in its composition, ways of operating, and taken-for-granted norms about behaviours and priorities. All seek to understand under what circumstances policy outcomes favourable to women can appear on the political agenda and be enacted and implemented; all identify the strong probability of resistance to change within existing institutions. Arguably the literature on women's policy machineries is underdeveloped in relation to thinking through how the policy machinery relates to the position of women in parliament and the core executive. It takes for granted that those within the women's policy machinery act for women, since that is its stated purpose, and, instead of interrogating the nature of representation, it sees the machinery in relational terms, analysing the extent to which it is networked inside government and outside government, principally through its links with women's campaign organizations.

Some scholars explicitly consider the respective contributions of the representation versus the policy machinery approach. Laurel Weldon has argued that women's policy machinery can offer an effective alternative to parliamentary representation, because it offers a way not just of linking to the demands formulated by women's organizations but of providing them with resources.[80] Other research focuses on the policy machinery as a force for women's rights in developing countries, where political power is concentrated and offers little chance of feminized representation, and where international organizations such as the UN can influence policy adoption through their programmes.[81]

However, when considering the British case, we need to consider the contextual specificities of the highly centralized Westminster model. This necessarily means giving attention to the presence and action of women throughout the policy process, beginning with the legislature and executive, and including the policy machinery and its links with women's organizations outside the state. This also entails awareness of the role played by individual women as 'critical actors' able to mediate between different spaces within the policy-making process, including outside the formal spaces of legislative action.[82]

As Lovenduski has argued, and this chapter has outlined, the British case shows the importance of political parties as gatekeepers of institutional innovation, which can have an impact on women's representation.[83] The adoption of all-women shortlists by the Labour Party brought about a 'sea change', which led many to expect significant change in women's substantive representation after 1997. Change in the formal rules of descriptive representation occurred alongside the strengthening in a relatively short space of time of the women's policy machinery alongside an existing agency of equality enforcement, the Equality and Human Rights Commission, within the British regulatory space (as discussed further in Chapter 4).[84] Moreover, the same period had seen constitutional change (devolution), which opened new spaces for women's activism. Labour's coming to power in 1997 therefore seemed to offer a favourable environment for women's interests to be represented descriptively and substantively.

However, as this chapter has also discussed, the expectation of a woman-friendly policy agenda was problematic, because institutional innovation requires more than a simple change in formal rules.[85] If it is grafted onto an existing set of informal 'rules of the game', it is unlikely to generate real change. The question of what conditions generate transformative change remains, as might be expected from the discussion here, elusive, but it seems to require both sustained top-level political leadership aimed at challenging discriminatory attitudes in all their forms, including the most invisible and insidious, and strong enforcement mechanisms with constitutional status. In the UK, as this chapter has shown, formal rules are only the visible section of a thicket of barriers to feminizing politics.

As will be explored further in Chapter 5, the adoption of all-women shortlists resulted from more than a decade of women's activism within the Labour Party, but was largely successful because of an appeal to instrumental rationality: for Labour leaders, who did not necessarily personally support the logic of positive action, the policy had the benefit of helping to justify moves to reduce the voting power of trade unions at conference and in leadership elections, within a package of measures under the heading of organizational reform. Dependence on instrumental rationality made substantive representation fragile and contingent. Nevertheless, the adoption of positive action helped to bring about a longer-term attitudinal shift within the party, alongside the increased presence of women MPs it had generated.

The following chapters consider in more detail the evidence for feminization of British politics after 1997 and the process by which change came about. As noted above, this discussion needs to take account of the spaces in which feminization has taken place and the ways in which those spaces themselves are subject to formal and informal ways of working. Those spaces include the Labour Party and the wider labour movement, including trade unions, parliament, government, and both the women's policy machinery and the equality (enforcement) machinery. Although this chapter has focused on representation of women in parliament and the executive, in line with the bulk of feminist scholarship, an empirical account of the development of policy on women and employment needs to be attentive to all the spaces in which opportunities for agenda-setting can occur, and the institutional 'rules of the game' that govern those spaces.

Moreover, as this chapter has discussed briefly, comparative research shows the need to distinguish between different categories of policy when examining the impact of institutions and bodies on policy outputs. The next chapter therefore looks at ways to approach understanding of policy, with particular attention to women and employment, and the emergence of the gender pay gap as a policy problem.

Notes

1. See M. Htun and L. Weldon, *The Logics of Gender Justice* (Cambridge: Cambridge University Press, 2018).
2. J. Lovenduski, *Feminizing Politics* (Cambridge: Polity, 2005), 208.
3. Inter-Parliamentary Union for Democracy, *Monthly Ranking of Women in Parliaments* (January 2022), available at https://data.ipu.org/women-ranking?month=1&year=2022 (accessed 9 February 2023).
4. European Institute for Gender Equality, *Gender Equality Index 2018: The United Kingdom* (Vilnius: EIGE, 2018).
5. The United Nations, *Women in Politics 2021* (Geneva: UN, 2021).
6. World Economic Forum, *Global Gender Gap Report 2021* (Geneva: WEF, 2021), 31.
7. H. Pitkin, *The Concept of Representation* (Berkeley and Los Angeles: University of California Press, 1967).
8. For a defence of Pitkin's work as integrating these four dimensions, see L. A. Schwindt-Bayer and W. Mishler, 'An Integrated Model of Women's Representation', *Journal of Politics*, 67 (2005), https://doi.org/10.1111/j.1468-2508.2005.00323.x.
9. For an overview, see L. Wängnerud, 'Women in Parliaments: Descriptive and Substantive Representation', *Annual Review of Political Science*, 12 (2009), https://doi.org/10.1146/annurev.polisci.11.053106.123839. On the British case, see, e.g., A. C. Weeks, 'Women

Acting for Women? An Analysis of Gender and Debate Participation in the British House of Commons 2005–2007', *Politics & Gender*, 5 (2009), https://doi.org/10.1017/S1743923X09000038.
10. A. Phillips, *The Politics of Presence* (Oxford: Oxford University Press, 1995).
11. K. Celis, S. Childs, J. Kantola, and M. L. Krook, 'Rethinking Women's Substantive Representation', *Journal of Representative Democracy*, 44 (2008), https://doi.org/10.1080/00344890802079573.
12. H. Harman, *A Woman's Work* (London: Allen Lane, 2017), 194.
13. Harman, *A Woman's Work*, 136, 192.
14. S. Childs, *New Labour's Women MPs: Women Representing Women* (London: Routledge, 2004).
15. F. Mackay, '"Thick" Conceptions of Substantive Representation: Women, Gender and Political Institutions', *Representation*, 44 (2008), https://doi.org/10.1080/00344890802079607, p.125.
16. Lovenduski, *Feminizing Politics*, 148.
17. Mackay, '"Thick" Conceptions of Substantive Representation', 128.
18. In this book I have used the term 'Black and minoritized' to describe people with characteristics associated with race and ethnicity, in line with current usage: see, e.g., A. Shepherd, L. Ville, C. Marren, A. Whitelock-Gibbs, and A. Bazeley, *A House for Everyone: A Case for Modernising Parliament* (London: Fawcett Society, 2023), 4. This term was not widely used when many policy developments analysed in this book were used, so usage will vary throughout, depending on source.
19. D. B. Hill, 'Political Culture and Female Political Representation', *Journal of Politics*, 43 (1981), https://doi.org/10.2307/2130244, 159, 168.
20. M. Tremblay, 'Democracy, Representation, and Women: A Comparative Analysis', *Democratization*, 14 (2007), https://doi.org/10.1080/13510340701398261.
21. M. M. Hughes and P. Paxton, 'The Political Representation of Women over Time', in S. Francescet, M. L. Krook, and N. Tan, *The Palgrave Handbook of Women's Political Rights* (London: Palgrave, 2019), 33–51.
22. M. L. Krook and F. Mackay, 'Introduction: Gender, Politics, and Institutions', in M. L. Krook and F. Mackay (eds), *Towards a Feminist Institutionalism* (London: Palgrave Macmillan, 2010), 1–20, at 6.
23. D. T. Studlar, 'Women and Westminster. Descriptive Representation in the United Kingdom', in M. Sawer, M. Tremblay and L. Trimble (eds), *Representing Women in Parliament* (London: Routledge, 2006), 83–100, at 83.
24. J. Lovenduski, 'Male Dominance Unbroken?', in D. Dahlerup and M. Leyenaar (eds), *Breaking Male Dominance in Old Democracies* (Oxford: Oxford University Press, 2013), 71–96, at 71.
25. J. Lovenduski, 'An Emerging Advocate: The Equal Opportunities Commission in Great Britain', in D. McBride Stetson and A. Mazur (eds), *Comparative State Feminism* (Thousand Oaks: Sage, 1995), 114–31, at 117.
26. M. C. Kittilson, 'Women, Parties and Platforms in Post-Industrial Democracies', *Party Politics*, 17 (2011), https://doi.org/10.1177/1354068809361012.
27. M. Sawer, M. Tremblay, and L. Trimble, 'Introduction: Patterns and Practice in the Parliamentary Representation of Women', in Sawer et al., *Representing Women in Parliament*, 1–23.

28. Childs, *New Labour's Women MPs*, 34. See also V. Atkinson and J. Spear, 'The Labour Party and Women: Policies and Practices', in M. J. Smith and J. Spear (eds), *The Changing Labour Party* (London: Routledge, 1992), 163–4; J. Lovecy, 'Framing Claims for Women: From "Old" to "New" Labour', in C. Annesley, F. Gains, and K. Rummery (eds), *Women and New Labour: Engendering Politics and Policy?* (Bristol: Policy Press, 2007), 63–92; S. Perrigo, 'Women and Change in the Labour Party 1979–1995', in J. Lovenduski and P. Norris (eds), *Women in Politics* (Oxford: Oxford University Press, 1996), 118–31; M. Russell, *Building New Labour: The Politics of Party Organisation* (London: Palgrave Macmillan, 2005), 96–128; C. Short, 'Women and the Labour Party', *Parliamentary Affairs*, 49 (1996), 17–25.
29. See F. Mackay, 'Gender and Political Representation in the UK: The State of the "Discipline"', *British Journal of Politics and International Relations*, 6 (2004), https://doi.org/10.1111/j.1467-856X.2004.00129.x.
30. Childs, *New Labour's Women MPs*, 35. See also M. Eagle and J. Lovenduski, *High Time or High Tide for Labour Women* (London: Fabian Society, 1998).
31. See J. Lovenduski, 'Sex, Gender and British Politics', in J. Lovenduski and P. Norris (eds), *Women in Politics* (London: Hansard Society, 1996), 3–18.
32. C. Durose, R. Combs, C. Easton, F. Gains, and L. Richardson, '"Acceptable Difference": Diversity, Representation, and Pathways to UK Politics', *Parliamentary Affairs*, 66 (2013), https://doi.org/10.1093/pa/gss085. On selectorate bias, see L. Culhane and J. Olchawski, *Strategies for Success: Women's Experiences of Selection and Election in UK Parliament* (London: Fawcett Society, 2018), 34–8.
33. See R. Kelly and I. White, *All-Women Shortlists*, House of Commons Briefing Paper, no. 5057, 7 March 2016.
34. M. L. Krook and M. K. Nugent, 'Intersectional Institutions: Representing Women and Ethnic Minorities in the British Labour Party', *Party Politics*, 22 (2016), https://doi.org/10.1177/1354068816655564.
35. J. Wäckerle, 'Parity or Patriarchy? The Nomination of Female Candidates in British Politics', *Party Politics*, 28 (2022), https://doi.org/10.1177/1354068820977242.
36. M. Kenny, *Gender and Political Recruitment: Theorizing Institutional Change* (London: Palgrave, 2013); Lovenduski, *Feminizing Politics*. See also Shepherd et al., *A House for Everyone*, 70.
37. See H. White, *Held in Contempt: What's Wrong with the House of Commons?* (Manchester: Manchester University Press, 2022).
38. UK Parliament, *Speaker's Conference on Parliamentary Representation* (2010), https://publications.parliament.uk/pa/spconf/239/23901.htm (accessed 22 June 2021).
39. All-Party Parliamentary Group Women in Parliament, *Improving Parliament: Creating a Better and More Representative House* (London: APPG, 2014), http://appgimprovingparliamentreport.co.uk/download/APPG-Women-In-Parliament-Report-2014.pdf (accessed 22 June 2021).
40. S. Childs, 'The Good Parliament' (University of Bristol, 2016).
41. See J. Lovenduski, 'The Good Parliament and Other Reports', *Political Quarterly*, 88 (2017), 306–10.
42. M. Kenny, 'Gender and Institutions of Political Recruitment: Candidate Selection in Post-Devolution Scotland', in M. L. Krook and F. Mackay (eds), *Towards a Feminist Institutionalism* (London: Palgrave Macmillan, 2010), 21–41.

43. See A. Brown, 'Gender and Political Institutions: "Twinning"—the Scottish Solution', in R. Campbell and S. Childs (eds), *Deeds and Words. Gendering Politics after Joni Lovenduski* (Colchester: ECPR Press), 113–15.
44. P. Chaney, 'Devolved Governance and the Substantive Representation of Women: The Second Term of the National Assembly for Wales, 2003–2007', *Parliamentary Affairs*, 61 (2008), https://doi.org/10.1093/pa/gsm063; T. Rees and P. Chaney, 'Multilevel Governance, Equality and Human Rights: Evaluating the First Decade of Devolution in Wales', *Social Policy and Society*, 10 (2011), https://doi.org/10.1017/S1474746410000564.
45. E. Uberoi, C. Watson, N. Mutebi, S. Danechi, and P. Bolton, 'Women in Politics and Public Life', House of Commons Briefing Paper 01250, 2 March 2021, 13.
46. Bevan Foundation, *The Position Today in Wales on Devolution* (Merthyr Tydfil: Bevan Foundation, 2015).
47. See V. Lowndes, 'How Are Political Institutions Gendered?' *Political Studies*, 68 (2019) https://doi.org/10.1177/0032321719867667.
48. M. L. Krook and D. Z. O'Brien, 'All the President's Men? The Appointment of Female Cabinet Ministers Worldwide', *Journal of Politics*, 74 (2012), https://doi.org/10.1017/S0022381612000382.
49. J. Erikson and T. Verge, 'Gender, Power and Privilege in the Parliamentary Workplace', *Parliamentary Affairs*, 75 (2022), https://doi.org/10.1093/pa/gsaa048.
50. See M. Russell, 'A Stronger Second Chamber? Assessing the Impact of House of Lord Reform in 1999 and the Lessons of Bicameralism', *Political Studies*, 58 (2010), https://doi.org/10.1111/j.1467-9248.2009.00810.x; M. Russell, *The Contemporary House of Lords: Westminster Bicameralism Revived* (Oxford: Oxford University Press, 2013).
51. C. Eason, 'Women Peers and Political Appointment: Has the House of Lords Been Feminised since 1999', *Parliamentary Affairs*, 62 (2009), https://doi.org/10.1093/pa/gsn049.
52. Uberoi et al., 'Women in Politics and Public Life', 3.
53. T. D. Barnes and M. M. Taylor-Robinson, 'Women Cabinet Ministers in Highly Visible Posts and Empowerment of Women: Are the Two Related?', in A. C. Alexander, C. Bolzendahl, and F. Jalalzai (eds), *Measuring Women's Political Empowerment across the Globe: Strategies, Challenges and Future Research* (London: Palgrave Macmillan, 2018), 229–55.
54. See C. Annesley, I. Engeli, and F. Gains, 'The Profile of Gender Equality Issue Attention in Western Europe', *European Journal of Political Research*, 54 (2015), https://doi.org/10.1111/1475-6765.12095.
55. Krook and O'Brien, 'All the President's Men?'.
56. See also D. Z. O'Brien, M. Mendez, J. C. Peterson, and J. Shin, 'Letting down the Ladder or Shutting the Door: Female Prime Ministers, Party Leaders, and Cabinet Ministers', *Politics & Gender*, 11 (2015), https://doi.org/10.1017/S1743923X15000410.
57. See, in particular, M. Escobar-Lemmon and M. M. Taylor-Robinson, *Women in Presidential Cabinets: Power Players or Abundant Tokens?* (Oxford: Oxford University Press, 2016).
58. C. Annesley, K. Beckwith, and S. Franceschet, *Cabinets, Ministers, and Gender* (Oxford: Oxford University Press, 2019).
59. Annesley et al., *Cabinets, Ministers, and Gender*, 197.
60. Culhane and Olchawski, *Strategies for Success*.

61. C. Byrne and K. Theakston, 'Leaving the House: The Experience of Former Members of Parliament who Left the House of Commons in 2010', *Parliamentary Affairs*, 69 (2016), https://doi.org/10.1093/pa/gsv053.
62. Byrne and Theakston, 'Leaving the House', 222.
63. P. Bartley, *Labour Women in Power: Cabinet Ministers in the Twentieth Century* (London: Palgrave Macmillan, 2019), 7–8, 177; P. Dorey, *Comrades in Conflict: Labour, the Trade Unions and 1969's in Place of Strife* (Manchester: Manchester University Press, 2019). As these authors point out, blatant sexism and the use of highly sexualized language in the treatment of Castle was widespread in the media and in her dealings with male colleagues and trade-union leaders.
64. PA News Agency, 'Harriet Harman Says Labour's Next Leader Must Be a Woman', *Northern Echo*, 10 September 2018.
65. For a discussion of how this environment affected the careers of seven prominent Labour ministers, see Bartley, *Labour Women in Power.*
66. See Celis et al., 'Rethinking Women's Substantive Representation', 103.
67. See S. M. Rai, 'Introduction', in S. M. Rai (ed.), *Mainstreaming Gender, Democratizing the State?* (Manchester: Manchester University Press, 2003), 1–12.
68. D. E. McBride and A. G. Mazur, *The Politics of State Feminism: Innovation in Comparative Research* (Philadelphia: Temple University Press, 2010), 3.
69. J. Outshoorn and J. Kantola (eds), *Changing State Feminism* (London: Macmillan, 2007). See also J. Kantola and J. Squires, 'From State Feminism to Market Feminism?', *International Political Science Review*, 33 (2012), https://doi.org/10.1177/0192512111432513.
70. N. Kardam and S. Acuner, 'National Women's Machineries: Structures and Spaces', in Rai (ed.), *Mainstreaming Gender, Democratizing the State*, 96–113, at 100.
71. S. L. Weldon, 'Beyond Bodies: Institutional Sources of Representation for Women in Democratic Policymaking', *Journal of Politics*, 64 (2002), https://doi.org/10.1111/1468-2508.00167.
72. M. Sawer, 'Femocrats and Ecorats: Women's Policy Machinery in Australia, Canada and New Zealand', Occasional Paper no. 6 (United Nations Research Institute for Social Development, 1996).
73. M. Sawer, 'The Life and Times of Women's Policy Machinery in Australia', in Rai (ed.), *Mainstreaming Gender, Democratizing the* State, 243–64.
74. Lovecy, 'Framing Claims for Women', 79.
75. Y. Roudy, 'Le Ciel des machos m'est tombé sur la tête', *France Culture*, 9 October 2008, https://www.franceculture.fr/politique/yvette-roudy-le-ciel-des-machos-mest-tombe-sur-la-tete (accessed 2 March 2022).
76. See McBride and Mazur, *The Politics of State Feminism*, 29.
77. S. Reynolds, 'Whatever Happened to the French Ministry of Women's Rights?', *Modern & Contemporary France*, 33 (1988), 4–9, at 4.
78. G. Allwood and K. Wadia, *Women and Politics in France 1958–2000* (London: Routledge, 2001), 33. Allwood and Wadia point out that, even under Roudy, her spending power, while far in excess of that of her successors, merely accounted for 0.025% of the government budget (p. 32).
79. K. Staudt, 'Gender Mainstreaming: Conceptual Links to Institutional Machineries', in Rai (ed.), *Mainstreaming Gender, Democratizing the State*, 40–65.

80. L. S. Weldon, 'Beyond Bodies: Institutional Sources of Representation for Women in Democratic Policymaking', *Journal of Politics*, 64 (2002), 132–54.
81. O. Avdeyeva and M. Melin, 'International Socialization, International Politics, and the Spread of State Bureaucracies for Women's Advancement', *Journal of Human Rights*, 20 (2021), https://doi.org/10.1080/14754835.2021.1940889.
82. Mackay, '"Thick" Conceptions of Substantive Representation', 129. See also Celis et al., 'Rethinking Women's Substantive Representation', 104; S. Childs and M. L. Krook, 'Should Feminists Give up on Critical Mass? A Contingent "Yes"', *Politics & Gender*, 2 (2006), https://doi.org/10.1017/S1743923X06251146.
83. Lovenduski, 'Feminising British Politics'.
84. Lovenduski, 'An Emerging Advocate'.
85. Lowndes, 'How Are Political Institutions Gendered?'.

3

Understanding Policy on Women and Employment

The Gender Pay Gap as a Policy Problem

Introduction

As outlined in Chapter 2, women's increased presence in political decision-making is broadly expected to lead to the emergence and possible adoption of a new 'woman-friendly' policy agenda, although other institutional and ideological–partisan factors mediate their influence on women representatives' policy priorities. However, it is necessary to qualify the discussion further, as the broad label of 'woman-friendly' policy covers many different types of policy, which are expected to result in different responses from parliamentarians and ministers.

Moreover, the relative status of policy issues covered by 'woman-friendly' policy needs to be considered. Research has shown that women representatives are under-represented, in relation to men, in discussions of policy areas with high status and to which a large amount of time is devoted in parliamentary debates, such as macroeconomics, foreign affairs, and defence (where women are also more likely to be under-represented at ministerial level).[1] This body of work highlights the difficulties faced by women representatives who wish to promote a 'woman-friendly' policy agenda, in terms of access to top-level decision-making, and the need for women to 'frame' their demands within the prevailing government agenda, and to form a range of alliances within and outside state institutions.[2] In this chapter, therefore, I focus on the question of which issues come to policy attention within the context of parliamentary debates, and how—that is, how they are framed and debated.

Beyond affirmation of women's equal rights before the law (including equal rights to own property), the list of policies usually held to fall under the broad heading of 'women's interests' include: maternity leave and pay; sexual harassment and violence; reproductive rights; equal treatment in the workplace, including equal access to training; equal remuneration; health and

Women and Employment in Public Policy. Susan Milner, Oxford University Press. © Susan Milner (2024).
DOI: 10.1093/9780191987359.003.0003

safety in the workplace, including maternity protection; family leave and other work–family measures; tax and benefits.[3] They extend from passive measures outlawing discrimination to positive measures such as those recognizing women's reproductive role and those that enable women to enjoy full rights, which might entail the removal of specific barriers or the need to address ways in which women are held back, such as stereotyping. In this chapter, I examine more closely the nature of policymaking in areas that relate specifically to the situation of women in employment. Even here, we will see that policy is complex and sometimes difficult to place in neat categories.

In their influential comparative analysis, Mala Htun and S. Laurel Weldon categorize policies aimed at eliminating women's disadvantage as either status based or class based. Status-based policies address the inferior and vulnerable status of women in relation to men and include: changes to family law; measures to combat gender-based violence; anti-discrimination and equality laws relating to the workplace and other aspects of the public sphere; liberalization of abortion and contraception laws; and positive action measures such as quotas, which are aimed at equalizing women's representation in decision-making.[4] Class-based policies involve an element of redistribution. Distinct from (regulatory) changes to abortion or contraception law, which are classified as status-based policies, funding for abortion or contraception is thus a class-based policy. Work–family policies such as maternity, paternity, and parental leave and support for childcare are also categorized as class-based policies.[5] Class-based policies aim to achieve greater gender equality by enabling women to secure financial independence in the labour market, outside the family.[6]

Policies vary by type in terms of the attention and resources allocated to them. Class-based policies affect the relationship between state, market, and society and are more likely to be adopted under left or social-democratic governments, and when the economy is doing well. They are also positively affected by the presence of women in parliament. The strongest driver of status-based policies, on the other hand, is the presence of women in government.[7]

However, this broad typology needs to be examined in more detail when considering specific cases, because—beyond women's movement mobilization, which appears to be a common factor across policy types—the weight of factors depends strongly on context. Although policies categorized as class based are generally associated with left-of-centre government and economic growth, they have been adopted in recent years under right-of-centre governments (led by men) and under adverse economic conditions. For example, in Australia and the UK, right-of-centre governments introduced or extended parental leave policies,[8] and in the UK gender pay gap reporting was introduced by a Conservative government, although it was initially tabled by the Equality Act 2010 adopted under a Labour government.[9] Several explanations could be put forward for this apparent divergence from the broader pattern. One possible explanation is that such measures represent 'diluted' legislation, which responds to political expediency arguments (such as the need to appeal to women voters, or other instrumental concerns such as welfare policy change) and reduces the redistributive dimension of policies. Arguably in some cases measures could even be seen as 'window-dressing' policy, which, particularly under right-leaning governments, purports to address gender equality against the backdrop of more widespread austerity measures having a disproportionately adverse effect on women.[10]

Another explanation relates to different sets of actors. While the influence of trade unions has declined sharply in liberal market economies, the rise of corporate feminism within transnational organizations and corporations may also increase attention to work–family policy, resulting in forms of regulation based on the 'business case', which reduces class-based redistributive conflict, or 'instrumental' policy, in which gender equality initiatives can be promoted in order to legitimate or materially support economic policy objectives.[11] Historical institutionalist analysis is helpful in this respect, because it identifies the impact of a shift towards a financialized 'knowledge economy', bringing about changes in welfare policy from traditionally class-based (redistributive) rights to individual (regulatory) rights.[12] Thus, while the structure of welfare regimes remains in place and ideological markers of left and right persist, new spaces for coalitions appeared (not just unions, for example, under left-of-centre governments, but also including previous 'outsiders' such as women), in a context where women's labour-market participation was actively sought.[13] Such opportunities create a space for women activists, if they are able to reframe their demands within the dominant frame of reference of the market.

In this chapter, I develop a framework for understanding treatment of the gender pay gap as a policy problem during the New Labour administration (1997–2010), focusing on debates within parliament. The chapter begins with an overview of the main typology used to categorize policies aimed at strengthening women's rights and goes on to examine the development of a distinctive approach to policy on the gender pay gap, which appeared as a policy problem during Labour's first term. Analysis of the parliamentary debates helps to identify which policy actors set the agenda and how they defined the problem within the parameters of the party-political debate. This chapter therefore aims to deepen understanding of the extent to which British politics was substantively 'feminized' during the New Labour years.

Regime Theories

Policies form only part of a wider system of gender (in)equality. They interact in complex ways with the family structures and cultures, labour markets, and countries' patterns of economic and social development. In response to social mobilization, states inserted regulatory and redistributive policies into existing national institutions of the family and the market. The result was different configurations of class, gender, and race inequality that together, as Lynn Prince Cooke argues, create 'an interlocking system of gender-class inequality in paid and unpaid work that blocks the ability to achieve progress in either domain'.[14] Sylvia Walby uses the concept of gender regimes to show how national trajectories of economic development led to specific configurations of gender relations in the public and private sphere, across four related domains: economy, polity, civil society, and violence. Patriarchy or structured male dominance takes different forms in this analysis, owing to patterns of modernization that increase inequality (neoliberalism) or decrease it (social democracy). In the British case, usually classified as a liberal market economy, the gender regime has moved even further towards neoliberalism.[15] This approach emphasizes political economy as an overarching structure of power relations, which includes norms and expectations about gender relations and gender roles in the private and public spheres. Feminist political economy makes a powerful contribution to understanding gender in the workplace by showing how the gender pay gap relates to structural features of the labour market, particularly wider pay inequality.

Other scholars emphasize the importance of welfare regimes as bundles of policy that together result in differing degrees of defamilialization. The concept of defamilialization goes beyond the usual reliance on decommodification—the extent to which individuals and households can maintain acceptable living standards independently of employment—by taking account of how far individuals can live independently of the family. It is important for feminist scholarship, because it goes beyond the idea of the welfare state as providing principally for non-employment and asks what policies can support women in employment, and it also highlights the unpaid work done by women.[16] Welfare regime theory is primarily concerned with class-based policies involving redistribution by the state through cash transfers or service provision (such as childcare or elder care). Liberal welfare states such as the UK (along with the USA and Australia) display weak decommodification and weak defamilialization. Moreover, this structural feature is found to be persistent over time regardless of the ideology of the party in power.

Returning to the question of how far women's increased presence in the legislature can affect change in policy, we can see how far this is mediated by the welfare-state regime. Anne Watson showed, through analysis of parliamentary speeches in Canada, Ireland, and the UK (Westminster) in the period from 1988 to 2017, that there was a lower incidence of attention to policy on family leave, childcare, working time regulation, and abortion regulation in the UK than in the other two countries.[17] Although all three countries are broadly considered to represent liberal welfare regimes, Ireland and Canada exhibited higher defamilialization scores for the same period, and also increased their defamilialization score, while in the UK it decreased. Watson's findings indicate weak attention to gender class-based policy in the British parliament, consistent with a persistently market-focused, residual welfare state.

Watson's analysis of speeches also identified a difference between attention given by women MPs, compared to men, to the type of policy, with women significantly more likely than men (when weighted to take account of number of MPs by gender) to speak on abortion regulation and childcare, but not so for family leave or working time regulation. Speech acts were mediated by party ideology, with Conservative men and women more likely to speak on abortion and childcare than on family leave or working time. Policy on abortion could be expected to follow a different trajectory, as it is classed as doctrinal policy, which is status based rather than class based. In the UK, it does not feature in party manifestos and is largely viewed as a matter of personal conviction, allowing MPs from all parties to table legislative bills (usually early day motions, which have low chances of being discussed and even lower chances of being adopted, or ten-minute-rule bills).[18]

However, it is less straightforward to understand why female MPs in the UK paid relatively less attention in parliament to family leave and working time than to childcare in the period 1997–2017, as all three areas are broadly categorized as class-based policy. The cross-national research presented by Htun and Weldon, enriched by national case studies, helps to explain why this should be so. They found that, while both strong feminist movements and left-of-centre government were associated with the adoption of childcare and family leave policy at a general level, contextual variation was strong. Given this finding, a further hypothesis already raised in the previous chapter is that agenda-setting in the Westminster parliament is strongly dependent on government, and on the role of critical actors. Policy on childcare had been prepared by the work of women activists within the Labour Party before 1997, in particular by Harriet Harman. It was integrated within a central plank of leadership thinking related to 'welfare to work', more specifically an agenda of helping and encouraging lone parents (the majority of whom were women) into paid employment.[19] Moreover, the redistributive aspects of childcare policy were relatively depoliticized in that the main employer organizations supported public childcare provision and did not frame policy in terms of costs or burdens.

Policy on family leave, working time regulation, and equal pay, on the other hand, remained highly conflictual and responded to traditional left–right (class) as well as gender divisions. The distinction between different levels of attention to types of policy dealing with women in paid employment is important. Here, I focus on two areas of policy as a starting point for further discussion in the book.

First, work–family policy is broadly defined as encompassing family (care-related) leave, working time regulation, and childcare support (which can be public provision or direct support to households in the form of cash transfers, vouchers, or tax credits). As set out above, although categorized overall as class-based policy, work–family policy comprises a 'menu of policy options'[20] or range of measures whose adoption results from different political factors (including cultural attitudes of voters and elites) and results in different outcomes with respect to gender and class.[21] In other words, it is the configuration of policies that matters, and its overall rationale in terms of gender norms.[22] As policy measures differ in terms of both origin and outcome, trade-offs are likely to occur, depending on the strength of women's organizations and party politics at any given moment.[23] A further set of contextual factors relate to the extent to which, in a market-oriented economy, redistributive aspects of work–family policy can be weakened and policy objectives reframed as 'business-case' arguments. In that case, policy is less directly dependent on left government and feminist mobilization, but still dependent on government leadership.

The second set of policies relate to legislation specifically designed not just to outlaw discrimination against women in the workplace but to provide means of redress to individuals (and in some cases to groups of women), and to place positive duties on employers to take steps to ensure that discrimination does not take place. As these policies relate primarily to women's status in the workplace as women, they are broadly categorized as status-based rather than class-based policies, and they are driven by societal pressure on parties in government. For such policies, Htun and Weldon found a 'sandwich effect', whereby women's movement mobilization combined with pressure from international organizations.[24] However, they found no significant association with labour movements. This finding confirms that trade unions have long been inconsistent on equal pay, often adopting a policy of pay equality in response to women's union activism while adhering to gendered differentials in pay bargaining in practice.[25] Overall, as for work–family policy, cross-national comparative analysis found strong contextual effects.

To summarize, while it is helpful to understand the logics of status-based and class-based policies in order to explain the adoption of policy on women and employment, it is also important to situate the discussion within a given national context. Theoretically, feminist institutionalism helps to identify the impact of formal and informal gender rules within the decision-making space, and regime theories based on feminist political economy and social policy shed light on national development trajectories shaping the gender–class nexus. To investigate further, I turn now to the gender pay gap and the way it is addressed as a policy problem.

Defining the Gender Pay Gap as a Policy Problem in British Politics: Agenda-Setting

As a policy problem, the gender pay gap has moved up the agenda as women's labour-market participation increased, and as policymakers explicitly sought to raise the female employment rate. For example, within the European Union it became a policy priority within the context of the EU's employment strategy after 1999, with the publication of Eurostat standardized data from 2002.[26] In this sense, the identification of the gender pay gap as a policy problem may be seen as at least partly instrumental and indeed is often framed in terms of labour-market efficiency and productivity.

Despite its identification as a priority by the EU and other international organizations, policy attention to the gender gap varies across countries. This variation reflects welfare regimes and the extent to which reliance on women's reproductive work is problematized in public policy, and the agency of policy entrepreneurs within the state machinery and outside it, in civil society. The efforts of the equality machinery and/or the women's policy machinery are particularly important in raising the policy profile of the gender pay gap.[27]

The identification of the gender pay gap as a policy problem relies on data on hourly earnings by gender. Statistics on the gender pay gap were first collected at UK national level in 1997, when the gap between women's median hourly pay and that of men stood at 27.5 per cent (25.3 per cent mean hourly gap), meaning that at aggregate level, for every pound paid to men, women earned on average 82.5 pence. It also reflects analysis of the gender gap in hourly earnings to identify the factors causing it, usually by regression methods. As discussed in Chapters 5 and 6, therefore, an important part of the work of the equality machinery and the women's policy machinery, following the publication of standardized statistics from 1997, was to commission and publicize research into the causes of the gender pay gap.

Comparative research indicates that, as well as the extent of attention given to the gender pay gap as a policy problem, the type of policy response varies significantly across countries. Three broad types of policy can be distinguished: equal-pay policy, aimed at tackling discrimination, through laws prohibiting discriminatory practice and/or awareness-raising activities; equal opportunities policy, aimed at helping women to remain in the labour market after childbirth and have continuous careers, and at breaking down occupational segregation; and wage policies, aimed at improving the situation of low-paid workers and reducing wage inequality. Although governments are often reluctant to intervene in wage-setting, the third of these policy types is thought by feminist economists to offer the best chances of tackling pay inequity.[28]

Here I track 'gender pay gap' as an item of parliamentary debates in the Westminster parliament (House of Commons). According to Hansard, the first mention of the gender pay gap in Westminster parliamentary debates occurred in May 1991, but the gender pay gap did not feature as an item of debate in itself until June 2002.[29] After that, it was the subject of one or two debates per year in 2007, 2008, 2009 and 2010, but attention increased after July 2015 (when the introduction of gender pay gap reporting regulations was announced). Mention of the gender pay gap in other debates began tentatively under the Conservative government of John Major with the launch of Opportunity Now, increased in the New Labour years, and became a more prominent policy under Conservative governments after 2015.

A number of factors appear to have led to the appearance of the gender pay gap onto the parliamentary agenda, and to the pattern of increasing—but still limited—attention. As noted above, both main parties have given attention to the gender pay gap, which first appeared and later substantially rose under right-of-centre government. It gained and subsequently increased attention under adverse economic conditions: shortly after the 1990–1 recession and the 2008 financial crisis.

Feminization of parliament helps to explain initial attention to the gender pay gap. In the period 1991–7, Labour politicians raised the gender pay gap as a problem in response to government bills or prior actions: abolition of wages councils (in a debate in February 1993), the trade union reform bill (in March 1993); Labour politicians also alleged lack of government action in following up two reports on sex discrimination by the EOC in 1988 and 1990 (March 1994), and the launch of Opportunity Now in 1990. In all cases, in the Commons or the Lords, the (Labour) member questioning the government on the gender pay gap was a woman: in particular, Maria Eagle, Alice Mahon, and Clare Short in the lower house, and Baronesses Lockwood (a lifelong campaigner for equal pay, and first chair of the EOC, made a life peer in 1978) and Turner (a former trade-union official, and member of the EOC between 1982 and 1988, ennobled in 1985) in the upper house. These were all prominent Labour women associated with the left of the party and in most cases with trade-union activity. For the period of the Major governments, then, partisan politics and women's parliamentary presence appear to be key factors explaining agenda-setting on the gender pay gap, responding also to the equality machinery in the form of the EOC.

In those parliamentary debates, there was little reference to reports or statistics outside the domestic context. However, the major intervention on the gender pay gap during the period 1992–7 took place in March 1994, when Clare Short (then shadow minister for women) deplored 'the Government's failure fully to implement European equality legislation or the recommendations of the Equal Opportunities Commission' and called on government to simplify, strengthen, and extend the Sex Discrimination and Equal Pay Acts.[30] Alongside stronger equal-pay legislation, Short argued for better childcare and maternity and parental leave provision, and criticized the government for blocking the European parental leave directive and only 'grudgingly' improving maternity leave when forced to do so by the EU. Short's speech also referred to the new women's policy machinery, which, although established under the Conservative government after the 1992 election, had been prepared by Labour's Jo Richardson in collaboration with Sir Robin Butler, head of the civil service. This institutional innovation had, she asserted, led to increased appointment of women to public positions.

This brief discussion of parliamentary debates in the first half of the 1990s, when the gender pay gap began to appear on the British policy agenda (as distinct from equal pay or equal opportunities), indicates the importance of female parliamentary presence, women's party activism, and lobbying by the equality machinery (in the form of the arm's-length enforcement agency, the EOC), using European equality legislation as a lever for political pressure. The creation of a new unit for women within the Department for Employment served as another reference point for parliamentary discussion. Analysis of Hansard debates also confirms the importance of partisan politics in carving out a political space for woman-friendly policy, associated with stronger equal-pay legislation, maternity and parental leave rights, and child-care provision. The political space was largely located within Labour Party politics, with all (female and male) Conservative MPs who participated in the debate presented above expressing satisfaction with existing legislation and opposing Short, on grounds of cost to taxpayers.

The terminology and methodology of the gender pay gap were still little used in political debate before 1997, however. When referring to the situation of women in paid employment, the vocabulary of equal pay and sex discrimination was most widely used, reflecting reliance on the equal-pay and sex-discrimination legislation, which had been enacted under a Labour government. In public discourse, British gender politics still rested on a passive approach to anti-discrimination, with the onus on individual women to prove discrimination in difficult circumstances, as I set out in the next chapter: the tribunal process was long and prohibitively costly, and the barrier for proving discrimination set high. The EU (then EEC) through its challenges to the British government helped the EOC to become a more effective support for litigants. Policy development at EU level also prepared the way for a more pro-active and wide-ranging approach to gender equality in the workplace, as the European policy agenda broadened and the links between different aspects of women's political, social, and economic empowerment were set out first in gender action programmes, then in gender equality strategies. Under the Amsterdam Treaty signed in 1997, gender equality became a guiding legal principle of the EU.

A shift towards a more pro-active approach had also been prepared in the UK by evidence gathered on the weak impact of equal-pay and sex-discrimination legislation in practice. To use the language of the gender pay gap was, among other things, to recognize that the existing legal framework was inadequate in addressing discrimination. Such a shift was, however, still marginal in parliamentary debates, whilst Labour policy framed women-focused policy primarily in terms of representation to political decision-making and public appointments. Wider areas such as women's unpaid work, and the specific disadvantage of black women, as well as disabled women, were not broached. Scholars began to ask whether the British equal opportunities regime could be opened up to consider intersectional disadvantage, although the term intersectionality was not then widely used. Cynthia Cockburn argued in 1989 that the radical potential of equal opportunities would not be realized as long as Labour retained its overriding focus on class.[31] Even raising the question of women's disadvantage as mothers and primary carers required a gender focus that was absent from official Labour Party discourse.

Labour's First Term: Developing Understanding of the Gender Pay Gap as a Policy Problem

Labour's 1997 manifesto made no reference to the gender pay gap, and referred to women workers in passing, in just two contexts: first, the particular benefit low-paid women would gain from the introduction of a national minimum wage, and, second, the need for flexible work–family rights derived from European legislation. However, the introduction of reliable gender pay gap datasets and the institutional innovation of a minister for women and equality and a stand-alone government department provided a knowledge and political infrastructure for public debate after 1997, although parliamentary debates continued to rely on the annual set-piece debate to mark International Women's Day, which marginalized policy for women. As discussed further in Chapter 6, the secondary nature of the women and equality brief in relation to the minister's main responsibility meant that debates primarily responded to that other responsibility and therefore depended on the relevance and authority of the lead government department, even in International Women's Day debates. Given women's ministerial location in traditionally 'feminine' departments such as social security and health, the gender pay gap was predominantly framed as a question of combining paid work and family care, mainly for mothers.

Despite the record intake of women MPs in 1997, mentions of the gender pay gap in debates did not increase until late into Labour's first term, and then only slightly. The debates were not led by women, with the exception of Tessa Jowell, then junior Minister for Women. Apart from the International Women's Day speech, which has become a parliamentary convention, debates that addressed the gender pay gap in the early first Labour term dealt with the minimum wage legislation, and were introduced and dominated by men. After 2000, the number of interventions dealing directly with the gender pay gap increased, in response to policy activism by the EOC. Men continued to lead several key debates, although in the House of Lords interventions by peers on matters relating to women and employment were more gender balanced. On 21 March 2001, Labour backbencher Vernon Coaker moved a ten-minute bill (supported by seven female and four male MPs) calling for the introduction of equal-pay audits, in a debate referring directly to the gender pay gap.[32]

Several explanations may be put forward to explain the low level of parliamentary attention to the gender pay gap. As noted above, the 1997 government had not defined it as a policy problem and saw action on behalf of women as resulting principally from the introduction of a national minimum wage and wider tax-benefits policy. As Childs argues in her analysis of the 1997 intake of Labour women, Labour women in 1997 saw themselves primarily through a party lens, even though they may also have identified as feminist.[33] The women's policy machinery was evidently not yet ready to make independent proposals or prepare the way for others to intervene, as will be discussed in Chapter 6. The increase in women's parliamentary presence seems to have made no difference to parliamentary attention. Childs suggests that the main reason was that women MPs saw the main priorities as being associated with care, particularly the childcare strategy. The gender pay gap as an indicator of how women were being treated on the labour market does not seem to have been salient as a policy priority, despite increased activism by the EOC in 2000.

Labour's Second Term: The Promise of Action on the Gender Pay Gap

In Labour's manifesto for the 2001 general election, the party committed itself to tackling the inequality between working men and women, which was indicated by the gender pay gap. It pledged to work with employees and employers in the public and private sectors to develop proposals 'building on good practice and the sound business case'. As discussed further in Chapter 5, this commitment had been prepared by women activists within the party, responding to the evidence that had been built by the equality machinery and the women's policy machinery. The campaign to strengthen and broaden debate within the party on equal pay had also been boosted by the beginnings, albeit weak, of union pressure on the party leadership through the National Policy Forum, as will be examined in Chapter 5.

The period following the 2001 general election saw brief but focused attention on the gender pay gap during preparations for the Employment Act 2002 and after its adoption on 8 July 2002 (with a total of three debates in this period on the gender pay gap). The main debate took the form of set-piece questions to the Minister for Women, Patricia Hewitt, on 13 June 2002, when she set out government policy.[34] The national minimum wage had already made a difference to low-paid working women, she argued, and she was working with colleagues in the Department for Education to develop childcare provision. Hewitt announced that the Employment Act would introduce, alongside paternity leave and pay and the extension of maternity leave and pay, a consultation on equal-pay questionnaires to help women seeking redress for sex discrimination at work. Meanwhile, all government departments would be required to carry out equality audits by April 2003, and the DTI was working with the EOC to provide support to private-sector employers to encourage them to conduct equal-pay audits.[35]

In the June 2002 debate, five Labour MPs (three women, two men) asked questions of the minister, and four Conservatives (all women). In this debate, two main policy concerns may be identified, in broad opposition to the government position. The first, represented by John Whittingdale (Labour), placed action on the gender pay gap within a broader set of employment rights, which this MP wanted to see strengthened under a Labour government: Hewitt in reply described his demand as 'nonsense'; the second defined the question as relating to women's representation in top posts, specifically senior civil service appointments. During Labour's second term, in contrast to these positions, the gender pay gap was placed on the government agenda with a broad set of objectives: narrowing of the pay gap for low-paid workers through the national minimum wage, improved access to childcare provision, flexible working, maternity and paternity leave, equality auditing in the public sector, and support for voluntary initiatives in the private sector.

With the inclusion of a commitment in the 2001 manifesto, activists had shifted the question of the gender pay gap from an anticipatory agenda (based on expectations of what might appeal to women voters) to a promissory one, creating pressure for the government to achieve its electorally mandated promise.[36] The issue had thereby been legitimated and there was an expectation of substantive action. However, a promissory agenda is mediated by political agency: who has the capacity to drive the agenda, and in what form. Analysis of parliamentary debates suggest that in Labour's second term the promissory agenda was still in the process of being defined and shaped, in ways that fitted the government's existing initiatives, but also including an emerging new agenda of public-sector duties.

Labour's Third Term: Strengthening Equalities Legislation

Two sets of initiatives shaped parliamentary debates on the gender pay gap in Labour's third term (with four debates in total headed 'gender pay gap'). The first responded to the recommendations of the Women and Work Commission (WWC), launched in February 2006. In January 2007, minister for women and equality Ruth Kelly reported that the government was working on its recommendations, including sponsorship of an exemplary employers network and preparation of the public-sector equality duty, which would be presented to parliament later that year.[37] The WWC's recommendations found their way into a debate on the gender pay gap on 19 June 2008, with a question from Labour's Jim Cunningham asking the Minister for Equality, Barbara Follett, what the government intended to do about gender stereotypes. Follett replied that the government would fund initiatives 'to encourage young people to consider atypical career choices when applying for apprenticeships'.[38]

The second set of initiatives was associated with the Equality Bill, which was published in its initial form in June 2008 and adopted during the last days of the Labour administration.[39]

The Equality Bill had been prepared by women within the Labour Party for the duration of the Labour administration (since 1997): inside government, by successive ministers and civil servants responsible for women and equalities; inside the prime minister's office, by political advisers; outside government, by a range of equalities campaign groups under the leadership of the EOC; and in the interface between government and outside agencies, by legal experts and equality campaigners commissioned by government after 2005 to review equalities and social mobility.

In its passage through parliament the Equality Bill encountered broad cross-party support for its principles.[40] However, important aspects of the bill, beyond the doctrinal issues around the tension between religion and sexual identity that are not examined here, were highly controversial. These included the innovative socio-economic duty assigned to the public sector as well as duties on private-sector employers. Duties on employers were justified by the Minister for Women and Equality, Harriet Harman, on the grounds that the public sector should lead by example and that private-sector employers should do more to increase transparency on pay.[41] Parliamentary discussion of the gender pay gap in the context of the Equality Bill presented employer duties to monitor gender pay gaps as necessary because of the deficiencies of the existing equal-pay legislation.[42] The framing of the gender pay gap within an overarching equalities framework opened the issue to a greater number of potential points of contestation, creating friction within the policy process.[43]

After Labour: From Gender Pay Gap to Gender Pay Gap Reporting

In the decade following Labour's period in office, with the House of Commons governed first by a Conservative-led coalition with the Liberal Democratic Party and after 2015 by a Conservative majority, parliamentary debates on the gender pay gap intensified, particularly after 2015. Under the coalition government, the gender pay gap was the subject of five debates, and between 2015 and 2020 twenty-six.

In October 2010 (just after the release of the film *Made in Dagenham*, which recounted the story of the 1968 strike by women workers at Ford), Theresa May as Minister for Women and Equalities (and Home Secretary) argued in response to a question from a Conservative backbencher (Harriet Baldwin) that, by extending the right to request flexible working to all employees, introducing shared parental leave, and encouraging girls to take up a range of career options, the government aimed to 'end' the gender pay gap.[44] These proposals were in line with the coalition agreement signed in May 2010, which did not, however, mention the gender pay gap specifically.[45]

In March 2011 (timed to coincide with International Women's Day), May answered a question from Simon Hughes (Liberal Democrat) on the gender pay gap to draw attention to the Davies review of women on corporate boards.[46] In December 2013, May again responded to questions from her own backbenchers and from Labour's Diana Johnson, Ann McKechin, and Gloria De Piero, returning to the theme of flexible working.[47] By July 2014, May had been replaced by Nicky Morgan as Minister for Women and Equalities (and Minister for Education), and Morgan's recently appointed deputy Jo Swinson (Liberal Democrat) answered questions from Labour MPs Heidi Alexander and Gloria De Piero, referring to the government's intention to extend the right to request flexible working and introduce shared parental leave, as well as to a voluntary initiative aimed at encouraging employers to report their gender pay gap.[48] When Morgan fielded questions from two male Conservative backbenchers and two female Labour MPs in January 2015, however, the minister's response emphasized collaboration with the Women's Business Council to develop the skills of female employees. Morgan argued that voluntary action by employers was 'much better' than mandatory duties.[49]

Before leaving government after the May 2015 general election, Swinson introduced a clause in the Small Business Act 2014 to enact the provision for mandatory gender pay gap reporting included in the Equality Act 2010. Like the Liberal Democrats, the Conservative Party for the first time included in their 2015 manifesto a commitment to reduce the gender pay gap and referred specifically to the introduction of regulations mandating gender pay gap reporting by organizations with 250 or more employees. Over the following five years, these regulations were the focus of parliamentary debates on the gender pay gap, as successive Conservative ministers for women and equalities repeated the 2015 manifesto pledge to end the gender pay gap 'within a generation'.[50]

Once the regulations had been introduced, parliamentary attention turned to compliance. In April 2018, the Minister for Women Victoria Atkins announced that over ten thousand employers had submitted reports in the first annual round of reporting. Parliamentary attention turned to ways of improving reporting by employers, in terms both of full compliance and of actions to address the gaps identified in the reports. Harman for Labour argued that secretaries of state for each department should be required to report directly to the Cabinet on the targets for reducing their gender pay gap and that the Equality and Human Rights Commission (EHRC) should be pushed to enforce private-sector compliance.[51] Swinson asked for future rounds of reporting to include gaps by race and ethnicity.[52]

In the second half of the decade, the presence of a new institutional actor was evident in parliamentary debates: the Women and Equalities Committee (WEC), appointed by the House of Commons in July 2015 to hold the minister for women and equalities and the Government Equalities Office to account. Despite the institutional constraints limiting the committee's ability to hold government fully to account, the WEC provided another point of contestation within the parliamentary debate, helping to broaden the terms of the debate beyond the narrow focus pursued by the government, and strengthening networks of women MPs and their male allies.[53] The committee's 2016 report on the gender pay gap formed a reference point for MPs wishing to push the government towards a stronger form of gender pay gap reporting, the inclusion of race and ethnicity alongside gender in reports,[54] and more emphasis on remedial actions such as better support for childcare.[55]

Conclusion

Parliamentary debates in the New Labour period defined the gender pay gap as a policy problem in relation to specific policy measures: public childcare provision, maternity and paternity leave and pay, the right to request flexible working (defined as a right depending on parental status), government support for voluntary initiatives by employers to conduct pay audits, and a range of requirements for public bodies to address gender equality in employment and pay. As Hewitt argued in parliament,[56] the rationale for these initiatives was based on research commissioned by the Women and Equality Unit in 2002, which showed an association between the gender pay gap and the impact of caring responsibilities, leading many women, particularly those with lower levels of education, into part-time employment.[57]

These debates largely set the path for subsequent discussions as the gender pay gap became an issue on which parties competed electorally. Partisan differences remained, with Conservatives in general showing a preference for voluntary over mandatory actions. However, the convergence of party positions reflects a combination of factors.

Feminization of parliament helped to keep the gender pay gap on the parliamentary agenda but was not by itself a decisive factor. The establishment of the WEC strengthened women's agency and that of male allies. Feminization of parliament spread beyond the Labour Party, although Labour remained the most highly feminized parliamentary party as a result of the adoption of all-women shortlists. Although more limited than in the case of Labour, feminization of the Conservative Party strengthened parliamentary networks of women and equality campaigners, both descriptively and substantively, as David Cameron's attempt to modernize his party involved a deliberate attempt to attract women voters and electoral candidates, not through rule changes, but through programmatic revision and a new communicative tone.[58]

Feminization of British politics took place within a circumscribed policy space in a relatively defamilialized but highly marketized regime, but also challenged it in several ways. The most obvious means by which it was challenged was through the women's policy machinery, which enabled purposive critical actors, most prominently Harman and Hewitt, to use all the resources available to them: party networks, direct access to prime-ministerial power, networking within the business community and with a range of civil society actors including trade unions and equality campaigners, and the formal equality machinery in the form of the EOC and its successor the EHRC, as well as the material resources of the civil service devoted to women and equality.

Rather than seeing legislative presence and the equality and policy machinery as competing drivers of policy, my analysis views them as complementary elements of a longer-term process of feminization. As feminist scholars of British parties of government have shown, descriptive and substantive representation of women form uneven but related parts of a recent and still unfinished process linked to party modernization, in the specific institutional context of British politics.[59] In the next chapter, I consider the role of the equality machinery within that process, before turning to changes within the Labour Party and the wider labour movement, and then the women's policy machinery.

Notes

1. L. Chaqués-Bonafont and C. Cristancho, 'The Gender Divide in Issue Attention', *European Journal of Political Research*, 61 (2022), https://doi.org/10.1111/1475-6765.12437; T. Osborn and J. M. Mendez, 'Speaking as Women: Women in Floor Speeches in the Senate', *Journal of Women, Politics and Policy*, 31 (2010), https://doi.org/10.1080/15544770903501384.
2. A. M. Goetz, 'Women's Political Effectiveness: A Conceptual Framework', in A. M. Goetz and S. Hassim (eds), *No Shortcuts to Power: African Women in Politics and Policy Making* (London: Zed Books, 2003), 29–80; A. M. Goetz and R. Jenkins, 'Feminist Activism and the Politics of Reform: When and Why Do States Respond to Demands for Gender Equality Policies?', UNRISD Working Paper 2016-13 (United Nations Research Institute for Social Development, 2016). See also C. Annesley, I. Engeli, and F. Gains, 'The Profile of Gender Equality Issue Attention in Western Europe', *European Journal of Political Research*, 54 (2015), https://doi.org/10.1111/1475-6765.12095; their article analyses issue attention in executive outputs, such as speeches.
3. The United Nations Convention on the Elimination of All Forms of Discrimination against Women (18 December 1979) is a good place to start. See also A. G. Mazur, *Theorizing Feminist Policy* (Oxford: Oxford University Press, 2002), 3.
4. M. Htun and L. Weldon, *The Logics of Gender Justice* (Cambridge: Cambridge University Press, 2018), 11.
5. Htun and Weldon, *The Logics of Gender Justice*, 13.
6. Htun and Weldon, *The Logics of Gender Justice*; see also the discussion in A. Sanders, C. Annesley, and F. Gains, 'What Did the Coalition Government Do for Women? An Analysis of Gender Equality Policy Agendas in the UK 2010–2015', *British Politics*, 14 (2019), https://doi.org/10.1057/s41293-018-00103-2.
7. Annesley et al., 'The Profile of Gender Equality Issue Attention'; Htun and Weldon, *The Logics of Gender Justice.*
8. M. Baird and M. O'Brien, 'Dynamics of Parental Leave in Anglophone Countries: The Paradox of State Expansion in Liberal Welfare Regimes', *Community, Work & Family*, 18 (2015), https://doi.org/10.1080/13668803.2015.1021755.
9. S. Milner, 'Gender Pay Gap Reporting Regulations: Advancing Gender Equality Policy in Tough Economic Times', *British Politics*, 14 (2019), https://doi.org/10.1057/s41293-018-00101-4.
10. See Sanders et al., 'What Did the Coalition Government Do for Women?'
11. See J. Rubery, 'Austerity and the Future for Gender Equality in Europe', *ILR Review*, 68 (2015), 715–41 https://doi.org/10.1177/0019793915588892.
12. See K. Thelen, *Varieties of Liberalization and the New Politics of Social Solidarity* (Cambridge: Cambridge University Press, 2014).
13. For a broad discussion, see J. Gingrich, 'Coalitions, Policies, and Distributions: Esping-Andersen's *Three Worlds of Welfare Capitalism*', in J. Mahoney and K. A. Thelen (eds), *Advances in Comparative–Historical Analysis* (Cambridge: Cambridge University Press, 2015), 67–96.
14. L. P. Cooke, *Gender–Class Equality in Industrialized Economies* (London: Routledge, 2011), 14.

15. S. Walby, 'Varieties of Gender Regimes', *Social Politics*, 27 (2020), https://doi.org/10.1093/sp/jxaa018.
16. G. Esping-Andersen, *Social Foundations of Post-Industrial Democracies* (Oxford: Oxford University Press, 1999); C. Saraceno, 'Gendered Policies: Family Obligations and Social Policies in Europe', in T. P. Boje and A. Leira (eds), *Gender, Welfare State and the Market* (London: Routledge, 2000), 135–56; D. Sainsbury, *Gender, Equality and Welfare States* (Cambridge: Cambridge University Press, 1999).
17. K. A. Watson, 'From Interests to Rights: Using CEDAW to Understand the Substantive Representation of Women', Ph.D. (University of Georgia, Athens, 2020).
18. See L. T. Larsen, D. T. Studlar, and C. Green-Pedersen, 'Morality Politics in the United Kingdom: Trapped between Left and Right', in I. Engeli, C. Green-Pedersen, and L. T. Larsen (eds), *Morality Politics in Western Europe: Parties, Agendas and Policy Choices* (London: Palgrave Macmillan, 2012), 114–36.
19. H. Harman, *A Woman's Work* (London: Allen Lane, 2017), 187–8.
20. B. Hobson, 'Gendered Dimensions and Capabilities: Opportunities, Dilemmas and Challenges', *Critical Sociology*, 44 (2018), https://doi.org/10.1177/0896920516683232.
21. See, e.g., A. Hegewisch and J. C. Gornick, 'The Impact of Work–Family Policies on Women's Employment: A Review of Research from OECD Countries', *Community, Work & Family*, 14 (2011), https://doi.org/10.1080/13668803.2011.571395.
22. T. Lauri, K. Põder, and R. Ciccia, 'Pathways to Gender Equality: A Configuration Analysis of Childcare Instruments and Outcomes in 21 European Countries', *Social Policy & Administration*, 54 (2020), https://doi.org/10.1111/spol.12562.
23. W. Korpi, T. Ferrarini, and S. Englund, 'Women's Opportunities under Different Family Policy Constellations: Gender, Class and Inequality Trade-Offs in Western Countries Re-Examined', *Social Politics*, 20 (2013), https://doi.org/10.1093/sp/jxs028.
24. Htun and Weldon, *The Logics of Gender Justice*, 100–8; see also D. E. McBride and A. G. Mazur, *The Politics of State Feminism* (Philadelphia: Temple University Press2010).
25. See S. Boston, *Women and the Unions* (London: Lawrence and Wishart, 2014).
26. J. Plantenga and C. Remery, *The Gender Pay Gap: Origins and Policy Responses: A Comparative Review of Thirty European Countries* (Luxembourg: European Commission, 2006); see also D. M. Figart, E. Mutari, and M. Power, *Living Wages, Equal Wages: Gender and Labour Market Policies in the United States* (London: Routledge: 2002).
27. Plantenga and Remery, *The Gender Pay Gap*, 28–30.
28. M. Karamessini and E. Iokimoglou, 'Wage Determination and the Gender Pay Gap: A Feminist Political Economy Analysis and Decomposition', *Feminist Economics*, 13 (2007), https://doi.org/10.1080/13545700601075088.
29. Hansard online search (http://hansard.parliament.uk) conducted 17 March 2022.
30. Hansard, HC, vol. 239, cols 423–98 (10 March 1994). The motion was lost by 303 votes to 257.
31. C. Cockburn, 'Equal Opportunities: The Long and Short Agenda', *Industrial Relations Journal*, 20 (1989), https://doi.org/10.1111/j.1468-2338.1989.tb00068.x.
32. Ten-minute-rule bills (Standing Order No. 23) allow MPs, usually backbenchers, to make the case for a new bill in a speech lasting up to ten minutes. In order to qualify, MPs must be the first through the door of the Public Bill Office on Tuesday or Wednesday

morning at least two weeks prior to the desired date of introduction. Most ten-minute-rule bills make it through to a first reading, but only a very small number make it through to legislative enactment: only two in 2001–2 (neither was Coaker's).

33. See S. Childs, *New Labour's Women MPs: Women Representing Women* (London: Routledge, 2004), 197–8.
34. By set-piece questions, I refer to the practice of placing backbencher questions as an opportunity for ministers to showcase initiatives. While these questions are often taken by junior ministers, it is noteworthy that Hewitt herself took questions relating to women and equality: see further discussion in Ch. 6.
35. Hansard, HC, vol. 386, cols 990–1, 997–8 (13 June 2002).
36. The distinction between anticipatory and promissory agendas was developed by J. Mansbridge, 'Rethinking Representation', *American Political Science Review*, 94 (2003), https://doi.org/10.1017/S0003055403000856.
37. Hansard, HC, Debate on the Gender Pay Gap, vol. 455, col. 916 (18 January 2007).
38. Hansard, HC, Debate on the Gender Pay Gap, vol. 477, col. 1071 (19 June 2008).
39. The title of the document presenting the main proposals of the bill, 'Framework for a Fairer Future', echoed the terms used in the WWC's reports.
40. See B. Hepple, 'The New Single Equality Act in Britain', *Equal Rights Review*, 5 (2010), 11–24.
41. Hansard, HC, vol. 478, col. 500 (26 June 2008).
42. Hansard, HC, vol. 494, col. 938 (25 June 2009).
43. See S. Bevan and W. Jennings, 'Representation, Agendas, and Interests', *European Journal of Political Research* (2014), https://doi.org/10.1111/1475-6765.12023.
44. Hansard, HC, vol. 517, col. 463 (28 October 2010).
45. *The Coalition: Our Programme for Government* (London: HM Government, 2010).
46. Hansard, HC, vol. 524, col. 1059 (10 March 2011).
47. Hansard, HC, vol. 572, col. 347 (12 December 2013).
48. Hansard, HC, vol. 583, col. 1074 (2 July 2014).
49. Hansard, HC, vol. 590, col. 1005 (15 July 2015).
50. Hansard, HC, vol. 606, col. 451 (25 February 2016); vol. 608, col. 506 (14 April 2016).
51. Hansard, HC, 639, cols 325–37 (18 April 2018).
52. Hansard, HC, vol. 646, col. 857 (13 September 2018).
53. See S. Childs, 'Feminist Institutionalist Change: The Case of the UK Women and Equalities Committee', *Parliamentary Affairs* (2022), https://doi.org/10.1093/pa/gsab066.
54. See questions by Labour MPs Dawn Butler and Naz Shah: respectively, Hansard, HC, vol. 638, col. 925 (29 March 2018), and vol. 649, col. 428 (15 November 2018).
55. Hansard, HC, vol. 620, col. 1125 (2 February 2017).
56. Hansard, HC, vol. 386, col. 991 (13 June 2002).
57. S. Walby and W. Olsen, *The Impact of Women's Position in the Labour Market on Pay and Implications for Productivity* (London: Women and Equality Unit, 2002).
58. R. Campbell and S. Childs, 'Conservatism, Feminisation and the Representation of Women in Politics', *British Politics*, 10 (2015), https://doi.org/10.1057/bp.2015.18.
59. I have referred in this chapter to the work of Rosie Campbell and Sarah Childs in particular, and also to the work of Joni Lovenduski (see Ch. 2), who emphasizes the slow process of feminzsation in an unfavourable institutional setting, with the possibility of resistance and setbacks as well as progress.

4

Reaching the Limits of the Equal Pay Act, 1970–2007

Introduction

The Equal Pay Act (EPA) 1970 was a 'momentous milestone'[1] in the history of the struggle for pay equality, applying to paid employment in all sectors of the economy. It was followed by the Sex Discrimination Act (SDA) 1975, which outlawed all forms of sex discrimination in employment, not just pay. These achievements reflected decades of equal-pay campaigning and the resourcefulness of a woman minister, Barbara Castle (Secretary of State for Employment and Productivity), working within the opportunity structure created by external pressure from international organizations (the International Labour Organization (ILO) and the European Economic Community (EEC)), the domestic context of incomes policy, and the failure of traditional reliance on collective bargaining.[2]

However, the adoption of equal-pay legislation was constrained by existing labour market practices and government's continued reluctance to foot the bill for public-sector equal-pay claims. The EPA 1970 specified that employers should give equal treatment to women and men in their employment and that

> a woman is to be regarded as employed on like work with men if, but only if, her work and theirs are of the same or a broadly similar nature, and the differences (if any) between the things she does and the things they do are not of practical importance in relation to terms and conditions of employment,

or where it had been rated as equivalent in an evaluation review.[3] This opened two avenues for individual equal-pay claims through employment tribunals: through reference to an existing evaluation scheme, or through evidence to support a claim of comparability between male and female jobs within the same work organization. Both avenues proved difficult to access in practice.

Women and Employment in Public Policy. Susan Milner, Oxford University Press. © Susan Milner (2024).
DOI: 10.1093/9780191987359.003.0004

Although the EPA allowed the UK to ratify the ILO's Convention no. 100 on equal remuneration, it did so in a very limited way, both in its definition and in its means of enforcement. The legal foundation was subsequently strengthened in some key respects, owing to pressure from European case law. Nevertheless, gaps and weaknesses remained, and the legislation has repeatedly been acknowledged by parliamentarians to be in need of reform, even unfit for purpose. As Labour MP Emily Thornberry stated in the House of Commons in March 2015, the Act was 'essentially reactive', crafted to meet the rampant discrimination of the time: it was not robust enough to allow systematic comparison of men's and women's wages, let alone to challenge wider discriminatory practices in the workplace.[4]

In this chapter, I review developments following the adoption of the EPA 1970, and the role of the equality agency in enforcing equal-pay legislation.[5] In Chapter 1, I outlined the concept of regulatory space, which, alongside government and parliamentary bodies, includes non-governmental agencies as well as civil society organizations. The policy field of equal pay forms a regulatory space characterized by a narrow form of enforcement that relies on individual claims to tribunals for judicial determination.[6] The procedural difficulties created by the law not only prevent many individual claimants from seeking redress but restrict the capacity of the equality agency to support individual claims. Moreover, the historical legacy of discriminatory structures and practices within the labour market means that the law has largely been used in a remedial way, causing backlogs and resistances, rather than in a way that actively promotes equality.

The capacity of the equality machinery to support claims and promote equality is also affected by its material resources, status in relation to government, and internal structure and leadership, as this chapter will discuss. In more general terms, as Jeanne Gregory argued in 1999, 'the single most important factor determining the success or failure of civil rights legislation is political commitment on the part of governments'.[7] In 1997, with Labour committed to establishing a ministry of women's rights, the conditions for a robust regulatory space seemed favourable. However, the situation during the Labour years was one of restructuring and flux, opening new avenues of debate but hampering in some key respects the equality agency's capacity to generate transformative change.[8] As this chapter will show, although the Labour government was more receptive to equal rights than the preceding Conservative governments, it displayed ambivalence towards gender-based claims and towards the equality body tasked with promoting them. Moreover, several policy trends with a powerful negative impact on women's labour-market situation, such as contracting-out within the public sector,[9] were not only continued but actively promoted under Labour. As a result, conflicts and tensions characterized the policy field of equal pay.

Implementing the Equal Pay Act

The Equal Pay Act did not take effect until 1975, as it set out a transitional timetable during which employers' representatives and trade unions were required to review all wage-setting practices to ensure that they conformed to equal pay according to the definition set out in the Act. Nevertheless, it had a strong initial impact: by 1977, women's wages, which stood at less than two-thirds of men's (63.1 per cent) in 1970, had risen to three-quarters (75.5 per cent) of men's average wages,[10] as many employers responded to the legislative impetus in the way desired by the government and reviewed pay structures in stages. However, the rate of change slowed subsequently, and the differential remained around 25 per cent into the 1980s.

At least part of the reason for the Act's limited long-term impact was the narrow definition of equal pay in the 1970 Act, which made it difficult to uphold claims of unequal treatment.[11] Only 11 per cent of sex-discrimination claims were successful between 1976 and 1983, and only 10 per cent of equal-pay claims.[12] Although Castle attempted to include the ILO definition—which explicitly goes beyond equal pay for the same or similar work, to allow for comparison of work that is different but can be shown to have equal value[13]—in the bill, she met opposition in parliament as well as from organized employers. In addition, comparison of men's and women's jobs for the purpose of establishing equal value requires detailed evaluation of jobs,[14] but the EPA 1970, while recommending job evaluation, did not make it compulsory, on the grounds that the British system relied on voluntary implementation through free collective bargaining.[15] Castle argued in 1970 that there was nothing to prevent unions from pushing for equal pay through job evaluation,[16] but job evaluation is a difficult and lengthy process and requires sustained commitment from all parties.

Membership of the EEC caused only minimal pressure to adapt British legislation initially, since the Treaty of Rome contained a narrow definition of equal pay (Article 119), referring to 'equal pay for equal work'. Subsequently, however, European case law led to successive extensions of the scope of equal pay and equal treatment. An implementation review by the European Commission in 1978 found that the Equal Pay Act 1970 was based on the most restrictive interpretation among all member states, and the commission commenced infringement proceedings against the UK in 1983. Following a ruling by the European Court of Justice that the UK had failed to implement Article 1 of Council Directive 75/119/EEC, which referred explicitly to the ILO definition of 'work of equal value', the EPA was amended in 1983 to include reference to equal pay where a women is employed 'in terms of the demands made on her (for instance under such headings as effort, skill and decision) of equal value to that of a man in the same employment'.[17] However, the 1983 regulations did not require job evaluation to determine whether the same demands were being made of men and women in such circumstances, but rather authorized industrial tribunals to conduct expert reviews to make the necessary comparisons where cases were brought before them.[18]

The amendment generated a significant increase in the number of equal-value cases: the Advisory, Conciliation and Arbitration Service (ACAS) received seventy-eight claims for upgrading women's work in the first three months of 1985 alone.[19] The case of the Ford Dagenham sewing machinists, whose 1968 strike for regrading pushed Castle into presenting the equal-pay bill, illustrates the difference made by the 1983 regulations. In 1968, their strike ended in failure, from the women's viewpoint, because the union settled for 'equal pay', which effectively left them in a pay grade below that of men doing work of equal value. Equal pay was widely understood at the time to allow different rates for jobs that were classified as men's or women's jobs, as long as men and women doing the same job were paid the same rate. The machinists had claimed, on the other hand, that their job was undervalued in Ford's pay grading structure precisely because they were women and their skills were not recognized. When a new generation of women went on strike for regrading in 1984, they were able to take the case to ACAS, which ruled in their favour: the women's skills were finally recognized, thanks to the principle of 'equal value'.

The first tribunal case won under the 1984 EPA (Amendment) was that of fifteen women fish-packers in Hull in 1985.[20] Supporting the fish-packers' case, Transport and General Workers' Union (TGWU) officer Pete Allen was backed by the Equal Opportunities Commission (EOC), and Allen went on to lead eighteen further cases, winning seventeen of them, in the period 1984–2002. Women workers' demands for equal pay increasingly caused trade unions to pay attention to their claims.[21] The Union of Shop, Distributive, and Allied Workers (USDAW) supported a case against Sainsburys supermarkets by checkout operator Geraldine O'Sullivan, who received an out-of-court award settling her claim for comparison with male warehouse workers.[22] However, employers could still justify unequal pay with reference to 'genuine material factor' defences, including the 'market rate' for the job.[23]

In the public sector, unions encountered fragmented pay systems and resistance from employers, resulting in long delays to bring cases through the tribunals. Landmark cases launched in this period were those of the canteen cook Julie Hayward and the speech therapist Pam Enderby, who both succeeded (in 1988 and 1993 respectively) in their claims that their work was comparable to male-dominated skilled trades and professions.[24] The Enderby case, which reached the European court, was particularly significant, because it established that collective agreements could not be used to justify unequal pay, and that employers could not use skills shortages as a defence for higher male wages.[25]

Union pressure led to new job evaluation initiatives aimed at avoiding equal-pay claims. In the private sector, leading retailers (notably Marks & Spencer, Tesco, and Sainsburys) reviewed their job evaluation schemes after the O'Sullivan case. In the public sector, with its high share of female employment (particularly in lower-paid jobs), pressure from the Confederation of Health Service Employees (Cohse) and the National Union of Public Employees (NUPE) sparked large-scale job evaluation.[26] The 'Whitley' councils set up after 1919, with separate bargaining for different occupational groups, represented by different trade unions and staff associations, resulted in a fragmented system, and job evaluation had not been undertaken for at least two decades. In the process of re-evaluation, further problems of comparability were uncovered, triggering conflicts between groups of workers set to gain and lose from regrading.

The biggest of the public-sector job-evaluation programmes, affecting over a million workers, was Agenda for Change in the National Health Service (NHS), which followed the Single Status agreement in local government. The Agenda for Change proposals, published in 1999, aimed to replace the complex Whitley grading structure with two national pay spines, underpinned by local job evaluation. Implementation was hindered by inadequate planning of costs,[27] delays, and gaps between expectations and results, but resulted in better pay for most nursing staff.[28] The long process of job evaluation in the public sector showed the incompleteness of the move towards equal pay begun with the passage of the EPA 1970.

The increased number of equal-pay claims in the public sector from the end of the 1990s was driven both by unions—in particular Unison (which resulted from the merger of Cohse, NUPE, and the National and Local Government Officers Association (NALGO)) and the General, Municipal and Boilermakers' Union (GMB, which had members in both the public and private sectors)—which now had better data on pay, thanks to job evaluation processes,[29] and by the introduction of new rules allowing solicitors to take claims on a 'no-win, no-fee' basis. The best known of these lawyers was Stefan Cross, who in the year 2004/5 alone was responsible for launching 10,000 claims, and 30,000 in 2007/8 (when in the 1980s and into the 1990s equal-pay claims numbered hundreds each year).[30]

Changes in the tribunal fee structure made litigation a more powerful tool. However, the conflict between individual claims and 'collective attempts to agree viable, affordable guarantees of long-term pay equality for all employees' in the financially constrained public sector was exacerbated.[31] Some trade unions themselves came under fire from Cross and other law firms, who backed claims against unions for embedding pay inequality in collective agreements.[32] During the New Labour years, therefore, equal pay became a significant and potentially costly problem for the state as employer, and the regulatory space a site of acute tension.

The Equality Machinery: An Agency with Enforcement Powers

With the adoption of the SDA 1975 came the creation of the EOC, a new regulatory body with statutory responsibility to oversee and enforce it (and the EPA). However, the EOC's capacity to effect change was hampered from the outset by difficult relations with both Conservative and Labour governments.[33] Although the EOC was an independent agency with powers laid down by law, government was able to influence its scope and priorities through the power to appoint members, and its budgetary discretion.[34]

As well as criticizing the appointments process, feminists argued that the role and powers of the EOC were ill defined,[35] and often badly managed, owing to lack of clarity about the role of the chair.[36] The legal powers of the EOC were also limited, and its budget small. The power to investigate complaints was little used by the EOC in the early years (only nine times in ten years) owing to lack of experience and the costs involved.[37] Altogether, the EOC's early operations often appeared to reflect those of 'a board with more limited scope than ... the more powerful body established in the legislation actually passed'.[38]

Faced with the constraints of implementing the EPA and the SDA, the EOC developed a strategy to challenge discriminatory practices by supporting claims through the European Court of Justice.[39] The move was risky, because of the danger of antagonizing the government to the point where it might reduce resources or dismantle the commission altogether, but it led to a series of victories that made it easier to pursue claims.[40] The EOC found that industrial tribunals were willing to integrate European case law into their rulings, leading to a more expansive interpretation of rights (on equal value and on maternity discrimination) than had hitherto been practised.

However, cases still took years to reach judgment, and the EOC had to be selective in its support, owing to limited resources. By 1987, when Joanna Foster became chair (insisting on 'chair' as the title rather than 'chairman', as her predecessor had been addressed), equality campaigners were disillusioned with the EOC and argued that its work was largely invisible, partly because individual cases took a long time to reach judgment. The 'prosaic reality', argued David Pannick QC, was 'that of a weak and underfunded EOC with powers unequal to the tasks it [was] asked to perform'.[41] The EOC responded by calling for stronger equality legislation, with 'one clear and comprehensive statute' to simplify procedures, and tougher enforcement powers for the commission itself: the authority to launch investigations without waiting for the consent of employers to do so; a simpler investigative process without the need for multiple opportunities for defence by employers; and the ability to take cases to tribunal rather than relying on individuals' capacity to seek redress.[42]

Foster's appointment was welcomed because it was not party political; she had expertise in equal opportunities as former head of the Industrial Society's Pepperell Unit.[43] Without waiting for government to grant the stronger legislation and enforcement powers it advocated, the EOC launched a series of preliminary investigations into public-sector organizations such as the Royal Mail, the NHS, and Birmingham City Council, as well as trade unions and collective-bargaining practices. The commission also sought to set the agenda by calling for initiatives to support working parents, including a childcare strategy and rights for part-time workers.[44] In this, as well as in its research on women in employment, which echoed policymakers' concern with productivity and training, the EOC selected its priorities to fit those of government, which under pressure from the CBI began to develop policy on childcare. Foster was appointed to a ministerial group on women's issues established in January 1989 and chaired by John Patten, then a minister at the Home Office (the EOC's sponsor department at the time), whose work focused on childcare policy.

However, while the EOC supported John Major's government's policy of tax credits for childcare places, it opposed moves to deregulate the sector by relaxing staff–child ratios. The EOC's call for work–family rights, in line with EEC proposals, also brought it into conflict with the Conservative government, which continued to veto such plans, along with its support for the draft European directive seeking to shift the onus of proof in equal-pay cases onto employers.[45] Such differences no doubt explained the government's refusal to increase its budget, which led the commission to appeal to public opinion to show how real-terms cuts damaged its ability to conduct research and investigations.[46] The creation of a new Women's Legal Defence Fund, through which legal practitioners and trade-union experts offered free support for equal-pay and sex-discrimination claims, was widely seen as a sign that the EOC could no longer afford to back cases.[47]

In 1991, with a general election in prospect, the EOC published an 'equality agenda', which it sent to political parties. Highlighting the largest gender pay gap in the EEC, and the highest rate of female part-time working, the EOC called on parties to present proposals for reform of equality legislation in their election manifesto, to accelerate procedures, and to raise the ceiling on awards.[48] The EOC's determination to press for reform had been sharpened by the high-profile and long-running case of Alison Halford, an assistant chief constable who claimed sex discrimination had obstructed her career in the police force. As Halford took early retirement before her claim was settled out of court, the victory was in some respects a Pyrrhic one, and the same was true of the EOC, whose financial resources were stretched by the case. However, the case had important indirect effects, not just on the police force itself (which cooperated with the EOC in establishing policies to improve its organizational culture—for example, by allowing greater use of part-time working) but also in raising wider public awareness of the prevalence of sex discrimination and the difficulties involved in addressing it.[49]

When the Conservative government explicitly ruled out such reform, the EOC took the 'unusual' step of openly criticizing all parties for their marginalization of women's economic status.[50] Through its more critical public interventions, the EOC had caused friction with the government but also placed it on the defensive, particularly as the Labour Party had developed a wider-ranging set of policies on women's political representation and work–family policy. For the first time, female ministers such as Virginia Bottomley and Gillian Shephard (then Minister of State for Health and Minister of State at the Treasury, respectively) took the lead in presenting policy initiatives on women. Equal pay and women's workplace rights had become issues on which parties began to compete electorally. Just before the 1992 election, EOC commissioners met opposition leaders Paddy Ashdown and Neil Kinnock, although its invitation to Major was not taken up.[51]

Difficult relations with the government and limited funding constrained the EOC, at a time when demand for its services was rising by on average 15 per cent annually. In an early draft of its 1992/3 corporate plan (which did not make it into the final published version), the EOC noted that 'the

Government's non-interventionist and voluntary approach poses a challenge to the Commission whose authority emanates from its statutory powers, and whose experience leads it to conclude that voluntarism is not an effective measure in combatting sex discrimination'.[52] The EOC intended to 'seize every opportunity to influence government policy',[53] but also sought to influence a wider policy community, including academics, trade unions, and employers, particularly the latter. The Equality Exchange was set up to promote communication with and between employers.[54] Foster in her media interviews emphasized that change in the business world was the biggest single factor enabling gender equality to become more mainstream. Although initially she saw Opportunity 2000 (established in 1991, and later renamed Opportunity Now) as a weak instrument for change,[55] with impetus evident only in a small number of very large companies, by the time Foster stepped down in 1993 she noted that 'concrete and often numerical targets' were being adopted.[56]

Foster's replacement by Kamlesh Bahl in 1993 was widely seen as a move to soften criticism of the government, given the latter's close relationship with the Conservative Party, and Bahl herself was the subject of campaigners' complaints about her lack of visibility (and internally about her management style),[57] but the commission had by now established a policy agenda that did not change under new leadership. Indeed, its work was strengthened by the United Nations conference in Beijing in 1995, which focused government's attention on empowerment of women and girls and led to a (temporary) increase in funding. The EOC's work was further boosted by the success of the Marshall case. Helen Marshall, a dietician, had in 1986 won her case against Southampton and South-West Health Authority on grounds of sex discrimination, having been forced to retire earlier than male colleagues and therefore lose income. Since the award was capped, owing to the ceiling in place at the time, Marshall appealed to the House of Lords and ultimately to the European Court of Justice, which challenged the ceiling and more than doubled the amount.[58] As the EOC had predicted, the higher ceiling on awards encouraged an ever-greater number of claims.

Yet in some ways the EOC was a victim of its own success, as it remained underfunded at a time in relation to demand for its services, and the high cost of claims. A quinquennial review conducted by the EOC's sponsor department (the Department for Employment) found that the commission 'spreads itself too thinly given its resources'.[59]

When Labour took office in 1997, the EOC faced one of its 'most demanding times', as it was asked to advise on an unprecedented number of parliamentary bills with equality implications (around forty within six months).[60]

The core of its work remained focused on the objective of replacing the EPA 1970 and the SDA 1975 with a single, comprehensive statute with stronger powers for tribunals, simpler procedures for claims, and the possibility of 'class actions' taken on behalf of groups of workers rather than relying on individual claims. In line with the UN's Beijing principles, the EOC also called for the mainstreaming of gender equality into all new laws, 'not bolted on'.[61] This wider agenda did not feature in Labour's first-term commitments, although the government promised to 'consider' the EOC's proposals.[62] Journalists noted that the government was likely to 'prevaricate' for fear of costs to business and political controversy.[63]

Julie Mellor replaced Bahl in November 1998, expressing her frustration that 'so many problems exist' twenty-three years after the EOC's creation.[64] She chaired an organization that struggled to meet the 'sheer weight of demands' placed on it.[65] Support for litigation had made a substantial contribution to the enforcement of equality law and would continue despite increased costs owing to the complexity of cases. Mellor secured an above-inflation increase in funding, which went some way towards making up for the erosion of resources the EOC had experienced under Conservative governments, but this was in the context of rising costs of enforcement work.[66]

The EOC's strategy continued to emphasize the need to work with employers to shift organizational culture, as well as to put pressure on government 'by asking why, despite thirty years of legislation, Britain's pay gap is the widest in Europe'.[67] Mellor's approach combined 'straight-talking' statement of the scale of the problem with persuasion based on the business case, and an understanding that employers needed time and support to make the necessary organizational changes.[68] The EOC had learnt from its work with employers that fear of legislation acted as a disincentive to initiate new workplace practices.[69] A major focus now became the question of how to 'place a legal obligation on employers' to carry out a full pay review and adopt an equal-pay policy[70] without simply encountering either outright blockage or foot-dragging on the part of employers.

Equal-Pay Audits: An Idea whose Time Had Come?

In 1999, the EOC launched a three-year campaign, 'Valuing Women', and established an Equal Pay Task Force to examine the causes of the persistent gender pay gap, and to make recommendations. The review was chaired by Bob Mason, human-resources director of British Telecommunications, and included representatives of employers and trade unions, as well as Rita Donaghy of ACAS, and independent experts, and Sally Hinkley from the Cabinet Office.[71] It based its work on research commissioned from Damian Grimshaw and Jill Rubery, which highlighted women's concentration in part-time, low-paid work as a specificity of the British labour market. Emphasizing the multidimensional nature of the gender pay gap, Grimshaw and Rubery recommended a mainstreamed policy approach encompassing a higher national minimum wage, investment in training for female part-time workers, actions to support women's career progression in the public sector, and limits on (male) long working hours, as well as employer pay reviews.[72]

The Task Force's report, published in 2001, identified three main causes of the gender pay gap: pay discrimination, occupational segregation, and the unequal impact of women's family responsibilities. Despite the scale of these structural problems, the report stated that 'we believe it is perfectly feasible, with concerted action by all the key players, that the gender pay gap due to discrimination should be reduced by 50% within the next 5 years and eliminated entirely within 8 years',[73] while policies to mitigate the second two causes of the pay gap could also be tackled by government straight away. Recommendations included funds to support awareness-raising through the 'Valuing Women' campaign; better data from the Office for National Statistics on the gender pay gap; a stronger role for the EOC in developing expertise among employers to assist them in preparing pay reviews; the creation of an Equal Pay Forum to promote good practice among employer organizations; a requirement for all companies to conduct equal-pay reviews and to report annually on them, with a complaints and arbitration system to address non-compliance; and complementary social and labour-market policies, in particular attention to policies and practices on childcare and flexible working, as well as maternity rights.[74]

Noting the slow pace of reduction in the gender pay gap (around one percentage point per year), the report found that 61 per cent of large public-sector organizations had conducted equal-pay reviews, compared to 39 per cent of large private employers; however, for all work organizations regardless of size, 28 per cent of public-sector employers had a pay review in progress, compared to only 1 per cent of private businesses. Little wonder, then, that a gap of ten percentage points stood between the public- and private-sector gender pay gaps. More generally, the Task Force report identified lack of employer awareness and expertise, lack of transparency about pay, ineffective equal-pay legislation, and inadequately supportive social and economy policy as explanations for the persistent gender pay gap.[75] The EOC in its commentary on the report argued that lack of compulsion to conduct pay reviews was preventing the EPA from being properly implemented. Mandatory reviews were, said Mellor, an idea 'whose time has come'.[76] Employment consultants echoed the EOC in describing the EPA as 'the shell of a law' unless it could be strengthened to create a legal duty to carry out reviews.[77]

The EOC's long-term vision was to introduce an equality duty for private-sector employers as well as public services, but it recognized that in the shorter term mandatory regulation might be a 'blunt tool', and therefore sought to provide practical support for employers in the form of technical expertise and pay review toolkits, and its position on regulatory action became more flexible, including a transitional period during which employers should be encouraged to conduct gender pay reviews and given an amnesty for any tribunal claims during that period.[78] Working with employers to encourage more systematic use of pay reviews therefore potentially opened a space for a stronger collaboration between the EOC and the Department of Trade and Industry (DTI). However, the government gave a cool reception to the Task Force, no doubt because it did not originate in a government initiative. Margaret Prosser, a former EOC commissioner who sat on the Task Force as deputy general secretary of the TGWU, later noted the political difficulties that hampered the Task Force from the start: 'I didn't feel the task force was going to achieve anything, as it didn't have any political backing.' Its report, she stated, 'never went anywhere'.[79]

In response to the Task Force report, junior Minister for Women and Equality Tessa Jowell[80] argued that 'much can be done by good practice, and by good example ... We want to ensure that pay reviews are both workable for business and effective for women.'[81] Instead of mandatory pay reviews, she set out an alternative strategy based on persuasion and incentives for 'good practice': the EOC was given an extra £100,000 to work with employers to assist them with pay reviews, including data management systems, and set up annual awards for employers. In addition, government said it would take action to streamline industrial tribunals procedures to make equal-pay claims easier.

Jowell then commissioned a second review, entrusted to former labour lawyer Denise Kingsmill, to focus on the question of how to shift employer practice. Since the relevant evidence had already been gathered by the Task Force, Kingsmill's review process was based on discussions with senior corporate leaders across the private, public, and voluntary sectors, and adopted the 'business case' approach to diversity: 'Any business that fails to ensure that women play a full part in its operations cannot hope to optimize its productivity and competitiveness.'[82] Kingsmill's recommendations responded to the government's preference for enabling and awareness-raising activities rather than legislation, but it also urged government to consider introducing individual employee rights to transparency over salaries, and it supported conditionality of public-sector contracts on the practice of equal-pay reviews.[83]

The Equal Pay Task Force had indirectly helped to set the policy agenda: Labour's election manifesto in 2001 contained a pledge to work with employers and trade unions to tackle the gender pay gap, and the measures announced by Jowell in April 2001 were carried into the DTI's programme for Labour's second term. However, the question of regulatory action had been sidestepped by the government.

The EOC's strategy was weakened by government's lack of responsiveness to its first track aimed at securing legislative change, which effectively undermined the second track aimed at shifting employer attitudes. Although mandatory pay reviews were recognized to be a blunt instrument, the introduction—or threat of introduction—of regulations provided an impetus for change, alongside the softer supportive measures advocated by the EOC. In the absence of stronger authority measures, change was likely to be much slower. The Chartered Institute of Personnel and Development (CIPD) observed an increase in the number of its member organizations (typically, larger organizations with human-resources departments) carrying out or intending to carry out equal-pay reviews following the publication of the Task Force report in 2001, but interest fell off in 2005, with nearly half of respondents saying that either that they had no desire to investigate pay discrepancies or that they felt their existing pay schemes were good enough.[84] Other research suggested even more limited take-up: a survey carried out for the EOC in 2004–5 found that only 21 per cent of employers carried out pay reviews, and 68 per cent said they had no intention of doing so.[85] This pattern continued: a survey carried out by consultants in 2013 found that only one in three private-sector employers had conducted equal-pay reviews, compared to over three-quarters in the public sector.[86]

Conclusion

As Paul Byrne and Joni Lovenduski observed in 1978, the question of equality between the sexes was a matter of government concern throughout the twentieth century, 'albeit sporadically'.[87] Yet, although governments shared the objective of equality of opportunity, their approach to it was filtered through party ideology and subject to concerns about costs to employers, resulting in ambivalent responses to campaigners' calls for stronger legislation and enforcement. Legislation was framed in increasingly expansive terms, bringing new groups under its protection. Legislation was also framed in terms of increasingly pro-active duties on providers of goods, services, and employment, rather than simply upholding an individual right to non-discrimination. However, strong enforcement powers did not follow this shift.

The main body established to promote and enforce equality between men and women, the EOC, developed specialist expertise in the use of the law to challenge discriminatory behaviour, and it deployed its expertise to lobby government for stronger legislation and to encourage employers to measure and act upon inequalities in the workplace. By 2007, its strategy of advocating strong public-sector equality duties had become government policy, and its long-term vision of duties on private-sector employers had begun to gain acceptance. However, governments continued to resist calls to make it easier for individuals to access justice, or indeed to allow bodies (like the EOC or trade unions) to pursue collective claims (or 'class actions', as in the USA). The system still relies on individual litigation, which is too costly and unwieldy to have significant effect across the economy, particularly in the private sector.[88]

Meanwhile, during the years of the New Labour administration, government attention turned at an early stage to the creation of a single equalities body. As will be discussed further in Chapter 6, preparations for the merger of existing commissions (the EOC, the Commission for Racial Equality, and the Disability Rights Commission) began in 1997, with proposals set out in 2002 for a single equality body. The shift towards a single body occurred across Europe, with some researchers arguing that it led to a downgrading of women's rights.[89] The EOC broadly welcomed the proposed change, but reiterated its call for stronger legislation and greater resources for enforcement.[90] In terms of resources, the disbandment of the EOC and creation of the EHRC meant a significant cut in budget (and therefore staffing).[91] The accompanying overarching legal framework was put in place much later, only after the EHRC had been established, and in the space of just two years, with several of the EOC's and campaigners' demands omitted in the process.

The most noteworthy achievement of these years was the general equality duty applying to all public authorities, covering all protected characteristics (including age, religious belief, sexual orientation, gender reassignment, maternity, and age, alongside the existing duties for gender and race and ethnicity). The public-sector equality duty, which will be discussed in more detail in Chapter 13, was enshrined in the Equality Acts 2006 and 2010, and committed public authorities not only to take actions to eliminate discrimination but to advance equality of opportunity, taking positive action if required.

While the adoption of gender pay gap reporting regulations in 2017 can be seen as a vindication of the EOC's long-term strategy combining lobbying and persuasion,[92] the duties they impose are weak in several respects, in particular the lack of requirements to act as well as report. The shift towards pro-active promotion of equality took place only partially and remains an unfinished policy agenda.

Policymakers and campaigners criticized the EOC (and later the EHRC) for failing to use the full range of powers available to it.[93] As discussed in Chapter 9, this criticism applies to the enforcement of gender pay gap reporting as well as other areas of work, such as investigations. It is widely acknowledged that the equality enforcement body was never equipped with the resources it needed to meet the demands of individual claims, or evidence of discriminatory practices. Under-resourcing of the commission reflects a wider ambivalence within government about the existence of a powerful, independent body able to challenge public bodies and private-sector employers. Ambivalence existed during the Labour years, even though in principle government shared the commission's objectives of promoting and enforcement equality law, and it undoubtedly affected the EOC's ability to drive forward its agenda.

Notes

1. R. Reeves, *Women of Westminster* (London: Bloomsbury, 2020), 127.
2. On the genesis of the EPA 1970, see, in particular, K. M. Fraser, *Same or Different: Gender Politics in the Workplace* (London: Routledge, 1999, reissued 2018), 121–44 (Ch. 5); E. Meehan, *Women's Rights at Work: Campaigns and Policy in Britain and the United States* (London: Macmillan, 1985).
3. The Equal Pay Act 1970, https://www.legislation.gov.uk/ukpga/1970/41/section/1/enacted (accessed 17 November 2020).
4. Hansard, HC, vol. 594, col. 293WH (18 March 2015).
5. EU, Directive 2006/54/EC of the European Parliament and the Council, on the implementation of the principle of equal opportunities and equal treatment of women and men in matters of employment and occupation (recast), L204/23 (26 July 2006). Article 20 states that 'Member States shall designate and make the necessary arrangements for a body or bodies for the promotion, analysis, monitoring and support of equal treatment of all persons without discrimination on grounds of sex. These bodies may form part of agencies with responsibility at national level for the defence of human rights or the safeguard of individuals' rights.' It emphasizes the independence of all actions of such bodies.

6. D. Barrett, 'The Regulatory Space of Equality and Human Rights in Britain: The Role of the Equality and Human Rights Commission', *Legal Studies*, 39 (2019), https://doi.org/10.1017/lst.2018.36.
7. J. Gregory, 'Revisiting the Sex Equality Laws', in S. Walby (ed.) *New Agendas for Women* (London: Macmillan, 1999), 98–118, at 98.
8. See J. Lovenduski, 'Unfinished Business: Equality Policy and the Changing Context of State Feminism in Great Britain', in J. Outshoorn and J. Kantola (eds), *Changing State Feminism* (Palgrave, 2010), 144–63.
9. Gregory, 'Revisiting the Sex Equality Laws', 102. Gregory's chapter drew on a 1996 report on 'equality-proofing' in Northern Ireland. In 1996, the EOC instigated a formal investigation into the impact of competitive tendering in education and health services in Northern Ireland, which resulted in a recommendation to halt the process; government, however, rejected the recommendation, arguing that its priority was cost-effectiveness. See Central Community Relations Unit, *Policy Appraisal and Fair Treatment: Annual Report 1996* (Belfast: CCRU, 1997).
10. A. Zanalza and Z. Tsannatos, *The Effect of Britain's Anti-Discrimination Legislation on Relative Pay and Employment*, Discussion Paper no. 155, London School of Economics (1983). The model used to support the argument that relative wage increases for women resulted from the legislation has been contested by other economists: see, e.g., B. Chiplin and P. J. Sloane, 'The Effect of Britain's Anti-Discrimination Legislation on Relative Pay and Employment: A Comment', *Economic Journal*, 98 (1988), https://doi.org/10.2307/2233919. Chiplin and Sloane agreed that Britain and Australia were exceptional in experiencing the same kind of wage increases coinciding with the introduction of legislation but argued that incomes policy flattening male wages may also have contributed to the narrowing of the pay gap.
11. See S. Fredman, 'Reforming Equal Pay Laws', *Industrial Law Journal*, 37 (2008), https://doi.org/10.1093/indlaw/dwn008.
12. F. Gibb, 'Battle for an Equal Break: The Pressure for Stronger Laws on Equal Pay', *The Times*, 1 September 1987.
13. See S. Olney and M. Tomei, *Equal Pay: An Introductory Guide* (Geneva: ILO).
14. Olney and Tolei, *Equal Pay*, 2–3.
15. E. Szyszczak, 'Pay Inequalities and Equal Pay Claims', *Modern Law Review*, 48 (1985), 139–57.
16. In the House of Commons debate: see Hansard, HC, vol. 795, col. 918 (9 February 1970).
17. See R. Townshend-Smith, 'The Equal Pay (Amendments) 1983', *Modern Law Review*, 47 (1984), 201–14.
18. The Equal Pay (Amendment) Regulations 1983, Statutory Instruments no. 1794, 6 December 1983.
19. J. Moss, *Women, Workplace Protest and Political Identity in England, 1968–1985* (Manchester: Manchester University Press, 2019), 158.
20. *Wells and Others* v. *F Smales & Son (Fish Merchants) Ltd* 25 April 1985 IT. A film produced by Sarah Boston and Jenny Morgan for the TUC, featuring Pete Allen as well as some of the women fish-packers, is accessible at https://www.youtube.com/watch?v=DdSLujnHFSU (accessed 15 June 2022).
21. A. G. Mazur, *Theorizing Feminist Policy* (Oxford: Oxford University Press, 2002) 94.

22. *O'Sullivan* v. *Sainsbury plc* 1990 IT. See S. Boston, *Women Workers and the Unions* (London: Lawrence & Wishart, 2014), 372–3.
23. S. Deakin, S. F. Butlin, C. McLaughlin, and A. Polanska, 'Are Litigation and Collective Bargaining Complements or Substitutes for Achieving Gender Equality? A Study of the British Equal Pay Act', *Cambridge Journal of Economics* (2015), https://doi:10.1093/cje/bev006; G. S. Morris, 'The Development of Statutory Employment Rights in Britain and Enforcement Mechanisms', in L. Dickens (ed.), *Making Employment Rights Effective: Issues of Enforcement and Compliance* (Oxford: Hart Publishing, 2012), 7–28.
24. See M. Berry, 'Pay up', *Thomson Solicitors Labour & European Law Review*, Weekly issue 121 archive (12 March 2008), https://www.thompsonstradeunion.law/news/lelr/weekly-issue-121-archive/pay-up (accessed 17 November 2020). The British Library has a set of resources on equal pay, including a video by Julie Hayward, at https://www.bl.uk/sisterhood/articles/equal-pay-and-equality-legislation (accessed 18 November 2020).
25. Judgment of the European Court of 27 October 1993. *Dr Pamela Mary Enderby* v. *Frenchay Health*. Case C-127/92.
26. M. Whitfield, 'Unions Challenge Health Service to Equal Pay Battle', *Independent*, 25 August 1990.
27. J. Buchan and D. Evans, 'Assessing the Impact of a New Health Sector Pay System upon NHS Staff in England', *Human Resources for Health*, 6 (2010) (open access).
28. J. Buchan and J. Ball, 'Evaluating the Impact of a New Pay System on Nurses in the UK', *Journal of Clinical Nursing*, 20 (2010), https://doi.org/10.1111/j.1365-2702.2010.03310.x.
29. Cécile Guillaume argues that unions turned to litigation as a last resort (or when pushed by women members) from a position of weakness in the workplace, including in collective bargaining: see C. Guillaume, 'Understanding the Variations in Unions' Litigation Strategies to Promote Equal Pay: Reflection on the British Case', *Cambridge Journal of Economics* (2015), https://doi.10.1093/cje/bev004.
30. C. Guillaume, *Organizing Women: Gender Equality Policies in British and French Trade Unions* (Bristol: Bristol University Press, 2021), 168.
31. L. Dickens, 'The Road Is Long: Thirty Years of Equality Legislation in Britain', *British Journal of Industrial Relations*, 45 (2007), https://doi.org/10.1111/j.1467-8543.2007.00624.x, 483. See also Deakin et al, 'Are Litigation and Collective Bargaining Complements or Substitutes for Achieving Gender Equality?', 400–2.
32. H. Conley, 'Trade Unions, Equal Pay and the Law in the UK', *Economic and Industrial Democracy*, 35 (2013), https://doi.org/10.1177/0143831X13480410.
33. J. Lovenduski, 'An Emerging Advocate: The Equal Opportunities Commission in Great Britain', in D. McBride Stetson and A. G. Mazur (eds), *Comparative State Feminism* (Thousand Oaks: Sage, 1995), 114–31.
34. V. Sacks, 'The Equal Opportunities Commission: Ten Years on', *Modern Law Review*, 49 (1986), 560–96, at 560.
35. The powers of the EOC proved highly controversial during the passage of the SDA 1975 (introduced in the House of Lords by Baroness Seear), with resistance in both houses of parliament to the plans drawn up by the House of Lords Select Committee, which Seear had established and to which women's rights organizations submitted evidence. The EOC was from the outset considered by these organizations (and feminists within the Labour

Party) to be a weak institution in need of reform: see Meehan, *Women's Rights at Work*, 112–16.

36. The first chair of the EOC was (later Baroness) Betty Lockwood, former secretary of Labour's Women's Advisory Committee: see J. Langdon, 'Lady Lockwood Obituary', *Guardian*, 6 May 2019. The second (from 1983 to 1988) was Lady Platt, a Conservative peer and former aeronautical engineer: see T. Corby, 'Lady Platt of Whittle Obituary', *Guardian*, 12 February 2015.
37. Sacks, 'The Equal Opportunities Commission', 584–5. In this respect Sacks contrasts the EOC with the Commission on Race Equality, which used its investigative powers more fully and to greater effect. See also Dickens, 'The Road Is Long'.
38. P. Byrne and J. Lovenduski, 'The Equal Opportunities Commission', *Women's Studies International Quarterly*, 1 (1978), https://doi.org/10.1016/S0148-0685(78)90,837-0, p. 132.
39. K. J. Alter and J. Vargas, 'Explaining Variation in the Use of European Litigation Strategies: European Community Law and British Gender Equality Policy', *Comparative Political Studies*, 33 (2000), https://doi.org/10.1177/0010414000033004002.
40. Alter and Vargas, 'Explaining Variation in the Use of European Litigation Strategies', 459.
41. D. Pannick, 'The Equal Opportunities Commission', *Guardian*, 1 November 1985.
42. Gibb, 'Battle for an Equal Break'; F. Gibb, '"Equality Act" Proposed to Curtail Sex Bias', *The Times*, 9 March 1988.
43. Foster's varied background in business and education (including a stint as researcher for the Conservative Party) marked her out from her two predecessors, who remained within the world of party politics. This difference gave her a public-relations advantage, which she exploited to the full, bringing the EOC into the media spotlight as part of a strategy of 'mainstreaming' gender equality. See, e.g., P. Toynbee, 'Starting over: The New Year Brings New Life to the EOC in the Able Form of Joanna Foster, but can she Salvage anything from the Wreckage?', *Guardian*, 31 December 1987.
44. S. Beavis, '"Once in a Lifetime" Equality Chance', *Guardian*, 19 January 1989.
45. B. Clement, 'EC Directive on Child Care is "Essential for Equality"', *Independent*, 14 June 1989.
46. H. Hague, 'Commission's Campaign for Equality "Threatened by Cuts"', *Independent*, 18 April 1989.
47. C. Dyer, 'Legal Fund Backs Equal Pay Cases', *Guardian*, 19 April 1989. The EOC received £3.8 million in grant-in-aid from the Home Office, but requested twice that amount. Over and above office operational costs, each investigation cost between £250,000 and £500,000, and support for equal-pay cases cost between £75,000 and £60,000, depending on complexity.
48. P. Myers, 'New Equality Law Urged', *Guardian*, 25 September 1991.
49. B. Clement, 'Campaigners See Strategic Advantages', *Independent*, 23 July 1992. See also EOC, *Annual Report 1993* (Manchester: EOC, 1994), 28.
50. B. Clement, 'Election 1992: Party Pledges over Equality Criticised', *Independent*, 19 March 1992.
51. Notes of the meeting with Paddy Ashdown, 18 February 1992, and with Neil Kinnock (accompanied by Jo Richardson), 2 March 1992; letter from Joanna Foster to John Major, 23 March 1992, and reply from Sir Geoffrey Finsberg, 24 March 1992; minutes of

commissioners' meeting, 10 April 1992, all in Joanna Foster archive at Oxford Brookes University library (Special Collections), Box JF/5/2.

52. Draft (typewritten, with some handwritten annotations by Joanna Foster), Equal Opportunities Corporate Plan 1993–6, p. 13: Joanna Foster archive at Oxford Brookes University library (Special Collections), Box JF/5/2.
53. Draft, Equal Opportunities Corporate Plan, 13.
54. EOC, *From Policy to Practice: An Equal Opportunities Strategy for the 1990s* (Manchester: EOC, 1988), 4.
55. In March 1992 (five months after the launch of Opportunity 2000), Foster wrote to Lady Howe, its founding chair, setting out critical observations based on a discussion within the commission, including 'considerable scepticism about the validity of the targets set by different organisations' owing to the lack of 'monitoring or evaluation process'. Foster concluded by offering support in elaborating monitoring and review processes and indicators: letter dated 17 March 1992, Joanna Foster archive at Oxford Brookes University library (Special Collections), Box JF/5/2.
56. Transcript, Joanna Foster interview for BBC Oxford, 18 January 1993: Joanna Foster archive at Oxford Brookes University library (Special Collections), Box JF/5/2.
57. Y. Alibhai Brown, 'Would you Buy an Equal Opportunities Policy from this Woman?', *Guardian Society*, 11 January 1995; P. Toynbee, 'RIP EOC?', *Guardian*, 23 August 1993.
58. Judgment of the Court, 2 August 1993, in Case C-271/91. See also K. Bahl, 'Equal Opportunities and the Law: Catalyst for Change?', *Nottingham Law Journal*, 3 (1994), 1–10, at 2–3.
59. DfEE, *Quinquennial Review of the Equal Opportunities Commission* (London: DfEE, 1998), 2.
60. K. Bahl, 'Foreword', in EOC, *Annual Report 1997* (Manchester: EOC, 1998), 1.
61. Bahl, 'Foreword'.
62. 'Government Drive for Women's Rights', *Guardian Weekly*, 15 November 1998.
63. B. Clement, 'Wanted: A Tough New Law to Protect Women', *Independent*, 21 January 1998.
64. J. Mellor, 'Chair Report', in EOC, *Setting the Agenda for Equality: Annual Report 1998* (Manchester: EOC, 1999), 3.
65. Mellor, 'Chair Report'.
66. By 2002/3, the EOC had received just over £7 million per year in grant-in-aid, which is what it had requested a decade earlier.
67. J. Mellor, 'Message from the Chair', in EOC, *Annual Report 2000–2001* (Manchester: EOC, 2001), 4.
68. H. Stewart, 'Counting the Cost of Sexism', *Guardian*, 9 January 2005.
69. S. Wild, 'Outline of the EOC Submission to the Women and Work Commission', internal EOC policy document, TNA: C/08/MAR/05, SH/DN5/Z.
70. EOC, *Equality in the 21st Century: A New Approach* (Manchester: EOC, 1988), 15.
71. Equal Pay Task Force, *Just Pay: Report of the Equal Pay Task Force* (Manchester: EOC, 2001), p. ix.
72. D. Grimshaw and J. Rubery, *The Gender Pay Gap: A Research Review* (Manchester: EOC, 2001).
73. Equal Pay Task Force, *Just Pay*, p. ix
74. Equal Pay Task Force, *Just Pay*, 14–25.

75. Equal Pay Task Force, *Just Pay*, 11–13.
76. S. Milne, 'Task Force to Beat Pay Bias', *Guardian*, 27 October 1999.
77. 'Equal Pay: Shell of a Law?', *Employee Benefits*, 18 April 2006, p. 66.
78. 'Equal Pay: Shell of a Law?'; see also J. Jones, 'Tackling an Old Problem Afresh: The Equal Opportunities Commission's New Code of Practice on Equal Pay', *Journal of Social Welfare and Family Law*, 26 (2004), https://doi.org/10.1080/01418030410001694440; D. Rowbottom, 'Rediscovering the Collective Application of the Equal Pay Act', 26 (2007), https://doi.org/10.1108/02610150710777033.
79. M. Prosser, *Your Seat is at the End* (London: Feather Publications, 2010), 193.
80. Tessa Jowell's position as Minister for New Deal straddled two government departments: Department for Work and Pensions and Department for Education and Employment.
81. J. Parker, 'EOC Urges New Action on Equal Pay', *Eurofound*, 27 April 2001, https://www.eurofound.europa.eu/publications/article/2001/eoc-urges-new-action-on-equal-pay (accessed 20 October 2020).
82. D. Kingsmill, *Review of Women's Employment and Pay* (London: DTI, 2002), 7.
83. Kingsmill, *Review*, 15–16.
84. CIPD, *Reward Management Survey* (London: CIPD, 2005). In the CIPD's 2019 survey, it found that 39% of organizations used pay reviews to look at pay equality: see CIPD, *Reward Management Survey* (London: CIPD, 2019). These tend to be larger organizations and are more likely to be in the public than the private sector.
85. L. Adams, K. Carter, and S. Schafer, *Equal Pay Reviews Survey 2005* (Manchester: EOC, 2005). See also F. Neathey, R. Willison, K. Ackroyd, J. Regan, and D. Hill, *Equal Pay Reviews in Practice* (Manchester: EOC, 2005).
86. S. Brett, 'Voluntary Approach to Equal Pay Reviews Isn't Working', Touchstone blog (TUC), 6 December 2013, https://touchstoneblog.org.uk/2013/12/voluntary-approach-to-equal-pay-audits-isnt-working/ (accessed 2 November 2020).
87. Byrne and Lovenduski, 'The Equal Opportunities Commission', 133.
88. Fredman, 'Reforming Equal Pay Laws'. It is interesting to note that one of the first councils (Lewisham) to put in place an equal-pay review was still seen as a case study of good practice over a decade later: see D. Brown, *The Power of Parity: A Study of how Lewisham Council Achieved Gender Parity at Senior Levels: The Learning and Implications* (Brighton: Institute for Employment Studies, 2016).
89. J. Kantola, 'Shifting Institutional and Ideational Terrains: The Impact of Europeanisation and Neoliberalism on Women's Policy Agencies', *Policy & Politics*, 38 (2010), https://doi.org/10.1332/030557310X521053; J. Outshoorn and J. Kantola, 'Assessing Changes in State Feminism over the Last Decade', in J. Outshoorn and J. Kantola (eds), *Changing State Feminism* (London: Palgrave, 2010), 266–85.
90. EOC, *State of the Nation on Sex Equality: Annual Report 2002–3* (EOC, 2003).
91. B. Hepple, 'Enforcing Equality Law: Two Steps Forward and Two Steps Backward for Reflexive Regulation', *Industrial Law Journal*, 40 (2011), https://doi.org/10.1093/indlaw/dwr020. Although the EHRC received £70 million in its first year, which was more than the combined budgets of the commissions it replaced, this was subsequently reduced each year to drop substantially below those previous budgets, standing at £20 million in 2015.

92. Dame Julie Mellor, private communication, 17 June 2021. See also S. Milner, 'Gender Pay Gap Reporting Regulations: Advancing Gender Equality Policy in Tough Economic Times', *British Politics*, 20 (2019), https://doi.org/10.1057/s41293-018-00101-4.
93. See Women and Equalities Committee, *Enforcing the Equality Act: The Law and the Role of the Equality and Human Rights Commission*, Tenth Report of Session 2017–2019 (London: House of Commons, 2019), 19–26.

5

Feminizing Labour

The Party and Trade Unions

Introduction

As previous chapters have shown, change in policy on women's economic empowerment was slow throughout the twentieth century in Britain, and the campaign for equal pay frequently encountered resistance at the level of party leaderships and government. However, from the late 1970s, a major shift occurred owing to two feminizing trends. The first was the growing influence of the women's liberation movement, directly through activism of feminists within grassroots organizations as well as mainstream political parties and trade unions, and indirectly through the diffusion of new attitudes about the role and place of women in society (the 'slow revolution').[1] Second-wave feminism challenged dominant attitudes, particularly in relation to the family, but it was also an exercise in new forms of democracy, disrupting established ways of organizing party politics.[2] The second, related shift occurred as political leaders responded to changes in social attitudes and new patterns of political behaviour, in particular voting, and realized that they needed to diversify their electoral offer.

Yet political modernization was relatively slow in Britain, compared to other European countries. Across all three main parties, parties maintained strong constraints against women's selection and progression, in an adversarial political culture that has been seen as inimical to feminization.[3] The Labour Party and wider labour movement held embedded masculine values and attitudes that for a long time had prevented women activists from making headway.[4] Although the Conservative Party had from the 1950s understood the potential benefits of appealing to women voters, Labour was slow to catch up, and the women's structures that had been established in the face of male exclusiveness, as in the trade-union movement, struggled to make their voices heard in the wider party.[5] However, from the 1980s the impact of political modernization became evident in the Labour Party, which was forced to rethink its political programme after over a decade shut out of power.

Women and Employment in Public Policy. Susan Milner, Oxford University Press. © Susan Milner (2024).
DOI: 10.1093/9780191987359.003.0005

By 2024, Labour remained the only Westminster party to have introduced mechanisms for positive action to increase the number of women MPs.

As Sylvia Bashevkin has argued, the confluence of feminist and party demands at a specific time when the Labour Party was renewing its policy programme cannot be taken to mean a durable influence of feminism within the party.[6] The party leadership stood far apart from feminism in several key respects, such as the organizational tension between centralization and grassroots mobilization, and the ideological preference for economic liberalism over provision of public services. Male dominance of policy preference formation persisted.[7] Nevertheless, the feminization of representation and decision-making is a long-term trend (the 'quiet revolution'[8]) that has had a lasting impact on deliberative politics, programmatic choices, and, albeit to a lesser extent, on policy outputs. This chapter reviews the changes that took place as feminist demands began to make inroads into the labour movement, including trade unions as well as the Labour Party. It focuses on Labour's preparations for power and its first two terms.

It also considers the relationship between party and union in supporting feminization and the policy changes it induced. Earlier than the party to which many were affiliated, unions realized that labour-market changes meant a feminized membership and the challenges of representing women workers.[9] The programmatic influence of feminism was evident in the Trades Union Congress's (TUC) 1975 Charter for Working Women, which mapped women's work onto traditional trade-union demands: equal education, jobs choice, promotion, maternity leave, sick pay, pensions, health and safety at work, convenient hours, back-to-work chances, full citizens' rights, and no discrimination.[10]

A key question here is to what extent the changing relationship between the Labour Party and trade unions created new spaces for feminists to influence policy. Party modernization for Labour stemmed from the need to win over new voters, but it was also strongly linked to weakening ties with the trade unions, which meant new opportunities to widen the policy formulation process procedurally (with policy increasingly discussed outside party conference and in more open forums with reserved places for women). The adoption of all-women shortlists was not prioritized by leaders—although Neil Kinnock and John Smith allowed themselves to be persuaded of the case—but accepted because it formed part of an agenda of modernization of the party's internal selection procedures aimed at reducing unions' block influence. Meanwhile, the changing role of the state meant both new challenges and new ways of working for trade unions, which saw them give greater attention to equality claims at a time when their own capacity to effect change was diminishing. Overall, as will be discussed further in this chapter, unions sought to increase their capacity for influence during a Labour administration, but in practice often found themselves 'on the back foot'.[11]

Feminizing Trade Unions

Trade unions can be important equality vehicles, through collective bargaining, influence over policy, and their equality resources at multiple levels (for example, workplace voice representation and legal expertise).[12] They are inconsistent equality advocates, sometimes giving voice to women's demands but often failing to give them full support, and, as organizations, they often resist internal change and challenges to cultures of male dominance. In the 1960s and 1970s, activism by women put pressure on the union leadership for a stronger approach, but also revealed 'what a slow, difficult business' it would be to change their ways of working.[13]

Gill Kirton has identified three periods of change between 1987 and 2012. The first period to 1992, when women's share of union membership grew from around 29 per cent to 35 per cent, saw only 'limited progress and much room for improvement'.[14] Women were under-represented in all representative and decision-making roles. During the second period, from 1992 to 2004, there was 'some progress, but still room for improvement'. Women's share of membership grew to 48 per cent; the biggest unions saw increasing numbers of women appointed to represent the union at congress and elected to executive bodies, but the top leadership remained male. The challenge to recruit female members entailed new organizational practices to find ways of encouraging and supporting women to become involved in unions, integrating women's demands into bargaining agendas and negotiating practices, and campaigning for women's demands. It underpinned the relaunch of the TUC in 1994, under its new general secretary John Monks.[15] The New Unionism project launched in 1996 to recruit new members was led by Frances O'Grady, later (2012) to become the TUC's first female general secretary.

In the third period, when female membership grew to around half the total (by 2010),[16] women made more significant inroads into the leadership structures of the ten largest unions. In 2003, the TUC appointed its first female deputy general secretary, Kay Carberry, and the deputy general secretary post in the biggest unions was now occupied by a woman: Debbie Coulter at the General, Municipal and Boilermakers' Union (GMB) and Liz Snape (assistant general secretary) at Unison, while at the Transport and General

Workers' Union (TGWU) Margaret Prosser was succeeded by Diana Holland. Still, by 2012, only five out of fifty-eight affiliated unions were led by a woman and only four had achieved proportionality (to membership) in their national executive.[17] Male officers continued to outnumber females by over three to one,[18] but this represented progress since 2002, when the ratio was four to one.[19]

From 2003, the TUC began to publish a bi-annual report on equality, tracking union efforts to put in place equality policies, and to promote equality objectives through actions such as awareness-raising as well as collective bargaining. Presentation of the equality audits at congress every two years ensured high-level engagement with and wider discussion of equality. The audits showed the importance of initiatives such as equality representatives in building equalities into mainstream union work. At the level of policy officer, and with the appointment of dedicated equality officers and representatives, attention to the representation of women's demands increased. Although these posts could be subject to organizational 'silos' marginalizing equality demands, they created opportunities for formal and information dialogue between unions and employers at different levels, and between unions and employees, as well as better-informed campaigning.[20] Training of local representatives was also found to result in greater attention to equal pay and more successful bargaining outcomes relating to gender equality.[21]

An equality agenda was developed at workplace level, although it was slow to be integrated into wage-bargaining practice. Fifty-four per cent of unions responding to the first TUC equality audit in 2005 said they had successfully negotiated on equal pay, and two-thirds reported achievements in work–life balance measures through bargaining.[22] By 2009, 30 per cent reported having secured an agreement on equal pay since 2005, and 44 per cent reported agreement on flexibility or work–life balance measures.[23] Increased attention to gender equality and work–family policy reflected both legislative change and better training for workplace union representatives.[24]

The Labour years therefore constitute a period of partial but significant long-term change within the trade-union movement. Feminization was incomplete and the trade-union movement had only recently begun to pay attention to poor pay and working conditions of black and ethnic minority workers.[25] It was also uneven across unions. Public-sector unions were among the first to open up their leadership structures to women in the 1970s, and the National Union of Public Employees (NUPE) was an early advocate of demands for low-paid workers during the 1978–9 strike wave, with the proposal for a national minimum wage set at two-=thirds of the median male hourly wage.[26] NUPE general secretary Rodney Bickerstaffe persisted in his efforts to persuade other unions to adopt this demand, repeatedly encountering resistance from construction and engineering unions determined to retain high wage differentials. Public-sector unions also took the lead in negotiating enhanced maternity leave and pay. Unions representing male-dominated manual occupations proved slower to feminize their decision-making structures, and, in the two biggest manual workers' unions, moves to integrate women's demands into local bargaining proved organizationally difficult to implement, despite activity such as support for groundbreaking equal-pay claims. Undoubtedly, masculine values and norms remained entrenched in some unions, and not only proved difficult to challenge but prevented women from making progress through the ranks.[27] Nevertheless, the partial feminization of the union movement empowered a new generation of women activists and influenced as well as accompanied change in the Labour Party, to which the biggest unions were affiliated.

The Labour Party

In 1997, record numbers (120, 101 of them Labour) of women were elected to parliament (doubling the number of women MPs), and eighteen were appointed to ministerial positions (five of cabinet rank, up from two under John Major). Within a decade, the Labour Party had moved from a period marked by 'a small minority' of women to one where women's parliamentary presence was becoming normalized, and attention shifted to representation at ministerial level.[28] The rise in the number of female Labour MPs was largely due to the adoption in 1993 of all-women shortlists—that is, women-only selection lists in half of all seats where members were retiring, and half of all target (winnable) seats.[29]

Feminization of the parliamentary party formed part of a broader agenda of measures aimed at improving the situation of women. Following defeat at the general election in 1987, the party had commissioned polling evidence showing how its perceived masculine style and values alienated women voters.[30] Earlier still, in 1979 Patricia Hewitt and pollster Deborah Mattinson had published data showing Labour's lower support among female voters, especially older women, than for Conservatives.[31] By 1992, competition for women's votes had become a commonplace feature of general elections, with proposals on women's representation in decision-making and specific policy concerns around childcare seen as more or less congruent with the three main parties' manifesto priorities.[32] In the Labour Party, the policy shift was motivated by an instrumental desire to modernize the party programme and broaden electoral support, but also reflected over a decade of campaigning by women within the party. High-profile politicians like Clare Short and Jo Richardson[33] were particularly influential, but women had become more active in the party at all levels, through women-only and mixed structures.[34]

Changes in the trade-union structures and policies also helped to pave the way for these developments. A group of women in the large Labour-affiliated unions worked together to plan how to persuade their unions to support all-women shortlists, including Angela Eagle, then in the Confederation of Health Service Employees (elected MP in 1992), Prosser in the TGWU, Bernadette Hillon in USDAW, and Maureen Rooney in the Amalgamated Engineering and Electrical union (AEEU).[35] Eagle recalled in 2018: 'We were just at the beginning of the huge shift of women into the labour market. The trade union agenda began to change while I was there. ... We were pushing at doors that were beginning to be unlocked at least, [although] you still had to give them a shove.'[36] As pressure within the unions grew, male party leaders increasingly became unwilling to be seen to block moves towards quotas and all-women shortlists.[37]

Programmatically, the feminization of policy coincided initially with a shift to the left after Margaret Thatcher's 1979 election victory and was based on three interrelated sets of initiatives: first, moves to increase women's political representation, through measures such as targets, quotas, and positive discrimination; second, institutional representation of women in government; and, third, policy measures to improve women's economic and social position. The first of these initiatives was influenced by moves within Socialist International Women, focused on quotas for women's representation on parties' internal decision-making bodies and candidate selection lists.[38] Quotas for decision-making bodies, particularly the National Executive Committee (NEC), proved surprisingly straightforward, thanks to organizational groundwork by activists.[39] The policy was agreed in 1989, and resulted in an increased number of women on the NEC from 5 out of 129 in 1991 to 18 out of 32 in 1998. Despite evidence in the early period of tactical voting by some men to keep women out, feminization of the party's executive helped to put women on Labour's front bench, as their profile in the party rose through such elections.

Changes to candidate selection rules were a 'harder sell', because, unlike in many European countries where it was possible to place men and women alternately on party lists, selecting a female candidate in a single-member constituency effectively meant all-women shortlists.[40] The 1989 conference set the goal of gender parity in the parliamentary party within ten years, reduced to 40 per cent at conference the following year, but advocacy of affirmative action was not widely shared among the party leadership.[41] The NEC did not feel able to implement the resolution.[42] When John Smith became leader, however, he attended the meeting of the Women's Action Committee (WAC, which joined together feminists on the hard and soft left of the party) to discuss ways of implementing it,[43] and expressed support for the WAC's proposal for all-women shortlists.

In 1993, Labour adopted a policy of all-women shortlists in vacancies in half of Labour-held seats and the most winnable seats, with local decisions to be coordinated at regional level. Neither Kinnock nor Blair was more than 'lukewarm' on positive action proposals.[44] A reluctant Blair was later reportedly happy to drop the policy on all-women shortlists when it was challenged on grounds of sex discrimination,[45] but its popularity in the party—and demonstrated effectiveness at the 1997 general election—meant that women were able to push for its reinstatement through the adoption of legislation allowing positive action in political parties.

The second feminist demand concerned the creation of a ministry for women. Richardson's 1986 discussion document 'Labour's Ministry for Women's Rights' argued that women's rights must have the full public backing of the leadership. Having junior ministers responsible for women in government departments had led nowhere, Richardson argued; instead, there was a need for a distinct, high-status department: 'The ministry should be small, but high-powered, with a clear set of political priorities—and based in the cabinet office with access to the prime minister. The minister herself must have status and backing, and a seat in the cabinet and on key cabinet committees.'[46] Labour's 1987 general-election manifesto contained a pledge to establish 'a Minister for Women, with a place in the Cabinet', tasked with ensuring 'that, framing their policies, all government departments listen and respond to women's needs and concerns'.[47] In 1991, the party issued a brochure putting the case for a ministry for women. Party activists assembled for Labour's women's conference that year argued that the proposal, alongside commitments to a minimum wage and 'decent childcare', constituted 'strong policies which attract great support among women.[48]

In preparation for the 1992 general election, Richardson (reappointed shadow minister for women in 1989) began discussions with the head of the civil service, Sir Robin Butler, to establish the basis for a ministerial department for women. Following the pre-election decision by the Conservative government that responsibility for women would move from the Home Office to the Department for Employment (DfE),[49] space for a full ministerial unit was allocated in Tothill House, opposite the DfE, as the civil service was apparently convinced that Labour would win: 'we cleared an entire floor of the building for the ministry that never was.'[50] The Labour Party's proposals on women (alongside lobbying by the EOC: see Chapter 4) had an impact on the incoming Conservative government, which had devoted a section of its 1992 manifesto to 'Women and Opportunity'. Major gave Gillian Shephard, the new Secretary of State for Employment, responsibility for women, and established a cross-departmental committee to coordinate policy.[51]

However, despite its apparent attractiveness to voters, the policy was the subject of scorn in the tabloid press and was disliked by Blair. Richardson's successor, Short,[52] realized that the proposal needed to have leadership backing, without which it could become a 'tokenistic dumping ground'.[53] Having already clashed with Blair over all-women shortlists, she sought a middle ground between a fully-fledged department and the status quo, arguing in a consultation document ('Governing for Equality') in 1995[54] that a government body for women needed a strong, networked structure, linked to both a strengthened Women's National Commission and the EOC, which should prepare a joint annual report, and to parliament through an annual statement and monthly questions, with the possibility of oversight by a dedicated parliamentary select committee in the future. This structure responded to the United Nations (UN) recommendations for a networked body with direct access to political decision-making. Short's document saw the main priority as a key position in government, located in the Cabinet Office and with ministerial presence in cabinet.[55]

Journalists saw the new policy, which replaced a ministry with a minister and civil-service support, as signalling the end of Richardson's 'feminist dream', but Short's pragmatism meant that a women's policy machinery could be retained in government.[56] Even these proposals, although accepted by the party, were dismissed by Blair's allies, who insisted that on becoming prime minister his hands would not be tied and any future minister for women would not be 'top-flight' but instead a 'junior or middle-ranking minister with non-cabinet status'.[57]

Short (who, having been elected to the shadow cabinet in October 1995, was given responsibility for transport) was replaced as shadow minister for women by Tessa Jowell, who, although widely seen as effective, was loyal to the leadership and not identified as feminist.[58] Journalist Melissa Benn called the post the 'Shadow of all Shadows', 'not quite a proper job', and suggested that Jowell, although thoughtful about the possibilities for the post, could not define its scope or remit.[59] Jowell occupied the post for a year before becoming Harman's deputy at health, and was replaced by Janet Anderson (previously opposition whip) in October 1996. Anderson, working with Jack Straw as shadow Home Secretary, focused on crime, which she presented as a women's issue,[60] having come to public attention by presenting a private member's bill on stalking.[61]

The third main feminist demand was linked to the first two: as Richardson had argued in her 1986 document, the policy agenda for women would be prepared by the (newly feminized) party and driven forward in government by the ministry for women. In 1989, Labour's policy review report included a call for 'six months' paid leave for every parent, a big expansion of child-care facilities, and full-time rights for part-time workers',[62] 'more flexible hours', and a 'series of measures to assist both women and men to combine family and work more fully'.[63] When Labour launched its idea for a ministry for women in 1992, Kinnock stated that the new structure would back the party's commitments to 'give part-timers the same legal rights as full-time workers, better training and opportunities for carers, a national minimum wage and improved maternity pay and parental leave'.[64] The 1992 Labour manifesto included these commitments, and made a specific appeal to gender equality: 'We will strengthen equality before the law and equality of opportunity for the majority of the population—women. Neither their legal status nor their chances in education, training and employment are full or free. We will ensure that the barriers to fairness are removed.'[65] It assigned a role to a new ministry for women most explicitly in relation to a national childcare strategy.

In broad terms, these 1992 commitments represented the basis for policy on women and employment after 1997, but they were developed unevenly within the policy review process thatfollowed Kinnock's defeat. Although the review process provided another opportunity to integrate feminist demands into party policy, and women were involved at all stages in the process, there was no review group looking specifically at women's situation.[66] The focus on gender equality began to disappear from policy commitments. In theory, the shift away from decision-making through NEC and party conference and towards a rolling two-year cycle of policy review through the NPF, which was promoted by leaders as a way of reducing the influence of unions over conference resolutions, provided a way of opening up policy within the party. In practice, the policy commissions—each with a 40 per cent quota for women's membership—mirrored the large government departments, starting with health, welfare and citizenship and justice.[67] Particularly in the early period when activists learnt to work with the new cycle, this meant a focus on 'big' questions in which women's specific interests could easily get left behind.

Just as the proposal for a ministry for women had been scaled down by the new leadership, Labour went into the 1997 election with a 'soft-focus' view of what women voters wanted. Jowell as shadow minister for women produced a strategy document 'Winning Words', which suggested that women did not have specific demands but wanted to hear a 'people-centred' presentation of all policies: 'Women do not live in a separate world, worrying about "women's issues"', she stated.[68] As journalist Angela Neustatter wrote, this meant that, without an understanding of structural inequality, and without authoritative voices to promote them, important issues such as domestic violence, housing, and poverty could 'be swept aside by the broader policies'.[69] The post of shadow minister for women had successfully overseen the adoption of all-women shortlists (a major change with lasting effects, although its future was unclear), but its impact on the policy of a prospective Labour government had become uncertain.

Without having formal responsibility for women, Harman (as shadow minister for health) and Short meanwhile worked to ensure that the 1992 commitment to a national minimum wage was not abandoned. The case was strengthened by Brown's policy on fiscal prudence: an independent commission to set the level of a national minimum wage was a useful way of defusing union demands for a stipulated level (which they wanted to establish at two-thirds of male median pay).[70] When Ian McCartney was appointed to a shadow role for trade and industry, with responsibility for the minimum wage, work on preparing both union and employer support for a commission to set its level began in earnest.[71]

Harman also appealed directly to Brown as shadow chancellor to secure a commitment to a national childcare strategy. From 1992, on Smith's election as leader, to July 1994 (when she was promoted by Blair to shadow Secretary of State for Employment), Harman worked closely with Brown as his deputy, and focused on a social investment strategy, which the shadow chancellor integrated into his programme for government.[72] Harmansought to produce a strong evidence base for her claims, and to meet employer organizations to persuade them of the business case. The employer lobby was receptive to the case for state childcare provision, because they saw it as productive investment funded by taxpayers rather than businesses (easing costs for small firms in particular).[73] Labour's proposals on childcare were widely popular and placed the Conservative government on the defensive.

Feminization of the Labour Party and the wider labour movement helps to explain why certain policies were adopted in the period of preparation for power, but they are only part of the picture. The new Labour leadership team of Blair and Brown and their close circle of advisers had a specific view of the type of policy that would not only get the party elected (by appealing to women voters) but set in train structural changes they wanted to promote. In the field of social and employment policy, women's rights activists could pursue proposals that fitted that agenda: the three main initiatives concerned the national minimum wage, childcare, and welfare-to-work. Of these, owing to its innovation and its reach, the national minimum wage made the most impact on the lives of low-paid women. Its adoption resulted from a combination of women's political leadership within the party, change within the union movement, and advocacy by influential party figures (in this case, McCartney) to persuade leaders of the political and economic benefits. The work–family policy agenda, on the other hand, originated not from within the party but from the European Union, which intensified opposition to it from the Confederation of British Industry (CBI).

Party–Union Relations under New Labour

Labour's 1997 manifesto stipulated there would be no return to the situation before the Thatcher governments' anti-union legislation of the 1980s: the key elements of Conservative legislation would remain in place, and, instead of collective (trade-union) rights, individual rights in the workplace would be promoted. Moreover, the relationship between party and unions had already undergone change (with the reduction of the unions' block vote at party conference from 70 per cent to 50 per cent in 1996), which would continue, although the party still depended heavily on unions for funding. The Blair–Brown leadership made clear that the Labour government would seek allies outside the trade unions: 'We have ... put our relations with the trade unions on a modern footing where they accept they can get fairness but no favours from a Labour government.'[74] This meant that, while the TUC was an 'insider' group in the sense that it would be consulted alongside business, its views were often treated with suspicion by party leaders while those of business were actively courted;[75] Labour-affiliated unions (also affiliated to the TUC) were also structural insiders in the party, but the leadership took strenuous action to control and circumscribe their ability to set agendas or block initiatives.

The changed party–union relationship reflected declining membership of trade unions, undermining their claim to speak on behalf of all workers: from its peak in 1979, when over 54 per cent of the workforce was unionized, union density had dropped to less than 30 per cent by 2001.[76] It was also driven by political considerations: party leaders were determined to avoid the failures that had characterized attempts at tripartite governance under the previous Labour government (1974–9). In addition, the economic context had changed with growing interdependence, not just through trade but through investment, leading to Blair's preference for a new style of 'business unionism' based on cooperation between trade unions and employers. Trade unions were divided about this shift, but the TUC executive (notably the general secretary John Monks and his successor Brendan Barber) took the lead in remoulding party–union relations and promoting a new style of business-friendly unionism.[77] As the three biggest unions still held nearly 40 per cent of the vote at party conferences, Blair needed their support to enact major constitutional changes such as the abandonment of Clause 4, which committed the party to public ownership.

The TUC turned increasingly to the EU as a policy resource, drawing on new rights in the Social Chapter, which the Labour government had adopted, following years of Conservative resistance. Union priorities concerning statutory trade-union recognition, new work–family rights, and a national minimum wage appeared in the 1997 Labour manifesto, but in weaker form than unions had hoped: statutory union recognition rules bowed to employer preferences, the minimum wage was set at a deliberately low level so that it could not be accused of harming employment, and on work–family policy the 1997 manifesto referred explicitly to a 'light-touch' approach. On all these policy priorities, the TUC leadership was able to claim influence over outcomes, but, although it remained a policy insider in that it continued to be consulted and given a place on deliberative bodies, its role fell short of the fully-fledged social partnership it sought,[78] and it was often frustrated by greater success of the CBI in achieving its policy objectives.

Whereas two initiatives had been promised and delivered in the first term (the national minimum wage and the employment relations bill, which introduced statutory union recognition), the 2001 manifesto contained no proposals on employment rights, and focused instead on reforms of welfare benefits and healthcare reform. Unions pushed for further rights, in line with European legislation on working time, rights for agency workers, and information and consultation rights, while the CBI took up an entrenched position against them.[79] Some unions began to take a more oppositional stance to government, particularly on contracting-out in local government and public services. At the party conference in 2002, Blair experienced his first major policy defeat when the big unions secured a commitment to review the involvement of profit-related finance in the running of public services. The four largest Labour-affiliated unions sought to regain policy influence, working through party liaison structures and the National Policy Forum (NPF), and bypassing the TUC, whose new general secretary, Barber, was close to Blair and more 'restrained' in his criticism of government[80] than the leaders of the Labour unions, themselves under pressure from their membership. Between 2000 and 2003, the older generation of general secretaries, many of whom had close personal ties with the Blair–Brown leadership, had been replaced by a new set of leaders tagged by the media as the 'awkward squad'. The label, which the leaders themselves rejected, overemphasized their unity: they were a 'disparate' group of (male) leaders,[81] but they were more independent from government than their predecessors, and they showed more capacity to coordinate their demands, partly because of personal affinities or 'micro-political' relationships.[82]

Affiliated unions were able to apply pressure on the party in the run-up to the 2005 election, when the party faced a funding shortfall and needed the voluntary efforts of union members to help canvas and provide other material support. As a result, intense negotiations took place in the NPF, leading to the Warwick agreement (so-called because the meetings took place at Warwick University) in July 2004. The Warwick agreement was secured because the big Labour-affiliated unions were able to keep a united front, learning from previous experiences at NPF when Downing Street insiders had been able to divide or outmanoeuvre them. It also reflected a weaker party leadership after the 2003 invasion of Iraq facing the erosion of public support and beset by an increasingly bitter division between the Blair and Brown teams. By then the Brown camp was courting support among unions and hinted at stronger employment rights under his leadership.

At the Warwick NPF, Labour-affiliated unions made clear that they expected greater input into the next party manifesto. However, party negotiators did not concede much ground to the unions, while they remained committed to working closely with the CBI. Key union negotiators (and Number 10 advisers) acknowledged later that the policies agreed were 'either insubstantial pieces of unfinished business left over from the first term or were things the government planned to do anyway'.[83] The Warwick agreement was important in keeping pressure on government on employment rights. Alongside pledges to protect public-sector pensions when services were contracted out, review privatization plans, and implement the European temporary workers' directive, the Warwick agreement contained a commitment to increase maternity and paternity leave and allow fathers to share a portion of maternity leave, to extend the right to request flexible working, and to expand the number of places for children in Sure Start centres (see Chapter 11). On the other hand, trade unions' hopes of pushing the government into committing to implement the European working time directive in full were disappointed.[84]

The Warwick agreement committed the government to set up a Women and Work Commission, and to address unequal pay in local government. The establishment of a commission had already been decided before the Warwick agreement, according to Baroness Prosser, who said that it had been decided at the NPF in 2003, in response to the TUC's call for equality representatives with statutory powers.[85]

The Warwick agreement showed that the policy agenda on women's employment rights was an area of tension and negotiation between unions and the Labour government, but, despite unions' opportunity for pressure in the run-up to the general-election campaign, they were unable to push hard on this agenda. This situation was at least partly due to the fact that the Department of Trade and Industry (DTI) had already set the agenda in its preferred direction, with the women's policy machinery steering the development of new rights within the limits of what it considered possible to achieve—that is, the regulatory preferences of the party leadership. It also reflected a crowded set of priorities on the union side, which allowed ministers and advisers to trade off concessions. Once the election had been won, the Warwick programme constrained government action to a lesser degree, so that it was possible for leaders to express adherence to it while pursuing it according to their own priorities.

Conclusion

This chapter has shown how feminization of the party and trade unions influenced policy formulation. The instrumental case for feminization of party structures and parliamentary and ministerial representation was accepted by leadership, but it depended on sustained work within the party by women activists. The case for positive action to enable gender balance in decision-making and representation proved to be not just empirically validated but electorally popular. The idea for a ministry for women, championed by Richardson as a way of guaranteeing high-status representation in government, was associated by the Blair leadership with the left of the party, and viewed suspiciously as representing 'sectional' interests. Without leadership backing, its proponents knew it would fail, so they accepted a watered-down version that depended on the individual authority and determination of its incumbent.

In policy terms, the result of activism within the party and within trade unions was a focus on the national minimum wage, rights for part-time workers (derived from European case law) and investment in childcare. These would be important gains for women, but they left aside other important questions and lacked the structural attention to inequality that had characterized earlier progressive politics of the centre-left, as well as a clear understanding of how the law could and should protect women from violence and discrimination. As women activists within the party and trade unions sought to raise those issues, conflicts over policy ensued. They played out within the party, particularly the NPF, and ensured that the women's rights reappeared on the agenda when pressure could be brought before a general election.

Chapter 6 considers what happened to the women's policy machinery once Labour was in power. This chapter has raised two key questions in relation to its capacity for effective action. The first relates to its resources in terms of ministerial authority, location and staffing of the civil-service unit, and network power in relation not just to government but to civil society and other actors in the policy space (such as the EOC). The second, following from this, relates to its framing of demands related to 'women-friendly policy'. As we have seen, by 1997 at least three strands of Labour feminist policy activism had emerged in the area of women and employment, all derived loosely from second-wave feminism: a rights-based feminism closely aligned with attention to women's economic empowerment, including equal-pay demands but also a concern with the specific conditions of women's low pay as well as with support for women's caring responsibilities; a trade-union agenda of collective workplace rights; and a pragmatic feminism framed in business-case arguments. These three strands were not mutually exclusive and could be complementary, depending on the political opportunities available.

Notes

1. J. Lewis, *Women in Britain since 1945: Women, Family, Work, and the State in the Post-War Years* (Oxford: Blackwell, 1992). See also L. Abrams, 'Liberating the Female Self: Epiphanies, Conflict and Coherence in the Life Stories of Post-War British Women', *Social History*, 39 (2014), https://doi.org/10.1080/03071022.2013.872904; J. Scott and E. Clery, 'Gender Roles. An Incomplete Revolution?', in A. Park, C. Bryson, E. Clery, J. Curtice, and M. Phillips (eds), *British Social Attitudes: The 30th report* (London: NatCen Social Research, 2013), 115–38.
2. S. Brookes, *Sexual Politics: Sexuality, Family Planning, and the British Left from the 1880s to the Present* (Oxford: Oxford University Press, 2011), 186.
3. See R. Campbell and S. Childs, 'Introduction: Deeds and Words', in R. Campbell and S. Childs (eds), *Gendering Politics after Joni Lovenduski* (Colchester: European Consortium for Political Research, 2014), 3–14.
4. See A. Black and S. Brooke, 'The Labour Party, Women, and the Problem of Gender, 1951–1966', *Journal of British Studies*, 36 (1997), https://doi.org/10.1086/386144.
5. S. Perrigo, 'Women and Change in the Labour Party 1979–1995', *Parliamentary Affairs*, 49 (1996), 116–29, at 119.

6. S. Bashevkin, 'From Tough Times to Better Times: Feminism, Public Policy and New Labour Politics in Britain', *International Political Science Review*, 21 (2000), https://doi.org/10.1177/0192512100214005.
7. J. Lovenduski, 'United Kingdon: Male Dominance Unbroken?', in D. Dahlerup and M. Leyenaar (eds), *Breaking Male Dominance in Old Democracies* (Oxford: Oxford University Press, 2013), 7296, at 82.
8. C. Short, 'Women and the Labour Party', *Parliamentary Affairs*, 49 (1996), 17–25, at 17. See also M. Russell, *Building New Labour: The Politics of Party Organisation* (London: Palgrave Macmillan, 2005), 96–128.
9. Brookes, *Sexual Politics*, 196.
10. 'The TUC's 12 Aims for Women at Work', held at TUC Library, London Metropolitan University. This replaced a 1963 six-point charter covering equal pay, equal opportunities for training and promotion, access to apprenticeships, retraining for older women and returners, and the health and welfare of women at work (also held at the TUC Library). Before the TUC's 1975 Charter, the London Trades Council's 1974 Working Women's Charter linked women's economic situation with their position in the home and in wider society.
11. Interview, Sarah Boston.
12. L. Briskin, 'Trade Unions, Collective Agency, and the Struggle for Women's Equality: Expanding the Political Empowerment Measure', in V. M. Moghadam, S. Franzway, and M. M. Fonow (eds), *Making Globalization Work for Women: The Role of Social Rights and Trade Union Leadership* (New York: State University of New York Press, 2011), 213–43.
13. A. Coote and B. Campbell, *Sweet Freedom: The Struggle for Women's Liberation* (London: Picador, 1982), 144.
14. G. Kirton, 'Progress towards Gender Democracy in UK Unions 1987–2012', *British Journal of Industrial Relations*, 53 (2015), https://doi.org/10.1111/bjir.12052.
15. See M. Simms, J. Holgate, and C. Roper, 'The Trades Union Congress, 150 years on: A Review of the Organising Challenges and Responses to the Changing Nature of Work', *Employee Relations*, 41 (2019), https://doi.org/10.1108/ER-09-2018-0242.
16. Department for Business, Innovation, and Skills, *Trade Union Membership 2014: Statistical Bulletin* (London: HM Government, 2014), 7.
17. S. Ledwith, 'Gender Politics in Trade Unions', *Transfer*, 18 (2012), https://doi.org/10.1177/1024258912439145.
18. E. Heery and D. Nash, 'Trade Unions and Collective Conciliation: A Secondary Analysis', Acas Research Paper nos 10–11 (London: Acas, 2011).
19. E. Heery, 'Union Workers, Union Work: A Profile of Paid Union Officers in the United Kingdom', *British Journal of Industrial Relations*, 44 (2006), https://doi.org/10.1111/j.1467-8543.2006.00508.x.
20. G. Kirton, 'Unions and Equality. 50 Years on from the Fight for Fair Pay at Dagenham', *Employee Relations*, 41 (2019), https://doi.org/10.1108/ER-09-2018-0239.
21. E. Heery, 'Equality Bargaining: Where, Who, Why?' *Gender, Work & Organization*, 13 (2006), https://doi.org/10.1111/j.1468-0432.2006.00321.x.
22. TUC, *Equality Audit 2005: Bargaining for Equality at Work* (London: TUC, 2005).
23. TUC, *Equality Audit 2009: Progress on Bargaining for Equality at Work* (London: TUC, 2009), 7.

24. TUC, *Equal Pay Pilot Project* (London: TUC, 2003). Three case studies were cited in the TUC's submission to the WWC: TUC, 'Women and Work Commission: TUC submission', 17 February 2005, pp. 30–2.
25. Kirton, 'Unions and Equality'.
26. Coote and Campbell, *Sweet Freedom*, 145.
27. Outright sexism and even sexual harassment remain problematic in several unions: in 2020, the GMB union was found to be institutionally sexist in an independent report conducted by the barrister Karon Monaghan QC, and in 2023 an independent inquiry led by Baroness Helena Kennedy QC showed the rail union Transport Salaried Staff Association (TSSA) to have a misogynistic culture that had allowed sexual harassment by leaders to continue unchallenged.
28. J. Lovenduski, 'Male Dominance Unbroken?', in D. Dahlerup and M. Leyenaar (eds), *Breaking Male Dominance in Old Democracies* (Oxford: Oxford University Press, 2013), 71–96, at 78–81.
29. See J. Lovenduski, 'Gender Politics: A Breakthrough for Women?' *Parliamentary Affairs*, 50 (1997), https://doi-org.ezproxy1.bath.ac.uk/10.1093/oxfordjournals.pa.a028766.
30. Short, 'Women and the Labour Party', 17.
31. P. Hewitt and D. Mattinson, *Women's Votes: The Key to Winning* (London: Fabian Society, 1979).
32. S. Gunn, 'Party Leaders Woo Women', *The Times*, 12 March 1992.
33. Richardson died on 1 February 1994, aged 70, having suffered from disabling rheumatoid arthritis for some time. As MP for Barking, she took a leading role in 'persuading the Labour Party to take women's issues seriously' (J. Adams, 'Richardson, Josephine', in H. C. G. Matthew and B. H. Harrison (eds), *Oxford Dictionary of National Biography* (Oxford: Oxford University Press, 2004), 831).
34. J. Lovecy, 'Framing Claims for Women: from "Old" to "New" Labour', in C. Annesley, F. Gains, and K. Rummery (eds), *Women and New Labour: Engendering Politics and Policy?* (Bristol: Policy Press, 2007), 63–92, at 71.
35. H. Harman, *A Woman's Work* (London: Allen Lane, 2017), 138.
36. R. Reeves, *Women of Westminster* (London: Bloomsbury, 2020), 171.
37. Russell, *Building New Labour*, 101.
38. Short, 'Women and the Labour Party', 18.
39. Russell, *Building New Labour*, 106.
40. Russell, *Building New Labour*, 113.
41. Lovecy, 'Framing Claims for Women', 89; V. Atkinson and J. Spear, 'The Labour Party and Women', in M. J. Smith and J. Spear (eds), *The Changing Labour Party* (London: Routledge, 2018), 151–70, at 159.
42. Short, 'Women and the Labour Party', 20.
43. Russell, *Building New Labour*, 97.
44. Russell, *Building New Labour*, 96.
45. He told reporters in July 1995 that all-women shortlists were 'not ideal' and would be discontinued. A spokesperson for Blair told reporters that the leadership formally opposed the policy.
46. J. Richardson, 'A Ministry for Women's Rights?' *Marxism Today* (March 1986), 36–37.
47. Labour Party, *Britain Will Win with Labour*, manifesto (1987).

48. C. Short, 'Introduction', 66th Labour Women's Conference, 13–14 April 1991, Wolverhampton, p. 2: OS Box 46, People's History Museum.
49. The EOC opposed the move when it was announced in the Conservative manifesto in March 1992, as Joanna Foster wrote to the prime minister: letter, 23 March 1992: Box JF/5/2, Joanna Foster archive, Oxford Brookes University. Richardson's discussions with Butler were influenced by this decision, the main difference between Labour and Conservative proposals being the size and status of ministerial responsibility, rather than location.
50. N. Williamson, 'Whitehall Holds Secret Briefings to Pave Way for Labour Government', *The Times*, 15 August 1995.
51. Without publicizing its work, the Conservative government established a dedicated unit within the Department for Employment, called the 'Sex Equality Branch', staffed by thirty-six civil servants, according to the Labour Party's 1995 document: Labour Party, 'Governing for Equality: A Labour Party Consultation On Government Machinery for Women (February 1995) (printed version): OS Box 46, People's History Museum, pp. 4–5. This sizeable unit was another indication of the influence of Labour's proposals on the other main party.
52. Richardson had been replaced by Mo (Marjorie) Mowlam in 1992, but, on taking over as leader, Smith appointed Short to the role, which suggests a recognition of feminists' demands by Smith: Short was strongly identified with women's organizing structures and had chaired the Women's Action Committee; she had high status within the party, having previously served on the front bench and been a long-standing member of the NEC, whose women's committee she chaired. However, it also reflected the low status of the post, as it followed Short's failure to be re-elected to the shadow cabinet; she was one of several women MPs to fall victim to what was widely seen as men's attempts to thwart the new rules instituting a form of quota (whereby MPs were required to cast at least three out of eighteen votes for women), whilst Mowlam's move to shadow national heritage secretary, having been elected by her peers, was seen as a promotion: see J. Langdon, 'The Shadow Women', *Herald* (Glasgow), 25 October 1993. Meanwhile Harman, politically closer to Smith, was appointed shadow chief secretary to the cabinet, despite also losing out in the election; she was the highest-placed woman in the most recent NEC elections. Harman was a particular target of male MPs voting tactically to keep women out of the shadow cabinet.
53. Short, 'Women and the Labour Party', 23.
54. Building on the work Richard had undertaken previously, the 1995 document was the product of research by party activists and academics close to the party, in particular Meg Russell, and several drafts were produced as it made its way through women's committees, Labour women's conference, and the NEC.
55. Labour Party, 'Governing for Equality', 11. Short herself admitted that she would prefer to retain the practice of a cabinet-rank minister and a civil-service unit attached to the Department of Employment but thought that location in the Cabinet Office would also give the posts the authority they needed: S. Womack, 'Labour Urged to Change Tack on Ministry for Women', Press Association News, 14 February 1995.
56. Editorial, 'The End of a Dream', *Guardian*, 15 February 1995.
57. A. Grice, 'Veto on Left's Plan for Minister of Women', *Sunday Times*, 28 May 1995.

58. See C. Raven, 'Brave New Socialist Whirl', *Observer*, 12 November 1995. In fact, Short did not identify herself as feminist, either, saying in a 1995 interview: 'I'm not a feminist. I never think of myself like that; never have done', but she often proved a fearless advocate of women's rights, as in her campaign against the *Sun*'s 'Page Three', and she particularly championed the cause of low-paid women: see N. Spivey, 'Thinking Man's Pin-Up', *Financial Times*, 27 May 1995. (The title of this article reflects widespread press obsession with Short's physical appearance.)
59. M. Benn, 'Will this Woman Win your Vote?', *Guardian*, 12 December 1995.
60. E. Creamer, 'Why New Labour Brings New Hope for Every Woman', *Mirror*, 2 October 1996.
61. C. Dyer, 'How to Stop Stalkers', *Guardian*, 26 September 1996.
62. Labour Party, *Meet the Challenge, Make the Change: Final Report of Labour's Policy Review for the 1990s*, manifesto (1989), 20.
63. Labour Party, *Meet the Challenge*, 22.
64. P. Wynn Davies, 'Labour Offers "a New Deal for Women"', *Independent*, 12 February 1992.
65. Labour Party, *It's Time to Get Britain Working Again*, manifesto (1992).
66. Atkinson and Spear, 'The Labour Party and Women', 151.
67. See Russell, *Building New Labour*, 146–51.
68. P. Ghazi, 'Labour Softens to Win Women's Hearts', *Observer*, 17 December 1995.
69. A. Neustatter, 'A Thorn in Labour's Side', *Guardian*, 24 April 1995.
70. D. MacIntyre, 'Brown Acts to Beat Tory "Tax and Spend" Jibes', *Independent*, 16 May 1996. The support of Short, as a leading left-winger, for postponing a decision on the level of the national minimum wage was seen as helpful to the leadership.
71. P. Wintour, 'Short Gets Transport Job in Shadow Shuffle', *Guardian*, 20 October 1995.
72. Harman, *A Woman's Work*, 148–9.
73. K. Farnsworth, 'Minding the Business Interest: The CBI and Social Policy', *Policy Studies*, 19 (1998), 19–38.
74. Labour Party, *New Labour because Britain Deserves Better*, manifesto (1997). The theme of 'fairness, not favours' was a Blair mantra—for example, at the Labour Party conference in 1996 ('There will be fairness, not favours, for employers and employees alike. The Labour government today is not the political arm of anyone other than the British people') and again at the TUC in 1999 ('For the first time in 20 years, trade union leaders came into Downing Street; they are consulted, they are listened to, just as the CBI are. No favours, but fairness').
75. J. McIlroy, 'The New Politics of Pressure: The Trades Union Congress and New Labour in Government', *Industrial Relations Journal*, 31 (2000), https://doi.org/10.1111/1468-2338.00143; J. McIlroy, 'Ten Years of New Labour: Workplace Learning, Social Partnership, and Union Revitalization in Britain', *British Journal of Industrial Relations*, 46 (2008), https://doi.org/10.1111/j.1467-8543.2008.00678.x.
76. C. Howell, *Trade Unions and the State: The Construction of Industrial Relations Institutions in Britain, 1890–2000* (Princeton: Princeton University Press, 2005), 131.
77. S. Coulter, *New Labour Policy, Industrial Policy and the Trade Unions* (London: Palgrave Macmillan, 2014).
78. McIlroy, 'The New Politics of Pressure'.
79. Coulter, *New Labour Policy, Industrial Policy and the Trade Unions*, 108–10.

80. A. Charlwood, 'The New Generation Of Trade Union Leaders and Prospects for Union Revitalization', *British Journal of Industrial Relations*, 42 (2004), https://doi.org/10.1111/j.1467-8543.2004.00319.x, p.387.
81. Charlwood, 'The New Generation of Trade Union Leaders', 387–8. The 'awkward squad' was usually held to include Bob Crowe (Rail, Maritime and Transport Workers), Kevin Curran (GMB), Andy Gilchrist (Fire Brigades Union), Dave Prentis (Unison), Billy Hayes (Communications Workers Union), Mark Serwotka (Public and Commercial Services Union), Derek Simpson (Amicus), and Tony Woodley (TGWU). Charlwood points out that these leaders all reflected the cultures of their specific unions rather than a wider mood of union unrest. See also P. Smith and G. Morton, 'Nine Years of New Labour: Neoliberalism and Workers' Rights', *British Journal of Industrial Relations*, 44 (2006), https://doi.org/10.1111/j.1467-8543.2006.00506.x.
82. I am indebted to Ed Blissett for this observation (interview). See also E. Blissett, 'Fatally Divided? An Analysis of the Role Micro-Political Divisions Played in the Loss of the 1986–7 News International Dispute', *Labor History*, 59 (2018), https://doi.org/10.1080/0023656X.2018.1467299.
83. Coulter, *New Labour Policy, Industrial Policy and the Trade Unions*, 126.
84. See H. Bewley, 'Raising the Standard? The Regulation of Employment, and Public Sector Employment Policy', *British Journal of Industrial Relations*, 44 (2006), https://doi.org/10.1111/j.1467-8543.2006.00504.x, p. 360.
85 Interview, Margaret Prosser.

6

The Women's Policy Machinery

Strengthening Women's Voice in Government?

Introduction

As outlined in Chapters 2 and 3, the women's policy machinery has been identified as a key driver of women's rights, especially in the Westminster political system, which gives a high degree of power to government in setting the agenda. In the UK, there have been two main phases in the development of the women's policy machinery. The first occurred in the 1970s, in response to advocacy from the European Economic Community (EEC) and the United Nations (UN). The second followed Labour's coming to office in 1997, as a result of sustained activism within the party over more than a decade, as outlined in Chapter 5.[1] The Labour period saw an unprecedented institutionalization of women's voice in political decision-making, thanks to the determined work of leading figures such as Harriet Harman, who learnt to work within the constraints facing them to persuade the circle of decision-makers (within the prime minister's office and the Treasury) to take up policy on childcare and work–family rights.

However, the Labour leadership resisted moves to strengthen women's voice mechanisms and ignored calls to resource them adequately. Consequently, the institutions set up after 1997 were hampered by fragmentation and under-resourcing, making it easier to deinstitutionalize them after 2010. Table 6.1 shows that the history of the ministerial post(s) with responsibility for women and equality has been an exceptionally unstable one, with frequent changes of personnel and department reflecting its subordinate position within government.[2] As a coalition of women's civil-society organizations commented in 2014, from the beginning 'the message sent out is that Gender Equality is not important enough to warrant a Secretary of State and a well-resourced department of its own'.[3] Alongside the moves undertaken after 1997, women's voice was institutionalized through the Women's National Commission (WNC), which reported to the Women's Unit (WU) and its successors. The WNC, in line with UN recommendations, was an

Women and Employment in Public Policy. Susan Milner, Oxford University Press. © Susan Milner (2024).
DOI: 10.1093/9780191987359.003.0006

advisory body that provided a formal mechanism for gathering the views of women's organizations and representing these views to government; it was disbanded in 2010. Although not meeting the criteria above for definition of a women's policy agency because it had no statutory responsibility for policy, its remit nevertheless covered agenda-setting.[4] It can be regarded as a quasi-agency in that it reported directly to the WU (and its successors), which set the terms of its remit and composition and oversaw its operation. The WNC's history reveals lasting ambivalences within the structures of political power concerning any external body with the capacity to criticize government or constrain its action. Women's voice mechanisms were curtailed or abandoned when government feared criticism or unwanted demands.

Considered together, these bodies give an indication of what a strong infrastructure could look like, and what it could achieve, if adequately resourced and with the capacity to be both independent and well networked. In practice, their development reveals subordination to wider government objectives that limits the potential for women's interests and perspectives to be taken seriously and integrated into policy. At times, the work of the women's policy machinery appears to have been overlooked, and it was always subordinated to other policy priorities. This overview confirms Claire Annesley and Francesca Gains's argument, based on their analysis of the early Labour years, that the core political executive has a gendered disposition 'as a consequence of years, decades and centuries of practices that traditionally excluded women'.[5]

Government Departments: A Minister (or Ministers), but no Ministry for Women

The creation of a distinct government department for women, headed by a minister of cabinet rank, was a long-standing demand of Labour women and had formed an important part of their agenda for programmatic change. However, by 1997 the demand had already been diluted in the election manifesto to a minister of cabinet rank, without a full department. In 1997, the initiative got off to a bad start when, instead of a full ministerial position, Harman was appointed alongside her role as Secretary of State for Social Security (and had to battle during that first year with her deputy, Frank Field). Joan Ruddock was also appointed as junior minister in a part-time (and unpaid) role.[6] Ruddock was given the job in the first place only because of Harman's intervention, as it had been a 'struggle with Number Ten' to secure a junior post to support her work.[7] Unsurprisingly, this perceived downgrading of women's issues in government drew significant adverse public attention, which the women ministers themselves were left to defend in public.

On appointment as Minister for Women, Harman stated that she would ensure that women's voice and interests were considered in all aspects of policy, promising to implement a national childcare strategy and monitor all policy proposals across government departments to assess their impact on women.[8] However, the ministry did not receive financial resources to accompany this work, instead relying on the host department, which effectively meant subordination to that department's policy programme. During Harman's short tenure as minister for women, her social-security brief dominated the agenda, with an emphasis on savings to the Treasury. Her work focused on single parents (overwhelmingly mothers) as the New Deal for Lone Parents was developed. Although Harman tried to emphasize the provision of childcare as a counterpoint to workfare,[9] the two policy agendas of supporting women and making welfare cuts were 'so obviously in conflict with each other'.[10] The agenda of women's rights was subordinated to a dominant logic of 'making work pay', with an instrumental objective underpinning it and excluding other approaches such as equality or care. But, even worse, the impact of the cuts fell most heavily on women, who, despite needing more funding for childcare than men, received less financial support through the New Deal programmes than men.[11]

Leaders' lack of support for Harman's position was starkly illustrated in December 1997, when she was left to defend the welfare cuts to single parents in the House of Commons, while the prime minister hosted a reception for celebrities at Downing Street. Harman, in presenting the bill while being booed by her fellow Labour MPs, was visibly 'close to tears'.[12] The situation worsened as Harman's deputy at the Department for Social Security developed his own agenda of contributions-based welfare, bringing him into open conflict with his nominal senior minister, which Blair did nothing to resolve.[13] Harman and Ruddock lost their jobs in a reshuffle within fifteen months, which was a public humiliation for the foremost woman in government. Both women were personally shaken by the experience.[14]

The Harman–Ruddock team was replaced by a more complex arrangement, with Baroness Margaret Jay, the leader of the House of Lords, rather than the head of a government department, sharing the role with Jowell, who in 1999 moved from her post as Minister of State for Public Health to Minister of State in the Department for Education and Employment. The post of women's minister was not only part-time and subordinate, but also ephemeral and shifting, meaning that its effectiveness depended not on its institutional status but on the determination and personal resources of the post-holder.[15] This was combined with a heavy workload: in effect, policy was starting from scratch in almost every area affecting the work of the minister for women and equality.

Jay went out of her way to emphasize her difference in personal approach from her predecessor, rejecting the term 'feminism', which Harman openly espoused,[16] although she and Jowell also stated that they wanted to build on three issues raised by Harman: childcare, work–family policy, and violence against women. Women who identified as feminist found themselves at odds with the circle around party leaders (including Peter Mandelson and pollster Philip Gould), who associated the 'women's vote' with 'Worcester woman'—that is, aspirational and traditionally minded middle-class women. This also created a tension within government between self-identifying feminist women and other women.[17]

At the Labour Party conference in October 1998, women's rights activists bemoaned the lack of policy proposals, with the Fawcett Society's Alison Ryan arguing at a fringe event that 'women's policy is in a state of paralysis'.[18] At the end of October, the ministers for women announced an action plan containing proposals to encourage girls and young women to look to positive role models like the Spice Girls, and to overhaul equalities legislation within a single overarching framework.[19]

Given the tension between feminist demands and leaders' views of women's rights, women ministers found that they needed to follow new methods, as they had little direct clout in the machinery of government, which remained heavily focused on a small group of insiders in the prime minister's office and the Treasury. They did this in a resourceful way, using existing networks and creating informational resources in the form they knew played well with the Labour leadership, particularly focus group and polling data. Harriet Harman, Patricia Hewitt, and their circle of friends, which included Jowell, worked closely with Deborah Mattinson to persuade party leaders that women voters, including those drawn to Blair in 1997, had turned away from Labour because of a perception of laddishness.[20] As discussed in Chapter 2, the use of instrumental logic to generate change often drives change in a male-dominated world of party politics.

However, the instrumental logic had its limits, as the women ministers themselves also had the job of presenting the response to the calls for more women friendly government. The existence of two women's ministers now proved useful for the leadership, as Jowell toured the country, sometimes with Jay, to listen to women. They met considerable scepticism during their roadshow, and the report that resulted from it provided an opportunity for Conservative and Liberal Democrat spokespeople for women to lambast the government for inaction, since no new measures were proposed.[21]

By now, Harman, who had initially been reluctant to criticize the party leaders, spoke publicly of the 'macho' culture surrounding Blair and his ministers, and the low priority attached to the issues she had championed as minister: childcare and family-friendly laws.[22] Harman's special adviser Anna Coote followed up with a *Guardian* article in May 1999, which argued that, while Labour had been women-friendly in opposition, in government they resisted moves to promote women's rights as 'rocking the boat'.[23] Unease at the 'laddish' behaviour and discourse of the policy advisers surrounding Blair spread among women MPs, early in Labour's first term.[24] A group of women, including some MPs, began to meet and work with influential policy researchers to put together an alternative policy agenda, which was set out in the 2000 book *The New Gender Agenda*.[25] Coote expressed this group's fears that, 'now the party was in government, it had lost the plot as far as women were concerned', and urgently needed to reconnect with women voters through the adoption of work–family policies such as paid parental leave.[26]

Despite remaining broadly loyal to the government and rarely rebelling openly in parliamentary votes, women MPs had already learnt to mobilize to put pressure on the government, even if only reactively. In 2000, they protested against the Home Office decision to issue a visa to the boxer Mike Tyson, a convicted rapist who faced fresh charges of sexual assault,[27] and high-profile backbenchers mobilized successfully against government plans to review family policy with an emphasis on 'marriage is best', with the support of ministers Jay and Margaret Hodge, as well as the families minister Baroness Hollis. Besides revealing the restiveness of women MPs, these incidents demonstrated a lack of gender sensitivity in the Blair circle, including the leader himself and the male ministers heading the major government departments.[28]

As outlined in Chapter 5, trade unions had also stepped up their criticisms of employment rights,[29] while, as outlined in Chapter 4, the Equal Opportunities Commission (EOC) under Julie Mellor launched a new campaign 'Valuing Women' in October 1999. Signalling the increased electoral salience of women's rights, Theresa May for the Conservative Party launched a policy review document aimed at winning female voters, including measures to attract women into local and national politics, the introduction of a career break for child-raising, and universal testing for the HPV virus, which causes cervical cancer.[30]

Increased pressure from a range of actors within the regulatory—and, more pointedly for the Labour leadership, electoral—space led to renewed activity by Jay and Jowell in the run-up to the 2001 general election. Even more than the earlier roadshow, which had sparked discussions in the media about women's priorities, the new communications initiatives—an online consultation on the Downing Street website and a glossy magazine—met with derision.[31] However, a new focus on the gender pay gap, referring to research compiled by the WU, was welcomed by campaigners. Jay and Jowell also backed moves by women in the Labour Party to present legislation allowing positive action by political parties, which opened the way for the re-adoption of all-women shortlists. Focusing on these two issues, the Labour Party conference in September 2000 saw greater attention to women's rights. Rumours circulated that Harman would return to cabinet after the general election, in a big-spending department, particularly after Mo Mowlam announced that she would step down both as MP and as Cabinet Office minister, leaving only Clare Short in a major spending department.[32]

In the event, Harman was invited to take the post of Solicitor General, which did not carry cabinet rank. Nevertheless, she saw it as a way back into government and an opportunity to achieve improvements in the prosecution of domestic-violence cases.[33] In the second Labour term, 2001–5, Hewitt was Minister for Women and Equalities, with Baroness Sally Morgan (former political aide to Blair who had just been ennobled) as the lead minister for women in the Lords.[34] Barbara Roche and later Jacqui Smith joined the team as deputy ministers, the former also as Minister of State in the Cabinet Office (June 2001–May 2002) and then Minister in the Office of the Deputy Prime Minister with responsibility for Social Exclusion (May 2002–June 2003), the latter also as Minister for Industry and the Regions (June 2003–May 2005). Jay's much criticized tenure as minister for women had resulted in widespread scepticism about the value of the role, which Hewitt sought to dispel.[35]

The period 2001–5 was the longest served by any single minister for women[36] and the post was now located at the Department of Trade and Industry (DTI), an activist and big-spending department. Moreover, Hewitt as a long-standing feminist activist was determined to 'lead from the front'.[37] As Secretary of State for Trade and Industry, she was a political heavyweight and a long-standing member of the 'New Labour' inner circle. Like Harman, she was on relatively good terms with Gordon Brown, which not only was important to gain Treasury support for any spending initiatives, but became more politically necessary as the shift in power from Blair to Brown gained momentum.[38] She had broad credibility in both the business and trade-union worlds, as the only minister with significant private-sector experience (at Accenture) and having previously been Minister for Small Business at the DTI. In her role as founding deputy director of the Institute for Public Policy Research, she had a track record of policy research and practice in areas of interest to the 'business case' for gender equality, particularly working time and family-friendly workplace measures.[39] This 'combination of feminism, Labour Party experience, policy expertise, and ... knowledge of business and technology' gave her the ability to mobilize different sets of stakeholders.[40] Hewitt's tenure therefore saw a combination of access to top levels of decision-making, strong links with key stakeholders (business and trade unions), and civil-society networks.[41]

At the same time, Hewitt was conscious of the need to present all policy ideas in a way that the Blair circle would understand and support. She was aided in this by changes in the business world that saw both greater feminization of decision-making roles and attention to the types of policy on the DTI agenda, including flexible working.[42] Hewitt's able steering of the ministerial brief for women meant that she was able to integrate work–family measures into the broader DTI agenda on employment regulation. As Melissa Benn commented in the *Guardian*, Hewitt 'has sold these changes as being in the simultaneous interests of a generation of frazzled fathers and some equally hard-pressed but well-meaning employers. It is clever, the way the f-word has shifted from feminism to fathers.'[43]

The reframing of women's demands came at a price, of course: it meant a right to request flexible working, rather than a right for mothers to reduce their hours on return from maternity leave, as campaigners had advocated; and it meant caution in the demands made on employers, with the bulk of changes being funded by the state in the form of increased statutory maternity leave pay. Hewitt's objective of shared parental leave, to encourage greater take-up by fathers, did not happen, despite strong links with fatherhood and family advocacy groups and the establishment of an evidence base showing positive child development outcomes:

> I inherited a manifesto commitment on maternity pay and leave.... What I wanted to do was something much more like I think Germany was starting to do at the same time, which was to advance parental rights for fathers as well as mothers, but of course the debate was so embryonic at that point. I simply didn't have any support in the cabinet if I'd taken it to them. ... And I really pushed it with my officials, because I thought that's what we ought to be doing. I got stuck. We did paid paternity leave, and we did the extra maternity leave, which was fine ... but it's absolutely helped to entrench the notion that women are the primary caregiver.[44]

Nevertheless, Hewitt's moves to integrate women's rights into the core work of the DTI represented a new and significant phase in the history of the women's policy machinery. Benn had spotted that there was 'an influential alliance of women, largely unrecognized, at the top and middle of government which is deadly serious about a core feminist agenda',[45] with Harman and Hewitt at its heart. Before the 2005 general election, this alliance had secured manifesto commitment to a single equalities bill, and further work–family rights, the latter thanks also to mobilization of trade unions within the party (as outlined in Chapter 5). Although Hewitt's tenure had some success in mainstreaming women's rights, it had made only first steps, which needed to be continued and strengthened. Women's organizations stepped up their criticism of the minister, arguing that the gender equality strategy published in 2003 contained only vague aspirations rather than measurable targets. Katherine Rake, chair of the Fawcett Society, complained that 'six years into a Labour government we should expect something more robust at this stage'.[46]

In this context of accommodation to the (male-)dominant Labour approach to policy, it is not surprising that activists expressed disillusionment. Their disappointment was shared by women voters, as revealed by a Mori poll in September 2004, which showed scepticism about the government's ability or willingness to make positive changes to their lives, as well as a negative assessment of policy on health and the economy.[47] Hewitt's response was to promise more radical action on parents' rights, and the Women and Work Commission (WWC) was established in September 2004 to examine the gender pay gap and make recommendations to address it. Meanwhile Harman continued to put pressure on party leaders to address women's rights, aided by new polling from Mattinson.[48]

After the 2005 general election, the same mistakes as in 1997 were made. When the new government was announced, a pause of nearly two weeks followed before Meg Munn (Parliamentary Under-Secretary for Trade and Industry) was appointed Minister for Women and Equality. If the creation of the post of minister for women and the establishment of the WU in June 1997 had been widely seen as a 'hasty afterthought', a second omission in 2005 was viewed as reflecting lack of interest and low priority. The fact that Munn, like Ruddock before her, was not initially paid for this job intensified press criticism.[49] The double oversight was rectified: Munn later received backdated pay for the role, and Tessa Jowell was appointed Minister for Women and Equality, giving the ministerial brief cabinet status.

Munn reported to Alan Johnson, the Secretary of State for Trade and Industry, who supported her in her role and was 'very committed to' the equalities agenda.[50] The continued location of the women and equalities brief in DTI made sense, because of the work it had already done since 2001. Vicky Pryce, senior economist at the DTI, ensured that the whole ministerial team understood the importance of women's employment and the need to close the gender pay gap:

> [Pryce] said if you address the pay gap, it's huge, it's 3% of GDP, which is equivalent to all our exports with Germany. And you could almost see everyone in the room sit up and take notice. So that kind of understanding of the importance of this agenda was there in the DTI.[51]

The period 2001–5 represented a high point in the representation of woman-friendly policy relating to the sphere of employment, thanks not only to the relative stability of the ministerial post but also to its location in a well-resourced, high-status department that was led by politicians committed to gender equality. As discussed in Chapter 8, the period between the 2005 general election and Harman's appointment as Minister for Women saw intense activity on both policy areas developed under Hewitt: the establishment of a unified equalities body, and the work–family agenda set out in the Warwick agreement. It also, however, saw institutional discontinuity in the representation of women's voice in government.

From the Women's Unit to the Women and Equality Unit and the Government Equalities Office

In June 1997, Harman announced: 'I will be supported by a dedicated Women's Unit which will promote women's issues across Whitehall and throughout the country.' [52] The Women's Unit (WU) was established after a delay of four weeks, following criticism from the Conservative opposition. Initially headed by Pauline Barrett, a career civil servant based in the Department for Social Security, it had a brief of coordinating policy on women across government departments, and consulting women's organizations. Owing to the delay in setting it up and the lack of independent resources, the unit was seen as marginalized and had difficulty in establishing policy priorities.[53] *The Times*, openly hostile to the idea of a proactive women's rights unit, thanked Blair for refusing to establish a fully-fledged department and instead creating 'a Portakabin unit' tacked onto the DSS.[54] According to press reports, the WU's work was delayed because of ministers' inability to agree guidelines, with Harman reported to have blocked draft guidelines on gender impact assessment prepared by civil servants. Civil servants speaking to journalists referred to an unhappy atmosphere and 'a wasted first year'.[55]

Commentators argued in the national press that 'Downing Street has always appeared to be embarrassed by its Women's Unit',[56] and it was widely expected that it would disappear when Labour took office for a second term. However, over time (and in various incarnations) the WU became a durable—albeit contingent—institution within the Whitehall system. In its various forms the women's policy unit has always undergone subordination to wider government priorities and struggled to make gender mainstreaming a proactive or consistent approach. It has also often, like the post of minister, suffered from instability in its institutional setting, resulting in a lack of continuity and wasted resources. In this context, the WU learnt to adapt its programme to the prevailing ideological and institutional setting, retaining expertise in the field of equality but at the expense of an independent agenda or the capacity to steer or even substantially to monitor wider policy.

Just ahead of the July 1998 reshuffle that lost Harman her ministerial post, Fiona Reynolds was appointed to head the WU. A high-ranking civil servant, Reynolds was a personal friend of Blair but had been unafraid to criticize the Labour government in her previous role as head of the charity Council for the Protection of Rural England.[57] The WU took over responsibility for coordinating policy on sex discrimination and equal pay, becoming a sponsor for the EOC and taking over lead responsibility for the Kingsmill review, which was then underway.[58] The WU had been under-resourced from the beginning, but with the new responsibilities came an increase in staffing and budget: by then the unit had a staff of thirty-five and an annual budget of around half a million pounds, with more promised the following year. Despite greater capacity, the WU's resources still fell short of the new workload.

The WU supported the public-facing role of the ministers for women, and under Jay and Jowell it was criticized for doing little more than public-relations exercises and a 'patronising' approach.[59] However, the decision to include a commitment to tackle the gender pay gap owed much to the evidence-gathering work conducted by the WU in 1999–2000, in particular a report on the lifetime earnings gap between men and women.[60] When Hewitt took over the role of minister for women and equality, the policy programme was already largely in place.

Despite this work, the prime minister's office briefed press that the WU would be disbanded after the 2001 election. However, women's activism ensured this did not occur. Instead, Hewitt pushed ahead with the agenda of merging gender with other equality strands, and renamed the body the Women and Equality Unit (WEU), with the intention to anchor women's rights within a broader equalities framework (see Chapter 9). The new unit had a substantial regulatory and policy agenda, in preparation for the creation of a single equalities body, announced in 2003. Angela Mason, a long-standing LGBT activist and director of Stonewall between 1992 and 2002, who was known to advocate the creation of a single equalities body, was appointed director of the WEU in November 2002.

This meant that, with Hewitt at the DTI, and Mason an activist head of the WEU, the women's policy machinery achieved some stability and a high profile in Labour's second term. However, the arrangement was less stable than might first appear, as became evident after the 2005 general election, which saw a succession of institutional changes.

Most damagingly, the unit had no independent infrastructure, and moved according to where the prime minister thought it would be best placed (see Table 6.1), usually but not always corresponding to the department where the lead minister was based. For example, the WEU was taken out of the DTI in 2006, following a government reshuffle, and followed ministerial responsibility to the Department of Communities and Local Government (DCLG), where there was a better fit with work on race and ethnicity;[61] in 2007, when it became the Government Equalities Office (GEO), it was 'spun out' to the Cabinet Office, on the grounds of bringing together the equality strands.[62] The rationale for moves often appeared unclear and relates to short-term operational rather than strategic needs.

Conservative (and Conservative-led) governments after 2010 retained the ministerial role for women and equalities, but personnel changes intensified, owing in part to greater turnover in government and ministerial posts, but also at times to political tensions around its remit. In 2018, when the Women and Equalities Committee (WEC) scrutinized the work of the GEO (and its forerunners) and the minister for women and equalities, it observed that 'the GEO has been unusually itinerant for a Whitehall function throughout its history, and there has been a high level of turnover among the people holding ministerial responsibility for it'.[63] This situation was not just a question of academic or bureaucratic interest, the committee noted; policy on women's rights directly affects people's lives, and it was regularly disrupted by the problems created by instability or 'churn' in staffing, resourcing, and institutional location. Instability slowed progress and diminished the status and perceived importance of policy on women and equality.

Janet Veitch, a civil servant working in the WU and the WEU as head of gender mainstreaming and then as director of the WNC (1999–2007),

Table 6.1 Women and equalities in the machinery of government, 1997–2022

Date	Minister/lead department	Women's/equalities office
May 1997	Harriet Harman (Secretary of State for Social Security and Minister for Women) Joan Ruddock (Parliamentary Under-Secretary, Department of Social Security, and Minister for Women)	Women's Unit (Department for Social Security)
July 1998	Baroness Jay (Leader of the House of Lords and Minister for Women) Tessa Jowell (Minister of State for Public Health with responsibility for women; Minister of State for New Deal and for Women)	Women's Unit (Cabinet Office)
May 2001	Patricia Hewitt (Secretary of State for Trade and Industry and Minister for Women) Baroness Morgan (Minister of State, Cabinet Office, and Minister for Women, June 2001–November 2001) Barbara Roche (Minister of State, Cabinet Office, May 2002; Minister for Social Exclusion, Office of the Deputy Prime Minister, June 2002–June 2003, and Deputy Minister for Women, May 2002–June 2003) Jacqui Smith (Minister of State, Industry and the Regions, and Deputy Minister for Women, June 2003–May 2005)	Women and Equality Unit (Department for Trade and Industry)
May 2005	Tessa Jowell (Secretary of State for Culture, Media and Sport, and Minister for Women)[a] Meg Munn (Parliamentary Under-Secretary for Trade and Industry, and Minister for Women and Equality)	Women and Equality Unit (Department for Culture, Media and Sport)
May 2006	Ruth Kelly (Minister of State for Communities and Local Government and Minister for Women and Equality) Meg Munn (Parliamentary Under-Secretary for Trade and Industry, and Minister for Women and Equality)	Women and Equality Unit (Department for Communities and Local Government)

Continued

Table 6.1 *Continued*

Date	Minister/lead department	Women's/equalities office
June 2007	Harriet Harman (Leader of the House of Commons and Secretary of State for Equality) Barbara Follett (Minister for Equality and Minister for the East of England) Maria Eagle (Minister of State, Government Equalities Office)	Government Equalities Office (stand-alone department)
May 2010	Theresa May (Home Secretary and Minister for Women and Equalities)	Government Equalities Office (Home Office)
September 2012	Maria Miller (Secretary of State for Culture, Media and Sport and Minister for Women and Equalities)	Government Equalities Office (Department for Culture, Media and Sport)
April 2014	Nicky Morgan (Financial Secretary to the Treasury and Minister for Women) Jo Swinson (Parliamentary Under-Secretary of State for Employment and Parliamentary Under-Secretary of State Women) Sajid Javid (Secretary of State for Culture, Media and Sport and Minister for Equalities)	Government Equalities Office (Department for Culture, Media and Sport)
July 2014	Nicky Morgan (Secretary of State for Education and Minister for Women and Equalities)	Government Equalities Office (Department for Education)
July 2016	Justine Greening (Secretary of State for Education and Minister for Women and Equalities)	Government Equalities Office (Department for Education)
January 2018	Amber Rudd (Home Secretary and Minister for Women and Equalities) Victoria Atkins (Parliamentary Under-Secretary, Home Office, and Minister for Women)	Government Equalities Office (Home Office)
April 2018	Penny Mordaunt (Secretary of State for International Development and Minister for Women and Equalities) Victoria Atkins (Parliamentary Under-Secretary, Home Office, and Minister for Women)	Government Equalities Office (Department for International Development, April 2018 to March 2019) (Cabinet Office Equalities Hub, from April 2019)

December 2019	Liz Truss (Secretary of State for International Trade and President of the Board of Trade and Minister for Women and Equalities) Baroness Berridge (Minister for Women) Kemi Badenoch (Exchequer Secretary to the Treasury and Minister for Equalities)	GEO (Cabinet Office Equalities Hub)
September 2022	Nadim Zahawi (Minister for Equalities, Cabinet Office) Katherine Fletcher (Parliamentary Secretary, Cabinet Office, and Minister for Women)[b]	Government Equalities Office (Cabinet Office Equalities Hub)
October 2022	Kemi Badenoch (Secretary of State for International Trade at the Department for Business, Energy and Industrial Strategy and Minister for Women and Equalities) Maria Caulfield (Minister of State and the Department of Health and Minister for Women's Health)	Government Equalities Office (Cabinet Office Equalities Hub)

[a]Of the three stints as minister for women (two junior, one senior), Jowell's ministerial responsibility for women is mentioned only briefly in her official parliamentary career record, with reference to her role at the DfEE (11 October 1991–8 June 2001): https://members.parliament.uk/member/159/career (accessed 5 July 2023).
[b]Fletcher's short term as minister for women does not appear on her parliamentary record.
Sources: Hansard; Lexis-Nexis newspaper database.

explained the consequences of this churn for civil servants working on gender equality:

> Over that period of eight years, I had eight different ministerial teams to work for. And that meant I spent a serious amount of my time just managing the machinery of government moves. ... It's like setting up an entirely new business with an entirely new employer, what happens is that you have to negotiate new office space, they will always try and get away with giving you ... the minimum they can get away with. ... But also you don't have any political clout if you're not going to stay somewhere permanently, so you never build up those reciprocal networks and arrangements that the civil service so closely relies on, where they know that you're going to be around and that the minister is interested in you .... They thought, in a year there'll be another reshuffle, and this lot will probably go, so why would we invest in them.[64]

As well as being weak institutionally, the WEU suffered during a critical period in its existence from difficulties in establishing its own policy focus. In the period leading up to the Equality Act 2010, the priority of achieving civil partnership necessarily entailed relative neglect of other policy priorities, including women's equality demands. As the EOC finished its programme in preparation for the creation of a new Equality and Human Rights Commission, feminist activists feared that specific women's demands would become marginalized. Veitch observed that 'they were trying to reduce the focus on women, and sweep it up along with everything else. Which I think has been the history of the women's machinery, really.'[65]

As well as putting forward legislative proposals in line with evidence and with demands coming from women's civil-society organizations, a key function of a women's policy unit is to promote gender mainstreaming, according to UN principles.[66] Gender mainstreaming—understood to mean monitoring of all policy proposals to ensure that gender inequality is not perpetuated—had always been a contested policy approach and struggled to make much headway in the British policymaking system. Harman and Ruddock were keen to promote gender mainstreaming, and the WU initially established processes to support it, including training of civil servants as well as assessment of policy across departments to ensure sensitivity to equality and diversity. However, in the early days it proved difficult to implement the new approach, partly because it was not yet institutionally embedded, but also because it was practised at the end stage of policy formulation rather than early on and throughout, leading to a perception that the unit was 'policing' ministers.[67]

Later, Hewitt's tenure as Minister for Women marked a renewed interest in gender mainstreaming, with an emphasis on providing expertise to different government departments, and the development of more systematic processes, in what has been called an 'expert-bureaucratic' phase of policy development.[68] However, the same period saw a shift away from a focus on gender to a wider view of equality, leading to confusion about the aims and scope of mainstreaming.[69] From its adoption onwards, the gender mainstreaming approach encountered a lack of understanding and a perceived weak prioritization by government that weakened its impact.[70]

Although the creation of a public-sector equality duty (PSED) and its integration into the Equality Act 2010 embedded gender mainstreaming in hard (that is, legally enforceable) law, in practice its implementation has been uneven. After 2010, implementation was further weakened under Conservative and Conservative-led governments, as the party had long contested the idea of what David Cameron, then prime minister, called 'bureaucratic nonsense' in 2012.[71]

Bringing Civil Society into Policymaking: The Women's National Commission

Non-governmental organizations (NGOs) fall outside the women's policy machinery but can form part of the wider machinery of governance, according to the UN's view of women-friendly political structures.[72] Their role is advisory, carrying no formal responsibility for policy, but they potentially have an important role to play in representing women's voice, bringing forward grassroots demands, and giving policymakers access to wider networks. They have been relatively little studied as women's policy actors, however.

During the Labour period of government, the Women's Budget Group (WBG) moved from criticism of John Major's Conservative government to a position of potential influence over policy.[73] Formed in the early 1990s, the WBG is a thinktank with limited, project-based funding, and takes the form of a network of associated academics. Its approach fitted more closely with Labour than Conservative policy, and after 1997 the group developed a close working relationship with the Treasury.[74] Research by the WBG highlighted the need to understand the relationship between individual earnings and household income, the gendered life course and the consequences of labour-market interruptions, and the undervaluation of caring work, both paid and unpaid.

According to Susan Himmelweit, founder chair of the WBG, the group was conscious that it could exert influence only by tailoring its message to the overriding concerns of the Treasury:

> We knew that we only got things if they were in line [with Treasury policy]. We had influence, but it wasn't that much really. … Having said that, they did come and talk to us quite a lot, they would respond to us, and they would sometimes invite us in. Especially [compared to] now when there is no consultation and it is hard to get the message across, there was quite a lot of discussion and input into policy.[75]

Only on one occasion did the WBG feel it had exerted an influence in its discussions with Treasury officials, and this concerned the need to make the tax-credit system more equality friendly by not penalizing partners for sharing employment hours.[76] According to Himmelweit, the WBG knew they had influenced Treasury decision-making because an official had told them that the WBG's insistence 'had cost [the Treasury] money'.[77]

The WU had a formal relationship with civil society through the Women's National Commission (WNC).[78] The WNC was established in 1969 under a Labour government.[79] A membership organization, it initially represented fifty member organizations and thirty-five associate organizations, and was served by a secretariat of civil servants whose role was to relay their views to government. A 'small, low profile, advisory agency',[80] it was widely seen as a rather conservative body seeking consensus between groups with sometimes conflicting agendas. One of the first things Harman did in 1997 was to announce a review of the WNC to make it more representative and effective. Enhancement of the WNC's voice capacity also fitted in with the government's obligations to the process set in train by the UN Fourth World Women's Conference held in 1995 in Beijing.

The review group, chaired by Ruddock and conducted by civil servants in the WU, recommended that the membership and remit of the WNC should be expanded, and its status enhanced. However, the recommendation that participation in the commission should be remunerated was ignored by government.[81] The WNC was restructured, with Veitch as director, Baroness Christine Crawley as chair, a fifteen-strong group of commissioners (including the director of the Fawcett Society, the former chair of the EOC in Northern Ireland, and the chair of the Family Planning Association), and a WU civil-service secretariat. Membership grew to around 200, including the hundred or so grassroots organizations that had formed an alliance in 1989 to coordinate responses to the government's reporting to the UN, and later expanded to around 500.[82]

In 2002 Margaret Prosser, who had retired as deputy general secretary of the Transport and General Workers' Union (TGWU) and was feeling 'a bit at a loose end',[83] was appointed to chair the WNC. Veitch remained as director. From 2007 the WNC became an advisory Non-Departmental Public Body of the GEO. Barbara Collins became the new director, replacing Veitch, and the board of commissioners was largely replaced. Baroness Gould[84] took over as chair from Prosser, who became deputy chair of the Equality and Human Rights Commission.

The WNC had a special role in coordinating comments on the government's annual report to the UN as part of the Beijing process. It also set its own priorities through its own representative structure, based on a board of commissioners of twelve to fifteen women representing member organizations, and working groups set up internally, as well as through its process of consultation of members, and it reported its priorities to the WU via its chair, and to the minister for women through regular meetings with its director, accompanied by members of the 'big six' women's organizations. The consultation process took place at conference ('rather than a proper survey of our members, which you always get poor responses to'), which was held every two years:

> they always really said the same story … there were three really strong top problems, and then a couple underneath. The first one was always women's poverty and income, so into that rolled women and work, women running their own businesses, the pensions gap, childcare, all of that stuff that goes with barriers to women's entry into the labour market, and then the second one was violence, and then the third one was women's voice.[85]

In 2000 for example, it established a set of priorities for actions to advance women's empowerment, on the gender pay gap, the need to redesign welfare to suit women's lives, funding for refuge services, women's representation in decision-making, and women's health and education.[86]

The WNC provided the network on which a strong women's policy machinery depends, and a useful sounding board for the WU and the minister for women. There is little evidence that its upward reporting and recommendations resulted in specific policy initiatives, or changes to the content of government initiatives. For women's organizations, the WNC nevertheless acted as an amplifier of voice and an opportunity to exert low-key influence—for example, in lending research insights or expertise to work being undertaken by the WU. The closure of the WNC by the

Conservative-led coalition in 2010 was denounced by its members as an unnecessary and ideologically motivated 'act of vandalism'.[87]

Conclusion

This chapter has shown how the women's policy machinery was institutionalized in the first two Labour terms. Two overarching policy objectives correspond to this institutionalization: first, the shift from separate equality strands to an overarching equalities framework; and, second, a focus on the gender pay gap as an indicator of women's labour-market disadvantage relative to men's. Both objectives had ambivalent effects on women's voice and the promotion of women's rights. As discussed in Chapter 4, the shift to an overarching equalities framework, promoted across EU member states, has been viewed by feminist scholars as resulting in a weakened voice for women as a specific policy constituency. This is not an inevitable outcome, however: a strong overarching framework, if accompanied by adequate expertise in specific structural inequality and appropriate resources, and by a strong legislative framework promoting both positive duties and the capacity to pursue multiple, intersecting claims, could improve individuals' access to social justice. The first two Labour terms constituted a period of development in which competing claims were still under consideration and a clear outcome was not yet certain.

The second objective was fraught with contestation at multiple levels. The Labour leadership had to respond to appeals based on instrumental logic (the need to win over women voters, based on the accumulation of polling and empirical evidence) but was resistant to specific policy proposals resulting from them. Consequently, the women's policy machinery was always subordinate and contingent to the dominant policy preferences. Women such as Harman and Hewitt who advocated a feminist agenda were often publicly mocked or sidelined, and could only succeed—thanks to their wider party and public standing—by adapting their demands to prevailing policy discourses, in particular a form of business feminism that emphasized voluntary initiatives as a way of achieving longer-term cultural change. This adapted 'gender agenda' undoubtedly set the groundwork for later policy reforms, but it is argued in this book that they did so in a way that created path dependency by locking in exclusionary mechanisms such as long qualifying periods, and self-limiting self-regulation.

Institutionally, the women's policy machinery undoubtedly suffered throughout its history from fragmentation and under-resourcing. It never became anything like a government department, nor did it have the capacity to work across departments through formal mechanisms. Instead, it worked by providing informational resources and through personal relationships. As Munn explained:

> The one thing that's really important to understand about the role of minister, the deputy minister for women and equality, is that you have very little in the way of people who report directly to you who are doing things. You are trying to influence across the whole of the parliament, across the whole of the government, that's what you're trying to do. And how do you influence, you influence by being the one in the room, and getting into those discussions, and raising it with the right people.[88]

The work of the women's policy machinery required sustained effort because of the institutional weaknesses outlined in this chapter. Visibility in the House of Commons was achieved by a dedicated timetabled slot for ministerial questions, as the architects of Labour's ministry for women had envisaged, but it entailed a large amount of work for the WU, which, unlike other civil-service teams, had to collate information across government departments.[89] The government itself remained male dominated in composition and outlook. For Hewitt, the main problem was that 'there were very few feminists around the cabinet table'.[90]

Nevertheless, this chapter has presented Harman and Hewitt as 'critical actors' capable of influencing policy through their networks of influence.[91] Harman remained a resolute agenda-setter during the period, regardless of whether she was in a formal position established to represent women's interests. After returning to the back benches in 1999, Harman used a mixture of formal and informal avenues to influence policy: chairing the parliamentary select committee on employment,[92] chairing an early years partnership in Southwark, and using these experiences to feed into Brown's work at the Treasury. Harman also used networks inside and outside parliament, including Labour-friendly journalists and those sympathetic to women's rights.[93] Along with other women MPs, she also worked within the Labour Party's decision-making structures.

This mixture of informal and formal pressure is important, because the literature on women's representation in parliament needs to take account of the ways in which influence over policy can be exerted outside the formal mechanisms of parliamentary debates, as discussed in Chapter 2, and particularly through opportunities within the party to influence manifesto commitments, using an instrumental logic at electoral times. The women's policy machinery could also support these opportunities through its informational resources. While as a group the women MPs elected in 1997 were often portrayed in line with the media cliché of docile 'Blair's babes', and indeed open rebellions in parliamentary votes were rare,[94] such rebellions grew behind the scenes, and resulted in manifesto commitments—for example, on maternity leave, flexible working, and the Equality Bill. This chapter has argued that women activists worked in a range of venues to exert pressure, which a reading of parliamentary debates alone is unlikely to capture.

Notes

1. W. Stokes, 'The Government of the United Kingdom: The Women's National Commission', in S. Rai (ed.), *Mainstreaming Gender, Democratizing the State?* (Manchester: Manchester University Press, 2003), 184–20, at 184.
2. When the WEC compiled this information in 2017, it was able to trace only part of the picture, focusing only on the lead minister. Table 6.1 and the information presented in this chapter are based on press reports, owing to the lack of reliable official information. Press reports are the most reliable source, because the women's policy machinery was outward facing, reporting constantly to media; parliamentary information, on the other hand, is scarce, and there is little or no trace in Cabinet documentation.
3. National Alliance of Women's Organizations (NAWO), *UK Women: Rights and Progress* (Edinburgh, NAWO, 2015).
4. See also J. Lovenduski, 'An Emerging Advocate: The Equal Opportunities Commission in Great Britain', in D. McBride Stetson and A. G. Mazur (eds), *Comparative State Feminism* (Sage, 1995), 114–31, at 114–15.
5. C. Annesley and F. Gains, 'The Core Executive: Gender, Power and Change', *Political Studies*, 58 (2010), https://doi.org/10.1111/j.1467-9248.2010.00824.x, p.914.
6. V. Elliott, 'Ruddock Takes Job as Minister without Pay', *The Times*, 12 June 1997.
7. H. Harman, *A Woman's Work* (London: Allen Lane, 2017), 197.
8. 'Harman Says Women Will Have a Greater Say on Policy', *The Times*, 4 June 1997.
9. See Harman, *A Woman's Work*, 186–7.
10. J. Smith, 'She's Minister for Women, so who Needs Chauvinists?', *Independent*, 14 December 1997. Smith had made the same point in an interview with Harman on her appointment: J. Smith, 'A Bit Further to Go Yet', *Independent*, 8 June 1997.
11. J. McAlpine, 'Women Let down by Blair's Babes', *Sunday Times*, 7 December 1997.
12. Smith, 'She's Minister for Women', 5.
13. Harman, *A Woman's Work*, 202–3.
14. Harman later in her memoirs referred to feeling 'raw', 'upset and humiliated' after the sacking and needing the support of close female friends (*A Woman's Work*, 210). Ruddock in a 1999 interview spoke of finding it hard to continue her long-standing parliamentary work after the experience: 'You ask yourself what did I do wrong?' (G. Lean, 'Saint Joan Launches GM Crusade', *Independent*, 19 September 1999).
15. S. Childs, *New Labour's Women MPs: Women Representing Women* (London: Routledge, 2004), 127.

16. See, e.g., R. Sylvester, 'Teen Girls Urged to Admire Role Model Spice', *Independent*, 8 November 1998, where Jay is reported as saying: 'In politics, feminism is seen as negative, complaining about things; it's perceived to be about separateness, putting up a brick wall between men and women. I don't think you have to be negative like that.' In other interviews too she described the term 'feminist' as divisive. Later Jay admitted that she had not identified with the policy area on her appointment: 'It wasn't something that I had ever been engaged in, but ministers are often asked to take up portfolios which aren't something that they necessarily worked on before' (A. Treneman, 'A Question of Balance', *The Times*, 30 July 2001).
17. Personal communication, Hewitt, 7 June 2023.
18. A. Treneman, 'The Incredible Disappearing Babes', *Independent*, 2 October 1998.
19. 'Government Drive for Women's Rights', *Guardian Weekly*, 15 November 1998.
20. R. Sylvester, 'Blair's Efforts to Woo Female Voters Fall Flat', *Independent*, 14 February 1999.
21. C. Norton, 'Modern Woman Worries Most about Juggling Home and Work', *Independent*, 7 October 1999.
22. R. Watson, 'Harman Hits at Macho Ministers', *The Times*, 9 March 1999.
23. A. Coote, 'It's Lads on Top at Number Ten', *Guardian*, 11 May 1999.
24. Already in June 1997, Polly Toynbee had written in the *Guardian* of 'dark mutterings about the maleness inside the lads' bunker. The key No 10 Policy Unit has 10 men and one woman, and Downing Street has its own all-boys' football team' (P. Toynbee, 'The Sneers Show Harman Has a Mighty Task', *Independent*, 12 June 1997). See also H. Wilkinson, 'The Day I Fell out of Love with Blair', *New Statesman*, 7 August 1998, pp. 9–10.
25. A. Coote (ed.) *The New Gender Agenda* (London: Institute for Public Policy Research, 2000).
26. A. Coote, 'Women: What about us?', *Guardian*, 11 September 2000.
27. P. Waugh and S. Schaefer, 'Women MPs in Rebellion over Visa for Tyson', *Independent*, 20 May 2000.
28. J. Deans, 'Jay Forces Blair Retreat on Marriage', *Daily Mail*, 13 November 2000.
29. See S. Milner, 'Gender Equality and Employment Regulation in the New Labour Years, 1997–2010: The Problem of the Gender Pay Gap', *Historical Studies in Industrial Relations*, 43 (2022), https://doi.org/10.3828/hsir.2022.43.5.
30. A. Woodcock, 'Tories Offer Choice for Women who Fled Labour', *Journal*, 31 March 2000.
31. J. Dillon, 'Home Page Roasting for Ministers', *Independent*, 9 July 2000; V. Low, 'The Government's Guide to Opportunities for All', *Evening Standard*, 9 October 2000; 'Voices', *Sunday Times*, 15 October 2000.
32. J. Dillon, 'Harman Is Set to Return to Cabinet', *Independent*, 10 September 2000.
33. Harman, *A Woman's Work*, 229–49.
34. Morgan's role was specifically linked to work within the Cabinet Office to ensure anti-discrimination across a number of strands, notably gender reassignment. This formal division of labour—with one minister responsible for equalities and anti-discrimination, the other focused on women—occurred first with the Hewitt Morgan pairing but became more common with the passage of the Equality Act 2010.
35. R. Paveley, 'Lords Leader Lady Jay Is Set to Leave the Cabinet', *Daily Mail*, 16 February 2001; L. Ward, 'Women: Hewitt's Way', *Guardian*, 18 June 2001.

36. The rapid succession of junior ministers, on the other hand, is striking and reflects the way in which the role was subject to trade-offs over posts at times of cabinet reshuffles. Roche suffered the same fate as Ruddock four years earlier, when she was sacked from her post without explanation, despite being personally engaged in the equality and anti-discrimination work she had done: J. Ashley, 'Equality Warrior Bloodied but Unbowed', *Guardian*, 30 June 2003.
37. Personal communication, Hewitt, 7 June 2023.
38. 'The Two Faces of Labour's Minister for Business', *Business*, 8 September 2002.
39. P. Hewitt, *About Time: The Revolution in Work and Family Life* (London: Institute for Public Policy Research, 1993).
40. Personal communication, Hewitt, 7 June 2023.
41. Annesley and Gains, 'The Core Executive', 923. See also S. Milner, 'Gender Pay Gap Reporting Regulations: Advancing Gender Equality Policy in Tough Economic Times', *British Politics*, 20 (2019), https://doi.org/10.1057/s41293-018-00101-4, p.125.
42. D. Demetriou, 'At Last, Women Break through to the Very Top', *Evening Standard*, 30 May 2002.
43. M. Benn, 'Don't Mention the 70s', *Guardian*, 10 April 2003.
44. Interview, Patricia Hewitt.
45. Benn, 'Don't Mention the 70s'.
46. D. Turner, 'Equality Plan "will not Halt Fall in Voting"', *Financial Times*, 12 June 2003.
47. M. Denes, 'What Women Want: A New Deal', *Guardian*, 24 September 2004.
48. J. Beattie, 'Harman Tells Blair: Women Could Cost us the Next Election', *Evening Standard*, 15 December 2004.
49. E.g., T. Branigan, 'Minister for Women to Work Unpaid', *Guardian*, 16 May 2005; J. Oliver, 'Meg, the (Unpaid) Minister Blair Forgot', *Mail on Sunday*, 15 May 2005.
50. Interview, Meg Munn.
51. Interview, Munn.
52. Quoted by J. Squires and M. Wickham-Jones, 'New Labour, Gender Mainstreaming and the Women and Equality Unit', *British Journal of Politics and International Relations*, 6 (2004), 81–98, at 83.
53. Squires and Wickham-Jones, 'New Labour, Gender Mainstreaming and the Women and Equality Unit', 84.
54. 'Blair's Babes', *The Times*, 26 August 1998.
55. P. Newton, 'Rows Hit Labour Plan to Be "Woman Friendly"', *The Times*, 26 August 1998.
56. Ward, 'Women: Hewitt's Way'.
57. Newton, 'Rows Hit Labour Plan to Be "Woman Friendly"'; D. Walker, 'Whitehall Women Help Green Labour', *Independent*, 19 April 1998.
58. Squires and Wickham-Jones, 'New Labour, Gender Mainstreaming and the Women and Equality Unit', p.85.
59. S. Hall, 'Tories Ready to Scrap "Patronising" Women's Unit', *Guardian*, 12 November 2000.
60. K. Rake, *Women's Income over the Lifetime* (London: Women's Unit, Cabinet Office, 2000).
61. Interview, Munn.
62. WEC, 'The Role of Minister for Women and Equalities and the Place of GEO in Government', Second Report of Session 2017–19, HC 356, 23 May 2018, p. 5.

63. WEC, 'The Role of Minister for Women and Equalities', 4.
64. Interview, Janet Veitch.
65. Interview, Veitch.
66. See also B. McPhail, 'A Feminist Policy Analysis Framework', *Social Policy Journal*, 2 (2003), https://doi.org/10.1300/J185v02n02_04, for a checklist of how to analyse public policy from a gender-equality perspective.
67. J. Veitch, 'Looking at Gender Mainstreaming in the UK Context', *International Feminist Journal of Politics*, 7 (2005), https://doi.org/10.1080/14616740500284615, 602.
68. J. Squires, 'The Challenge of Diversity: The Evolution of Women's Policy Agencies in Britain', *Critical Perspectives on Gender and Politics*, 3 (2007), https://doi.org/10.1017/S1743923X07000360, 518.
69. Squires, 'The Challenge of Diversity', 532.
70. See Squires, 'The Challenge of Diversity'; Squires and Wickham Jones, 'New Labour, Gender Mainstreaming and the Women and Equality Unit', and Veitch, 'Looking at Gender Mainstreaming in the UK Context'; also O. Hankivsky and A. Christoffersen, 'Gender Mainstreaming in the UK: Current Issues and Future Challenges', *British Politics*, 6 (2011), https://doi.org/10.1057/bp.2011.1.
71. D. Cameron, 'Prime Minister's Speech to CBI', 19 November 2012, https://www.gov.uk/government/speeches/prime-ministers-speech-to-cbi. In this speech, Cameron announced the end of the use of equality impact assessments.
72. C. Durose and F. Gains, 'Engendering the Machinery of Governance', in C. Annesley, F. Gains, and K. Rummery (eds), *Women and New Labour: Engendering Politics and Policy?* (Bristol: Policy Press, 2007), 93–116.
73. S. Himmelweit, 'The Experience of UK Women's Budget Group', in Dipartimento per le Pare Opportunità (DPO), International Workshop on Gender Auditing of Government Budgets (Rome: DPO, 2000), 3–25.
74 S. Himmelweit, 'Making Policymakers More Gender Aware: Experiences and Reflection from the Women's Budget Group in the UK', *Journal of Women, Politics & Policy*, 27 (2005), https://doi.org/10.1300/J501v27n01_07, p. 111.
75. Interview, Susan Himmelweit.
76. See Himmelweit, 'Making Policymakers More Gender Aware'.
77. Interview, Himmelweit.
78. Unfortunately, the WNC left no archive behind. Its website is archived by The National Archives, but this consists of a seemingly random selection of website captures for each year; the links to documents on the website are not always functional. I have used this resource here, alongside my interviews with Janet Veitch and Margaret Prosser.
79. Stokes, 'The Government of the United Kingdom', 185.
80. Lovenduski, 'An Emerging Advocate', 114.
81. Stokes, 'The Government of the United Kingdom', 192.
82. Interview, Veitch.
83. M. Prosser, *Your Seat is at the End* (London: Feather Duster Publications, 2012), 200.
84. Joyce Gould, made a Labour life peer in 1993, was a long-standing party insider, starting out as a regional organizer and becoming a trusted party fixer in the 1980s during the conflict with Militant. See J. Gould, *The Witchfinder General: A Political Odyssey* (Hull: Biteback, 2016). She was chief women's officer from 1975 to 1985.
85. Interview, Veitch.

86. Interview, Veitch.
87. Prosser, *Your Seat is at the End*, 203. The then chair of the WNC, Baroness Gould, called the move 'a mistake' and 'yet another blow to women across the UK' (WNC, 'Closure of the Women's National Commission', press release, 14 October 2010, WNC online archive, GEO 3, The National Archives). The closure of the WNC was announced at the same time at massive cuts to the Equality and Human Rights Commission budget: see P. Curtis, 'Quangos Cull', *Guardian*, 14 October 2010.
88. Interview, Munn.
89. Personal communication, Veitch, 7 June 2023.
90. Interview, Hewitt.
91. See Milner, 'Gender Equality Gap Reporting Regulations'. On 'critical actors', see Chs 2 and 3.
92. Harman, *A Woman's Work*, 213–14.
93. Journalist Jackie Ashley refers to a female political network: 'the women MPs are often in touch with female journalists and academics, who can usefully work together to bring an issue to the fore. Academics ... produce the statistics and research; MPs raise the question in Parliament and the journalists can then push a good story' (J. Ashley, 'The Story of Critical Mass—Women at Westminster', in R. Campbell and S. Childs (eds), *Deeds and Words: Gendering Politics after Joni Lovenduski* (Colchester: ECPR Press), 165–6, at 166).
94. P. Cowley and S. Childs, 'Too Spineless to Rebel? New Labour's Women MPs', *British Journal of Political Studies*, 33 (2003), https://doi:10.1017/S0007123403000164.

7

The Women and Work Commission

Bridging Different Approaches to the Gender Pay Gap

Introduction

Independent commissions are convened by governments to examine policy problems seen as complex, deep-rooted, and politically sensitive. As previous chapters of this book have discussed, the question of the gender pay gap, raised in Labour's 2001 general election manifesto, had become highly sensitive by 2004: 'There was a lot of discussion in government at the time and certainly in the Labour Party about how best to approach the gender pay and opportunity gap that persisted.'[1] The Women and Work Commission (WWC) was established, in the run-up to the 2005 general election, as a way of finding alternative solutions to mandatory equal-pay audits, which unions strongly advocated, but which the party leadership had no intention of granting, and as a way of responding to pressure from Labour-affiliated unions more generally. As well as work–family policy, stronger rights for workplace equality representatives featured on an agenda of union demands that became increasingly vocally expressed at party policy forums.

Meanwhile, several equal-pay claims were still outstanding in local government, with potentially large costs associated with remedial actions if the claims proved successful. Such cases were making their way through tribunals as the commission sat: in March 2005, women health workers in Cumbria received a record award after an eight-year legal battle.[2] Women police officers had won an equal-pay case earlier that year. The public-sector union Unison vowed to increase efforts to support equal-pay claims and urged employers, particularly in local government, to address equal pay through annual awards rather than await tribunal cases. The commission was even directly involved in a dispute: Prosser, in her capacity as chair of the WWC, was asked to mediate in a long-running equal-pay case in the prison service, and the 2006 report noted that the parties had subsequently returned to negotiations with a settlement 'likely'.[3]

Women and Employment in Public Policy. Susan Milner, Oxford University Press. © Susan Milner (2024).
DOI: 10.1093/9780191987359.003.0007

There could be no question of using a commission merely to deliberate without recommendations, or to postpone policy decisions. On the contrary, the political stakes were high, as were expectations among campaigners and activists. In such circumstances, the membership and remit of the commission, as well as its working methods and general approach to the question, shaped deliberations and outcomes. In line with the literature on the workings of independent commissions (summarized in Chapter 1), this chapter examines the way the WWC was established and how it worked, and how these characteristics influenced the recommendations that followed.

Composition

Membership of the commission was largely decided within the prime minister's office, although the Confederation of British Industry (CBI) and Trades Union Congress (TUC) were invited to propose representatives, subject to approval. Prosser's name was suggested as chair by Sally Morgan, then Tony Blair's chief of staff, but was more widely thought by all the political staff to be the ideal candidate.[4] As well as enjoying wide support within the party and union movement, Prosser had been an Equal Opportunities Commissioner and was in 2004 chair of the Women's National Commission (WNC; see Chapter 6), so she had strong networks within the women's movement. As a previous trade-union deputy general secretary, she was known to have sympathies on the union side, but she was trusted by the party leadership as a safe pair of hands, and she had made known on several occasions her impatience with union leaders on equal pay.

The CBI and TUC were invited to propose four commissioners each. John Cridland, then deputy CBI director, was its lead negotiator on all aspects of social policy and had established a good working relationship with the prime minister's office. Experienced in negotiations with trade unions, he was seen by them as pragmatic. Christine Ray was the most senior corporate figure, as head of human resources at the leisure and entertainment company Rank Group. Sarah Anderson, who ran her own specialist catering employment agency Mayday, had sat on the Better Regulation Task Force. Sally Hopson was one of the youngest members of the commission, having only recently become regional retail managing director at Asda (then the second largest supermarket in the UK), which was at that time a leading member of Opportunity Now. All three women were active members of CBI committees, and Anderson and Ray regularly attended meetings with government on behalf of the CBI, on employment and skills.

Anderson was an important figure for government because she represented the voice of small businesses, a community policymakers found difficult to access. Hopson, on the other hand, was relatively unknown to government and had to undergo a vetting process she remembered as 'bizarre':

> You get a letter inviting you to a meeting with Downing Street, but you don't know what the meeting's about. … And then you get into the room, and other people turn up, including John Cridland … and some very senior civil servants … and half way through you think, I'm being interviewed! … And there's a secret sign, because … they move into selling the Commission … would you do this? And I distinctly remember saying, it's a fascinating topic, but if it's all just about equal pay, I'm not interested; equal pay comes as a result of lots of other things. So that's it, you're in![5]

Among trade-union appointees, Kay Carberry was the obvious choice as the most experienced top-level negotiator (and the most senior woman at the TUC). As well as extensive knowledge of the union landscape in her role as assistant general secretary, she also had extensive expertise in gender equality, as she had led the TUC's equality efforts, including the commitment to pursue gender equality in all aspects of work and report on these efforts biannually to congress. Nita Clarke (Tony Blair's policy adviser on trade unions) emphasized that the commission benefited from the relationships between CBI and TUC that had already been developed during Labour's first two terms:

> You also have to remember that John Cridland and Kay Carberry worked very closely together anyhow, on a day-to-day basis.[6] It was a very small world of people at the top of business, top of the TUC, and politics. … It was important that the key people had strong pre-existing relationships. Of trust.[7]

Carberry as assistant general secretary had responsibility for TUC representation on bodies and therefore decided which of their affiliated unions would be represented on the commission. These were unions with large female membership: GMB (assistant general secretary Debbie Coulter), Unison (director of policy and public affairs Liz Snape), and Usdaw (general secretary John Hannett). Hannett and Snape also sat on the TUC's General Council. Carberry, Coulter, and Snape were important figures in the union movement as part of a still small number of women in senior national leadership positions. Through their personal experience but also through their powerful positions within these large, strategically important unions, union representatives on the Commission were strong voices:

> We had the general secretary of the shop workers' union, we had the deputy general secretary of the GMB, we had a powerful national official of Unison ... it wasn't just something driven by the TUC office, there were people very much equipped and entitled to speak about low-paid women workers.[8]

However, there was some disagreement within TUC about nominations to the commission, and this may have later affected union responses to the WWC's report, particularly as one of the big four unions (Amicus) was not represented, and another (TGWU) was represented only informally by Prosser as chair: she no longer held an official position within the union, which had seen a major change of leadership after she left.

In addition, three appointees represented public-sector employers. Naaz Coker, one of only two women from ethnic minority backgrounds on the commission, had twenty years' experience of working in the NHS and was appointed chair of St Georges Healthcare NHS Trust in November 2003. The winner of several awards for her services to the Asian community, she had set up the Muslim Council's leadership programme, and also chaired the Refugee Council at the time the WWC was established. Local government was represented by Stella Manzie,[9] who had caught the eye of national policymakers because of her work improving services at Labour-led Coventry City Council. There, Manzie had hit the national news through the council's thoroughgoing implementation of job evaluation, which had been complex and controversial owing to the loss of pay of some historically male-dominated groups of workers (see Chapter 13):

> It was very, very fraught. We had about ten thousand employees at the time ... large numbers, and it was very high profile at the time, because there was industrial action. I had been quite prominent in speaking out in favour of equal pay, and I'd been in front of big staff meetings explaining to front-line staff why we had to do this.[10]

The remaining commissioners were appointed because of their representation of specific sectors, such as the head of the Learning and Skills Council Chris Banks, and the chair of the Equal Opportunities Commission (EOC), initially Julie Mellor, who was replaced by her successor Jenny Watson in June 2005. Adeeba Malik represented community organizations, as deputy chief executive of QED-UK, a Bradford-based charity aiming to improve the position of south-east Asian communities. Malik had already participated in several government initiatives, including the Department of Trade and Industry's (DTI) Ethnic Minority Employment Forum and its Muslim Women's Advisory Group. Finally, Ruth Silver, principal of Lewisham college and a national expert on vocational training policy, had worked with both the prime minister's and chancellor's offices on welfare-to-work programmes and on training as a vehicle for social inclusion.

Commissioners were 'largely known to Number Ten and we [in the prime minister's office] had experience of working with them in different spheres—in that sense there was confidence that they could form an effective circle of people.'[11] They were seen by policymakers, unions and employers as forming a 'strong'[12] and authoritative body: they were individually 'powerful people, thoughtful people',[13] 'the key players';[14] 'people who had a real understanding of the live issues on the ground' rather than 'the great and the good';[15] 'the right people round the table';[16] 'people that were going to produce interesting, profound stuff'.[17] Commissioners were known to be likely to work within the boundaries of 'what was possible'[18] in the prevailing political context, and—based on their previous public service—to engage fully with the subject, despite not being paid for the work.

As this list shows, the commission was large in its composition, and, as discussed further below, it faced a sizeable workload. However, the secretariat was relatively small, given the amount of data to process and work to coordinate. Whereas the commissioners were appointed by the prime minister, the process was managed by a team within the DTI, which at the time of the commission's establishment also housed the Women and Equality Unit (WEU). The secretariat was headed by Tracy Vegro, a senior civil servant at the DTI (who also worked on other areas of DTI responsibility), and Matilda Quiney, who had left her previous job as policy officer at the GMB union to join the civil service, and who had acquired considerable equal-pay expertise in her former role.[19] They were supported by a third civil servant, Gina Martinelli, and subsequently assisted by a wider team within the DTI once the evidence had to be processed. Initially, in the setting-up phase in June and July, the three main civil servants responsible for the secretariat were therefore 'working flat out' until more staff could be allocated.[20] At the time of the interim report, the secretariat remained small, and civil servants faced a major upheaval as the WEU moved from DTI: 'We were writing the interim report on the day we had to move office. We had to turn up, turn on new computers, take papers out of the boxes.'[21]

Once the commission had been established, the DTI recruited an economist from within the civil service, Helen Grimshaw, who was to follow the process through all the way to the submission of the follow-up report in 2009. Professor Diane Houston of the University of Kent, who was working on secondment at the DTI, was appointed as academic adviser and formed part of the DTI team. In this way, the establishment of the WWC helped to build expertise in the DTI on the question of women's employment.

Remit and Approach

The remit of the commission was strikingly broad and open, as all my interviewees observed: it covered investigation into the 'wide-ranging' causes of the gender pay gap, including occupational gender segregation, how educational experiences feed into occupational segregation, working time, tax and social security, sex discrimination, women's labour-market experience before and after having children, and the role of the public sector as a substantial employer of women. This breadth of approach reflected thinking in the prime minister's office, where the question of women's employment was seen as being difficult to approach from one single angle:

> A lot of it was, when we were thinking and talking about this, it looked a lot more complicated in its origins, you needed to look at the origins of all these things, gender segregation and career choice, the careers advice people get, you needed to look at these things in the round, rather than focusing on some legislative thing.[22]

The broad remit had advantages in that it gave a large degree of latitude to commissioners and especially the chair to determine working priorities, but it also created problems, not least in terms of the sheer amount of ground to be covered. Having a broad agenda also, arguably, allowed policymakers to avoid hard decisions by referring to the scale and complexity of the problem.

With hindsight, commissioners saw the breadth of the remit as creating difficulties: 'It's much easier for a bespoke commission dealing with a bespoke issue to come up with a bespoke solution. Commissions that have a very wide remit, it's harder for them.'[23] One commissioner spoke of the terms of reference being 'loose', which meant that areas where consensus was harder to reach could be set aside in favour of the 'easier' subjects of agreement. Those within the commission who resisted 'harder' outcomes would feel less pressure to compromise. Breadth of remit was, therefore, likely to favour 'softer' outcomes putting less onus on government to act: 'It's sufficiently loose in the terms of reference that—I'm being pretty critical here, but—well,

I can think of one or two things but it certainly won't be high-value cost issues.'[24]

The terms of reference also lacked strong mechanisms for reporting back:

> If it had been set up ... in a way that, if people thought there was a major gap in this area, and there are many, what we're going to do is put some real political clout behind this, and therefore the terms of reference are going to be that this is going to be reported into the government or whoever. ... The terms of reference, have they sufficient authority?[25]

The terms of reference had a high degree of political authority, because they referred to a remit to make recommendations to the prime minister within twelve months, but they did not specify the method or timeframe for implementation of the recommendations. In contrast, the Low Pay Commission (LPC), which is seen as the most effective policy commission from the same period, specified that the body would make recommendations on the level at which the national minimum wage should be set, and the objectives to which the recommendations should respond, making it highly likely that government would respect the advice of the commission (particularly since its remit made clear that its advice would be based on the best possible evidence). The terms of reference made it difficult for government to resist its recommendations, because a triangle had been created (objectives, authority, evidence), with no other possible point of entry into the problem. With the WWC, there was 'not the same pressure'.[26]

The difference between the two commissions should not in itself be read as a difference of status in the treatment of the two sets of issues. The LPC and the WWC were clearly 'two different animals'[27] established for different purposes. The LPC represented over a decade of preparatory work, which had narrowed the remit of any advisory body. The WWC, on the other hand, was seen by all concerned as a first step in setting out policy in all its complexity, despite the work already done by the EOC and the WEU: 'I think it was seen by many as an exercise of learning, more than doing';[28] 'It was baby steps actually. This was a newer issue ... in commission terms. It wasn't an issue that had had air time.'[29]

At the same time, this sense of innovation was in itself problematic, for the reason already given, that some participants felt much of the ground had already been covered: 'That sounds a terrible admission, but it was reinforcing much of what we knew.'[30] This view was not shared by all policy actors, however, or even those on the commission. A key difference in this regard existed between trade-union participants, who already had a high degree of expertise and experience in dealing with issues around women and employment, and employers, for whom the question was relatively new: as Cridland stated:

> The pressure for [the WWC] was from women in the labour movement and women in the Labour Party, there wasn't a similar debate going on in CBI. ... There wasn't a countervailing pressure. So—'oh yes, I recognize this as an important issue, yes of course, we should do something about it, we'll put some resource into it', but we weren't the driver. Perhaps we should have been, but ... we weren't.[31]

This differential learning was recognized and mutually respected within the commission, but it inevitably slowed its work, at least in the early phase.

The Interim Report (2005)

Initially, the WWC was established for twelve months, but the amount of work and complexity of the data necessitated a longer period than initially anticipated: 'I don't think that any of us had truly anticipated the scale of the task.'[32] Prosser reflected on this wryly in her address to TUC in 2005: 'The magnitude of the task did not escape me: 35 years of legislation and a pay gap still wide enough to accommodate the proverbial coach and horses, and we were given 12 months to solve it all!'[33] By way of comparison, the Royal Commission on equal pay had taken two years (in 1944–6) and the Royal Commission on trade unions and employers' associations (the Donovan commission) had taken three years. Given the breadth of its remit, therefore, the commission sat over a relatively short time span (in terms of meetings, less than a year).

Five months into the commission's work, and with the expectation that it would report in September according to the original schedule, it was decided to issue an interim report on 8 March 2005, to coincide with International Women's Day. In her foreword, Prosser justified the decision by the importance of the subject, and 'some of the recently announced related policy developments.'[34] These developments were, first, the 'next steps to enable women to achieve greater work–life balance' in the pre-budget report for 2005, including the extension of paid maternity leave from six to nine months from April 2007; the possibility of transferring some maternity leave to fathers; and a consultation on flexible working. In addition, the government had announced its ten-year childcare strategy.[35] The commission welcomed these moves while noting that its terms of reference had set aside such questions because of the DTI review, and ruling out any major focus on childcare owing to time constraints.

Second, the interim statement noted three developments in the area of skills and training: the White Paper in response to the 2004 Tomlinson report on education for 14–19-year-olds, which had emphasized the need to strengthen vocational skills training; the Green Paper on services for young people, which had been initially planned for November 2004 and postponed into the spring of 2005; and the final report of the EOC's investigation into occupational segregation in apprenticeships and the government's response to it.[36]

Third, the inclusion of a section on the public sector as employer signalled the WWC's interest in the public-sector gender-equality duty, which was being prepared at that time. In particular, the interim statement welcomed the intended inclusion in the equality duty of an obligation on public authorities to ensure that adequate pay evaluation systems were in place, to avoid the need for individual complaints to tribunals.[37]

By March 2005, evidence had been invited and collated, and commissioners had heard presentations in November 2004 from academics, mostly selected because of research they had conducted for the EOC, the WEU, or other public bodies (such as the Learning and Skills Council).[38] Houston also presented her research on mothers and work–life balance. A preliminary literature review had been conducted, together with analysis of Office for National Statistics (ONS) data on the gender pay gap (using the Annual Survey of Hours and Earnings) and Labour Force Survey data.[39] By Christmas 2004, the interim statement stated, 'we have absorbed much of the academic evidence base'.[40] Prosser later confirmed that the commission had never intended to gather new data but rather to conduct a rapid review of existing evidence before carrying out a comprehensive consultation of stakeholders, including women in the workplace.[41] The evidence showed that the gender pay gap for full-time workers had been falling since the late 1980s, but still remained at 14.4 per cent for median hourly pay, and 18.4 per cent for mean hourly pay, while the gap for part-time workers continued to rise. This meant that the pay gap between women working full-time and those working part-time was increasing.[42]

The decision to release an interim statement also reflected a recognition of the high expectations placed on the commission by stakeholders, in particular trade unions. At the time the interim statement was published, and in the period leading up to it, Prosser and other commissioners took part in external events intended to widen the discussion. The DTI hosted a gender and productivity summit in October 2004, which responded to three key pieces of EOC investigation released that year, into maternity discrimination, women's labour-market position, and gender segregation in vocational training. The meeting, opened by Gordon Brown and closed by Patricia Hewitt, was addressed by commissioners Mellor and Cridland, and Prosser and Carberry led workshops.

The CBI hosted a workshop on equality and diversity at its Centrepoint conference centre in November, chaired by Ray and addressed by Cridland and Mellor. Jacqui Smith, Deputy Minister for Women and Equalities, spoke on behalf of the DTI, with Vegro, Grimshaw, Houston, and Martinelli also in attendance, along with seven of their DTI colleagues. In these meetings, the CBI, which prior to the establishment of the WWC had rarely publicly tackled the subject of women's employment, set out its position on the issues the commission was investigating—'job segregation and women's traditional role as carers, and thus their interrupted labour market participation, are the most influential factors in creating a pay gap'[43]—while gender stereotypes narrowed the range of choices for women. Cridland called for state funding of childcare, better-quality careers advice, and positive action by employers and government to encourage women to apply for jobs in sectors traditionally dominated by men. Mellor at the same event, and in line with the EOC's research reports published that year, highlighted the same factors but also emphasized the need for flexible working arrangements. Together, these interventions gave a flavour of the approach that was starting to take shape within the commission.

Meanwhile, the TUC's annual congress in 2004 saw the question of women and work move to centre stage, in the context of a confident post-Warwick set of renewed union demands. Both GMB and Unison moved successful resolutions on women at work, which called on the TUC and affiliated unions to raise their campaigning voice and integrate gender-equality actions into all aspects of their work, including collective bargaining, and demanded government action to introduce mandatory pay audits, invest in skills training for women, ensure all parents had access to flexible working arrangements, and fund initiatives on work–life balance. Demands for mandatory pay audits and better-paid leave arrangements also featured in a successful composite motion proposed by the TGWU, which called for stronger collective rights within the context of a new employment relations act.

Tony Blair's response to Congress pledged that 'building on Barbara Castle's Equal Pay Act, Margaret Prosser's Women and Work Commission will enable us to ensure that in our generation we close the gap in pay and opportunity between men and women at the workplace.'[44] Coulter, in moving the GMB resolution, spoke directly after the prime minister's address and did not mince her words: 'I do not want to see unequal pay ended within a generation. Did he say that? I nearly fell over. It is illegal, it is immoral and it is unjustifiable. We cannot allow our women members to be discriminated against any longer—never mind within a generation.'[45] Diana Holland, Prosser's successor at the TGWU, hammered home the point: 'We need to ensure that this Commission is not another chance to measure the pay gap, but a final chance to close it.'[46]

However, the commission's interim statement, and the communications that accompanied it, showed clearly that it already identified mandatory pay audits as an area where commissioners were unlikely to reach agreement. In particular, the CBI's comments on the interim statement strongly opposed such a measure and stated a preference for a voluntary approach, as set out in its submission to the WWC.

Instead, the press release accompanying the interim statement highlighted other areas where the commission was likely to focus its recommendations. These included a 'strong steer' to government that the public sector should carry out pay audits 'in order to prevent equal pay cases from ever having to reach the courts'; a concern around girls' limited career choices; and the need to improve the quality of part-time work, as well as training opportunities for women working part-time.[47] Press coverage was generally favourable, and most of the public figures quoted in reports gave a cautious welcome to the ideas floated in the commission's press release. However, Katherine Rake, director of the Fawcett Society, expressed the hope that the commission would be 'much bolder' when it came to its final report, and supported the TUC's and EOC's call for mandatory pay audits, adding that 'we need a fundamental rethink of the way women and men share responsibilities for paid employment and the unpaid work in the home.'[48]

Working Methods: Towards Consensus

There is no established formula for the way in which commissions work, although they owe much to established civil-service practice, precedents, and methods used in other relevant settings such as parliamentary bodies of inquiry such as those set up by select committees. By 2004, the Labour governments had created several similar bodies. Two of these were widely seen as successful: the first, the LPC, by now already a well-established feature of pay regulation; the second a short-lived but influential Work and Parents Task Force (WPTF) (see Chapter 11), which formed part of a wider set of stakeholder reference groups used by the DTI. The WWC secretariat informally consulted the civil servants who supported those two bodies to gain insights on how to organize the evidence and work towards recommendations. More generally, the secretariat treated the commissioners as they would ministers, preparing the material for them and circulating it before meetings, collating views, and summarizing data and views at each stage. Grimshaw (supported by Houston, Martinelli, and Quiney alongside others in the DTI team) did the bulk of work on the evidence submitted to the commission, which was processed rapidly between the deadline for submission in February and the interim statement in March.

As Hopson reflected, the amount of paperwork meant that commissioners relied heavily on civil servants:

> You realize just how smart civil servants are. ... The meetings were so brilliantly organized. There were papers, and you had to have read them, there was no winging it. The summaries of the meetings were so short but they had everything, and if you hadn't read them, in the meetings you were out of your depth. They were very, very well ordered, very well thought through.[49]

Even with a secretariat to summarize and synthesize information, commissioners were aware of the huge volume of material to read before and after meetings: 'the amount of paper we had, you could have wallpapered a cathedral with it.'[50] The commission sat, of course, at a time before such material would have been sent electronically, so the secretariat had to send out thick packages of papers by post.

Given the breadth and complexity of the subject matter, the chair and civil servants needed to establish a programme of work straight away: 'It's called the Women and Work Commission, it has the terms of reference it has, but that is a huge bundle of stuff, so what are we going to focus on?'[51]

The first working meeting after the launch, which took place in a London hotel, was intended to settle on an approach that would allow commissioners to focus gradually, with the aid of the academic presentations and civil-service digest of evidence. The DTI approach, based on statistical analysis, was to break down the causes of the gender pay gap in a way that would demonstrate that there were many areas where action was needed and on which the commissioners could therefore find common ground, thus steering a course between the trade unions' focus on equal pay and the employers' focus on training.

It was not just trade unions who wanted to focus on equal pay. For Stella Manzie, the two main issues of concern were pay and working conditions, including evidence of discrimination. Mellor also wanted to take up the issue of equal pay, in line with the EOC's work programme and its evidence-based analysis of the gender pay gap.[52] On the other hand, employer representatives, in particular Cridland, who represented CBI members, saw their role as being circumscribed by the narrow mandate they had been given, which did not include pay audits; instead they focused on issues where they felt there was room for common positions, around training and the dissemination of good employer practice on flexible working.

In such circumstances, it is not surprising that education and training, which veered away from the controversy over equal-pay audits, received most attention from commissioners. It also resulted from the deliberately broad remit of the commission, which encouraged discussions on the roots of occupational segregation, in early career choices. The broad approach was encouraged by the prime minister's office, as Geoffrey Norris (Blair's special adviser for trade and industry) reflected:

> This is a big and complicated area, but in order to have impact we wanted the canvas to be broad. Had we narrowed the canvas, there would have been a bit more 'so what?' or 'this is only one thing. It's a massive failure because it's not looking at the root causes.'[53]

This approach was approved by most of the commissioners as having the potential to provide real insights into why workplace disadvantage occurred: 'Margaret made the choice not to focus on pay reviews, but to broaden it out, to look at the context of women's pay, the ecosystem. I think, yes, that was a good idea.'[54] Others felt in hindsight the commission had been too ambitious in taking on such a broad agenda: 'I think if it hadn't been so ambitious—seriously—if we'd started with practice, and that's my rule in commissions. Three things: the world we're in, the state we're in, and the state we want to be in. And we started with the state we want to be in.'[55]

This route also took commissioners towards particular areas of policy, notably education and training. The choice was influenced by the CBI's preferences, which created common ground, but, according to interviewees, it was also determined by the evidence they heard, in particular from the visits, where they heard statements from girls and young women about the lack of careers advice and opportunities open to them, which for some commissioners at least were shocking:

> The conclusions were much broader than I think I would have guessed, going in. You know it's complex, but it's more complex. And my biggest learning was, it actually all starts in school. It starts with girls making poor choices, it starts with them having the wrong influences around them. Who are they going to take their influence from? Their parents, their teachers and their friends.[56]

The breadth of the remit, and the choice to focus on education, which took conclusions and recommendations outside the purview of the DTI, helped to build consensus but at the expense of targeted solutions:

> The emphasis on the education system was because, the more we looked at things that people were representing, the more we came to the view that these were deeply seated cultural issues. And because they were deeply seated cultural issues, anything you did with legislation in the workplace, however important and necessary, was effectively remedial. You were fixing something that had been pre-cooked. And what we wanted to do was change how things were cooked.[57]

Resolving, Avoiding, or Managing Conflict?

As noted in Chapter 1, a key function of policy commissions is to defuse conflict in areas where protagonists' positions diverge fundamentally, but there is no template for how to achieve this. Much depends on interpersonal relations as well as the working method established by the chair, both creating a 'dynamic' that may be explicitly or implicitly understood by all commissioners. Both the LPC and the WPTF were chaired by Sir George Bain, an academic employment-relations specialist and university senior manager (then vice-chancellor of Queens University Belfast) who was close to the Labour leadership. Bain's energetic direction of these bodies is widely seen as crucial in focusing commissioners' minds on outcomes (which encourages participants to understand the need for compromise positions) and fostering a sense of common purpose.

Cridland, who had served on both bodies, reflected that

> what I'd really learned from the success of the Low Pay Commission … what made the commission effective was the bonding of the commissioners, and building trust. To the point where, when we did our regional visits as Low Pay commissioners, sometimes we would go in, and it wouldn't be obvious who was the voice of employers and who was the voice of trade unions. … Although we still had constituencies and although it would come down to a negotiation, we did have a mission and we did try to agree a mutually agreed purpose.[58]

In the case of the LPC, the sense of a mutually agreed purpose was reinforced by the chair's actions and by working procedures, but it had been prepared by the representative bodies established while Labour was still in opposition. In the case of the WWC, it had to build from scratch, and in more difficult conditions of a wide-ranging remit and a deliberately broad-based set of individual commissioners' positions:

If the size of the commission's composition and the breadth of its remit created obstacles to be overcome, so too did the grandeur of the setting, at least for the large meetings, which also included civil servants in the initial period, and often took place in imposing venues within Whitehall or in London hotels. Some of the commissioners, particularly the younger members or those with less experience of this type of public body, felt that this inhibited frank and open discussion, and made it difficult to engage fully with all aspects of the work:

> It was a Number Ten commission, absolutely everybody was there around that table [at the launch]. ... You had every kind of department, every kind of equal opportunity authority, it was absolutely unmanageable. ... Reflecting on it, we were too grand, too posh, too ambitious, too far from the ground.[59]

Necessarily, given this dynamic, several commissioners reflected that the discussions often revolved around the views of large organizations rather than those of small businesses or the voluntary and community sector, or indeed the voices of individual women. This power imbalance had advantages, as the voice of large employers gave authority and was useful in testing recommendations that could lead to practical implementation initiatives, but it also tended to steer discussions in a broader rather than tightly focused direction. Another consequence of a large, wide-ranging commission was that in practice much work was left to a small group of very engaged 'insiders'. Several interviewees in their reflections wondered if more effective—and inclusive—working could have been enabled by the formation of smaller working groups, with tight procedures for reporting back centrally. In addition, Silver also suggested that, rather than the dispersed authority expressed in civil-service participation across different departments, one political leader (ideally the prime minister himself, or the head of a prestigious lead department) should have visibly been the focus of reporting back during key meetings.[60]

For these reasons, Prosser as chair had been given a more difficult task than Bain in the LPC or the WPTF. One way of managing, rather than resolving, conflict was to steer discussions towards areas more conducive to consensus. As noted above, consensus-building was enhanced by early agreement on a focus on the area of education and training, where there was broad convergence of positions:

> We rallied round things like that, and as soon as we'd rallied round them, it actually didn't matter where we were coming from, we didn't have different views. Sort of, the veil was lifted. ... We didn't realize how bad it was. Now we do, we've got to talk about this, because it's so important.[61]

Steering, aided by the secretariat, was also important because of the sheer amount of material to be worked through and the technical nature of some of it. However, it could not necessarily resolve conflicts. Nor did the evidence presented in writing or in the presentations or visits help to resolve areas of conflict. Knowledge of two fundamentally different positions on equal-pay reviews formed part of the work of the commission from the outset, although that knowledge was not shared equally among participants:

> The one thing that [the CBI] were determined to achieve was for there not to be a recommendation for mandatory pay audits, so they were going to be happy as long as that was not the outcome. ... That was part of the whole dynamic of the commission. So there was goodwill, and cooperation, and agreement with the objective to narrow the pay gap, and do something about all the structural factors that contributed to it, but they didn't ... want to be beaten around the head with invasive, as they would see it, legislation.[62]

For the trade unionists on the commission, this observation formed a central part of the commission's mode of working, as Carberry explained:

> Everything you heard from the unions at that point was that the gender pay gap would be dealt with if employers were forced to audit, do equal pay audits, and there was less emphasis being given by the unions to all the other factors that were at play. ... That's not to say that unions didn't understand the whole picture, but there was a strong conviction that the biggest difference you could make would be if you could expose what was going on in pay structures in workplaces. And that did not in any way dominate discussions in the commission, because we were getting so much information, and gaining so much insight into the other factors.[63]

The TUC in this respect had set out to support the commission by producing a wide-ranging submission which set out mandatory pay reviews within a broader set of measures:

> What I think we could do best was take up all the questions on all the areas they were looking at, and bring in all the union, workforce, shopfloor dimension ... We thought that would be a unique perspective. ... We were very careful about that, and we struggled a bit with the [TUC] Women's committee, because I think there were some members on there who just wanted us to reiterate our ten-point plan, you know, to tell government all the things where we thought they weren't doing fast enough. And we thought really ... the best way to be helpful would be to be supportive in tone, and add a few areas in.[64]

While Coulter was a knowledgeable, impassioned, and fluent advocate of mandatory pay audits, backed by other union members and Watson for the EOC, Ray provided evidence from her own corporate experience of why in her view they could be counterproductive. The conflict between unions and employers created a stalemate that could not be resolved by appeals on either side to the remaining commissioners. Although others on the WWC shared the unions' support for mandatory pay reviews, they did not advocate for them in the same way, resulting in a 'bifurcation' and 'an inability to land' a majority view in favour of mandatory action.[65]

The stalemate position was finally taken outside the full commission, and Carberry and Cridland, veterans of direct negotiation in the Labour period, tried to come to an agreement, but ended up 'agreeing to disagree':

> We were getting to the stage where we were formulating our recommendations, and it was very, very clear that we were not going to get recommendations that there should be mandatory pay audits, and those of us in the trade union movement had an obligation to articulate the unions' aspirations, even if our own opinions were different.... So we had to decide what we were going to do.... I spoke to my counterpart at the CBI who was also on the commission ... and to Margaret, and it wasn't a very sophisticated solution, but the obvious solution was to agree to disagree, and to try and find a form of words, which we did, which left it open to people to use equal pay audits in workplaces where they themselves judged that that might be useful.[66]

Arguably, this decision blocked off other—maybe more imaginative—compromise solutions, as more than one interviewee reflected (see Chapter 9). But it was central to the commission's brief to ensure a consensus position.

The result was a decision to present both sides of the argument in the report, which ultimately meant accepting no recommendation on mandatory reviews in the private sector but rather an encouragement to take the discussion further through trials in exemplar companies. For the trade unionists this meant accepting defeat on their main equal-pay demand. However, good relations within the commission were maintained, according to Cridland:

> I don't remember difficult moments, I don't remember pregnant pauses where people had stopped speaking to each other because they couldn't agree. That sometimes happens, you know. It certainly happened on statutory trade union recognition, it came down to: well, I won't agree to this word, and I won't agree to that word. I don't remember those moments [in the WWC].[67]

As Cridland had participated in many stark conflicts between unions and employers during the period after 1997, the WWC disagreements appeared relatively mild to him. Other commissioners remembered sharp clashes over the issue of mandatory pay reviews: 'yeah, there was tension, at times.'[68]

In comparison with the clash between unions and the CBI over union recognition that Cridland recalled, the WWC developed a style of working based on cordial interpersonal relations that developed over the course of meetings, particularly those held over two days with dinner and a residential stay in the evening. Several interviewees suggested that a majority of women commissioners made it easy to find commonalities of experience. Others recalled that it was precisely difference of experience that made membership of the commission a personal learning experience:

> Having people coming along with different views or presenting their kind of expertise, having people on the ground who were delivering projects, was a very positive thing. I like to believe that we all learnt from each other as well, whilst we were sat there, because ... we all have different experiences. ... There are some very strong distinctions and differences in people's experiences that are very important when you're putting a report like that together.[69]

The creation of a mutually respectful space for deliberation was due in no small part to Prosser's role as chair, as all interviewees emphasized. Prosser had political clout and knew from long experience how to handle difficult situations: 'She was a great speaker, unafraid to challenge, even unafraid to challenge John [Cridland] at one stage, because she could really get her sleeves rolled up.' [70] She also had an approachable manner, and acute skills as a sensitive and even-handed intermediary between unions and the party in her work for the Labour Party.[71] These skills allowed her both to steer the commission in the direction she wanted and at the same time to listen to a wide range of opinions: 'She's got a very good personal manner. ... I suppose it's that thing that women don't have that much formal power, so we rely on our informal power. ... [Prosser] made full use of that, sharing recognition.'[72] All commissioners similarly attributed strong interpersonal skills to Vegro, who as the senior secretary to the commission had responsibility for liaising with commissioners, listening, and responding to any concerns they raised.

Another way the commission avoided intense conflict was to postpone recording decisions or 'banking' conclusions.[73] This practice—attributed by some interviewees to traditional employer–union bargaining procedures—left many issues open and created a significant decision-making burden for a small group of insiders at a later date, once others had effectively moved on to other responsibilities.

Writing the Report

The final meeting of the commission was an event that all participants remembered, over fifteen years later. It took place at a hotel in Richmond, on 6–7 July 2005. On the first day, commissioners took stock of their work and a draft version of the report, and had dinner together. On the second day, they were due to discuss the recommendations. Over breakfast, they learnt of the terrible events in central London where bombs had been detonated on public transport, killing fifty-two people and injuring many more. The city was now locked down. Although advice was to stay indoors until the threat was cleared, commissioners were anxious to return home to their families, so the decision was taken to send everyone home by taxi.

This left a considerable amount of work to do collating recommendations and getting the final report into shape. Grimshaw and Quiney, supported by Houston and Martinelli, wrote the final report, with commissioners commenting on further drafts by mail. The report's publication, scheduled for the autumn, was now postponed until the following year.

Meanwhile, Prosser undertook the political work of gaining support for the commission's output. As well as talking to officials from government departments,[74] she worked on preparing the ground for the report's recommendations among stakeholders, principally trade unions and employer organizations whose views on equal-pay audits were in conflict. Before TUC in September 2005, she confessed to the *Guardian* that she felt 'nervous', as delegates might feel disappointed with the commission's outcome.[75] Her concern was to present the question of women's employment and pay as a broad set of deep-rooted problems, rather than just equal pay (discrimination against women doing the same job as men).

Prosser told the Chartered Institute of Personnel and Development (CIPD) annual conference in November that the commission remained divided on the issue, with 'a swell of opinion' on one side for mandatory audits, but others believing 'it would be a sledgehammer to crack a walnut'.[76] The commission would recommend statutory rights for workplace representatives, she told delegates. Although she was personally against the idea, she would go with majority views. As late as November 2005, press reports showed Prosser stating publicly that the commission had still not resolved the question of mandatory pay audits. 'We haven't resolved anything,' she told the

Scotsman, adding that 'it's certainly on the table'.[77] Effectively, the commission's internal debates on the advantages and disadvantages of mandatory pay audits were being played out in public, alongside the idea of equality representatives. Given the rush to complete the report, as noted above, these thorny issues could not be resolved through the final writing process and were instead framed in terms of a difference of views, and the need for workplace initiatives to test the case for mandatory action.

A final way of relieving the tension caused by divergent views was to transfer them outside the commission, as moves to strengthen the equalities legislation had been set in train by the Equalities Review established in 2005. At TUC in September, Prosser had highlighted the work of the Equalities Review as a way of taking up the stronger legal rights demanded by unions. In particular, she floated the idea of amending equalities legislation to allow class actions, which Prosser told *Personnel Today* in November 2005 would be 'an effective way' of addressing the pay gap, although government seemed less keen.[78] At the time, and in view of the time pressures facing the WWC, this appeared a reasonable strategy to adopt, although, as discussed in Chapter 9, it did not guarantee that the Equalities Review would approach the question of gender equality in the same way.

Conclusion

The recommendations of the WWC, presented in its final report in February 2006, will be discussed in Chapter 8. In this chapter, I have outlined several distinctive characteristics of the commission, compared to other commissions and similar bodies established in the same period. Labour in office after 1997 developed an approach to governance of employment that has been described as broadly pluralist, with a central role for employers and trade unions, but that also kept organized interests at arm's-length, as distinct from traditional neo-corporatist modes of governance where employers' organizations and trade unions have privileged access to decision-making.[79] Rather than having a template for these deliberative bodies, the government established them ad hoc, with differences in composition, remit, and modes of working. They were underpinned by wider, sustained networks of contact that enhanced mutual understanding and created informal ways of resolving conflicts, although these informal relations could generate mutual suspicion, depending on the way they were handled by government as well as by the employer and union protagonists.

When the journalist Polly Toynbee's reaction to the WWC's report was published, it highlighted the commission's composition as a reason for what she saw as 'good' but weak recommendations: largely representing a stalemate between the CBI and trade unions, it effectively gave veto power to the former.[80] This chapter has found some support for Toynbee's view in that the CBI's lesser 'stakes' in policy discussions about women and employment created a power asymmetry within the commission that resulted in the choice of certain options over others, in particularly a preference for voluntary over statutory initiatives.

However, this view addresses only one aspect of the WWC's approach to the gender pay gap. The CBI's veto was effective, because it went with the grain of other characteristics of the commission, such as its broad remit, its congruence with DTI thinking about the gender pay gap, and the choices made by decisive actors, in particular the chair and union representatives. Outcomes were also shaped by the operational mode of the WWC, as this chapter has shown: its relatively short duration in comparison with the depth and breadth of the problems it examined, and the relatively few resources available to it while it sat. As several interviewees reflected, the broad approach arguably required a more thoroughgoing investigation over a longer period, with time-specific points for monitoring, review, and follow-up by named government departments, all set out explicitly at the outset.

A striking feature of the WWC's work, as interviews presented in this chapter show, is that investigation of women's employment as a policy problem was new to the British policy environment, at least in the way it came onto the agenda in the early twenty-first century. For much of the twentieth century, it had been addressed in a defensive way, to counter or limit claims to equal pay. While equality campaigners, actors within the equality machinery, and trade-union officers were all familiar with the policy problem and had spent decades looking at solutions, mainstream politics had dealt with it in a circumscribed and cautious way. Consequently, policy advisers and many commissioners saw the need to advance in 'baby steps', setting out an agenda to be followed up incrementally.

The WWC was the first public body invested with the authority of the prime minister to investigate the gender pay gap, and by doing this it brought the gender pay gap into mainstream public debate, including into the top levels of employer organizations for the first time. Its comprehensive approach was new. It also brought one particular aspect of the gender pay gap in particular into mainstream public debate for the first time: as discussed in

Chapter 11, it defined women's part-time work, not as an expedient solution to labour-market shortages, but as a reflection of the constraints facing women as carers.

Novelty did not mean that the commission worked *ex nihilo*: on the contrary, the 2006 report showed the importance of evidence built up from research commissioned both by the EOC and by the WEU (and the Women's Unit before it), as well as from pilot projects in the workplace. In this sense, the agenda had already been set by the equality and women's policy machineries and by civil society. However, the WWC was important in setting a marker for a more comprehensive approach to gender inequality in the workplace. The incremental approach it proposed required sustained investment, monitoring, and oversight. The next chapter turns to its recommendations and their follow-up by government

Notes

1. R. Ward, 'The Women and Work Commission Legacy in the Age of Austerity', *Local Economy*, 27 (2012), 864–71.
2. C. Buckley, '£300m Equal Payout for Women', *The Times*, 15 March 2005.
3. WWC, *Shaping a Fairer Future* (London: DTI, 2006), 91.
4. All political advisers interviewed stated this.
5. Interview, Sally Hopson.
6. The position of Carberry and Cridland as second-in-commands in their respective organizations was significant: it allowed them freedom to negotiate while the director or general secretary could claim 'plausible deniability'. See G. Bain and J. Jones, 'The Bullock Committee and the Low Pay Commission: Some Reflections' (University of Warwick, 2001); W. Brown, 'The Process of Fixing the National Minimum Wage, 1997–2007', *British Journal of Industrial Relations*, 47 (2009), https://doi.org/10.1111/j.1467-8543.2009.00722.x.
7. Interview, Nita Clarke.
8. Interview, Kay Carberry.
9. See J. Bunn, 'Stella Manzie: An Elite Troubleshooter', *Local Government Chronicle*, 11 June 2018. Manzie was awarded an OBE for her services to West Berkshire council, then a CBE in 2007 for the improvements she had led in the management of Coventry city council, and was made a dame in 2018.
10. Interview, Stella Manzie.
11. Interview, Carey Oppenheim.
12. Interview, Clarke.
13. Interview, Carberry.
14. Interview, Janet Veitch.
15. Interview, Clarke.
16. Interview, Adeeba Malik.
17. Interview, Geoffrey Norris.

18. Interview, Clarke.
19. In her GMB role, Quiney had participated in the EOC's Equal Pay Task Force: see Ch. 4.
20. Interview, Matilda Quiney.
21. Interview, Quiney.
22. Interview, Norris.
23. Interview, John Cridland.
24. Interview, John Hannett.
25. Interview, Hannett.
26. Interview, Hannett.
27. Interview, David Coats.
28. Interview, Hannett.
29. Interview, Cridland.
30. Interview, Carberry.
31. Interview, Cridland.
32. WWC, *A Fair Deal for Women in the Workplace: An Interim Statement* (London: DTI), 3.
33. TUC, *Congress Report 2005: The 137th Annual Trades Union Congress, 12–15th September, Brighton* (London: TUC, 2005), 170.
34. WWC, *A Fair Deal for Women in the Workplace*, 3.
35. WWC, *A Fair Deal for Women in the Workplace*, 10.
36. WWC, *A Fair Deal for Women in the Workplace*, 11.
37. WWC, *A Fair Deal for Women in the Workplace*, 13.
38. These were Dr Susan Harkness (University of Bristol) on the part-time work penalty; Professor Alan Manning and Dr Barbara Petrongolo (LSE) on the pay gap for women working full-time and part-time; Dr Andy Dickerson (University of Warwick) on future labour-market needs; Professor Heather Joshi (Institute of Education, University of London), on employment outcomes over the life course; Professors Jill Rubery and Sylvia Walby (University of Manchester) on gender pay-gap analysis; and Professor Shamit Shaggar (University of Sussex), on race and policy.
39. As well as the EOC reports highlighted in n. 53, the DTI's analysis was informed by research it had commissioned from a team at the Institute for Employment Studies. The report used wage regression analysis of Labour Force Survey data, and identified occupational segregation and part-time working as drivers of women's lower pay relative to men's: T. Anderson, J. Forth, H. Metcalf, and S. Kirby *The Gender Pay Gap: Report to the Women and Equality Unit* (London: DTI, 2001). The report was cited by the WWC's 2006 report (p. 55) as evidence for widespread undervaluing of women's skills.
40. WWC, *A Fair Deal for Women in the Workplace*, 14.
41. Prosser, *Your Seat is at the End*, 205.
42. WWC, *A Fair Deal for Women in the Workplace*, 5.
43. John Cridland's notes, Workshop, CBI, 30 November 2004: CBI archive, MSS 200/C/2014 Box 174, Modern Records Centre, University of Warwick.
44. TUC, *Congress Report 2004: The 136th Annual Trades Union Congress, 13–16th September, Brighton* (London: TUC, 2004), 61.
45. TUC, *Congress Report 2004*, 62.
46. TUC, *Congress Report 2004*, 141.
47. Media summary, attached to M2 presswire, 8 March 2005.

48. A. Jones, 'Women "in Limited Work Opportunities"', Press Association, 8 March 2005.
49. Interview, Hopson.
50. Interview, Carberry.
51. Interview, Manzie.
52. The EOC had commissioned a series of studies providing statistical analysis of the gender pay gap, using all available datasets (British Household Panel Survey, Labour Force Survey, and New Earnings Survey). The 2004 report by Wendy Olsen and Sylvia Walby for the EOC was a major reference for the WWC in its analysis of causes of the gender pay gap: WWC, *Shaping a Fairer Future*, 30. Olsen and Walby showed that part-time work had a cumulative negative effect on women's earnings (taking into account likely wage progression had they been working full-time) and that occupational segregation was a significant feature of part-time working. Overall, one-third of the total gender pay gap was found to be associated with lifetime working patterns. Direct and indirect discrimination also played a part but was more difficult to quantify. The report listed a range of possible policy solutions including pay audits: W. Olsen and S. Walby, 'Modelling Gender Pay Gaps', Working Paper no. 17 (London: EOC, 2004). The other important EOC study on the gender pay gap was by Damian Grimshaw and Jill Rubery. Commissioned by the Equal Pay Task Force, it analysed data from the European Structure of Earnings Survey and identified a combination of concentration of women in low-paid sectors and fragmented, opaque pay systems as major drivers of the gender pay gap in the British case: D. Grimshaw and J. Rubery, *The Gender Pay Gap: A Research Review* (London? EOC, 2001).
53. Interview, Norris.
54. Interview, Watson.
55. Interview, Ruth Silver.
56. Interview, Hopson.
57. Interview, Cridland.
58. Interview, Cridland.
59. Interview, Silver.
60. Interview, Silver.
61. Interview, Cridland.
62. Interview, Carberry.
63. Interview, Carberry.
64. Interview, Veale.
65. Interview, Watson.
66. Interview, Carberry.
67. Interview, Cridland.
68. Interview, Hannett.
69. Interview, Malik.
70. Interview, Silver.
71. See, e.g., L. Minkin, *The Blair Supremacy: A Study in the Politics of Labour's Party Management* (Manchester: Manchester University Press, 2014), 244–8.
72. Interview, Veitch.
73. Interview, Watson.
74. The secretariat, based in the WEU in the DTI, liaised regularly with Geoffrey Norris and other advisers in the prime minister's office, and with Treasury special advisers

(according to Matilda Quiney, Ed Miliband, and later Spencer Livermore): personal communication, Quiney, 30 May 2023.

75. H. Mullholland, 'Interview: The Big Payback', *Guardian*, 7 September 2005. The interview caused Prosser difficulties, as her view of trade-union efforts on equal pay, as presented in the *Guardian*, was highly critical, and she was obliged at TUC to soften the criticism, arguing that the journalist had misrepresented her words.
76. *Personnel Today*, 1 November 2005.
77. E. Harrell, 'No Hiding Place for the Firms that Pay Women Less', *Scotsman*, 8 November 2005.
78. 'Commission to Call for Group Litigation', *Personnel Today*, 8 November 2005.
79. See S. Milner, 'Gender Equality and Employment Regulation in the New Labour Years, 1997–2010: The Problem of the Gender Pay Gap', *Historical Studies in Industrial Relations*, 43 (2022), https://doi.org/10.3828/hsir.2022.43.5.
80. P. Toynbee 'It Really Won't Do to Blame Women for Britain's Pay Gap', *Guardian*, 28 February 2006.

8

The Women and Work Commission

Implementation, Influence, and Effectiveness

Introduction

As Martin Bulmer has observed in relation to royal commissions: 'The greatest dissatisfaction ... has been at the implementation stage.'[1] Bulmer distinguished between direct and indirect, and short-term and longer-term influence of royal commissions and similar bodies. Much depends on the way government intended the commission to operate. If government gives a commission a very specific remit and adequate resources and authority, this can result in a targeted, substantive resolution to a given policy problem. If governments wish to use a commission to explore a new policy area, outcomes may have a less immediate but still significant longer-term influence.

In their study of British commissions on migration integration policy, Alistair Hunter and Christina Boswell defined three main functions of independent commissions: problem-solving, substantiating, and legitimizing. The latter two functions are largely symbolic: commissions can provide evidence for governments' preferred course of action (substantiating) and communicate the appropriateness of government action (legitimizing).[2] Hunter and Boswell also distinguish between dissemination of commission findings (the nature of the public debate they spark) and government take-up (in terms of tone, swiftness, and completeness).

As Bulmer emphasized, symbolic influence does not mean lack of influence, as commissions can act as 'a signpost or beacon to an area of policy, which will affect the future course of policy in that area without necessarily shaping it directly in the short-term.'[3] Commissions can be influential without necessarily leading to specific, concrete actions on the part of government, if they help to shape public debates. However, where commissions are asked to make recommendations, the expectation would be that they should have some problem-solving as well as symbolic impact.

Chapter 7 analysed the way the Women and Work Commission (WWC) operated, highlighting its inability to resolve areas of hard conflict, but also

Women and Employment in Public Policy. Susan Milner, Oxford University Press. © Susan Milner (2024).
DOI: 10.1093/9780191987359.003.0008

its efforts to set out a broad agenda for policy on women and employment, identifying the respective responsibilities of government departments, public-sector and private-sector employers, and other actors such as trade unions and training providers. As Chapter 7 showed, the WWC set out to influence government policy particularly in the areas of public-sector employment and public procurement, and called on the government to fund pilot projects aimed at demonstrating the value of 'good practice' in the private sector on training for career progression and on 'quality' part-time jobs (that is, those with equivalent pay and conditions to those worked full-time).

Chapter 7 showed that the WWC operated in ways that enhanced its effectiveness: it had a strong and highly respected chair; it established interpersonal relations of trust; it gathered authoritative evidence; and it worked within a wider network to raise awareness and gain influence in public debates. On the other hand, the WWC's remit emphasized learning about the causes of the gender pay gap, and left the nature of recommendations unspecified. The breadth of its remit created a risk of dispersed recommendations, rather than the targeted approach characteristic of recommendations likely to have effective impact on public opinion and pressure for authoritative government action. It also lacked specific response mechanisms for ensuring that the recommendations would be coordinated across government departments. The WWC chair, Baroness Prosser, evidently feared lack of active championing of the proposals across government departments. In a *Guardian* interview in September 2005, she spoke of the need 'to determine who is going to be the watchdog of our recommendations'.[4]

In this chapter, I consider the impact made by the WWC report in public debates and assess the government's response to it, before examining the WWC's follow-up report in 2009, which reviewed the government response. In the final sections of this chapter, I discuss the longer-term impact of the WWC, and lessons to be learnt from its work, concerning the effectiveness of independent commissions.

The Report and its Launch

The WWC report, *Shaping a Fairer Future*, contained no fewer than forty recommendations. Using the typology of policy instruments developed by Helen Ingram and Anne Schneider,[5] Table 8.1 summarizes the recommendations under three broad categories: authority (measures that require or prohibit action); capacity-building (information, awareness-raising, and

Table 8.1 Summary overview of WWC recommendations (2006), by policy instrument type

Policy area	Authority	Capacity-building	Hortatory	Procedural/administrative
Education and training		Better support for women in New Deal programmes (DWP), including personal advisers Train to Gain: personalized support for women in and out of work, based on skills level already acquired; £20 million package to enable women to change occupation or job and secure better career progression; pilot projects for women in areas of skill shortages (Treasury funding; Learning and Skills Council delivery)	Promotion of apprenticeships among young women (sectoral skills councils)	National strategy for tackling gender equality in education (particularly pre-14 schooling) (DfEE) Better coordination of skills infrastructure (DfEE) Better careers guidance and information (DfEE) New guidelines for early years staff on how to avoid/challenge gender stereotyping (DfEE) Strategy for social-care sector to improve career progression
Flexible and part-time working	Extension of right to request flexible working	Better training of line managers (employers) Publicity on good practice on 'quality' part-time jobs (Opportunity Now) Pilot initiative on 'quality' part-time jobs, with £5 million funding (DTI/GEO/Treasury)	Monitoring of right to request (trade-union representatives)	Better monitoring of right to request (DTI)

Workplace employment regulation private sector	Targeted enforcement of national minimum wage in low-wage sectors (HMRC)	Regular reporting on gender impact of national minimum wage (Low Pay Commission) £1 million through Investors in People for fair pay and reward, equality, and diversity Additional £5 million through Union Modernization Fund to train workplace equality representatives		
Workplace employment regulation: public sector	Public-sector equality duty (PSED), to include gender pay Use of public procurement to ensure good equality and diversity practice	Annual reports should contain equality and diversity reports		
Childcare				Childcare strategy should take account of diverse needs
Equal-pay laws				Consideration of generic actions in equal-pay cases (Discrimination Law Review)
Monitoring				New Cabinet Sub-Committee (chaired by Minister for Women) WWC to be reconvened within one year

Source: Author analysis, based on WWC, *Shaping a Fairer Future*.

technical assistance); and symbolic and hortatory tools (activities aimed at encouraging target populations to avail themselves of opportunities provided by existing agencies). Use of public funds (redistribution) is not considered here as a separate category, as the proposed measures involving public expenditure all take the form of pilot projects and fall within the category of capacity-building tools, rather than direct cash transfers. I have added a fourth category, headed 'procedural/administrative', to denote recommendations targeting government department or agencies, or concerning process rather than output.

The majority of recommendations can be classed as capacity-building measures, in line with the WWC's approach, as discussed in Chapter 7, which showed that several commissioners—and policy advisers in the prime minister's office—viewed the policy problem of the gender pay gap as relatively new and complex. The question of how to address the gender pay gap also proved divisive, in that commissioners could not reach agreement on statutory pay reviews. This finding is in line with Ingram and Schneider's framework: they argued that capacity-building instruments are chosen by policymakers when problems are viewed as complex and intractable. In addition, Ingram and Schneider posited that policymakers were more likely to prefer self-regulation over authority instruments where the target population (in this case, employers) are viewed positively, and are advantaged in policymaking.[6] The WWC's preference for capacity-building measures showed a good fit with the approach of the Department of Trade and Industry (DTI) and government preferences more widely, so it would be expected that government would receive the recommendations positively and seek to implement them in full or to a large extent.

However, three inhibiting factors suggested the likelihood of difficulty in gaining government acceptance of all the recommendations. First, although the WWC had not recommended legislative change to allow group-based litigation or generic equal-pay claims, employer bodies and related publications were quick to spot its inclusion—in generally favourable terms—in the report, with a recommendation that the Discrimination Law Review consider the possibility. Employer resistance to such a move made at least parts of the report politically controversial.[7] Second, two sizeable public-expenditure items were included in the recommendations: £20 million earmarked expenditure through the Train to Gain programme (although it was not clear how much additional funding would be needed beyond the already agreed national budget for training and skills) and £5 million funding for a new initiative on quality part-time jobs, as well as £1 million for Investors in People. The WWC's remit had instructed commissioners to consider the impact of recommendations on public expenditure— in other words, to refrain from recommending significant expenditure-inducing measures.

Third, the recommendations placed significant duties on government departments to lead, coordinate, and monitor initiatives in the private sector, and to establish robust practices in the public sector, including through public procurement policy. This emphasis on strong state leadership required decisive championing by an authority figure within government able to command respect and marshal resources across several key departments, including the Treasury (at a time when relations between the Treasury and other government departments—including increasingly the prime minister's office—were tense).

The Report's Launch and Press Impact

On 28 February 2006, Tessa Jowell (Minister for Women and Equalities) announced in writing to the House of Commons that she had received the final report of the commission. The commission, she stated,

> proposes a wealth of practical ideas on how to close the gender pay and opportunities gap. … The commission has described a complex problem which requires progress on a number of fronts. This is an imperative, not least because of the waste of women's skills and potential and the negative impact this has on the UK economy. … The Government are determined to take action to address all causes of the pay gap highlighted in the report.[8]

The WWC report was launched the same day at a well-publicized, top-level reception in Downing Street, chaired by the Prime Minister Tony Blair, who called it a 'superb, ground-breaking piece of work'.[9] Many commissioners remembered this event, like Adiba Malik, who travelled from Bradford to attend:

> Tony Blair chairing the meeting, Gordon Brown on one side, and Tessa Jowell on the other. I'll never forget that. And Margaret Prosser, as [commission] chair, talking about the findings. There was the chief executive from the Royal Mail and some big employers there, chief execs of the big companies. And we were all around this massive table, and the Prime Minister was welcoming the report, and the publicity around it was phenomenal.[10]

According to journalists, civil servants briefed the press that the Downing Street launch of the report signalled the government's intention to implement its recommendations, 'unlike those of other papers such as the Tomlinson report on education reform'.[11] This signal from the government encouraged media interest in the WWC report.

The political salience of equal pay had increased in 2005 (the thirtieth anniversary of the Sex Discrimination Act and the coming into force of the Equal Pay Act), partly because of the efforts of Prosser and others to take its work into the wider public space, but also because of high-profile equal-pay claims in both the public and the private sectors. In December 2005, the General, Municipal, and Boilermakers' Union (GMB) accused Morrisons of sex discrimination when it paid male warehouse workers more in redundancy payments than women working in the company's finance office.[12] Earlier that year, seven women managers in the South Wales Police Authority had won a sex-discrimination claim supported by Unison.[13] The Public and Commercial Services Union also saw its claim on behalf of female members working in administrative and managerial roles in the prison service upheld at appeal tribunal in 2005.[14] In addition, 2005 was the year of the Gate Gourmet dispute over redundancies, involving a largely female workforce of South Asian origin.[15]

The years 2005 and 2006 saw hundreds of press articles discussing the recommendations of the WWC report. Press reports followed closely the messages presented by ministers in speeches at events organized to publicize the WWC findings, with Jowell supported by DTI minister Alan Johnson in the initial period, and her deputy, Meg Munn, taking on the bulk of presentation subsequently. The WWC report's headline finding that the gender pay gap cost the British economy up to 2 per cent of GDP was widely circulated, alongside attention to its proposals on skills, and to a lesser extent on gender stereotypes in education, and on the poor quality and pay of part-time jobs.

Across the range of political positions occupied by the mainstream press, the WWC report was received generally favourably, but also sparked a wider debate about whether action was needed to address the gender pay gap, and if so what type of action. Several trade-union leaders expressed support for the recommendations but also 'disappointment' that they did not include proposals for mandatory actions: 'they don't go far enough in addressing the scandal of pay inequality'.[16] The Fawcett Society's criticism was widely cited, with its director, Katherine Rake, arguing that 'it's not enough to encourage employers to change—that's been happening for years, but change is too slow'.[17] *The Times* similarly voiced 'sceptical' views about the effectiveness of the recommendations on part-time work, quoting Professor Alan Manning (who had presented evidence to the Commission).[18]

Harriet Harman, then Minister of State at the Department for Constitutional Affairs (but beginning her campaign to become deputy leader of the Labour Oarty), also suggested that the report's recommendations were too diffuse and could lead to the government wringing its hands about the gender pay gap and saying 'we are against it'; instead, she argued, the government should 'set a target to close the gender pay gap and close it right away'.[19] In addition to mandatory equal-pay reviews, the way to close the gender pay gap was to raise the national minimum wage and child benefits, Harman argued.[20]

Government Follow-up

The prime minister gave specific cabinet responsibility to Jowell, as Minister for Women and Equalities, to produce an action plan to take forward the commission's recommendations. However, the chancellor made an immediate response to the WWC report in the March 2006 budget, announcing that the number of skills-coaching pilots would be doubled, 'with a specific focus on helping low skilled women return to work' and an additional pilot scheme within Train to Gain, aimed at helping skills councils in sectors with labour shortages to 'test new recruitment pathways' for women.[21]

On 4 May 2006, in response to opposition questions, Jowell and Munn reported to the House of Commons that the Women and Equality Unit (WEU) had established an implementation group to take forward the report's recommendations, and the government was committed to producing an action plan within six months, with emphasis on the need for policies to address the quality of part-time jobs. They stated that Baroness Prosser would reconvene the commission in a year's time, to evaluate progress.[22]

A team of six civil servants was established in the WEU to prepare an action plan, which was announced in September 2006, as discussed further below. However, as Geoffrey Norris commented, 'there is a difference between having a work programme, which they diligently work their way through, and that work programme being animated by leadership which lifts it off the paper. And it strikes me that ... [in this case] it didn't have much leadership.'[23]

This point has two aspects: the first relates to the 'clout' of the ministers for women who were leading on the commission's recommendations (and that of the WEU, which was particularly poorly resourced and situated at that time). Munn worked within DTI, while the minister with cabinet responsibility, Jowell, headed a different department (Media, Culture and Sport), which was both a traditionally less authoritative department and one that bore less obvious direct relevance to the commission's recommendations. In May 2006, Munn moved to the Department of Communities and Local Government (DCLG), reporting to Ruth Kelly who had taken over as Communities Secretary and Minister for Women.

Munn, a popular and well-regarded parliamentarian and minister, worked hard to follow up the report, both within and outside government, but lacked high-level authority:

> It's a very, very difficult thing to do in Whitehall, if you're a minister outside the department. If you're a junior minister it's very difficult to get anything done within your own department, let alone another department. But actually trying to get another department to give a higher priority to something is extraordinarily difficult. Even if you're prime minister.[24]

This consideration was particularly important, because the WWC report had covered a large area, and therefore potentially a significant number of government departments. It therefore required very high-level ministerial authority in order to elicit an appropriate response from the various departments.

> Tackling the extent of the problem was probably more ambitious than we thought, and an aspect of that is possibly we needed to have given more thought to how we were going to act on the findings of the report once it was delivered, as opposed to bringing together a great group of people.[25]

The 2006 report had recognized the scale of the government response needed in order to tackle the problems set out by the commission's work: 'Closing the pay gap between men and women requires a significant and concerted effort on the part of a number of people if real and lasting change is to be achieved.'[26] The second aspect therefore concerned monitoring. Rather than an informal working group of civil servants chaired by the junior minister for women, the WWC report recommended that 'a new Cabinet sub-Committee of Ministers should be formed, chaired by the Minister for Women, to oversee the implementation of our recommendations.'[27]

The absence of high-level oversight was compounded by personnel (ministerial and civil service) turnover. By mid-September, most of the original DTI team had moved on to other responsibilities, and the Ministry for Women and Equalities, as well as the Government Equalities Office (GEO, which had replaced the WEU: see Chapter 6), had undergone yet another office move. At the highest level of government, the (conflict-ridden) shift from the Blair to

Brown premiership was already underway,[28] sapping energy and reshuffling priorities.

The Government Action Plan (2006)

The government (the DCLG, the home of the ministry for women and equalities) announced an action plan in September 2006.[29] Kelly announced that she would implement 'almost all the recommendations', including support for workplace equality representatives.[30] Launching the action plan during a visit to Tesco workers in east London, Kelly emphasized government support for a campaign to sign up business 'exemplars' willing to take forward the commission's recommendations on quality part-time jobs and flexible working.[31]

Most of the recommendations were accepted, but expenditure items were scaled down significantly. Only a tenth (£500,000) of the recommended £5 million fund for initiatives on quality part-time jobs was provided; no additional funding was found for Investors in People initiatives; and the government did not specify how much additional spending had been made available in the Train to Gain programme for initiatives earmarked for women. According to Prosser, funding for the quality part-time jobs initiative had been secured through her personal approach to Ed Balls, then Economic Secretary at the Treasury (May 2006–June 2007) and Brown's closest political ally.[32] The main authority measure recommended (mandatory reporting on pay by gender in the public sector) became an 'optional' element of the public-sector equality duty (PSED).[33] Most of the capacity-building measures were accepted, but with some exceptions: actions to tackle occupational segregation in schools were limited; the right to request flexible working would be extended but only to parents of older children; actions on work–family policy and childcare were left outside the remit of the action plan.

Prosser's public view of the government response, as reported to the House of Lords in its annual International Women's Day debate in March 2007, was positive: 'I was immensely proud to be asked by the Prime Minister to chair the commission and even more pleased at the way in which its report was received and, indeed, is being implemented.'[34] Of the commission's forty recommendations, she stated, all but two had been accepted by government, and more than a hundred companies had joined the Exemplar Employer programme, committing to review their practice to support female employees, while the Trade Union Modernization Fund was being used to support the work of trade-union equality representatives.[35] The commission would meet again within a month to assess progress on its recommendations, Prosser reported.[36]

However, the government's action plan was criticized by the parliamentary Trade and Industry Committee, which expressed concern that the government did not announce a timetable for implementation of the WWC's recommendation or funding to support it. The committee had in 2005 published a report on occupational segregation[37] that advocated a set of recommendations similar to those formulated by the WWC a few months later. Following the 2005 general election, and despite the transfer of the women and equalities ministerial brief to the DCLG, the committee (subsequently renamed the Business, Enterprise, and Regulatory Reform Committee (BERR)) decided (with the agreement of the Communities and Local Government committee, which monitored the work of DCLG) to continue to press for implementation of its, and the WWC's, recommendations. The WWC had, it noted, advocated specific funding for women's skills development, which it wished to see implemented.

In April 2007. the government published a report on progress towards implementing the commission recommendations.[38] The BERR committee called an inquiry into the government's response to its earlier report as well as the WWC recommendations, at which government ministers gave evidence. In its conclusions it strongly criticized the government on areas where implementation lagged behind the commission's recommendations. On training, it said that government paid inadequate attention to the specific needs of women in its skills programme (in particular, the attention drawn by the WWC to the needs of older women), and cited the Confederation of British Industry (CBI) and the Trades Union Congress (TUC), which had 'both lamented' underfunding of the Quality Part Time Work initiative.[39] It urged government to extend the right to flexible working further, to cover all employees.

On actions to tackle pay discrimination, the BERR committee noted the mixed evidence about the effectiveness of mandatory duties, and argued that government should be prepared to introduce mandatory duties if it transpired in a few years that employers' voluntary actions to carry out pay audits were insufficient, or if the PSED was not being adequately implemented. Progress in narrowing the gender pay gap would be an important indicator of whether these actions were by themselves sufficient. It expressed disappointment that government's endorsement of union equality representatives was 'lukewarm', given the importance of such initiatives in bringing out cultural change in the workplace.[40] Even in the area where government preferences aligned with the WWC's recommendations, dissemination of best practice and role models, the committee argued that executive action had still not been put in place.

Finally, the BERR committee turned its attention to the public sector. It noted that the gender equality duty had made a promising start but that this needed to be monitored, as there were signs of a highly variable response by public authorities, and more needed to be done to spread good practice. It criticized the new guidelines for public procurement for a 'timid' approach and urged government to review them.[41] Altogether, the committee's report highlighted what it called a lacklustre, 'half-hearted' government response to the WWC's recommendations.[42] It expressed concern that the women and equalities minister lacked a coordinated approach and asked whether this reflected the weak institutional position of the post and the low priority given to the question of women's economic situation 'amidst her other tasks'.[43]

In introducing the report at the parliamentary liaison committee on 16 October 2008, the committee chair, Judy Mallaber, was more conciliatory towards the government, observing that a number of positive developments had occurred since the inquiry took place, including an increase in the number of apprenticeships, and reports from government departments on their implementation of the gender equality duty. However, she called for further action on the Quality Part-Time Jobs funding, which government had committed to increasing but had still not done. Mallaber asked how to move beyond short-term pilot projects: 'We can do good projects and pilots, and get a range of employers as exemplars, as we have, that try to do positive work, but the difficulty is extending it.'[44] Despite the extension of the right to request flexible working (to all parents of children under 18), which had been introduced since the committee's report, Mallaber urged that it needed to go further and extend it to all employees, supported by several MPs in the debate.

Maria Eagle, who had been in post as parliamentary under-secretary and joint women and equalities minister for just a week, responded for the government that the Quality Part-Time Jobs pilots would be evaluated shortly and that the WWC, which had just been reconvened (eighteen months after it had been expected to meet again), would no doubt look at this. Eagle's response dealt mainly with legislation against sex discrimination, which she said would be reinforced in the Equality Bill through the introduction of the concept of positive discrimination and stronger rules on public procurement.

Following the 2007 general election, the chancellor, Alistair Darling, announced a new commitment to reduce the gender pay gap, leading the Minister for Women and Equalities Harriet Harman in late 2008 to instruct

Prosser to reconvene the commission. No reason was given for the failure to reconvene the commission within a year. Based on the timeline set out above, it seems reasonable to conclude that the lack of strong, continuous leadership at ministerial level had a significant adverse impact on the way the commission's recommendations were taken up in 2006. After the 2007 general election, however, with Harman as Leader of the House (and deputy leader of the Labour Party), the profile of equalities within government had risen considerably.

Despite this change, the tone of the WWC's 2009 report was noticeably downbeat, in comparison with the earlier report, reflecting the restricted policy environment in the context of the post-2008 economic downturn. The 2009 report revealed commissioners' disappointment at the way their 2006 recommendations had been received. In considering progress made since 2006, the commission used a 'traffic light' (red, amber, green) rating to assess four areas: education and culture; training and development; balancing work and family life; and the public sector. Two of these, education and work–family policy, were rated red, meaning significant progress had yet to be achieved; training and the public sector were viewed as needing further work despite some progress.[45] This rather pessimistic evaluation led to no fewer than forty-three new recommendations.

The 2009 recommendations were integrated into the GEO's work plan, led by the Solicitor General Vera Baird, alongside the results of a National Equality Panel conducted the same year, and in the context of the Equality Bill's passage through parliament. The National Equality Panel found that, although girls' educational attainment matched that of boys, they soon encountered poorer pay and job prospects once they entered the labour market.[46] Increasing numbers of women were working part-time. The GEO's work plan set out a number of proposed actions, including more flexibility in the use of maternity leave for mothers and fathers, but it contained many measures that committed government only to 'consider' rather than to propose policy initiatives. At this stage of the Labour administration, and given the strength and range of the bank of evidence now available, the language of the action plan was robust but the planned output weak and thin.

From the Women and Work Commission to the Equality Bill (2009)

Two key political developments overshadowed the WWC's follow-up report in 2009. The first was that Brown's premiership was already in difficulties. After the resignation of James Purnell, Secretary of State for Work on

Pensions, on 4 June, followed by that of Minister for Europe Caroline Flint several days later, fifteen MPs met to express criticism of Brown, although they failed to gain the wider support needed to force a leadership contest. A feature of the rebellion was the relatively large numbers of women prepared to criticize their leader publicly, including Munn and, from the Lords, Prosser.[47] Flint, in announcing her resignation, claimed that she and other women had been used as 'a smokescreen' and 'female window dressing', and she denounced a culture of bullying.[48]

The second political development was that the main opposition parties had significantly strengthened their attack on Labour on its gender-equality record. Theresa May as Conservative spokesperson for women and equalities, and her Liberal Democrat counterpart Lynne Featherstone, developed proposals that went beyond Labour policy on work–family measures and on equal pay. This placed the Labour leadership on the defensive, and it led to a more fractious atmosphere in parliament when discussions on women and employment occurred.

It was not an auspicious time to relaunch the WWC's recommendations. Even worse for Prosser herself, policy on gender equality had been politicized further by Trevor Phillips's leadership of the Equality and Human Rights Commission (EHRC), on which she sat as his deputy. In July 2009, Harman trimmed the EHRC's staff budget but reappointed both Phillips and Prosser, causing the resignation of three commissioners, just as a damning report by the National Audit Office on Phillips's management of the EHRC was published.[49] Although Prosser herself was not the object of criticism, she was nevertheless damaged to some extent by association with Phillips, whom she defended publicly while acknowledging that mistakes had been made in the EHRC's early days.[50]

Compared to the high profile of the WWC's report launch in 2006, there was relatively little comment on the recommendations contained in the 2009 follow-up report. The *Guardian*'s Anne Perkins was sympathetic in her view that the commission was 'prodding away at the reasons underlying the choices women and men make that end up with them working in quite separate occupations, and then alerting everyone to them'. Having to remind policymakers that the gender pay gap remained high did not constitute failure, Perkins argued, but 'the bread and butter of progress, and it is indispensable'. The 2009 report was 'a really meaty piece of work from the commission, full of good practical ideas'.[51]

In presenting the WWC report in 2009, the GEO chose to focus on the lack of progress in education and training, rather than work–family policy, the other area where a 'red' warning was issued in the report. In some respects, this political choice was understandable, because it highlighted the success of the Women and Work Sectoral Pathways Initiative and put pressure on the chancellor to fund its second phase, as a bill on apprenticeships made its way through parliament.[52] With this approach, however, the WWC's recommendations in 2009 fell onto politically stony ground. The WWC lacked a sympathetic leader within the two relevant departments (business and education), which in June 2009 merged to become the Department for Business, Innovation and Skills, headed by Lord Mandelson. Meanwhile, as the Equality Bill began to make its way through parliament, the political debate began to engage again with the question of mandatory pay audits, which the WWC had earlier left to one side.

The WWC's approach of dealing with the causes of the pay gap was criticized by feminist activists like Beatrix Campbell, who argued that it was tantamount to reducing inequality to a matter of individual choice and capacity.[53] For the Fawcett Society, Rowena Lewis similarly pointed out that, while it was useful to support women moving into male-dominated occupations, this did not address the wider undervaluation of women's work.[54] The WWC's recommendations still had supporters within parliament, but in the debates that took place over the next few months they struggled for attention.

Conclusion

In the previous chapter, it was argued that the broad remit and large size of the commission made it difficult to focus on a single set of hard-hitting recommendations. However, several interviewees saw this as a strength, not just because it set out an authoritative, evidence-based and multidimensional agenda for action, but because the recommendations were rooted in practical, 'sensible' solutions that combined both 'quick wins' (measures that could be implemented quickly and at relatively low cost) and a longer-term programme of cultural change. If fully addressed, funded, and rolled out with attention to monitoring and follow-up, arguably the commission's recommendations could have made a significant improvement to working women's lives and career chances over time.

However, to succeed, this programme required two essential factors. First, it relied on financial investment, which, although provided, fell short of the necessary amount. Prior agreement on funding for capacity-building instruments would have enabled swift implementation of the two major policy recommendations.

Secondly, the programme of recommendations required close monitoring and continuous high-level leadership, otherwise the risk of failure was high, given the need to coordinate work across different government departments. Neither of these essential factors applied to the WWC's recommendations. As this chapter has shown, the programme lost momentum after 2006. The commission was not reconvened in 2007, as it had itself recommended. Instead, after a period of discontinuous and relatively low-level ministerial leadership, the policy agenda was reset under the Brown premiership, resulting in a loss of focus, as the commission's agenda competed with a new set of priorities for the incoming ministerial team responsible for women and equalities.

As will be discussed later in the concluding chapter, feminist institutionalism helps us to understand what happened in the period between 2006 and 2009 because it puts the spotlight on what can only be seen as a lack of attention to the women and equalities policy brief by political leaders caught up in other areas that claimed priority, as well as in power calculations and rivalries. The women and equalities ministerial role had in the period 2001–5 been embedded in the relatively powerful DTS, albeit at the cost of having to frame all claims within the overarching policy rationale, which was market driven and which denied the legitimacy of women-specific demands. In the period after 2005 it lost this authoritative departmental seat, became fragmented, and was more dependent on the personal clout of individual ministers in weaker departmental settings.

After 2007, the Conservatives and Liberal Democrats both sought to appeal to women voters with proposals to extend work–family policy. Whereas in principle the WWC's recommendations constituted the basis for a longer-term agenda for change as well as 'quick wins', Labour had little to propose at the 2010 general election, other than the provision in the Equality Act 2010 to 'encourage' employers to carry out pay audits.[55] The 2010 Conservative manifesto, in contrast, made repeated reference to the need to make Britain 'the most family-friendly country in Europe' by extending the right to request flexible working to all in stages and introducing shared parental leave.[56] The Liberal Democrat manifesto in 2010 also pledged to introduce shared parental leave and extend the right to request flexible working, and set out a series of proposals to address discrimination in the workplace, including mandatory 'fair-pay' audits in all organizations with over a hundred employees, and anonymous job applications.[57]

However, although this shift in the politics of work–family policy allowed it to continue to develop under subsequent governments, the overarching thrust of Conservative policy shaped it in a narrow form, as the following chapters will show, while-t women in work and out of work increasingly bore the brunt of austerity-driven cuts to public services. The next chapter focuses on the campaign for equal pay, which was the most controversial area discussed by the WWC, but where the Equality Bill appeared to provide a fruitful avenue to take forward some of the measures where commissioners were able to find agreement.

In subsequent chapters, the book will consider to what extent the WWC influenced policy debates over the longer period. In the short to medium term, the broad agenda established by the WWC had significant influence, because it took the multilevel approach set out by the EOC's Equal Pay Task Force in 2001 and took it both into government via the GEO, and outwards, into mainstream media discussions (thanks to prime-ministerial backing) and especially into the business world. Undoubtedly, the threat of mandatory action on equal-pay audits and trade-union equality representatives, as well as the prospect of strengthening equal-pay legislation in the Equality Bill, focused the minds of employers and helped to ease discussions about what they could do through voluntary means, as press coverage of the WWC's 2006 report showed. How far the voluntary approach could be relied upon to deliver significant change has continued to dominate debates since then, as the rest of this book will examine.

Notes

1. M. Bulmer, 'Increasing the Effectiveness of Royal Commissions: A Comment', *Public Administration*, 61 (1983), https://doi.org/10.1111/j.1467-9299.1983.tb00538.x, p.441.
2. A. Hunter and C. Boswell, 'Comparing the Political Functions of Independent Commissions: The Case of Migrant Integration Policy', *Journal of Comparative Policy Analysis: Research and Practice*, 17 (2015), https://doi.org/10.1080/13876988.2014.896117.
3. Hunter and Boswell, 'Comparing the Political Functions of Independent Commissions', 442.
4. H. Mullholland, 'Interview: The Big Payback', *Guardian*, 7 September 2005.
5. H. Ingram and A. Schneider, 'The Choice of Target Populations', *Administration and Society*, 23 (1991), https://doi.org/10.1177/009539979102300304.
6. A. Schneider and H. Ingram, 'Social Construction of Target Populations: Implications for Policy and Politics', *American Political Science Review*, 87 (1993), https://doi.org/10.2307/2939044, p.336.
7. M. Millar, 'Closing the Gender Divide', *Personnel Today*, 7 March 2006, p. 8.
8. The statement was lodged on 27 February but was received too late for publication that day: Hansard, HC, Written Statements, col. WS9.
9. P. Johnston, 'Blair Promises to Improve Girls' Job Prospects', *Daily Telegraph*, 28 February 2006, p.8.
10. Interview, Adeeba Malik.
11. 'Women and Work Commission Ready to Publish Report on Gender Pay Gap', *Personnel Today*, 28 February 2006, p. 3
12. S. Laville, 'Call for New Laws to Beat Sex Discrimination at Work', *Guardian*, 29 December 2005.

13. G. H. Davies, 'Women Still Need to Fight for Equal Pay', *Sunday Times*, 4 September 2005.
14. 'No Quick Fix for Gender Pay Gap', *Guardian*, 9 September 2005.
15. See J. Arrowsmith, 'British Airways' Heathrow Flights Grounded by Dispute at Gate Gourmet', *Eurofound*, 19 September 2005, https://www.eurofound.europa.eu/publications/article/2005/british-airways-heathrow-flights-grounded-by-dispute-at-gate-gourmet (accessed 11 November 2021).
16. Miller, 'Closing the Gender Divide', summarized reactions from business and unions. This quotation came from Janice Godrich, president of the Commercial and Public Services Union. Criticism by Derek Simpson, general secretary of Amicus, was widely cited in the press. Simpson, who had given oral evidence to the WWC, argued that 'without compulsory pay audits women will have to wait until doomsday for equal pay' (A. Grice, 'Gender Pay Gap Costs UK Economy £23 Bn a Year', *Independent*, 27 February 2006, p. 16).
17. Miller, 'Closing the Gender Divide'; see also P. Curtis and T. Branigan, 'Women Told to Raise their Sights on Pay', *Guardian*, 3 March 2006, p. 14.
18. N. Woolcock, 'Women Will Earn the Same as Men—if they Wait 150 Years', *The Times*, 28 July 2006, p. 24. See also 'UK Pay Gap among Worst in Europe', *Guardian*, 27 February 2006; G. Rozenberg and R. Bennett, 'At Last—Women Overtake Men in the Pay Race, but Still Lose out as Careers Progress', *The Times*, 27 October 2006, p. 5.
19. 'Harman: Failure to Pay Women's Minister "Embarrassing"', *Guardian*, 20 April 2006.
20. T. Branigan, 'Boost Pay to Help Working Mothers, Says Harman', *Guardian*, 14 September 2006, p. 13.
21. 'A Strong and Strengthening Economy: Investing in Britain's Future', *Local Government Chronicle*, 22 March 2006.
22. Hansard, HC, Questions to the Minister for Women, cols 1099–1103 (4 May 2006).
23. Interview, Geoffrey Norris.
24. Interview, Meg Munn.
25. Interview, Norris.
26. WWC, *Shaping a Fairer Future* (London: DTI, 2006), 100.
27. WWC, *Shaping a Fairer Future*,101.
28. See L. Minkin, *The Blair Supremacy: A Study in the Politics of Labour's Party Management* (Manchester: Manchester University Press, 2014), 642–54. This context was referred to by several interviewees.
29. DCLG, *Government Action Plan Implementing the Women and Work Commission Recommendations* (London: HMSO, 2006).
30. Branigan, 'Boost to Help Working Mothers, Says Harman', 13.
31. 'Kelly Sets out to Help Working Mothers', *Yorkshire Post*, 12 September 2006.
32. Interview, Margaret Prosser.
33. DCLG, *The Government Action Plan*, 35.
34. Hansard, HC, 'Women', debate, vol. 690, cols 326–406 (8 March 2007).
35. Although Kelly expressed support for union equality representatives, it was suggested in 2006 that the full £5 million recommended by the WWC would not be made available: the TUC in September 2006 pushed for the whole amount, noting that the cash commitments in the WWC recommendations had been only partly implemented. Trade-union lobbying ensured that £3 million was allocated to the second round of Union Modernization

Fund (UMF) projects (up from around £2 million in the first round), launched in November 2006, but training and resources for equality representatives formed only one of four main themes of the projects funded. The main contribution of the WWC, apart from applying pressure to maintain funding for the UMF, was to ensure funding of networks of equality representatives: see M. Stuart, M. Martinez Lucio, J. Tomlinson, and R. Perrett, *The Union Modernisation Fund—Round Two*, Employment Relations Research series, no. 111 (London: Department for Business, Innovation and Skills, 2010), 2.

36. See also Vera Baird's statement to the House of Commons in the International Women's Day debate there: 'we are about to do a women and work commission one year on programme for progress': ibid. This would, she said, feed into the gender-equality strategy that had to be published by the end of April.
37. BERR Committee, *Jobs for the Girls: The Effect of Occupational Segregation on the Gender Pay Gap*, Sixteenth Report of Session 200–5, HC 300.
38. GEO, *Towards a Fairer Future* (London: HMSO, 2007). The term 'a fairer future', used by the WWC, was taken up in the preliminary framework documents leading to the Equality Bill: GEO, Framework for a Fairer Future: The Equality Bill (HMS), 2008).
39. BERR Committee, *Jobs for the Girls: Two Years on*, Second Report of Session 2007–8, HC 291, 29 January, p. 22.
40. BERR Committee, *Jobs for the Girls*, 29.
41. BERR Committee, *Jobs for the Girls*, 36.
42. BERR Committee, *Jobs for the Girls*, 38.
43. BERR Committee, *Jobs for the Girls*, 38.
44. Hansard, HC, Jobs for the Girls, Two Years on', vol. 480, col. 338WH (16 October 2008).
45. WWC, *Shaping a Fairer Future: A Review of the Recommendations of the Women and Work Commission Three Years on* (London: GEO, 2009), 7.
46. The National Equality Panel was established in October 2008 by Harriet Harman, following the report of the Equalities Review in 2007, in order to examine evidence on the equality 'strands' (gender, race, disability, age, sexual orientation, and religion or belief), the relationship between them and how they had changed over time. Chaired by Professor John Hills of LSE and comprising nine other academics, it received submissions from the major NGOs in the field, commissioned ten independent research reports, made twenty-four visits to government departments, research centres, and other relevant institutions, and held two stakeholder round tables. See J. Hills/National Equality Panel, *An Anatomy of Economic Inequality in the UK: report of the National Equality Panel* (London: GEO, 2010).
47. 'Labour Rebels Regroup for Push against Brown', *Guardian*, 5 June 2009.
48. G. Hinsliff and C. Cadwaller, 'Angry Flint in Fresh Attach on Brown', *Observer*, 7 June 2009.
49. A. McSmith, 'Revolt against Phillips at Equality Watchdog Grows', *Independent*, 20 July 2009; H. Muir, '"How do you Alienate that Number of People?"', *Guardian*, 28 July 2009.
50. In her autobiographyProsser gives a flavour of the problems faced within the new body, which faced what she termed 'sectionalism' (it brought together several strong equalities constituencies, each with its own established ways of working) and a 'lack of straight talking', perhaps due to the sensitivities involved (p. 210): M. Prosser, *Your Seat is at the End* (London: Feather Duster Publications, 2012. Nicola Brewer, a former civil servant at the Foreign and Commonwealth Office, was as EHRC chief executive 'out of her depth'

(p. 10), while Phillips was a 'great blue skies thinker' but lacked the managerial skills to navigate the tensions (p. 11).

51. A. Perkins, 'Plugging away at the Gender Pay Gap', *Guardian*, 29 July 2009.
52. The Apprenticeships, Skills, Children, and Learning Act was presented in February 2009 and adopted in November. See Lady Prosser's intervention in response to the Queen's Speech in November 2009: Hansard, HL, Debate on the Queen's Speech, vol. 715, col. 440.
53. B. Campbell, 'Promised with a Forked Tongue', *Guardian*, 16 March 2019.
54. L. Nousratpour, 'Britain— the Gender Pay Gap Gets Larger', *Morning Star*, 30 July 2009.
55. Labour Party, *A Future Fair for All: The Labour Party Manifesto 2010*, manifesto (2010), 21.
56. Conservative Party, *Invitation to Join the Government of Britain: The Conservative Manifesto 2010*, manifesto (2010), 41.
57. Liberal Democratic Party, *Liberal Democrat Manifesto 2010*, manifesto (2010), 31, 45.

9

The Unfinished Campaign for Equal Pay in the UK

Introduction

Unequal pay remains a problem in the UK. In the period from 2007 to 2020, more than 368,000 complaints were made to tribunals relating to equal pay, an average of almost 29,000 per year,[1] and these cases may represent the 'tip of the iceberg', with many cases withdrawn or settled before reaching tribunal.[2] Such a high number of claims has undoubtedly been stimulated by increased awareness created by successive attempts to adapt and strengthen the legislation. But, although regulatory initiatives have drawn attention to the problem of unequal pay, they have evidently not resolved it.

As discussed in Chapter 4, the thirtieth anniversary of the Equal Pay Act (EPA) in the year 2000 saw the launch of a campaign to remedy its weaknesses through stronger rights for claimants, on the one hand, and supportive measures for employers facing claims, on the other. Although the Equality Act 2010 opened the way for gender pay-gap reporting (introduced in 2017), campaigners in 2020 identified the same defects in the law as twenty years earlier: long, costly, and discouraging procedures for redress; lack of rights to information about the pay of colleagues doing the same or similar job; lack of intersectional understanding of multiple discrimination;[3] and weak positive duties on employers, creating a culture of inaction.[4]

This chapter begins by looking at discussions on equal-pay legislation within the Women and Work Commission (WWC), which, as the previous two chapters have set out, was established to examine causes of the gender pay gap and possible solutions, including full equal-pay audits, as recommended by the Equal Opportunities Commission (EOC). Differences of views within the WWC raised wider questions about how to effect change, which the EOC in its Equal Pay Task Force had already begun to consider, informed by communications with employers in its Equality Exchange network.

As this chapter outlines, while the policy debate has moved on since 2006, with the introduction of gender pay-gap reporting regulations, the same

Women and Employment in Public Policy. Susan Milner, Oxford University Press. © Susan Milner (2024).
DOI: 10.1093/9780191987359.003.0009

questions persist about the effectiveness of legislation. In the absence of compulsion, employer engagement with full pay reviews (or audits) showed little progress, and the weaker form of mandatory instrument chosen in 2017 (gender pay-gap reporting requirements applicable to organizations with 250 employees or more) does not provide sufficient incentive for employers to generate detailed pay data. Nor does it satisfy the requirement for remedial action outlined in the comparative work of the International Labour Organization (ILO) on effective equal-pay policy: that is, action plans as well as diagnostic data.[5]

The Women and Work Commission (2004–9) and the Question of Mandatory Pay Reviews

Organizational gender pay reviews (or audits) are widely viewed as a necessary step for tackling pay inequality, for three main reasons. First, data analysis helps to uncover where any problems of unequal treatment exist and to work out strategies for dealing with them, following the well-known maxim that 'what gets measured, gets managed'.[6] Second, they increase transparency, provided that the results are communicated within the organization. Third, the process of generating and analysing data can empower change agents, such as employee representatives or equality professionals in human resource (HR) management departments.[7]

Yet employers are generally reluctant to engage with pay reviews, for fear of costs and potential conflicts.[8] Moreover, in practice, pay reviews can be counterproductive if measurement is mismanaged or poorly communicated, and they can be subject to internal resistance, which not only limits impact but can create backlash.

Canada's two largest provinces, Ontario and Quebec, provided early examples of legislative action to promote pay equality through reviews, which suggested that, although they were effective in the public sector, where job-classification schemes were already in place, they were more difficult to implement in the private sector. The Pay Equity Act of 1987 in Ontario introduced a proactive duty on all public-sector employers and all private-sector employers with ten or more employees, consisting of a four-step process starting with the identification of predominantly female and male jobs, the classification of these jobs using numerical scores, the comparison of the jobs in relation to established wage rates, and, finally, pay adjustments where it was found that predominantly female jobs were undervalued. Rather than relying on individual claims of discrimination, as in the British case, the Act put strong pressure on employers to take specific actions, with consequences for non-compliance. It created the Pay Equity Commission to oversee implementation, enforce compliance through sanctions if necessary, and arbitrate in disputed cases.

Relatively high levels of compliance were found among larger companies, those with trade-union presence, and in the public sector, but only around half of organizations surveyed reported plans to put in place pay-classification systems in the decade following Ontario's 1987 Act. Smaller firms with between fifty and ninety-nine employees were significantly less likely to have implemented pay-review processes (30 per cent), and even fewer very small firms with between ten and forty-nine people on the payroll reported having done so (12 per cent).[9] Investigation of the reasons for non-compliance identified employer avoidance of administrative costs but also lack of awareness about concepts underlying the implementation of classification systems. In very small firms, the lack of effective male comparators posed problems for compliance.[10] Enforcement was not strong enough to impel employers to overcome these barriers.

Quebec's Act on Pay Equity followed Ontario's in 1996 and is seen as the most advanced legislation in the world.[11] It applies to all employers with ten or more employees. Small organizations with between ten and forty-nine employees must identify pay disparities between men and women and correct them, but the Act does not specify how they should do so. Those with fifty or more employees are obliged to follow a four-step process, as in Ontario, with a four-year deadline for pay adjustments, following the formulation of a pay-equity plan. Those with 100 or more employees must establish a pay-equity committee, two-thirds of whose members must represent employees, half of them women. The Act was, therefore, more prescriptive than the Ontario legislation in setting out duties for employer action, and the financial sanctions for non-compliance were set at a high level. Consequently, compliance was found to be higher than in Ontario, but gaps in coverage remained. Pay adjustments to women began after 2001 and had a small but identifiable effect of reducing the gender pay gap.[12]

The Canadian examples showed that 'no single piece of legislation can do it but some methods are undoubtedly better than others'.[13] They were influential in British discussions of the merits of mandatory pay reviews, highlighting both the benefits and the pitfalls of statutory intervention:

> [Pay reviews] did some good, especially in the public sector, but in the private sector employers did them, but then they went, oh look, there's no problem. This

was quite influential. It influenced my thinking on pay reviews. Just making a law doesn't solve the problem, you can't just wave your wand.[14]

The EOC's Equal Pay Task Force in 2001 concluded that equal-pay reviews could be helpful in directing employers' attention to pay inequity in a focused way, resulting in the proposal that all employers should carry out a two-step process, beginning with a full pay review to identify whether inequalities existed. Only if inequalities were uncovered would it be necessary for employers to produce an action plan and to communicate the plan to employees and their representatives. The EOC would be able to request a copy of the plan to check its compliance with sex-discrimination legislation, but otherwise no public reporting was foreseen. The Task Force recommended intensive support for employers, including training, software provision, and the deployment of external expertise.[15]

The voluntary approach adopted by the government in response to the 2001 Task Force recommendations had some impact, but not enough to make a difference in the private sector. Research commissioned by the EOC suggested that a majority of organizations conducting pay reviews had done this for the first time in 2003–4, spurred on by awareness of gender pay gaps generated by press coverage and, in the case of public-sector organizations, prompts from government or regulatory bodies; trade-union pressure was also an important factor.[16] While improvements in women's pay relative to men's had been observed in only a fifth of the organizations studied, most employers planned to continue with further reviews and invest in better training and data collection to assist the process. Contrary to what employers may have feared, the research found that costs of producing data were relatively low, and no internal conflicts had been sparked by the production of data.[17] Overall, two-thirds of employers classed the experience as positive.[18]

The number of organizations engaging in gender pay reviews continued to rise, from 12 per cent in 2005 to 17 per cent in 2008. However, this trend mostly concerned the public sector, where 43 per cent of organizations surveyed in 2008 had carried out or were conducting reviews.[19] As discussed further in Chapter 13, the Department for Trade and Industry (DTI) had in 2001 instructed public-sector employers to conduct gender pay reviews, so this survey indicated that the public sector was not fully compliant with its duty, as well as showing that reluctance to carry out reviews was prevalent in the private sector.

Given the slow pace of employer engagement with pay reviews, unions' policy position hardened in favour of a mandatory requirement, resulting in a wide distance between the union and employer positions when the WWC was convened to consider the question. The case for mandatory action, supported by unions and equal-pay experts giving evidence to the commission, was based on evidence of reluctance to conduct reviews in the absence of compulsion. The case against rested on costs, particularly for smaller companies, and lack of expertise and even basic awareness among employers and HR managers.[20] Employers giving evidence to the commission also argued that equal-pay reviews might divert resources from other ways of addressing the needs of female workers, and could lead to a 'tick-box' approach.[21] In summary, the commission concluded that 'equal pay reviews can benefit women, provide clear incentive systems and reduce the costs of litigation. But they only address part of the problem.'[22]

Instead of considering ways of combining mandatory action with supportive measures, as the EOC advocated, the WWC therefore chose to focus instead on actions already underway. These included dissemination of good practice through existing networks such as Investors in People (for which it recommended additional funding from government), Opportunity Now's annual benchmark, and the EOC's plans to trial a 'light-touch equality check', which would help employers to identify where there were problems potentially requiring a fuller pay review.[23] In the public sector, on the other hand, commissioners had all agreed on the need for pay reviews.

The WWC grappled with, but did not resolve, the question of how change could be effected in the private sector, as the Kingsmill review had done in 2001. Sarah Anderson expressed this question from the perspective of a small business employer:

> The law, if nothing else, just makes people talk about it more, but there are unintended consequences, and that's why you need to use carrots rather than sticks. With small businesses ... I would divide them into the good, the bad and the ignorant. The good ... will be good whatever. The bad will be bad whatever, and therefore you have to deal with the ignorant. And that's the piece of work which is more about iterative processes and culture than it is about the silver bullet of law, which doesn't work.[24]

In this respect, the WWC could have considered how the EOC's experience of working with private-sector employers could be harnessed to identify ways of finding lighter-touch or multilevel regulatory solutions. Two of my interviewees, Matilda Quiney (a former trade-union policy officer with expertise in equal pay, who contributed to the Equal Pay Task Force, and later worked in the DTI secretariat supporting the WWC) and Jenny Watson (chair of the EOC in the period leading up to its replacement by the Equality and Human

Rights Commission (EHRC)), referred to ideas that were being discussed outside the WWC at the time but did not surface there. Quiney stated that, based on the work she had done as a policy officer at the General, Municipal, and Boilermakers' Union (GMB), she thought there was a case for allowing tribunals to order full equal-pay reviews in organizations where an individual equal-pay award had been made.[25] This idea fitted the EOC's call for stronger tribunal powers, based on the observation that existing equality law did little more than provide individual redress in a small number of cases, without any wider impact on pay equality in the UK.[26] 'So much more could have been done,' Quiney reflected.

According to Watson,

> What we realised in talking to businesses was that they supported pay reviews, a lot of them, but they were scared of the legal actions.... Pay reviews just weren't going to happen. ... So we realised that employers needed a breathing space. We thought that you could have pay reviews if employers had a breathing space when they were allowed to take action to redress disparities without being open to legal action. It's not totally straightforward from a legal point of view, but we took legal advice, and the advice was that it can be done.[27]

The EOC idea of a temporary amnesty or 'breathing space' was innovative, and it potentially provided a means of unblocking the stalemate over equal-pay reviews. The EOC's legal advice was that such a solution was possible. However, although the idea was discussed in the Cabinet Office (which regularly brought together public-sector employers and trade unions on the subject of equal pay), it was viewed as risky, because of the possibility of an equal-pay claim based on any acceptance of unjustified disparities. The WWC sought additional legal advice, which raised doubts about the legality of any action to condone pay inequality.[28]

When the WWC launched its report, it was strongly criticized by trade unions and equality campaign groups for not making a stronger case for mandatory equal-pay reviews. The stalemate between employer and trade-union views prevented it from doing so, despite impassioned advocacy from the union representatives. Trade-union representatives on the commission could have issued a dissenting minority report. However, not only would a minority report have made no difference to government readiness to consider mandatory pay reviews; it could have jeopardized the rest of the recommendations, with which all commissioners broadly agreed.

The Fawcett Society also criticized the WWC for not recommending mandatory equal-pay audits. But Watson (previously chair of Fawcett) defended the WWC report, using the opportunity in press interviews to reiterate the EOC's position on a range of supportive measures, including 'self-regulation, flexibility and pay amnesties—giving employers with a problem time to sort it out'.[29]

In media interviews, Baroness Prosser as chair of the WWC presented the question of mandatory pay reviews as a divisive one that it was impossible to bridge. When in 2012 Prosser gave evidence to the parliamentary committee on Business, Innovation and Skills, she expressed a favourable view on pay reviews but stressed that they form only part of the solution:

> If you have few, if any, opportunities for well-paid part-time employment, all the equal pay audits in the world are not going to change that. They are extremely useful and important, and transparency is very important, but you need all those other social structures to be implemented before the issue is going to be cracked.[30]

Prosser's holistic view of unequal pay as an ecosystem influenced the WWC's report but was not picked up in most public discussion of the report's recommendations, which focused almost entirely on either mandatory equal-pay reviews or gender stereotypes in education. Nor did it find its way into the GEO's response.

However, as a way of defusing conflict on the question of statutory duties, the WWC recommended it should be considered by the Discrimination Law Review (DLR) announced in February 2005. The rest of this chapter traces how in three main areas—reform of the tribunal system for individual claims of unequal pay, proactive reporting duties on employers, and workplace equality representatives—proposals for change were largely dismissed by the DLR but later resurfaced in discussions on the Equality Bill, tabled in 2008. As the following sections show, a preference for voluntary action remained policymakers' default position and was strengthened after the 2008 financial crash, but the case for statutory intervention remained strong owing to the slow progress made in narrowing the gender pay gap, and employers' general failure to respond to appeals for voluntary action.

Reforming the Tribunal System

The EOC's demands for reform of the tribunal system focused on ways of making it easier to show comparative value of work, as well as ways of increasing the impact of individual judgements. In 2003, the DTI introduced a formal questionnaire template to help complainants elicit information about comparators from their employer. In line with the EPA 1970, information gathered through the questionnaire could allow claims to be settled in the workplace without recourse to tribunals, but if it proved impossible to reach a settlement and the case was taken to tribunal, this information would make it easier for a decision to be made. Although the questionnaire was not compulsory, if employers refused to supply information or gave an evasive or equivocal reply, their failure to respond adequately could be taken into account by the tribunal.

The questionnaire itself was straightforward, consisting of two sections: in the first, the complainant set out the grounds for an equal-pay claim and gave details (job title, or name if known) of any person they thought was carrying out 'the same or similar work, work rated as equivalent, or work of equal value' but paid at a higher rate or otherwise treated more favourably in their terms of employment (such as bonuses or holiday entitlement); in the second, the respondent (the employer) should reply with details of how each element of pay and conditions differed between the complainant and the comparator, and for what reasons.[31]

The WWC considered evidence that the questionnaire was not working as well as it should, because employers sometimes refused to give comparative information on pay, citing data-protection requirements. The WWC recommended that government guidance should make explicit that pay disclosure did not breach data-protection rules.[32]

In addition to directing attention to the equal-pay questionnaire and setting out a strong case for workplace equality representatives (albeit without recommending statutory rights for the latter), the WWC report made a specific recommendation that the DLR should 'consider more fully the issues of whether or not to extend the hypothetical comparator to equal pay claims, and of generic or representative equal pay claims'.[33] This recommendation was significant because of its explicit reference to the EOC's, trade unions', and equality campaigners' long-standing demands for substantive strengthening of equal-pay claims through employment tribunals.

The DLR, which resulted in a consultative paper published in June 2007, represented an opportunity to strengthen equality legislation while also placing it within an overarching framework bringing together the hitherto separate equalities strands. However, it took place in inauspicious circumstances, at the same time as the existing commissions were being dismantled and a new equalities body established, which limited their input into the proposals. The response of the existing commissions was muted, and the parliamentary Communities and Local Government committee (the Women and Equality Unit (WEU) having moved from DTI to the Department for Communities and Local Government) expressed criticism of the inadequate preparation for the new equalities body in terms of management and resources, and the delay between setting up the new body and presenting proposals for a new single body of legislation.

Regarding stronger equality legislation, the committee noted that the DLR had been hampered in its recommendations by the government's 'hesitancy towards permitting combined multiple discrimination claims', which 'rests on the additional complexity this might add to any legislation and the consequent additional burden it would place on employers'.

While such fears were understandable, the committee urged government to acknowledge the need for action to address the weakness of existing law, which left many people effectively without recourse to redress.[34] The case for claims on grounds of multiple discrimination was supported by a broad range of bodies, including many law firms, who argued that changes to the law could be relatively simple.[35] Lawyers and campaigners also expressed strong support for the inclusion of reference to hypothetical comparators alongside actual comparators in equal-pay cases, in order to make it easier and quicker for tribunals to reach decisions, but the WEU consultation expressed a preference to retain the existing regulation rather than allowing hypothetical comparators. Finally, trade unions and other collective bodies received little attention in the DLR[36] and none in the consultation that followed it. This meant that the idea of representative (or generic, or 'class' actions as in the USA) was omitted from its scope.

Altogether, the DLR viewed legislation as warranted only 'where there is a clear case and bearing in mind the potential burden on employers, particularly small employers'.[37] In this respect, it was hard to escape the conclusion that the shift towards a single institutional framework for equalities reflected an individualized, laissez-faire (even deregulatory) view of equality and anti-discrimination.[38] However, the DLR did not have the final say on equalities legislation.

The Equality Act 2010

Despite campaigners' disappointment with the DLR, pressure within the Labour Party (resulting in a last-minute manifesto commitment)[39] and changes within government, with the nomination of Deputy Leader Harriet Harman as minister for women and equalities, raised hopes that stronger legislation could yet be adopted in the Equality Bill presented to parliament in autumn 2008, 'beyond the limited scope' of the DLR.[40] The bill had a difficult gestation, and Harman later spoke of the resistance she encountered 'in every single department' of government to the proposals in the Equality Bill, on the grounds of cost. It was 'odd', she reflected, that, 'if you have been elected and you are in government with your colleagues, you have to rely on outside organisations to persuade your own colleagues with whom you have been working for more than 20 years'.[41]

Ayesha Hazarika, who was then Harman's special adviser working on the Equality Bill, later recounted that 'everybody' in government "hated us", including 'lots of people at Number 10'.[42] According to Matilda Quiney (Harman's parliamentary private secretary between 2008 and 2010), senior men in the Cabinet Office assumed that the bill would fall before the end of parliament.[43] Although Harman's team 'pressed on, determined not to take no for an answer',[44] the passage of the bill required skilful handling and several concessions, to retain its core features.

The content of the Equality Bill shifted during its passage through parliament, under pressure from opposition amendments and from additional demands raised by Labour peers and backbenchers at committee stage. In the process, the demand for representative actions failed to make it into the final text of the Act, as did the proposal to give workplace equality representatives statutory rights (as discussed below), and, while the demand for combined (dual) discrimination claims was included in the Act, its effect was severely reduced by the overriding emphasis on discrete equality strands or 'protected characteristics', and the clause was subsequently abandoned under the Conservative–Liberal Democrat coalition government. The WWC's recommendation to consider the use of hypothetical comparators in equal-pay claims was only partially included in the final text of the Equality Act 2010, in Section 71, which allows equal-pay claims based on a hypothetical comparator where it is impossible to find a real comparator. This innovation has proved difficult to deploy in practice, as tribunals have little sense of how information on pay in such cases could reliably be secured.[45]

The question of claims on grounds of multiple discrimination claims had already proved controversial in the DLR, which bowed to government reluctance to encourage costly claims. The DLR asked for evidence of difficulties in obtaining redress where it was claimed discrimination had taken place on multiple grounds, following the 2004 case of *Bahl* v. *Law Society*, in which the Court of Appeal ruled that the claimant should make claims separately for each ground, whereas Ms Bahl had claimed discrimination as a woman of Asian ethnicity and sought to compare herself to a white man.[46] The volume of evidence submitted by lawyers and organizations such as Citizens Advice led the government to reconsider the question of how claims on grounds of multiple discrimination could be allowed 'without making the law overly complex or placing an undue burden on those with responsibilities under the law', in the words of the Solicitor General, Vera Baird.[47]

There appeared to be cross-party support for recognition of discrimination on two grounds, such as gender and disability or gender and race. At the eighth committee sitting on 17 June 2009, the Liberal Democrat spokesperson for women and equality, Lynne Featherstone, moved an amendment allowing claims of direct discrimination on multiple grounds.[48] Baird responded that, subject to further consultation, particularly with employers, the government could accept the principle of legislation allowing claims of dual (rather than multiple) discrimination. Section 14 of the Equality Act included provision for claims of 'combined discrimination' on grounds of two characteristics,[49] whereby a claimant could show they had been discriminated against in comparison with someone who shares neither of the two characteristics.

Section 14 therefore marked a (temporary) victory for campaigners, particularly since employers had opposed its introduction, but it was only a partial victory, as the new right was restricted to claims of direct (not indirect) discrimination, and therefore fell short of the recommendations in the 2000 Cambridge review, and indeed of European Union (EU) law, which since 2000 had recognized the multiple discrimination to which women are often subjected.[50] This partial victory was short-lived, because the Labour government decided not to enact Section 14 immediately. In 2013, the Conservative-led coalition government announced that provision for claims on grounds of combined discrimination would not go ahead.

Provision for generic actions did not make it into the Equality Act 2010 at all. At the thirteenth and fourteenth committee hearings on the Equality Bill, Labour MP Sandra Osborne, backed by Featherstone, introduced a new clause to allow the EHRC, trade unions, or charities representing specific groups (such as disabled people) to apply to a tribunal for a claim representing a group of workers. As well as preventing stigmatization of individual claimants, she argued that representative actions would have a greater impact on pay equality than reliance on individual claims.[51] The government first responded that it needed to consult further, but, at the bill's second reading, it indicated that the clause would be brought forward. However, when the Equality Bill went to the House of Lords in January 2010, the clause was dropped. Although Lord Lester made a powerful case in favour and was supported by several other peers, Baroness Royall for the government rejected the amendment, on the grounds that it polarized views and required further reflection, and it was withdrawn.[52]

The failure of long-standing campaign demands, in what initially appeared to be a favourable context heralded by Harman's authoritative championing of a single equality bill, can be seen as the result of intense political trade-offs on a highly sensitive policy area, which had become sharpened because of the financial crisis and the political weakness of Labour in its final years of government. As discussed below, Harman's priorities were focused on expanding duties on public bodies and on new measures to promote pay transparency. In any case, government had not been persuaded of the merits of stronger powers for tribunals or representative actions, as seen in their omission from the original text of the bill and their later inclusion only at committee stage, and it had adopted provision for combined discrimination claims only hesitantly.

Following the change to Conservative-led coalition government, the parameters for action were reset, with some unexpected results. In 2014, the statutory equal-pay questionnaire was abandoned and could no longer be used in any tribunal claims relating to the period after 2014, although it could still be used informally as a guide to gathering information. The move formed part of a broader agenda of reform of employment tribunals proposed by the Conservative–Liberal Democrat coalition government. The Deregulation Act 2015 repealed the provision in the Equality Act 2010 to allow tribunals to make general recommendations for action (such as training for line managers) as part of their ruling in discrimination cases. The Enterprise and Regulatory Reform Act 2013 made it harder for employees to access justice by raising the qualifying period of continuous service (accompanied by the introduction of fees for raising a tribunal case) from one year—already the longest qualifying period in Europe—to two years.[53] Women and younger workers were predominantly affected by this change owing to the less stable nature of their employment.

On the other hand, the Enterprise and Regulatory Reform Act 2013 amended the Equality Act 2010 to include a new power for tribunals to order an employer (with ten or more employees) to carry out a full equal-pay audit 'where the tribunal finds that there has been an equal pay breach', in order to avoid further breaches occurring.[54] The Conservative Party in opposition and in government supported the idea that employers who had been found guilty of pay discrimination should be ordered by the tribunal to conduct a full equal-pay audit. In December 2008, Baroness Morris (Patricia Morris, then Conservative shadow minister for women) introduced a private member's bill to this effect, but it failed to progress beyond its second reading (first debate). In the debate held in January 2009, Morris argued that it was not reasonable to impose a duty on all employers to conduct a full equal-pay audit, as these are 'costly, time consuming and demand that organisations publish their findings'. However, for the small minority of employers who were found not to comply with equal-pay legislation (mostly unintentionally, she added), action was needed. The bill found support across the chamber, but, by including a proposal to add a requirement for employers to demonstrate that any difference between comparators' pay was 'reasonable', it encountered opposition from peers—including Prosser—who found the adjective too vague to be operational. Prosser also objected that the duty on employers in cases of proven discrimination was not likely to make much difference. Overall, the bill was commended by the Lords despite its 'fundamental flaws', as Lester stated,[55] and it was passed to committee stage, but was later superseded by the Equality Bill.

Morris's successor as shadow spokesperson for women, Theresa May, reminded the House of Commons of the Conservatives' proposal when she opposed the Equality Bill at its second reading in November 2009, contrasting her party's 'fair and measured' initiative with Labour's 'heavy-handed and obstinate' approach.[56] When May led the introduction of a duty to conduct equal-pay audits, she enacted at least one of the ideas that had been floated in the period after the Equal Pay Task Force in 2001, but did so as part of a move to restrict recourse to employment tribunals. Nevertheless, as had been recognized when Morris first presented the idea in December 2008, trading stronger duties on recalcitrant employers against lighter regulation of wider group organizations formed an important part of the policy experimentation of this period, and helped prepare the way for the introduction of gender pay-gap reporting.

Gender Pay-Gap Reporting: A New Approach?

The Equality Act 2010 sought to promote greater transparency on pay as a way of furthering gender equality, and this aspect of the bill was emphasized by Harman in parliamentary debates. Section 77 stated that so-called gagging clauses in employment contracts or agreements could not be used to prevent claimants from soliciting information from colleagues about their pay or terms and conditions. This section of the bill was intended to ensure that 'there is greater transparency and dialogue within workplaces about pay'.[57] However, Section 77 is a limited instrument, because it restricts the circumstances in which it is legitimate to solicit information: it does not outlaw pay secrecy. It falls short of legislation adopted in other countries that gives individuals the right to request pay information concerning colleagues, as in

Germany, where a 2017 law giving all workers in organizations with a workforce of 200 or more the right to comparative pay information concerning a specific group of workers, although take-up of the measure is rare, not least because of the company size threshold.[58]

By itself, a right to request comparative pay information is unlikely to fulfil the aim of encouraging greater transparency and dialogue. Measures and practices that provide more general and systematic ways of comparing pay, such as job-evaluation schemes, are more likely to achieve that aim.[59] Another approach that has gained traction is reporting duties on employers, particularly large employers, where it is felt the administrative burden of data-gathering is more easily carried. However, although reporting duties are widely supported and have the potential to build employer awareness and capacity, in practice their impact has often been found to be small. The effect of reporting duties depends on regulatory design and the extent to which the mix of incentives and sanctions has the power to change employer behaviour: over-complexity, restrictions and exemptions, weak enforcement, or poor communication by government or regulators encourage foot-dragging and 'lip-service' compliance.[60]

The Equality Act 2010 included provision for gender pay-gap reporting duties on private-sector employers with 250 employees or more. However, when the bill was debated in parliament, Harman stated that government would enact a statutory duty only if employers failed to respond voluntarily. Reluctance to impose the duty reflected hostility from the Conservative opposition and the CBI as the financial crisis hit businesses. It also stemmed from the wider discussions about how to achieve organizational change, and how to move away from the litigation approach that had characterized equal-pay enforcement to date and had failed to narrow the gender pay gap.

The Cambridge law review in 2000 had proposed a shift to reflexive legislation, which would oblige employers not only to report on their gender pay gaps but also to report on ways to address those gaps, and to engage with stakeholders (most obviously, employees, but also potentially shareholders) on such proposed actions. By tailoring actions to the disparities uncovered by the data, and involving a range of workplace actors, this approach sought to encourage and support as well as steer, and to promote learning among all actors about what works best.

Reflexive regulation has a hybrid character, between imposed legal obligations and voluntary self-regulation.[61] Yet the approach set out in the DLR, although ostensibly referring to reflexive regulation, did not move beyond a purely voluntary and capacity-building approach, unlike the Cambridge review that had proposed it earlier. The DLR ignored evidence from

Northern Ireland, whose experience of reflexive regulation in the form of the Fair Employment and Treatment (Northern Ireland) Order 1998 and the public-sector equality duty (PSED) introduced in the Northern Ireland Act 1998 showed that certain preconditions for effective action applied: in particular, mandatory reporting and regular monitoring.[62] The failure of purely voluntary actions, in the case of equal-pay audits, had also been demonstrated in the wake of the 2001 Kingsmill review, which had criticized employer inertia.

With the introduction of Section 78 of the Equality Act, Harman showed awareness of this regulatory gap and provided a legal basis for future action. The possibility of future mandatory duties was intended to stimulate the 'ignorant' employers referred to by Anderson, above, to adopt their own measures before they were pushed to do so. However, even with this explicit threat ('the shadow of hierarchy'[63]), the absence of compulsion resulted in a lack of voluntary action. Only six employers voluntarily published equal-pay data (in rudimentary form), although some 280 signed a voluntary code of practice under the 2011 'Think, Report, Act' initiative committing them to do so. Several interviewees referred to the failure of the highly publicized 'Think, Report, Act' approach. As Janet Veitch (former director of the Women's National Commission, WNC) reflected:

> You have to consider the market you're working in, and if it's mandatory then it's a cost that everyone shares, and in that sense it's not a cost to the sector, but if it's not mandatory then of course they're going to resist doing it, why would they take on a cost unless they absolutely have to. ... When you're in a competitive market you make something mandatory for people who are competing against each other, it's the only way, otherwise the benefits of freeloading and the benefits of not being part of the club are just too great.[64]

Another reason the threat of coercive action did not work in this case is that experience told employers the threat was likely to be empty: the 2001 Kingsmill report had also suggested mandatory regulations if employers did not act voluntarily, but it was not followed up.

In 2014, Jo Swinson, the Liberal Democrat Parliamentary Under-Secretary for Business, Innovation and Skills, rescued Section 78 of the Equality Act 2010 by including its enactment in the Small Business Act. One of David Cameron's first acts on being reappointed prime minister after the 2015 general election was to announce the introduction of regulations on gender pay-gap reporting for organizations with 250 or more employees in the public, private, and voluntary sectors.

Three party-political reasons help to explain this shift towards statutory intervention. First, Cameron's modernization of the Conservative Party included attempts to feminize the party through the adoption of informal measures championed by May and others, particularly training and support for women candidates (short of targets and quotas) and 'priority' lists of future *ministrables* (short of formal positive discrimination). Second, Labour's adoption of a ministry for women, retained under Conservatives in various forms, helped to feminize government, as a succession of women occupied ministerial posts with responsibility for women and equality, notably May. Third, some aspects of gender pay-gap reporting were based on common ground between centre-left and centre-right, particularly the emphasis on reporting over action.

Another set of explanations emphasizes the institutional aspects of change, in particular relationships with organized and leading employers that had been established and developed during the Labour years within the regulatory space, both by government (notably the DTI, when Hewitt was also minister for women) and by the EOC and later the EHRC.[65] Employer organizations and large corporations were also under pressure from within and from the wider business world, with the spread of international benchmarking on gender-equality indicators.

Following the adoption of gender pay-gap reporting in 2017, and with the benefit of learning from successive rounds of data, the advantages of this regulatory approach have become evident, as well as the gaps within it. There is some indication that the legislation is effective, in that organizations subject to the regulations have seen a higher degree of narrowing of their gender pay gap than others, consistent with the idea that greater transparency has an egalitarian impact on pay outcomes.[66] Less positively, it appears that this effect stems largely from stagnation of male pay levels, consistent with US evidence that employers respond to reporting duties by depressing average wage increases, rather than by taking proactive steps to support women's career progression and raise female pay.[67]

The EHRC and Fawcett Society argue that the regulations need to include a stronger duty to report on actions aimed specifically at supporting women in the workplace.[68] At present, employers are encouraged to submit accompanying narratives explaining the gender pay-gap data and showing how gaps will be addressed, but EHRC research found that only around half of those submitting reports supplied narrative statements, and of these only a small minority specified actions with measurable targets.[69] Monitoring of action statements as well as data would add substantially to the EHRC's workload. Given evidence that many employers slip through the net with inadequate or misleading information,[70] any further expansion of reporting duties would require a major investment in the EHRC's enforcement capacity, backed up by parliamentary scrutiny of enforcement practice.

The fate of these proposals demonstrates the importance of political will on the part of government. To date, cross-party parliamentary pressure to extend the scope of reporting to lower the organizational size threshold, and to extend reporting to include data on employment contract status (full-time and part-time) and organizational work–family policies, have been ignored by government,[71] as have calls from within the business community as well as equality campaigners and parliamentarians to extend reporting to cover race and ethnicity.[72] A report on a first full review of gender pay-gap reporting regulations, timetabled for publication by April 2022 at the latest, did not take place as the regulations required.

In the absence of stronger duties and enforcement, the reporting regulations remain a 'blunt tool'.[73] They have had a significant awareness-raising impact in work organizations and in wider society. They have legitimated employer reporting as a regulatory tool. Employers have found that data-gathering is not overly burdensome and can bring organizational benefits. Equality actors within organizations have seen their resources and authority boosted in many cases.[74] Yet the Chartered Institute for Personnel and Development (CIPD) reported in 2022 that, despite the awareness and capacity built by statutory reporting requirements, the proportion of organizations implementing equal-opportunities policies is low: the CIPD refers to 'pockets of good practice' (in less than a quarter of private-sector organizations and around a third in the public sector).[75] Without statutory intervention, even this slow and uneven long-term change would not have happened.

Trade-Union Equality Representatives

Short of backing mandatory pay reviews, the WWC in 2006 gave broad support to trade-union equality representatives, which, 'working with employers to support equal pay and opportunity, can resolve problems at the sharp end'.[76] Trade unions, based on their experience and independent evaluations conducted on the work of equality representatives funded by the Union Modernization Fund (UMF), argued that statutory rights to protection from dismissal and ring-fenced time were necessary, primarily to prevent workload pressures driving equality down the agenda.

Early discussions in the WWC had indicated a consensus in favour of statutory rights for union equality representatives, as Prosser told the CIPD's annual conference in November 2005.[77] However, the question of statutory rights ultimately divided commissioners, with the final report leaving the question to the DLR. Prosser knew that the prime minister would not accept a recommendation for statutory rights.[78]

Following the WWC's 2006 report, a further eight union-led projects were initiated to recruit and train 500 equality representatives by 2009, through a dedicated pot within the UMF. An evaluation of the initiative, based on surveys of representatives, found that a majority of representatives reported enhanced expertise and a positive impact of their activity on employer practices, through dialogue and monitoring. However, like earlier evaluations, it noted significant constraints on their activity, owing to the lack of statutory rights for time off for representative duties and for training, particularly as representatives often combined this role with others.[79]

Unions continued to press for statutory rights for representatives and were backed in their demands by women's equality organizations as pressure built to influence the content of the Equality Bill. The first draft of the bill included provision for collective rights to support the work of equality representatives. The WNC, in its assessment of the bill, welcomed the inclusion of these rights in clause 123, dealing with employment tribunals.[80]

Sarah Veale, former head of equality and employment rights at the TUC, reflected 'with hindsight' that unions should have pushed harder for rights for equality representatives when the question was discussed in the WWC. The TUC worked with government on the Equality Bill: 'we even drafted all the clauses on equality reps for them.' However, unions could not persuade the Labour front bench to present the clauses to parliament, and worked instead with Baroness Gibson to introduce them in the House of Lords, 'going in backwards'.[81] Gibson, a former TUC women's officer and former EOC commissioner, argued in favour of equality representatives in the upper house at the bill's second reading in December 2009. Expressing surprise at the lack of government support for equality representatives, Gibson gave notice that she would table an amendment giving them statutory rights. Once the Equality Act came into force, Gibson argued, the work of equality representatives would increase, and they needed rights to dedicated time in order to be effective.[82]

At committee stage, Gibson, supported by Lester and former EOC Commissioner Lord Hunt, argued that equality representatives needed stronger rights in order to carry out their work effectively, referring to a TUC survey that the government had promised to consider. For the government, Baroness Thornton responded that the GEO had held a round table to discuss the TUC report but had been unable to overcome differences of opinion between employers and unions. The amendment was withdrawn. Although Thornton had hinted that action might be possible in the future, the TUC knew that in Veale's words this 'was our last chance, that was last knockings'.[83]

Government opposition to union equality representatives was deep-rooted, despite the TUC's efforts to use the UMF to demonstrate their value in helping employers to avoid expensive and damaging litigation. According to Nita Clarke, Tony Blair's adviser on trade unions from 1997 to 2004, equality representatives were viewed within the prime minister's office as representing sectional interests, rather than the workforce as a whole.[84] They were also seen as forming part of an agenda of collective rights that the TUC and Labour-affiliated unions pushed strongly around the time of the Warwick agreement—for example, in advocating expansion of the bargaining agenda to include pensions and equality. This agenda was strongly opposed by the CBI[85] and helps to explain the hard line taken by the employer organization against statutory rights for equality representatives when the Equality Bill was debated. Moreover, the CBI rejected proposals to allow class actions, and the presentation of the clause on equality representatives alongside that on generic or class actions also hardened the employer position with respect to the former.

The WWC undoubtedly boosted the funding available to train equality representatives at a crucial time, but unions' failure to secure a stronger recommendation on equality representatives meant a missed opportunity to gain statutory rights, which they were unable to recoup when the Equality Bill was presented, because government was unwilling to face down employer opposition on this issue, when it needed to negotiate a way through employer reluctance on other aspects of the bill it deemed more important.

By 2018, around 3,000 union equality representatives were found to be active, a considerable increase since the previous survey carried out in 2010 (which put the number at 600), suggesting that unions were prepared to put resources into this function, even in difficult economic times. However, this remains a small minority of workplaces. In comparison, in 2018 there were over 40,000 union learning representatives, which were given statutory backing by the Labour government.[86]

Conclusion

Campaigners, lawyers working within the tribunal system to support equal-pay claims, and the EOC (the body set up to enforce the equality legislation) and its successor the EHRC, as well as parliamentarians, very quickly saw the limits of British equal-pay law, as discussed in Chapter 4, and set out an agenda for reform. Yet governments showed no willingness to carry out the substantial reform needed either to simplify and accelerate existing procedures, or to establish an alternative means of addressing equal pay proactively. Rather, change has occurred in piecemeal fashion, and sometimes been accompanied by measures restricting access to means of redress. The main initiative reviewed here, included in Labour's Equality Act 2010 and enacted by a Conservative government, is the introduction of the gender pay-gap reporting regulations (2017). Although gender pay-gap reports are publicly available and stimulate public debate on pay equity, the regulations are limited to larger companies, require only basic reporting with no duty regarding remedial actions, and are relatively weakly enforced, although they carry a strong public awareness element by virtue of being published in full on a government website.

As this chapter has shown, reluctance to pursue reform of an inadequate legal framework reflects strong employer resistance. It also indicates an absence of instrumental pressure on political parties throughout the policy cycle, including at agenda-setting stage. Quite simply, reform of equal-pay legislation never found its way into mainstream party programmes. Neil Kinnock, then Labour leader, during a 1992 meeting with Equal Opportunities commissioners (see above, Chapter 4), expressed a view that it was difficult to engage voters with legislative reform. Although public attitudes towards pay inequality have changed, with more men and women acknowledging the gender pay gap as a problem since 2010 and stating that action should be taken to remedy it, they remain divided on the actions to be taken.[87]

Party-political ambivalence has also hampered the work of the equality agencies and created deep and lasting tensions within the regulatory space. At the same time, as this chapter has shown, case law and the policy development work of the EOC (and later, although to a lesser extent, the EHRC) have not only kept pay inequality on the policy agenda but also led to interventions at certain times. As will be discussed further in Chapter 14, these moments of intervention hold important lessons about how change can be achieved, albeit often at the price of dilution of the original objectives or highly circumscribed initiatives. One lesson concerns leadership (or entrepreneurship) by key individuals within the regulatory space: the EOC's effectiveness has often depended on the resourcefulness of its chair. This dependence on political agency is a source of weakness, because individual agency cannot compensate for structural lack of capacity, but it highlights the possibilities created by networking within the wider regulatory space.

Notes

1. Equal-pay claims are the second most common complaint to employment tribunals, representing almost 20% of the total number in 2022. While overall the number of cases at employment tribunals has decreased, for equal pay it has risen continuously. Data are published by the Ministry of Justice: see https://www.gov.uk/government/collections/tribunals-statistics (accessed 18 May 2022).
2. S. Goodley, '29000 Claims a Year despite 50 Years since the Equal Pay Act', *Guardian*, 25 May 2000.
3. A. Bazeley and G. Rosenblatt, *Why Women Need a Right to Know: Shining a Spotlight on Pay Discrimination* (London: Fawcett Society, 2019). Multiple here means discrimination on more than one ground, which grounds then together combine to produce specific forms of discrimination. Today we would use the term 'intersectionality' to describe such situations; I have used the term that was used at the time of discussions leading up to the Equality Bill 2010 and during its passage through parliament. On intersectional pay discrimination, see C. Woodhams, B. Lupton, and M. Cowling, 'The Snowballing Penalty Effect: Multiple Disadvantage and Pay', *British Journal of Management*, 26 (2015), https://doi.org/10.1111/1467-8551.12032.
4. Equality Trust, *UK Gender Pay Gap Reporting 2017–2020: Patterns and Progress* (London: Equality Trust, 2020); Equality Trust, *Unequal Pay: 'The Place where Pay Discrimination is Hiding'* (London: Equality Trust, 2020).
5. M. Oelz, S. Olney, and M. Tomei, *Equal Pay: An Introductory Guide* (Geneva: ILO, 2013), 85.
6. The maxim was originally used to refer to the need for client data, but it has been widely used in the context of workplace equality and diversity.
7. G. Kirton, 'Unions and Equality: 50 Years on from the Fight for Fair Pay at Dagenham', *Employee Relations*, 41 (2019), https://doi.org/10.1108/ER-09-2018-0239.
8. M.-T. Chicha, *A Comparative Analysis of Promoting Pay Equity: Models and Impacts* (London: ILO, 2006), 1.
9. M. Baker and N. M. Fortin, 'Comparable Worth in a Decentralized Labour Market: The Case of Ontario', *Canadian Journal of Economics*, 37 (2004), https://doi.org/10.1111/j.0008-4085.2004.00251.x, p.858.
10. Baker and Fortin, 'Comparable Worth', 859–60.
11. M.-T. Chicha, *A Comparative Analysis of Promoting Pay Equity: Models and Impacts* (London: ILO, 2006).
12. J. A. McDonald and R. Thornton, 'Have Pay Equity Laws in Canada Helped Women? A Synthetic-Control Approach', *American Review of Canadian Studies*, 46 (2016), https://doi.org/10.1080/02722011.2016.1265568.
13. P. Armstrong, 'Back to Basics: Seeking Pay Equity for Women in Canada', *Labour and Industry*, 18 (2007), https://doi.org/10.1080/10301763.2007.10669363, p.27.
14. Interview, Matilda Quiney.
15. Equal Pay Task Force, draft recommendations, November 2000, pp. 1–2: EOC archive, 595 Box 3/3, Modern Records Centre, University of Warwick.
16. F. Neathey, R. Willison, K. Akroyd, J. Regan, and D. Hill, *Equal Pay Reviews in practice* (Manchester: EOC, 2005), 10–12.
17. Neathey et al., *Equal Pay Reviews in Practice*, 42.

18. Neathey et al., *Equal Pay Reviews in Practice*, 43.
19. L. Adams, P. Hall, and S. Schäfer, *Equal Pay Reviews Survey 2008* (IFF/EOC, 2008), p. v.
20. Adams et al., *Equal Pay Reviews Survey 2008*, 80.
21. Adams et al., *Equal Pay Reviews Survey 2008*, 82.
22. WWC, *Shaping a Fairer Future* (London: DTI, 2006), 71.
23. WWC, *Shaping a Fairer Future*, 85–6.
24. Interview, Sarah Anderson.
25. Interview, Quiney.
26. B. Hepple, M. Coussey, and T. Chowdhury, *Equality: A New Framework. Report of the Independent Review of the Enforcement of UK Anti-Discrimination Law* (London: Hart, 2000), 98.
27. Interview, JennyWatson.
28. Personal communication, Matilda Quiney, 30 June 2023.
29. S. Gainsbury, 'Profile Jenny Watson: Opportunity Knocks', *Public Finance*, 2 March 2006, https://www.publicfinance.co.uk/2006/03/profile-jenny-watson-opportunity-knocks (accessed 3 November 2020).
30. House of Commons, 'Oral Evidence Taken before the Business, Innovation and Skills Committee on Tuesday 18 December 2012', HC 754-v, p. 25. https://publications.parliament.uk/pa/cm201213/cmselect/cmbis/c754-v/c75401.htm.
31. Government Equalities Office, 'Equal Pay Act 1970: the questionnaire' (London: HM Government, 2003). The questionnaire was published on the WNC website as well as on the DTI website.
32. WWC, *Shaping a Fairer Future*, 96 (Recommendation 36).
33. WWC, *Shaping a Fairer Future*, 97 (Recommendation 37).
34. House of Commons, *Communities and Local Government: Sixth Report, Session 2006–7* (2007) para. 34.
35. See, e.g., Employment Lawyers Association, 'Response to Consultation: Discrimination Law Review: A Framework for Fairness: Proposals for a Single Equality Bill for Great Britain', 4 September 2007.
36. C. McCrudden, 'Equality Legislation and Reflexive Regulation: A Response to the Discrimination Law Review's Consultative Paper', *Industrial Law Journal*, 36 (2007), https://doi.org/10.1093/indlaw/dwm015.
37. Discrimination Law Review, *A Framework for Fairness* (London: Department of Communities and Local Government, 2007), ch. 3, para. 3.5. Cited by S. Fredman, 'Reforming Equal Pay Laws', *Industrial Law Journal*, 37 (2008), https://doi.org/10.1093/indlaw/dwn008, p.193.
38. McCrudden, 'Equality Legislation and Reflexive Regulation', 258.
39. See S. Milner, 'Gender Equality and Employment Regulation in the New Labour Years, 1997–2010: The Problem of the Gender Pay Gap', *Historical Studies in Industrial Relations*, 43 (2022), https://doi.org/10.3828/hsir.2022.43.5
40. Fredman, 'Reforming Equal Pay Laws', 218.
41. D. Thornton, 'Interview, Harriet Harman' (London: Institute for Government, 2007), 11. In this interview, Harman claimed that campaign organizations had become so 'dulled' by years of having to work to government preferences that she needed to 'shake them up a bit' (p. 12); a similar claim is made in H. Harman, *A Woman's Work* (London: Allen Lane, 2017), 290.

42. S. Hattenstone, 'Ayesha Hazarika: "Who's Labour's Best Drinker? I Couldn't Say"', *Guardian*, 6 July 2016.
43. Personal communication, Quiney, 30 May 2023.
44. Harman, *A Woman's Work*, 295.
45. J. Hand, B. Davis, and P. Feast, 'Unification, Simplification, Amplification? An Analysis of Aspects of the British Equality Act 2010', *Commonwealth Law Bulletin*, 38 (2012), https://doi.org/10.1080/03050718.2012.695001, pp. 523–4.
46. *Bahl* v. *Law Society*, {2004] IWCA Civ 1070; [2004] IRLR 799.
47. Hansard, HC, 'Equality Bill', vol. 495, col. 682 (2 July 2009).
48. Hansard, HC, 'Equality Bill', General Committee Debates, vol. 495, cols 235–48 (17 June 2009).
49. The characteristics covered the range of protected characteristics set out in the Act, apart from pregnancy and maternity and marital status: see B. Hepple, *Equality. The New Framework* (London: Hart, 2011), 62.
50. I. Solanke, 'Putting Race and Gender Together: A New Approach to Intersectionality', *Modern Law Review*, 72 (2009), https://doi.org/10.1111/j.1468-2230.2009.00765.x.
51. Hansard, HC, 'Equality Bill', General Committee Debates, vol. 495, cols 493–7 (25 June 2009).
52. Hansard, HL, Debate on the Equality Bill, vol. 716, cols 965–86 at cols 976–82 (19 January 2010).
53. L. Dickens, 'The Coalition Government's Reforms to Employment Tribunals and Statutory Employment Rights—Echoes of the Past', *Industrial Relations Journal*, 45 (2014), https://doi.org/10.1111/irj.12055. Also in 2013, fees were introduced to take a case to employment tribunals, which together with the longer qualifying period resulted in a steep decline in the number of cases; however, unions successfully challenged the fees order, and the Supreme Court quashed it in July 2017: see D. Pyper, F. McGuinness, and J. Brown, 'Employment Tribunal Fees', House of Commons Briefing Paper 7081 (2017).
54. House of Commons, 'Enterprise and Regulatory Reform Act 2013', C 24 (2013), sect. 98.
55. Hansard, HL, 'Equal Pay and Flexible Working Bill [HL]', vol. 706, cols 1875–1902, at col. 1890 (23 January 2009).
56. Hansard, HC, Equality Bill, vol. 492, cols 553–655, at col. 567 (11 May 2009).
57. 'Equality Act 2010. Explanatory Notes', https://www.legislation.gov.uk/ukpga/2010/15/notes/contents, c.271.
58. P. Ahrens and A. Scheele, 'Game Changers for Gender Equality in Germany's Labour Market? Corporate Board Quotas, Pay Transparency and Temporary Part-Time Work', *German Politics*, 31 (2022), https://doi.org/10.1080/09644008.2021.1984428, 166–7.
59. V. Frey,*Pay Transparency Tools to Close the Gender Wage Gap* (Paris: OECD, 2021).
60. Frey, *Pay Transparency Policies to Close the Gender Wage Gap*; M. Cowper-Coles, M. Glennie, A. Mendes Borges and C. Schmid, *Bridging the gap? An analysis of pay reporting in six countries* (Kings College London, 2021). The Austrian case is also instructive as its regulatory design has been found to be weak—due largely to lack of monitoring and absence of compulsion to publish results, as well as initially high company size thresholds—and therefore to have had little effect: see R. Böheim and S. Gust, *The Austrian pay transparency law and the gender pay gap*, Discussion Papers no.14206 (Bonn: Institute for Labor Economics, 2021).

61. S. Deakin and C. McLaughlin, 'The Regulation of Women's Pay: From Individual Rights to Reflexive Law?', Working Paper No. 350 (University of Cambridge, 2017), 6–8.
62. McCrudden, 'Equality Legislation and Reflexive Regulation', 265–6.
63. See A. Héritier and D. Lehmkuhl, 'The Shadow of Hierarchy and New Modes of Governance', *Journal of Public Policy*, 28 (2008), https://doi.org/10.1017/S0143814X08000755.
64. Interview, Janet Veitch.
65. S. Milner, 'Gender Pay Gap Reporting Regulations: Advancing Gender Equality Policy in Tough Economic Times', *British Politics*, 14 (2019), 121–40.
66. M. Jones and E. Kaya, '*Organisational Gender Pay Gaps in the UK: What Happened Post-Transparency?*', Discussion Paper No. 15342 (Bonn: Institute for Labor Economics, 2022).
67. M. Bennedsen, B. Larsen, and J. Wei, 'Wage Transparency and the Gender Pay Gap: A Survey', Working Paper No. 17-2022 (Copenhagen Business School, 2022).
68. Fawcett Society, *Equal Pay Day 2022: What Does the Gender Pay Gap Mean for Women in the Cost-of-Living Crisis?* (London: Fawcett Society, 2022).
69. EHRC, *Closing the Gender Pay Gap* (London: EHRC, 2018).
70. M. Bailey, S. Glaeser, J. D. Omartian, and A. Raghanundan, 'Misreporting of Mandatory ESG Disclosures: Evidence from Gender Pay Gap Information', SSRN Papers (2022), https://ssrn.com/abstract=4192257 or http://dx.doi.org/10.2139/ssrn.4192257.
71. See Women and Equalities Committee, *Gender Pay Gap*, Second Report of Session 2015–16, HC 584 (House of Commons, 2016). Government foot-dragging on reporting regulations since 2019 marks a break with previous Conservative policy and contradicts my expectations as stated in Milner, 'Gender Pay Gap Reporting Regulations', 136.
72. Women and Equalities Committee, *Ethnicity Pay Gap Reporting*, Fourth Report of Session 2021–2, HC 998 (House of Commons, 2022).
73. CIPD, *Not Just a Number: Lessons from the First Year of Gender Pay Gap Reporting* (London: CIPD, 2019), 3.
74. See G. Kirton, 'Union Framing of Gender Equality and the Elusive Potential of Equality Bargaining in a Difficult Climate', *Journal of Industrial Relations*, 63 (2021), https://doi.org/10.1177/00221856211003604.
75. CIPD, *Inclusion at Work* (London: CIPD, 2022).
76. WWC, *Shaping a Fairer Future*, pp. ix, 71.
77. 'Women and Work Commission Doubts Value of Equal Pay Audits', *Personnel Today*, 1 November 2005, p. 7.
78. Interview, Veitch.
79. N. Bacon and K. Hoque, 'The Role and Impact of Trade Union Equality Representatives in Britain', *British Journal of Industrial Relations*, 50 (2012), 239–62.
80. Women's National Commission, 'Equality Bill: Women's National Commission Position Paper' (January 2010), 5, accessed via Women's National Commission web archive, GEO 3, The National Archives.
81. Interview, Sarah Veale.
82. Hansard, HL, Debate on the Equality Bill, vol. 715, cols 1433–1516, at col. 1471 (15 December 2009).
83. Interview, Veale.
84. Interview, Clarke.
85. See 'Brakes on Employment Reform', *Business Voice* (May 2006), 10–11, at 11.

86. J. Mamode, 'All Together Now? Renewal, Revitalisation and the Trade Union Equality Representative', Ph.D. thesis (University of Warwick, 2019), 121.
87. See, e.g., for example, YouGov survey, 'Gender Pay', fieldwork, December 2021, https://docs.cdn.yougov.com/atcyxs8mi6/Internal_GenderPay_Results_211217_W.pdf (accessed 21 December 2022).

10
The Part-Time Working Penalty and the Undervaluing of Women's Work

Introduction

Part-time employment presents a dilemma to policymakers: it is widely seen as a way of helping parents (particularly mothers) to reconcile work and family life, and therefore helps to boost the employment rate, but it often has negative consequences. It is more likely than full-time employment to have the characteristics of labour-market 'outsiders': precarious or insecure contractual status, poor working conditions, and low pay. It is more likely to be located in specific sectors and occupations, and to be carried out by women and workers at the extremes of the age range.[1] For these reasons, it is a factor of labour-market segmentation and inequality. From a gender perspective, attention to part-time work is essential, because it is female dominated and more likely to be associated with poor working conditions than when carried out by men.[2]

Part-time employment is not always 'bad', of course. High-quality part-time work is characterized by relatively high levels of pay, job security, control over working time and schedules, opportunities for skills training and career progression, and pro-rata access to the same benefits as those available to full-time employees,[3] such as measures to help them balance work and family life (such as leave for parents). It may also include the possibility of increasing hours if desired—for example, to suit changing family care needs.[4] Part-time jobs vary, and they can combine good and bad characteristics.[5] There is evidence that part-time work forms two broad types, which are dependent on socio-economic status: 'good' jobs, where conditions are aligned with those of full-time employment, and 'bad' jobs, where the part-time workforce has little time autonomy or job security and pay is low.[6] Women form the majority of those in 'bad' part-time jobs, and they are less likely than men to have access to 'good' part-time jobs.

Regulation can affect the incidence of part-time employment, by influencing decisions on both the supply and the demand sides, and it can

Women and Employment in Public Policy. Susan Milner, Oxford University Press. © Susan Milner (2024).
DOI: 10.1093/9780191987359.003.0010

have an impact on the degree of inequality between full-time and part-time employees. By legislating for minimum hours and minimum wages, the state can limit the precarious conditions suffered by many part-time workers.[7] By regulating the contractual status of part-time employees, providing social protection in the form of childcare and welfare benefits, and ensuring access to training opportunities, the state can influence the choices made by women about whether to work full-time or part-time. Differences in regulatory approaches help to explain cross-national variation in the incidence of part-time work.[8]

In the British case, in 2019, 38.1 per cent of employed women worked part-time. This represents only a small decrease since 1997, when the figure stood at 43 per cent.[9] Around 80 per cent of part-time workers are women, a proportion that has remained stable. The high proportion of female part-time working, in comparison to other European countries, is explained by three broad, interrelated factors. The first is cultural: attitudinal resistance to women working after marriage and childbirth remained strong throughout the twentieth century.[10] Part-time employment for women was designed initially to meet temporary labour shortages during wartime and the post-war years (with minimum disruption of the sexual division of labour in the workplace and home).[11]

This particular 'gender contract'[12] allowed married women into the labour market but on a limited and secondary basis, perpetuating the idea of male breadwinners and female caregivers. The deliberate policy choice of expanding women's employment opportunities through part-time work effectively created a dual labour market, which, once in operation, became embedded in the regulatory space, including in employment relations practice.[13] Although women's full-time employment rose from the 1980s, part-time employment remained largely segregated by gender, despite the spread of male part-time employment from the 1990s.

The second, related reason is constraints caused by the affordability and accessibility of childcare provision, as discussed in Chapter 11. Lack of available childcare to fit around full-time or variable working hours is probably the strongest obstacle to women's career progression, in a country with among the most expensive childcare places in the world. Post-war policymakers in seeking to increase women's part-time employment explicitly rejected childcare provision to support female wage-earners.[14]

The third relates to employers' labour-market behaviour: part-time working is a major source of employer-driven flexibility and is used extensively in service sectors that employ large proportions of women.[15] This approach was initially encouraged by the British state, which exempted those working very low hours (less than sixteen per week) from the main provisions of employment legislation, such as protection against dismissal. In the 1980s, women's part-time working hours peaked at just under sixteen. Even when in 1986 the government proposed raising the threshold for employment protection (including from redundancy after childbirth) to twenty per week, those working for the same employer for less than two years (the great majority of part-time women) were excluded.[16]

As Sylvia Walby testified to the House of Commons Select Committee on Education and Employment in March 1998,

> Part-time work in Britain has become equated with relatively casual work, in which the employer can vary the hours of those workers as they choose; and that type of flexibility has often been seen as of benefit to an employer. Now that is not a necessary consequence of working part-time but has been a contingent feature of most of the development of part-time working in Britain.[17]

Part-time working is associated, in the British context, with lower-than-average wages as well as with employment insecurity, while higher-paying jobs are characterized by long hours and presenteeism. Jill Rubery and colleagues have shown that part-time working is defined in relation to the full-time norm, and, if full-time work is increasingly defined by results or organizational norms rather than reference to a fixed number of hours, it becomes defined primarily in relation to its indeterminacy and peripheral status.[18] As Rubery argues, 'it just seems to me absolutely essential that you can't have quality part time jobs if quality full-time jobs involve very long hours or uncertain hours'.[19] Policymakers have, however, been unwilling to view part-time working as a structural feature of the British labour market, let alone challenge its status.

The way in which employment is regulated in the UK directly affects the supply of part-time jobs, and indirectly also recognizes and embeds it (for example, by providing top-up tax credits or welfare benefits that effectively acknowledge below-subsistence wages). Part time working in the UK, therefore, often takes the form of extremely marginal, insecure employment that falls below the threshold for access to rights such as maternity and paternity leave, or even paid sick leave. The growth of zero-hours contracts exemplifies this trend towards extreme forms of employer-driven flexibility.

Owing to the low pay, insecurity, and low status of part-time working and the working hours gap between men and women, part-time employment is structurally central to the undervaluation of women's economic contribution. Susan Harkness's 1996 analysis of women's pay relative to men's showed that women working full-time and those working part-time had similar levels of qualification but that those working part-time had significantly lower rates of pay. In 1993, the mean hourly pay of female part-time workers was equal to 63 per cent of that of men, whereas female full-timers had started to close the pay gap in relation to their male counterparts.[20] Women working part-time were older than those in full-time employment, reflecting the impact of childbearing years on employment status, and they were more likely to remain in their jobs for longer, suggesting constraints on changes in work schedules.

In this chapter, I review debates on part-time working during the Labour years and show how they led to greater awareness of its low status and its gendered nature, but to very limited policy solutions, owing to conflicts over the extent of regulation. The chapter focuses on the way in which these debates played out in the Women and Work Commission (WWC) and in the years following its recommendations. Finally, it considers why the question of part-time working has proved so difficult to address in policy.

The 1990s: The New Policy Salience of Part-Time Work

The question of part-time working became politically salient in the period of New Labour government, owing partly to its growth but mainly to pressure from European legislation, which in turn was influenced by the International Labour Organization's (ILO) Convention on Part-Time Work (adopted in 1994 and in force from 1998).[21] Between 1989 and 1998, the number of part-time employees (defined as those working fewer than thirty hours per week) rose from 24 per cent to 29 per cent of all British jobs, accounting for the majority of new posts.[22] In retail and accommodation, the proportion stood at 58 per cent and 60 per cent respectively in 1999, in line with the share of female employment in those industries.[23] Female part-time working was a counterpart to male working cultures of long hours, with over three-quarters of full-time employees reporting that long hours were expected in their organization.[24] MPs therefore agreed in 1999 that 'discussions about part-time work are at the centre of the current debate about the future of work'.[25]

The ILO's Convention no. 175 sought both to encourage part-time working and to prevent the development of a two-tier workforce, reflecting conflicts within the ILO between a desire to stimulate employment and a wish to protect labour standards. The text resulting from intense negotiations between employer and trade-union representatives was a compromise that upheld the principle of equal treatment of part-time and full-time workers, but neglected structural disadvantage by including only basic pay (excluding bonuses and access to overtime payments, where there is a significant gap in favour of men) and referring to the same or similar work, rather than work of equal value (which applies to ILO conventions on sex discrimination and equal pay).[26]

Similarly, the European Union's (EU) policy sought to encourage part-time working by normalizing it, and at the same time to challenge the culture of long hours that entrenched the divide between long full-time hours (usually worked by men) and short part-time hours (usually worked by women). Beneath this basic rationale lay several policy tensions. The commission had sought to reconcile contradictory positions on labour-market regulation, with trade unions, the European Parliament, and some countries like France preferring to reduce working time, and other countries and the employer lobby rejecting minimum standards or maximum limits. By adopting the 'social-partner' route for discussion of the proposals, it sought to manage the conflict. The result was a compromise text that emphasized individual choice and flexibility and left aside social-justice claims.[27] The directive based on the social-partner agreement was an exceptionally weak instrument, including many qualifying terms that effectively limited part-timers' recourse to it.[28]

Despite this weakness, the Part-Time Work directive was resisted by John Major's Conservative government. Labour's pledge to transpose it had formed an important part of the party's claim to be women friendly in 1992, as we saw in Chapter 5. But, in transposing the text as a legal obligation rather than as an active choice, the Labour government selected a minimalist interpretation in line with the promise made in the 1997 manifesto to implement European legislation in a light-touch way.[29] The transposition of the directive in the Part-Time Workers (Prevention of Less Favourable Treatment) Regulations adopted in 2000, with effect from July 2002, gave a broad definition of part-time work (not restricted to those regarded as employees and therefore also including those in casual and seasonal employment) and therefore had potentially far-reaching significance for the approximately six million part-time workers in Britain.[30] However, in line with British employment law, enforcement depended on individual claims to employment tribunals for discrimination, which in turn relied on comparison between full-time and part-time work for the same job, whereas part-time jobs are often located in highly specific sectors and occupations, making it difficult to prove comparability.[31]

Owing to occupational segregation, the need for a full-time comparator effectively excluded most part-time workers from the benefit of the regulations. Government explicitly chose a narrow definition of discrimination to cover part-timers working alongside full-timers in the same role, leaving to one side the problem of the structural features of part-time employment.[32] Indeed, the new regulations aimed at ensuring fair treatment of part-time workers offered a less effective remedy than the Sex Discrimination Act already provided. In 1981, Brenda Clarke, who worked part-time in a munitions factory, had successfully claimed that it was discriminatory for the employer to negotiate with unions a deal whereby part-time workers would be made redundant first.[33]

The question of regulation of part-time employment became politically charged, as trade unions and feminist campaigners, on the one hand, pushed for stronger rights for women part-timers, and trade unions advocated tighter regulation of working hours, while, on the other, employers' organizations sought to block regulatory moves. When parliament debated the implementation of the directive, the Confederation of British Industry (CBI) spokespeople made clear that they opposed any attempt to regulate conditions of part-time workers, as part-time employment for them constituted a key form of employer-oriented flexibility, with an emphasis on weak contractual security and employee control over hours.[34]

Nevertheless, in some business and policy circles it was acknowledged that low pay and poor career prospects of part-timers was not only a social-justice issue but a contributory factor to weak productivity. The 1999 White Paper on Fairness at Work, which put forward proposals on regulating the labour market and employment relations, did not mention part-time working but acknowledged regulatory problems caused by the growth of zero-hours contracts in female-dominated sectors such as healthcare, retail, and catering. The government did not, however, propose legislation to curb the growth of such contracts, which it said provided welcome flexibility; instead, it argued, the new statutory minimum wage and the transposition of the working time directive would prevent the worst abuses.[35]

Transposition of the Working Time Directive generated further conflict. Even more than the Part-Time Work Directive, the need to transpose European legislation raised awareness of the social problems still caused by weak regulation, but it resulted in minimalist regulations and conflicts over implementation. The UK had no previous tradition of significant regulation of working time, which was instead left to collective bargaining. As a result, employers in the private and public sectors relied on long working hours, with overtime often weakly regulated or enforced, particularly since the dismantling of wage councils and in the context of declining collective bargaining. However, this alone could not explain governments' resistance to European-derived legislation, which was ideologically embedded.[36]

The complexity of the regulations, with their qualifying clauses, exceptions, and opt-outs, made it easier for employers to evade compliance, particularly in sectors with low union membership (typically casualized, low-pay sectors), and it also caused difficulties of interpretation more generally, resulting in increased recourse to employment tribunals.[37] British opt-outs from sections of the European directive, negotiated by Major, were under review by the commission (along with those of other countries) during the period of the Labour government, with unions pushing for full implementation and an end to exemptions. The CBI, on the other hand, resisted any extension of the regulations; it criticized the 'ill-crafted directive'[38] but accepted its transposition as long as the opt-outs were retained. This long-running tension kept the regulation of working time a live political issue and opened up the policy debates, without resolving them.

The Part-Time Work Directive referred to the need for men and women to have access to part-time work in order to reconcile work and family life, although it fell short of giving parents a substantive right to variation of contract. The UK regulations that transposed the directive left out this possibility, but campaigners called for its introduction. The parliamentary select committee on Education and Employment in March 1999 argued that further action was needed to strengthen the rights of women, particularly mothers, and recommended

> that the Government introduce legislation guaranteeing women the right to return to work after maternity leave on a part-time basis, whilst retaining their right to transfer to full-time work, unless the employer is able to demonstrate that it would be to the detriment of the operation of the employer's business.[39]

This demand gathered steam in the debates around working time sparked by both European directives, and it led the Department of Education and Employment—and later the Department of Trade and Industry (DTI)—to establish a working group to examine possible legislation. However, the CBI's resistance to regulation included opposition to any employee rights to shift from full-time to part-time work: 'Employers should have flexibility and have the discussion and try to reach a resolution of each individual issue in a way that makes sense for us, the employer, and then the employee... [That] is really the way forward.'[40] The result, as discussed further in Chapter 11, was the right to request flexible working, which was introduced in the Employment Act 2002.

By shifting the terms of the regulatory initiative from working time reduction to temporal flexibility, the DTI had narrowed the question of why women are disproportionately located in casualized, low-pay sectors. The lack of quality part-time jobs formed part of the situation of labour-market disadvantage in which many women found themselves: unable to adapt their working hours after return from maternity leave, many left their post and sought part-time jobs elsewhere, usually at a lower rate of pay and with fewer progression prospects; some left the labour market entirely. In theory, the right to request changes to work schedules, if sufficiently strongly designed to be enforceable in practice, could therefore help to reduce the earnings gap between men and women in the middle of the wage distribution, just as the national minimum wage was about to do for those employed at the bottom of the pay scale.

However, the right to request flexible working did not result in a significant decrease in gender segregation within or between occupations. Two main reasons for this were put forward in the early years of the right's operation: uneven application, with the right more commonly accepted in large organizations and associated with stable employment; and a 'flexibility stigma' owing to the gendered nature of take-up.[41] More women than men requested changes to hours, and men when adopting flexible hours were more likely to use remote working or flexitime, whereas women were more likely to use reduced hours.[42] Overall, the right to request flexible working initially had relatively little take-up, despite evidence of a widespread demand for changed hours, because it followed the grain of existing organizational practices and was subject to business needs.[43] Moreover, the emphasis on flexibility did not tackle the long-hours culture, which is also gendered; indeed, it may have exacerbated it.[44]

Understanding Part-Time Employment: The Evidence Base

An important feature of the policy space in the first decade of the new millennium was a strong evidence base establishing the characteristics and drivers of women's part-time employment, commissioned by the women's policy (Women's Equality Unit (WEU), and later the Government Equalities Office (GEO)) and equality (Equal Opportunities Commission (EOC)) machineries. The WWC's 2006 report referred to four pieces of research in particular. The first, by Alan Manning and Barbara Petrongolo for the WEU in 2004, investigated the 26 per cent earnings gap between women working full-time and those working part-time. Using Labour Force Survey Data, Manning and Petrongolo showed that the occupational segregation of women into low-paid occupations explained a very large part of this gap, which had widened over the previous fifty years. Women in professional jobs tended to be downgraded into lower-paying jobs when they shifted to part-time hours after childbirth.[45] Manning and Petrongolo, in presenting their work to the WWC in November 2004, compared the British situation to other countries, concluding that 'the UK does seem to have a particular problem with downward occupational mobility among part-time women'.[46] They concluded that any policy that did not address occupational segregation would fail to tackle the pay gap between part-time and full-time work.

The second study, by Linda Grant, Sue Yeandle, and Lisa Buckner for the EOC in 2005, took a localized, qualitative approach to the same problem, and showed how women trapped in part-time, low-status jobs lost confidence in their ability to progress and lacked opportunities to gain skills and qualifications. Managers not only overlooked these women's abilities but saw part-time work as intrinsically low skilled. The study demonstrated that part-time employment, rather than a choice, was due to the lack of affordable childcare and the absence of better-paid, higher-skilled jobs in their local labour market. Their recommendations focused on the need for better skills training opportunities for women, and actions to encourage employers to open up a wider range of jobs with part-time hours, in line with the 2001 Kingsmill report.[47]

The third piece of influential research from this period, by Katherine Rake, Hugh Davies, and Heather Joshi, with Randa Alami, for the Women's Unit in 2000, modelled women's income over the lifetime. It showed a marked gap between women's and men's lifetime incomes at the level of low-skilled and mid-skilled jobs, with a smaller gap for higher-qualified women, beyond any gap attributable to motherhood. They attributed the income gap to the length of time women in lower-skilled jobs spent working part-time following childbirth.[48]

A fourth piece of research contributed significantly to the WWC's broader analysis of the gender pay gap, and also provided insights into the impact of part-time working. Harkness's analysis (see above) showed that, although women's average earnings had increased, this improvement was not commensurate with their levels of education and training. Younger women had similar earnings to men with equivalent qualifications, but the earnings gap between men and women grew with age and was associated with the presence of children in the household. Women working part-time had also seen less improvement in their earnings relative to men's than had those working full-time.[49] A large part of this gap for part-time women could be explained by lower education levels, relative to women working full-time, but there also appeared to be a wider link between part-time working and low pay, linked to its sectoral location.[50]

Finally, Jill Rubery in evidence presented to the WWC, based on comparative European research, emphasized the association between women's part-time work and lack of childcare provision, alongside the long hours expected of many full-time jobs. Consequently, Rubery argued, part-time jobs, more often than in other European countries, are 'found in specific enclaves, designed as part-time jobs to meet the flexibility demands of employers, instead of being "reduced hours jobs" within standard full-time job areas'.[51]

Taken together, this body of research showed that the policy problem of part-time work had two main elements. The first comprised the lack of availability of 'quality' part-time jobs in professional and managerial occupations. The main policy intervention to address this problem was the right for parents of small children to request flexible working, which, as researchers noted, was weakly framed and subject to employers' assessment of business needs. The second element was the persistence of a sizeable secondary labour market where women part-timers found themselves trapped in low-paid jobs with few or no routes into better-paid jobs or longer hours.

The WWC: How to Address the Part-Time Work Penalty

As well as the academic evidence, many submissions from trade unions to the WWC focused on the case for better-quality part-time jobs.[52] First Division (the union for senior managers and professionals in public services) highlighted the negative impact of a long-hours culture in the civil service and the lack of senior women role models, while the Society of Personnel Officers in Local Government (SOCPO)) told of presenteeism in male-dominated organizational cultures that did not tolerate flexible work schedules.[53] The Trades Union Congress (TUC), based on evidence from affiliated unions, argued that women in the workplace found it difficult to secure reduced hours to fit childcare.[54]

The commission's interim report published in March 2005 (before the written submissions had been analysed) therefore focused on the part-time pay gap, measured as a 43.2 per cent difference in median hourly pay of men working full-time compared to women working part-time (40.3 per cent mean). Moreover, the pay gap between women working full-time and women working part-time was increasing.[55] Already commissioners had concluded that 'we need to address the lack of availability of "quality" part-time work'.[56]

The 2006 report followed the same line, citing a pay gap between female part-time workers and male full-time workers of 41 per cent in 2005. Asking why women worked part-time, it observed that they were more likely to do so when they had children.[57] The report also noted an association between working hours and vertical segregation: 'Many women who gave evidence cited the lack of quality part-time work as being a major barrier to taking on senior roles.[58] However, having identified part-time working as a major driver of gender pay inequity, the commission was divided on how policy should deal with it. Sarah Anderson, representing small businesses, felt that it was too simplistic to focus on the gendered nature of part-time work:

> One of the things that I was rather more controversial about was to do with part-time work, and to do with the fact that women so often choose part-time work to fit in with their childcaring arrangements, [but as to] to what extent it was a factor of part-time work as opposed to gender ... when you start with the overall numbers they're not necessarily very helpful.[59]

This showed a fundamental difference in approach from the trade-union position, which was to see the part-time pay gap as a structurally gendered problem calling for actions to strengthen regulation of labour markets. For example, the TUC in its submission called for a stronger right to request flexible working, making it more difficult for employers to reject requests, and authorizing closer government monitoring of requests and their outcomes. Its call was not taken up by the commission, although the report echoed the TUC's argument that better training for line managers and union representatives could help not just to promote awareness of the right to request flexible working, but to give unions more power to oversee it in the workplace.

Instead, the commission went along with Anderson's view that more could be done to use the example of good employers to persuade others to adopt a more flexible approach to individual employee requests: 'I've always thought it's about working with the grain and not against it, and therefore you have to look at what people want to do, and how can we help them to do that, and what's their motivation.'[60]

John Cridland was keen to develop the quality part-time work agenda, but within the specific context of higher-paid jobs:

> The thing that I banged on the table for was, you have to have some recommendations which will facilitate higher-paid part-time work. Why do these higher responsibility roles have to be done full-time? Is it essential, is it inevitable? Can it be done more flexibly? And that was tough. That was where, in a sense, employers

did dig in their heels a bit. If it was a high value-added employee, they wanted her or him full-time.[61]

This necessarily meant in his view recommendations for pilot work that could be carried out by those employers willing to take the agenda forward:

> You're trying to set out good practice, you're trying to pilot things, you're trying to encourage things and you're trying to facilitate things. ... There were some very good people on the commission, people like Sally Hopson, then at Asda, who were prepared to pilot things, to show things could be done differently. That's the best we could do. ... I think the pilot on quality part-time work was the right thing to do, but it was a bit of an underwhelming proposal. It wasn't going to change the world. We just couldn't identify a better way of moving things forward at that time.[62]

Diane Houston, the WWC's academic adviser, saw the commission's reluctance to view part-time work as a structural problem, partly as the result of more conservative voices on the commission, but also as a reflection of a wider concern in New Labour circles not to question business practices:

> There were things that kept emerging. For example, I remember there was a discussion about supermarkets and how the government is essentially subsidizing them, large multinationals, through the benefits system, because they won't pay a living wage. I felt this was part of the discussion we needed to have. But there was political sensitivity about expanding on this and a hesitancy to examine things at a more fundamental level.[63]

The WWC took the question of part-time work seriously: it devoted much of its investigational time to it, and the two main spending recommendations responded to its findings. In its recommendations, the commission addressed two aspects of part-time work: first, 'quality' part-time work; second, low-paid jobs. The commission saw the former as driving the latter: 'Those looking for part-time work crowd into a narrow range of lower-paying occupations due to a lack of quality part-time jobs.'[64] The WWC made two main recommendations. First, it urged the DTI to

> establish a UK-wide Quality Part-Time Work Change Initiative of £5 million to support new initiatives aimed at achieving a culture change, so that more senior jobs—particularly in the skilled occupations and the professions—are more open to part-time and flexible working. This should start from junior management level upwards, and include the roles considered 'stepping stones' to senior management.[65]

Second, the commission recommended government sponsorship of a network of 'best-practice' employers, along the lines of Opportunity Now. This approach implicitly acknowledged employer resistance to aligning full-time and part-time work and aimed to incite cultural change through pilot initiatives. Indeed, the 2006 report referred to the Parliamentary Select Committee on Trade and Industry, which had in 2005 found evidence of hostile attitudes among employers to part-time work for highly paid roles.[66] Pilot initiatives were intended to break down such attitudes by providing evidence of the benefits of change, but exhortatory measures would necessarily take many years to have an impact.

Exhortatory and capacity-building measures were thought by government ministers to be more effective than legislative intervention (authority measures), as Meg Munn, the minister responsible for implementing the WWC's report, highlighted:

> I'd say that a problem generally in politics, and with the Prime Minister's Delivery Unit and all of that, they want big high-profile things that they think are really going to make a difference, but the reality is with all this stuff that it isn't big high-profile things that make a difference, it's working away at lots and lots of little issues, over a long period, which change culture. That's what makes a difference.[67]

The second dimension of part-time work investigated by the WWC was its close relationship with occupational segregation: 'Lower rates of pay for part-time work are linked to general lower rates of pay in those sectors offering the most part-time opportunities.'[68] Here the main solution was seen as improving career progression through better training opportunities. As will be discussed in Chapter 12, the commission wanted to see the recently launched vocational training programme, Train to Gain, focus on women in the low-paid female-dominated sectors (often referred to as the five Cs: catering, cleaning, cashiering, clerical, and caring), particularly those working part-time, with the provision of free Level 3 training. Again, the report referred to the practice of exemplary employers, in particular Tesco, which provided in-house training to fit employees' working hours, including those on part-time contracts.[69]

When the WWC's report was published, it came under fire for its cautious approach. Manning, the economist who had presented his research on part-time working to commissioners, argued that, without a clear understanding of why women were held back in their careers (including, for example, why more men than women are promoted to high-level positions), funding to promote organizational efforts in favour of 'quality' part-time jobs would have little effect: 'The Women and Work Commission is right to recommend that more should be done to open up high-level jobs to flexible working arrangements. But it is not very specific about what should be done.'[70] Manning asserted that the focus on high-quality part-time jobs also left aside the wider question of why so many women are trapped in low-paid employment in particular sectors characterized by low pay.

Implementation: How to Improve the Quality of Part-Time Jobs

As outlined in Chapter 8, the lack of strong government champions weakened the impact of the relatively modest initiatives recommended by the WWC. The recommended £5 million funding to run the Quality Part-Time Jobs initiative resulted in an allocation by the Treasury of £500,000, around half of which was spent on twelve projects selected for initial funding. These included two campaign/consultancy organizations working with employers to promote flexible and a small recruitment company specializing in flexible working; two large local authorities; a large regional police force; a medical professional organization; a youth training charity and an adult education association; Royal Mail (then a public company); and just one private-sector company, the multinational food manufacturer Kelloggs.[71] Of the twelve projects, evaluation found that only two organizations had successfully responded to employees' needs for reduced or flexible hours, and these were the large local authorities. The lack of private-sector participation in the initiative, despite the 2006 report's emphasis on exemplar employers, severely undermined it. Few concrete lessons emerged from the initiative to be taken forward by policymakers.

In the commission's 2009 follow-up report, disappointment was expressed that the Quality Part-Time Jobs initiative had not led further. 'The lack of quality part-time work should be a key focus for Government action in future,' stated the report.[72] Disappointment was also expressed that the government had not done more actively to promote flexible working through specific information activities and support for businesses.

In the area of working hours and working time flexibility, a general sense of disappointment pervades the 2009 report. The commission's faith in the capacity of voluntary actions to generate long-term cultural change, which was underpinned by the exemplar scheme, had largely been frustrated, and actions remained limited to a handful of leading companies such as BT. Whereas the commission had in 2006 suggested many ways in which government could help to support voluntary business action, such as through training provision and business support, Munn had worked hard to promote business initiatives through her speeches and visits, but little or no concrete support measures had been established. As previously discussed, a common theme in many interviews was a feeling of regret that the commission's recommendations simply got lost and there was no top-level follow-up to keep them on track. Adeeba Malik, for example, expressed this regret:

> I think ... that it was a really substantial piece of work that unfortunately just didn't continue in the way that I thought it was going to continue. Which is, maybe give it life for four or five years in terms of making some of the changes. Because a lot of it does not happen in one year. ... I think that momentum was lost.[73]

Cridland, the chief advocate of recommendations on quality part-time work within the commission, also expressed disappointment at the scale of the response:

> An awful lot of these government initiatives ... there has to be some action, it has to lead to something, let's get a small pot of money and set up a pilot. And quite often, to be honest, those things do not necessarily lead to major change, they don't get multiplied, they don't get developed, because public policy moves on so fast, ministers move on, there's another [Comprehensive Spending Review].[74]

Consequently, as Malik reflected, the same problems exist today, both the question of high-quality part-time work and in particular the problem of low-paid part-time work:

> We're seeing more women running organizations. I think the lower end are the ones that need the most support. ... They might have part-time jobs, they're very often getting jobs they don't like doing, but they're doing it to bring money into the house. Now what is it that's being done to help them and support them and make sure they have their rights, they are protected, they have opportunities? ... And you know what? They're making up a huge percentage of our work market.[75]

The Continued Problem of Part-Time Employment

By 2010, the gap between the pay of women working part-time and men working full-time still stood at 39.4 per cent (down from 43.2 per cent when the WWC started).[76] Progress after 1993 (when it stood at 63 per cent) appeared to result mainly from the introduction of the national minimum wage, which, thanks to the transposed EU directive on part-time work, was applicable to part-time workers as well as those employed full-time. Since then, no policy initiatives have made significant inroads on the part-time working penalty.

The gender part-time employment gap narrowed after 2000. Linked to the spread of insecure low-hours contracts, male part-time employment rose from 8.5 per cent of total employment in 2000 to 11.6 per cent in 2010 and 11.4 per cent in 2020. As women's part-time employment fell slowly but steadily over the same period, the gender gap in part-time employment decreased from 32.2 per cent in 2000 to 27.1 per cent in 2010 and 23.1 per cent in 2020.[77] This change sets the UK apart from two other countries with high part-time employment rates, Netherlands and Switzerland, where part-time work is more heavily gendered, and closer to the conservative welfare states of Germany and Japan. It indicates higher numbers of women in full-time employment, as might be expected from rising levels of female educational attainment, but it also reflects the normalization of 'bad' part-time employment and the entrenchment of the gendered dual labour market.

An indicator of the quality of part-time employment is rates of pay in relation to full-time remuneration. This shows that part-timers' median hourly pay has risen in relation to full-time employees but remains significantly below the full-time rate, at 69 per cent of the full-time median rate (60 per cent in 2000). The gender pay gap for part-time employment reverses the full-time pattern, with women earning on average 4 per cent more than male part-timers.[78] Unlike the full-time gender pay gap in favour of men, which has narrowed since 2000, the slight part-time gender pay gap in favour of women has increased but only by a tiny amount. Overall, women's over-representation in the part-time workforce still explains a significant part of the gender pay gap. Female part-time employment remains predominantly located in the five Cs.[79]

The main policy change in the period since 2010 is the extension in 2014 of the right to request flexible working (discussed in Chapter 11), and ongoing policy debates about its further extension. While the right to request flexible working has evidently allowed many working mothers to gain more flexibility in their working hours, and remain in full-time employment, this change has mostly occurred in the public sector.[80] Case law shows that several organizations still see full-time working as the norm and resist considering how full-time jobs could be adapted to suit the needs of parents. In September 2021, British Airways (the leading employer in the Quality Part-Time Jobs initiative) was found to have discriminated against a senior in-flight manager working for its CityFlyer service, by rejecting her request for reduced hours following the birth of her daughter in 2017; the company had 'barely engaged' with her request, the tribunal judge found, and was unable to provide evidence that it ever responded favourably to requests for flexible hours for childcare reasons.[81]

Such cases have become increasingly frequent. Even after the Covid-19 pandemic, which saw an unprecedented shift to remote and flexible forms of working for many employees, the campaign organization Timewise noted in its annual index of flexible working practices that many employers still resist requests to reduce working hours, and that part-time working remains primarily a characteristic of the low-paid, peripheral workforce.[82]

Conclusion

The question of how to improve women's part time work remains an important one, and, as the WWC found, it raises a substantial set of policy issues. As observed in this chapter, it resulted during the Labour years from external adaptive pressure, from the ILO and more directly from the EU's Part-Time Work Directive. The policy environment was favourable to those seeking to gain attention for the issue, because Labour had signed up to the inclusion of European social and employment policy in the Amsterdam Treaty (marking a break with the approach of the previous Conservative administration), albeit in a 'light-touch' way that limited the impact of transposition, and because a wider range of civil-society actors had access to decision-makers. European case law also embedded in British law the principle of indirect discrimination, which allowed women to challenge worse conditions for part-time than full-time workers.

In the context of the UK's withdrawal from the EU, and of government by a Conservative party that has consistently resisted EU-derived social and employment rights, rights for part-time workers have received less policy attention since 2010. There is even a risk of loss of existing anti-discrimination protection should derived rights be revoked.[83] While policy attention has been directed to extreme forms of contractual and temporary flexibility such as zero-hours contracts, there has been little attempt to regulate their use or to understand how structural inequalities in the labour market are exacerbated by it.

Matthew Taylor's 2017 report on 'Good Work' recognized the disproportionate impact of low and uncertain hours on women's pay and progression, and framed policy discussion in terms of a need to improve the quality of work for all. The Taylor report also advocated stronger protection against maternity discrimination and measures to increase the number of young women in male-dominated apprenticeships, and urged government to look at ways of boosting productivity in the (female-dominated) sectors of retail, care, and hospitality.[84] Labour opposition MPs Dan Jarvis[85] and Yasmin Qureshi tabled private members' bills in 2022 to strengthen rights of workers against maternity discrimination and to extend the right to request flexible working, respectively, and the Conservative government announced support for both bills, which enabled them to pass through parliament. These initiatives constitute partial adoption of the agenda set out by the Taylor report, which recognized many of the problems associated with 'bad' part-time work.

At a more fundamental level, the UK's distinctive use of women's part-time labour raises questions about why women find themselves so often in the position of having to take whichever part-time positions are available to them. In the UK, comparative analysis indicates that part-time working is overwhelmingly explained by observable characteristics, in particular educational level and childcare responsibilities.[86] Better childcare would, therefore, constitute a significant policy response to this question. Investment in training opportunities could also help women in 'bad' part-time work to move into better jobs, but it has never been systematically pursued in the UK.[87]

Another way would be to look at why, nearly twenty years after the introduction of a right to request flexible working, governments have not succeeded in taking up the challenge posed in the WWC's 2009 follow-up report to investigate thoroughly the reasons why employment tribunals still find that leading employers are not taking requests seriously. Although, as discussed in Chapter 11, the right to request was extended with effect from April 2014, current gaps in implementation highlight the weaknesses of the approach underpinning the right to request flexible working, and it raises an overarching question about how best to change business practices, which is taken up in the concluding chapter of this book.

The wider issue of job quality, which came back onto the agenda after the G20's Ankara declaration in 2015, and again in the context of the Covid-19 pandemic, remains to be addressed. Recent research has suggested that women's increased full-time employment between 2008 and 2019 is largely a result of having fewer children, rather than having better choices at work.[88] This seems a tenuous basis on which to drive labour-market change and a painfully slow route towards greater equality between men and women. Job insecurity has risen, while poor work–life balance is likely to result in poor mental and physical health outcomes.[89] Instead, available evidence indicates that improving job quality requires top-level ministerial commitment to set the framework for employer practice, through enforcement actions (by investigating abuses and taking action to stop them), investment in the training infrastructure, standard-setting as an exemplary employer in the public sector (including through the use of public procurement), and the promotion of good practice in the private sector, including through regulation.[90]

Finally, the British case has shown the importance of the national minimum wage but also suggested that it could do more to improve the purchasing power of the low paid.[91] This observation chimes with Jill Rubery's argument, presented to the WWC in 2004, that the institutions of pay-setting need to be reformed to make them fairer and more adapted to the contemporary labour market.[92] As Heather Joshi and colleagues note in their investigation of the gender pay gap, a sectoral approach to wage regulation could help to bring the pay of those with the least bargaining power into line with the average.[93]

Notes

1. L. Vosko, *Managing at the Margins: Gender, Social Citizenship and the International Economy* (Oxford: Oxford University Press, 2010).
2. J. Tomlinson, 'Part-Time Occupational Mobility in the Service Industries: Regulation, Work Commitment and Occupational Closure', *Sociological Review*, 54 (2006), https://doi.org/10.1111/j.1467-954X.2006.00602.x.
3. H. Nicolaisen, H. C. Kavli, and R. S. Jensen, 'Introduction', in H. Nicolaisen, H. C. Kavli, and R. S. Jensen (eds), *Dualisation of Part-Time Work. The Development of Labour Market Insiders and Outsiders* (Bristol: Policy Press, 2019), 20–46, at 25.
4. C. Lyonette, B. Baldauf, and H. Behle, *Quality Part-Time Work: A Review Of the Evidence* (London: GEO, 2010).
5. Nicolaisen et al., 'Introduction', 29.
6. T. Warren and C. Lyonette, 'Good, Bad and Very Bad Part-Time Jobs: Re-Examining the Importance of Social Class for Job Quality since the "Great Recession" in the UK', *Work, Employment & Society*, 32 (2018), https://doi.org/10.1177/0950017018762289.
7. J. Rubery, D. Grimshaw, P. Méhaut, and C. Weinkopf, 'Dualisation and Part-Time Work in France, Germany and the UK: Accounting for Between And Within Country Differences in Precarious Work', *European Journal of Industrial Relations* (2022), https://doi.org/10.1177/09596801221120468.
8. E. Bardasi and J. C. Gornick, 'Women and Part-Time Employment: Workers' "Choices" and Wage Penalties in Five Industrialized Countries', Working Paper no. 223 (Luxembourg Income Study, 2000); see also M. Yerkes and B. Hewitt, 'Part-Time Strategies of Women and Men of Childbearing Age in Netherlands and Australia', in Nicolaisen et al. (eds), *Dualisation of Part-Time Work*, 233–52.
9. Eurostat, *Part-Time and Temporary Contracts—Annual Data*, https://appsso.eurostat.ec.europa.eu/nui (accessed 30 November 2020).
10. See H. McCarthy, *Double Lives: A History of Working Motherhood* (London: Bloomsbury, 2020).

11. C. J. Briar, 'Part-Time Work and the State in Britain, 1941–1987', in B. D. Warme, K. L. P. Lundy, and L. A. Lundy (eds), *Working Part-Time: Risks and Opportunities* (Westport, CT: Praeger, 1992), 75–86, at 83.
12. See L. Vosko, *Managing the Margins: Gender, Citizenship, and the International Regulation of Precarious Labour* (Oxford: Oxford University Press, 2010), 6–9.
13. B. Burchell, A. Dale, and H. Joshi, 'Part-Time Work among British Women', in H.-P. Blossfeld and C. Hakim (eds), *Between Equalization and Marginalization: Women Working Part-Time in Europe and the United States of America* (Oxford: Oxford University Press, 1997), 210–46, at 211.
14. Briar, 'Part-Time Work and the State in Britain', 80–2; J. Lewis, 'The Failure to Expand Childcare Provision and to Develop a Comprehensive Childcare Policy in Britain during the 1960s and 1970s', *Twentieth Century British History*, 24 (2013), https://doi.org/10.1093/tcbh/hws011.
15. J. Tomlinson, 'Employment Regulation, Welfare and Gender Regimes: A Comparative Analysis of Women's Working Time Patterns and Work–Life Balance in the UK and the US', *International Journal of Human Resource Management*, 18 (2007), https://doi.org/10.1080/09585190601167466.
16. Briar, 'Part-Time Work and the State in Britain', 79; A.-M. Daune-Richard, 'How Does the "Societal Effect" Shape the Use of Part-Time Work in France, the UK and Sweden?', in J. O'Reilly and C. Fagan (eds), *Part-Time Prospects: An International Comparison* (Routledge, 1998), 214–30, at 217.
17. House of Commons, Select Committee on Education and Employment, *Minutes of Evidence*, Questions 43–59, 12 March 1998.
18. J. Rubery, K. Ward, and D. Grimshaw, 'The Changing Employment Relationship and the Implications for Quality Part-Time Work', *Labour & Industry*, 15 (2005), https://doi.org/10.1080/10301763.2005.10669315.
19. Interview, Jill Rubery.
20. S. Harkness, 'The Gender Earnings Gap: Evidence from the UK', *Fiscal Studies*, 17 (1996),1–36.
21. *Convention Concerning Part-Time Work*, Convention no. 175, 1994.
22. Select Committee on Education and Employment, Second Report, *Part-Time Working*, 30 March 1999.
23. Select Committee on Education and Employment. *Part-Time Working*, table 1, p. 5.
24. See J. Kodz, B. Kersley, M. T. Strebler, and S. O'Regan, *Breaking the Long-Hours Culture* (Brighton: Institute for Employment Studies, 1998).
25. Select Committee on Education and Employment, *Part-Time Working*, para. 2, p. 2.
26. J. Murray, 'Social Justice For Women? The ILO's Convention on Part-Time Work', *International Journal of Comparative Labour Law and Industrial Relations*, 15 (1999), https://doi.org/10.54648/238282; Vosko, *Managing at the Margins*, 89.
27. I. Bleijenbergh, J. de Bruijn, and J. Bussemaker, 'European Social Citizenship and Gender: The Part-Time Work Directive', *European Journal of Industrial Relations*, 19 (2004), https://doi.org/10.1177/0959680104047023.
28. M. Jeffery, 'Not Really Going to Work? Of the Directive on Part-Time Work, "Atypical" Work, and Attempts to Regulate it', *Industrial Law Journal*, 27 (1998), https://doi.org/10.1093/ilj/27.3.193.
29. See Milner, 'Gender Equality and Employment Regulation'.

30. HM Government, *The Part-Time Workers (Prevention of Less Favourable Treatment) Regulations 2000*, Statutory Instruments no. 1551.
31. M. Bell, 'Achieving the Objectives of the Part-Time Work Directive? Revisiting the Part-Time Workers Regulations', *Industrial Law Journal*, 40 (2011), https://doi.org/10.1093/indlaw/dwr010.
32. A. McColgan, 'Missing the Point? The Part-Time Workers (Prevention of Less Favourable Treatment) Regulations 2000 (SI 2000, No. 1551)', *Industrial Law Journal*, 29 (2000), 260–7.
33. H. Harman, 'Feminism Finds a Foothold in the Centre Left', in N. Lawson and N. Sherlock (eds), *The Progressive Century: The Future of the Centre-Left in Britain* (Palgrave, 2001), 162–72, at 163.
34. S. Anderson, evidence to Select Committee on Education and Employment, *Minutes of Evidence*, Questions 31–39, 2 May 2001, Q31, p. 1.
35. J. Lourie, 'Fairness at Work', Cm 3968, House of Commons Research Paper 98/99, 17 November 1998.
36. R. Rogowski, 'Implementation of the Working Time Directive in the UK', in J.-C. Barbier, R. Rogowski, and F. Colomb (eds), *The Sustainability of the European Social Model* (Cheltenham: Edward Elgar, 2015), 231–52.
37. Rowgoski, 'Implementation of the Working Time Directive'; see also TUC, *Working Time: A Guide for Trade Union Activists* (London: TUC, 2017), 5.
38. J. Cridland, 'An Employers' Perspective of Trends in Employment Regulation', speech to West Midlands Employment Relations Forum, 17 November 2004, p. 3: CBI archive, MSS 200/C/2014 Box 174, Modern Records Centre, University of Warwick.
39. Select Committee on Education and Employment, *Part-Time Working*, para. 77, Summary of Recommendations, p. 2.
40. R. Collinge, evidence to Select Committee on Education and Employment, *Minutes of Evidence*, Questions 31–39, 2 May 2001, Q37, p. 3.
41. S. Himmelweit, 'The Right to Request Flexible Working: A "Very British" Approach to Gender (In)Equality)?', *Australian Bulletin of Labor*, 33 (2007), 246–63.
42. H. Chung, 'Gender, Flexibility Stigma and the Perceived Negative Consequences of Flexible Working in the UK', *Social Indicators Research*, 151 (2018), https://doi.org/10.1007/s11205-018-2036-7.
43. A. Hegewisch, 'Employers and European flexible Working Rights: When the Floodgates Were Opened', *Work Life Law Issue Brief* (University of California, 2005).
44. H. Chung, *The Flexibility Paradox: Why Flexible Working Leads to (Self-)Exploitation* (Bristol: Bristol University Press, 2022); J. Tomlinson and S. Durbin, 'Female Part-Time Managers: Work–Life Balance, Aspirations and Career Mobility', *Equality, Diversity and Inclusion*, 29 (2010), https://doi.org/10.1108/02610151011028859.
45. Their research was echoed by that of Sara Connolly and Mary Gregory, who showed using individual and household panel data that only in two female-dominated professions—teaching and nursing—were women able to retain their jobs on reduced hours: 'Moving Down: Women's Part-Time Work and Occupational Change in Britain 1991–2001', *Economic Journal*, 118 (2008), F52–F76.
46. A. Manning and B. Petrongolo, 'The Part-Time Pay Penalty', Powerpoint slides (kindly supplied by Professor Manning). See also D. Grimshaw and J. Rubery, *The Gender Pay Gap: A Research Review* (Manchester: EOC, 2001).

47. L. Grant, S. Yeandle, and L. Bruckner, 'Working below Potential: Women and Part-Time Work', Working Paper no. 40 (Manchester: EOC, 2005).
48. K. Rake (ed.), *Women's Incomes over the Lifetime* (London: The Stationery Office, 2000).
49. See also T. Anderson, J. Forth, H. Metcalf, and S. Kirby, *The Gender Pay Gap: Report to the Women and Equality Unit* (London: WEU, 2001).
50. Harkness, 'The Gender Earnings Gap'.
51. Notes of presentation to WWC, kindly provided by Jill Rubery.
52. WWC, *Shaping a Fairer Future* (London: DTI, 2006), 34–5.
53. WWC, *Shaping a Fairer Future*, 36.
54. TUC, Submission to Women and Work Commission, 17 February 2005, para. 22, p. 10.
55. WWC, *A Fair Deal for Women in the Workplace: Interim Report* (London: DTI, 2005), 4.
56. WWC, *A Fair Deal for Women in the Workplace*, 7.
57. WWC, *Shaping a Fairer Future*, 30.
58. WWC, *Shaping a Fairer Future*, 35.
59. Interview, Anderson.
60. Interview, Anderson.
61. Interview, Cridland.
62. Interview, Cridland.
63. Interview, Houston.
64. WWC, *Shaping a Fairer Future*, p. viii.
65. WWC, *Shaping a Fairer Future*, 37.
66. WWC, *Shaping a Fairer Future*, 12–13.
67. Interview, Meg Munn.
68. WWC, *Shaping a Fairer Future*, 4.
69. WWC, *Shaping a Fairer Future*, 63.
70. A. Manning, 'The Gender Pay Gap', *Centre Piece* (London School of Economics, Summer 2006), 13–16.
71. One organization refused to take part in the evaluation study, so it is not possible to identify it: see C. Lyonette, B. Baldauf, and H. Behle, 'An Exploration of Quality Part-Time Working in Europe, with a Focus on the UK Case', in M. Connolly and J. Wu (eds), *Handbook on Well-Being of Working Women* (New York: Springer, 2016), 489–502.
72. WWC, *Shaping a Fairer Future. A Review of the Recommendations of the Women and Work Commission Three Years On* (London: Government Equalities Office, 2009), 38.
73. Interview, Adeeba Malik.
74. Interview, Cridland.
75. Interview, Malik.
76. Lyonette et al., *Quality Part-Time Work*, 9.
77. OECD, *Part-Time Employment Rate*, https://data.oecd.org/emp/part-time-employment-rate.htm (accessed 16 September 2022).
78. ONS, *Annual Survey of Hours and Earnings Time Series of Selected Estimates*, https://www.ons.gov.uk/employmentandlabourmarket/peopleinwork/earningsandworkinghours/datasets/ashe1997to2015selectedestimates (accessed 16 September 2022).
79. ONS, *Part-Time Work by Occupation*, https://www.ons.gov.uk/employmentandlabourmarket/peopleinwork/employmentandemployeetypes/datasets/parttimeandtemporaryworkersbyoccupationemp10 (accessed 8 September 2022).

80. W. Olsen, V. Gash, S. Kim, and M. Zhang, *The Gender Pay Gap in the UK: Evidence from the UKHLS* (London: GEO, 2018), 7.
81. M. Sharma, 'Working Mother wins £40000 after Employer Refuses to Accommodate Part-Time Hours', *HR Review*, 29 September 2021.
82. Timewise, *The Timewise Flexible Jobs Index 2021* (London: Timewise).
83. See J. Rubery and C. Fagan, 'Advancing Gender Equality through European Employment Policy: The Impact of the UK's Membership and the Risks of Brexit', *Social Policy and Society*, 17 (2018), 297–317, https://doi.org/10.1017/S1474746417000458.
84. M. Taylor, *Good Work: The Taylor Review of Modern Working Practices* (London: UK Government, 2017).
85. Protection from Redundancy (Maternity and Family Leave) Act 2023. On Qureshi's bill, see Ch. 11.
86. Bardasi and Gornick, 'Women and Part-Time Employment'.
87. B. D. Warme, K. L. P. Lundy, and L. A. Lundy, 'Introduction', in Warme et al., *Working Part-Time*, 1–17, at 5.
88. See P. Bourquin and T. Waters, 'Jobs and Job Quality between the Eve of the Great Recession and the Eve of Covid 19', *Fiscal Studies*, 43 (2022), https://doi.org/10.1111/1475-5890.12279.
89. CIPD, *CIPD Good Work Index 2021* (London: CIPD, 2021).
90. See, e.g., C. Fagan, H. Norman, M. Smith, and M. C. González Hernández, *In Search of Good Quality Part-Time Employment* (Geneva: ILO, 2014); P. Findlay, C. Warhurst, E. Keep, and C. Lloyd, 'Opportunity Knocks? The Possibilities and Levers for Improving Job Quality', *Work and Occupations*, 44 (2017), https://doi.org/10.1177/0730888416689813.
91. See also J. Besamusca and M. Yerkes, *Part-Time Work: Risk Or Opportunity? Policy Brief* (Utrecht: Utrecht University, 2021), 5.
92. Notes of presentation to WWC, kindly provided by Jill Rubery.
93. H. Joshi, A. Bryson, D. Wilkinson, and K. Ward, 'The Gender Gap in Wages over the Life Course: Evidence from a British Cohort Born in 1958', *Gender, Work & Organization* (2020), https://doi.org/10.1111/gwao.12580.

11

Families and Childcare

An Unfinished Revolution

Introduction

At the 2009 Trades Union Congress, Prime Minister Gordon Brown made a speech in which, with a general election on the horizon, he sought to distinguish between the Conservatives' austerity approach to the crisis and Labour priorities of investment-led recovery, public infrastructure, and employment support through training. There was no mention of women, but an emphasis on families, including the 'family-friendly' policies that had been a hallmark of the Labour years. Announcing the new Additional Paternity Leave coming into force in April 2011, which would give fathers up to three months' paid parental leave where mothers returned to work not having used their full statutory maternity leave and pay, Brown set out the achievements of the Labour administration:

> Since 1997 we have increased paid maternity leave from 18 weeks to 9 months. And we retain our ambition to extend it further. This is not only good for mothers but helps give children the best start in life. But fathers have responsibilities too. No Tory government has ever given a single day of paternity leave. This Labour government gave men the right to two weeks paternity leave.[1]

These measures built on a broader strategy for children and parents in a cross-departmental ten-year strategy introduced in 2004,[2] with the dual aim of improving children's life chances and making work–life choices easier for parents. The strategy focused on maternity and paternity leave, and the expansion and improvement of early years provision.

Labour policies on families and childcare were 'path-shifting',[3] departing from the traditional reluctance of the state to intervene in the 'private sphere' of the home and presenting policy on children and parents as investment rather than costs. This policy shift was the result of two decades of activism by women within the Labour Party, and it reflected awareness by

Women and Employment in Public Policy. Susan Milner, Oxford University Press. © Susan Milner (2024).
DOI: 10.1093/9780191987359.003.0011

political leaders of the electoral popularity of work–family policies.[4] It also responded to policy advocacy by international organizations such as the Organization for Economic Cooperation and Development (OECD), which recommended supportive measures to boost women's employment as a way of improving national productivity.[5] Financial support for childcare was significantly increased in 2004, earning Brown praise as a 'childcare champion' from the charity the Daycare Trust.[6]

However, doubts remained about whether funding and policy matched the scale of the problems faced by parents.[7] The strategy stalled in Labour's third term, making relatively small adjustments rather than forging ahead. Subsequently, while the Conservative and Liberal Democratic parties continued along the path shaped by Labour, and expanded provision, they failed to move significantly beyond the limits set earlier. Consequently, the same needs for flexibility, affordability, and availability of care provision face working parents twenty years later and constitute a major obstacle to achieving gender equality.

Moreover, while maternity and paternity leave provision was embedded in national policy for the first time, the level of provision remained low, and significant exclusions persisted. This policy trajectory fits the idea of a 'stalled revolution', set out in Chapter 1, whereby feminist demands succeeded only to the extent that they followed the prevalent logic of the liberal market economy, as a support for women's increased labour-market participation, and delivery of provision remained dependent on the market.[8] In this sense, the departure from the previous policy path was limited, and policy failed to challenge the prevalent gendering of care.[9]

This chapter reviews the development of families and childcare policy in the Labour years and its legacy.[10] While welcoming Labour's childcare strategy, feminists criticized the absence of a broader vision of care as an organizing principle of society, in the name of social justice as well as of effective reproduction of society.[11] The lack of a gender perspective in policy[12] meant that defamilialization of care remained limited, and a maternalist view of care within the family prevailed.[13]

As will be argued in this chapter, Labour's commitment to leave for working parents was constrained from the start by opposition from employer organizations on grounds of cost, which set limits on investment in parents' ability to reconcile paid work and unpaid family responsibilities. However, this was not the only constraint. Trade unions were slow to campaign for rights for fathers (as opposed to mothers), in a policy area that developed piecemeal from work-based rights to maternity leave and pay. The lack of an effective campaign voice for fathers also hampered policy development.[14]

Feminist scholars argue that countries with a universal caregiver policy model—such as Sweden and Norway—provide the most gender-equal outcomes (albeit with shortcomings in practice) owing to a high level of universal childcare provision, and relatively generous leave for working parents, which reduces (but does not eliminate) the 'care gap' between men and women—that is, the amount of time each spends on unpaid care work. Countries with a partnership caregiver policy model—such as continental European states such as Germany and the Netherlands—also offer lessons for liberal regimes like the UK, as they have developed a flexible and decentralized approach to care provision, combining strong formal rights that encourage parental sharing of care and state-funded incentives within a market-based system of provision.[15] The concluding section of this chapter assesses the British policy model in comparison with these 'woman-friendly' policy models.

Regime theories help to explain why the UK was relatively late in adopting work–family policies, and why, even at times of left-of-centre government, 'inaugural' laws creating new rights for parents were highly controversial and limited in their impact. Institutionalist theories provide an alternative set of explanations, emphasizing the power resources of institutional actors within the policy space: negotiations within and between political parties, and the influential role of women policy entrepreneurs.[16]

Formal Childcare Provision (Nursery and Early Years)

The omission from Brown's 2009 speech of childcare is all the more surprising as it was widely seen as a flagship policy, and one that proved popular with voters.[17] As noted in Chapter 5, a major part of the feminization of Labour policy undertaken from the 1980s was the development of a national childcare strategy where previously, to all intents and purposes, none existed.[18] Prominent Labour women such as Margaret Hodge and Harriet Harman had been actively involved in and influenced by municipal government, which, particularly in the London boroughs, became laboratories of good practice in early years provision.[19]

At the end of the twentieth century, the UK was a 'notorious laggard' in childcare and early years policy.[20] The 1967 Plowden report was a milestone in recommending the expansion of part-time nursery education for 3- and 4-year olds, but it was not implemented in the 1970s owing to the oil crisis (despite the Labour Party's commitment to nursery provision in its 1974 manifesto), and in the 1980s early years policy had no appeal to the

Conservatives. This gap stood in contrast to countries with relatively extensive nursery provision prior to the oil crisis, which continued to develop childcare services as well as innovative rights for working parents. As Jane Lewis has shown, 'by end of the 1970s, the foundations for the kind of mixed economy of provision and fragmented service that have continued to characterize childcare in Britain were firmly in place'.[21] As employers' support for better childcare provision grew, and in the face of a weak response by the Conservatives, both Labour and the Liberal Democratic Party presented proposals for universal provision in their 1992 manifestos.[22] Labour's policy, prepared in opposition, was established relatively early in government, with the withdrawal of the Conservatives' nursery voucher scheme, and the adoption of a five-year National Childcare Strategy in 1998 (followed by a ten-year strategy in 2004). Led by the Department for Education, and established in partnership with local authorities, the strategy included the provision of free part-time care for 3- and 4-year-olds, for two and a half hours daily, and further tax credits for childcare costs for lower-income families, reaching up to 80 per cent of costs.[23] Funded by £125 million per year of public money, this initiative was supplemented by £170 million for out-of-school care by the National Lottery's New Opportunities Fund, which was intended to support the expansion of provision and creation of new places. A survey in 2009 found that the number of full-day care providers had increased by 81 per cent since 2001.[24]

The national childcare strategy set three overarching aims for childcare: availability, affordability, and quality. On availability, it pledged to introduce by 2008 a duty on local authorities to ensure sufficient places for local needs; to work towards twenty hours of free childcare for thirty-eight weeks per year for all 3- and 4-year-olds, starting with a first step of fifteen hours by 2010; and a place for all 3-year-olds in standard working hours by 2010. Affordability remained a major problem: British parents had to face the most expensive childcare of all OECD countries. Expansion of provision alone could not tackle this.[25] To enhance affordability, the strategy included moves to increase the childcare allowance in Working Families' Tax Credit and announced £5 million funding for a pilot project to make childcare more affordable in London.

To improve quality, the government established a 'transformation fund' of £126 million per year from 2006 to support professionalization of early years jobs, and consultation on a new qualification and career structure. It set a target of at least one graduate employee per childcare setting by 2015; by 2009, less than a quarter of settings were found to meet the target, but the general level of qualifications of staff had risen.[26] Professionalization of the early years workforce formed part of Labour's childcare strategy, which intensified in the second phase after 2004. However, it was not until Labour's third term, following a series of child abuse scandals, that the workforce strategy became more comprehensive, with funding to match.[27] Government policy focused on ensuring graduate-level training in childcare, with the aim that every setting should have at least one graduate leading practice by 2015. The workforce strategy also aimed to provide training, so that 70 per cent of early years workers would have at least Level 3 qualifications by 2010. But, although funding had increased, this was in the context of high workforce turnover and a high rate of closure of settings.[28]

By 2009, the reconvened Women and Work Commission (WWC (see Chapter 8)) observed that little had changed in the early years workforce, particularly in respect of pay levels. It therefore urged the Department for Children, Schools, and Families (DCSF)[29] to consider further what more could be done to increase the wages of childcare workers, many of whom received low/minimum wage, while ensuring that childcare costs remained affordable. In particular, the DCSF was urged to consider work to drive forward the 'professionalization' of the childcare sector, given that 'the majority of its employees are female and the sector is still struggling to attract men'.[30]

Overall, Labour's national childcare strategy was transformational both at a symbolic level, in bringing childcare into mainstream policy, and substantively, through the expansion of nursery provision and subsidies to parents. It brought about a change in approach, from seeing childcare as a private cost to viewing it as a social investment. It was remarkably detailed in its commitments, in terms of both the targets (including on expenditure) and the timetable. However, it suffered from a key structural weakness owing to the legacy of underfunding and dependence on private provision.[31] Campaigners consistently drew attention to the need for larger-scale public funding to overcome this legacy.[32] Reliance on the private sector was amplified by the Labour leadership's dominant mode of thinking about policy delivery through the market rather than through public services and local authorities. Margaret Hodge, who served as children's minister from the department's creation in 2003 to 2005, later said that 'we got this wrong' and argued, in line with a series of reports evaluating the strategy, that it would have been better to focus on improving the supply rather than expanding demand through subsidies to private providers.[33]

A second major tension concerned the balance between selective provision aimed at improving the life chances of the poorest, and universal services, which had the potential to place the family at the centre of policy.[34] Affordability of childcare was principally achieved through the tax credits system, which targeted support on those households with the lowest incomes.[35] Timo Fleckenstein and Martin Seeleib-Kaiser argue that Labour's focus on childcare support for low-paid workers (alongside a preference for occupational rather than statutory leave and pay) reflected business support for the policy, based on the British economy's need for low-skilled jobs that are predominantly filled by women. This policy choice needs to be understood as reflecting both the complexities of the policy area and the challenges of innovating in the context of long-term underfunding and structural weakness.[36]

Following Labour's time in office, Conservative policy continued along the same path in some respects, while diverging in others. The 2016 Childcare Act, adopted under David Cameron's Conservative-led coalition government, extended working parents' entitlement to free childcare for children over 3 years old to thirty hours (for thirty-eight weeks a year) from September 2017. At the same time, the government introduced tax credits whereby parents earning less than £10,000 per year could open a tax-free childcare account enabling them to claim back a quarter of costs. Yet spending on childcare for under-5s fell continuously after 2011.[37]

An annual survey of childcare by University College London's Coram Centre has shown costs continuing to rise each year at rates above inflation, owing to the 'patchwork' of funding arrangements. In England, parents were in 2023 entitled to claim up to fifteen hours of free childcare for their 3- and 4-year-olds, for thirty-eight weeks a year, and, where both parents work, entitlement rose to thirty hours a week. Working parents of 2-year-olds could claim up to fifteen hours of free childcare. However, as government funding has not matched the full cost of providing free places, providers have either withdrawn from the market or passed costs on in other ways.[38] Partly as a result of this shortfall, availability of childcare remains limited, even for those entitled to the universally funded hours for 3- and 4-year olds.[39] In March 2023, the Conservative government announced plans to provide thirty hours of funded childcare for all parents of children from the age of 1, by the end of 2024. The success of this initiative will depend on a comprehensive strategy to address the falling number of places and the continued recruitment crisis affecting the sector.[40]

Maternity Leave and the Maternalization of Care

Maternity leave and pay developed in the UK 'in rather a haphazard way',[41] initially dependent on employee and employer national insurance contributions to a maternity fund. From 1948, contributors were entitled to thirteen weeks (increased to eighteen in 1953) of maternity allowance on giving up work at childbirth, and from 1975 to six weeks of maternity pay (at 90 per cent of basic weekly pay, less the maternity allowance) from an employers' maternity fund, available to mothers who had been employed continuously for two years by the same employer. Maternity pay and allowance were merged in 1987, but many mothers remained uncovered by the entitlement.

In 1992, the European directive on the protection of pregnant women at work was amended to give all working mothers the right to at least fourteen weeks' maternity leave, paid at least at the equivalent of statutory sick pay.[42] As the revised directive had to be transposed by October 1994, the relevant changes to maternity pay and allowance legislation were made in 1993, adding the right for all mothers to fourteen weeks of paid leave to the existing provision. This meant in practice a right to up to forty weeks of leave, with six of these paid at the higher rate (90 per cent of basic weekly pay) and a further twelve weeks at a statutory leave pay equivalent to statutory sick pay if the mother had worked for the same employer for at least twenty-six weeks prior to childbirth, alongside the legal entitlement of fourteen weeks' paid leave for all. The resulting patchwork was confusing, and Labour was committed to aligning entitlement to eighteen weeks of paid leave for all working mothers.[43]

This commitment was enacted in the Employment Relations Act 1999, which established paid maternity leave of eighteen weeks, at the statutory rate (raised from £57.70 to £64.40 per week), retaining the six weeks' pay at a higher rate for those who had been continuously employed for at least six months. The number of mothers receiving statutory maternity pay (SMP) increased from 90,000 in 1998 to over 300,000 in 2001.[44] The European Union had applied adaptational pressure, resulting in a degree of alignment of British maternity leave provision with best practice in northern Europe. By 1997, a consensus existed in support of this change, with only organizations representing small businesses complaining of costs associated with rights to extended leave, periods of notice required, and protections during the period of leave. The new consensus rested on an employment-anchored view of the welfare state, which emphasized the benefits of maternal employment for the economy.[45]

A fairer and less complex (therefore more accessible) regime was emerging, and formal maternity leave entitlements were successively extended. From April 2002, paid maternity leave was extended from eighteen to twenty-six weeks, and the rate of SMP was increased in 2001 and 2002. In 2006, the Department of Trade and Industry (DTI) conducted a consultation on further extension of paid maternity leave to a full year.

The 2006 consultation revealed that beneath the consensus lay significant tensions. Despite increases in SMP (to reach £111.28 by 2007), it remained low by European standards, and, for most mothers, taking maternity leave continued to mean a prohibitive drop in income. The measures introduced therefore constituted only a 'partial response' to demands for better paid maternity leave.[46] Treasury caution no doubt explained the reluctance to increase the welfare bill further.

Instead, the choice of a long, poorly remunerated leave for mothers kept the UK apart from its European neighbours, with three negative consequences. First, access to maternity leave remained strongly inegalitarian, with those in lower-income households and low-paying jobs less able to afford time away from work, and those in insecure employment excluded from the higher-paying maternity allowance. Second, employers, particularly smaller businesses, disliked long leave, owing to the uncertainty over women's return. The incremental approach to what was a relatively new universal right, grafted onto a conditional—and in practice highly exclusionary—set of existing rights, left many mothers and employers uncertain about legal entitlements, with the result that maternity and pregnancy discrimination could be left unchallenged. In 2003, the Equal Opportunities Commission (EOC) launched a formal investigation into pregnancy discrimination at work, which found that around half of expectant mothers experienced some form of work-related discrimination by their employer, owing to low awareness but also in some cases hostile attitudes by managers.[47] As a result, around 30,000 mothers every year unfairly lost their job, and women missed out on millions of pounds in statutory maternity pay.

Third, extending leave for mothers was by then shown internationally to reinforce gender inequality by reducing their attachment to the labour market and making it harder to rejoin full-time employment later, and also by overemphasizing mothers' role as primary caregivers at the expense of a fuller role for fathers.[48] Moreover, this mother-focused leave policy was reinforced by weak leave entitlement for fathers.

Paternity and Parental Leave: A New and Slowly Developing Policy Agenda

Maternity leave was in 1997 a patchwork depending on individual national insurance contributions, but no paid leave provision existed at all for fathers. The UK was a latecomer to both paternity and parental leave (available to both parents, sometimes with a portion reserved for fathers), and it was

European legislation that created the pressure for change, following the adoption of the Parental Leave Directive (1995). Initially, the solution to this adaptational pressure was to transpose the directive in a minimalist fashion by introducing a right to three months of unpaid parental leave available to either parent. However, this passive right did not enable parents to take up leave, and it created confusion in relation to existing rights to maternity leave.

Labour had not entered office in 1997 with a conceptualization of leave as support for working parents or a strategy to enact it. On the one hand, this created a potential space for family-rights campaigners to influence policy; on the other, the lack of a strategic vision meant that policy developed piecemeal, added on to existing provision on maternity leave. The overall effect of policy development was to reinforce the idea of fathers as secondary carers, dependent on mothers for the exercise of their rights and their parenting responsibilities.[49]

In 2000, the Green Paper 'Competitiveness and Choice' proposed new rights for fathers in the context of parental leave, and in 2002 paid paternity leave of up to two weeks (paid at the rate of statutory maternity pay) was introduced. However, the right, although welcomed by campaigners, proved difficult to access in practice in the period immediately following its introduction: far from the 80 per cent of fathers anticipated by the DTI, fewer than 20 per cent of new fathers took paid paternity leave at the statutory rate.[50] Between 2003 and 2005, fathers increased their time off work around the time of the birth of a child, but were more likely to do so if they were in professional jobs where employers often paid leave in full, or they had access to unpaid leave. Fathers in lower-paid jobs and in smaller workplaces took less leave.[51]

One of the reasons for low take-up of statutory leave was that it was conditional on twenty-six weeks' continuous service, thus excluding men in insecure employment.[52] In addition, surveys showed both low awareness of the new right and a view among many fathers that the rate of statutory pay was too low to enable access.[53] The effect of paid paternity leave appeared to be indirect, relying on changes in both demand for leave by fathers and supply by employers, rather than direct through the creation of a universal right.

Women in and close to government, alongside the EOC, pushed for a stronger right for fathers to access leave on terms that were more closely aligned to those available to mothers, allowing a more equitable share of care. Ruth Kelly, who served on the Treasury select committee and was appointed Economic Secretary to the Treasury after the 2001 general election, argued publicly for paid parental leave,[54] and Patricia Hewitt as Secretary of State for

Trade and Industry and Minister for Women and Equalities sought to promote it. Although both women were close to the Labour leadership, the case was not supported within cabinet, as Hewitt explained:

> We had a manifesto commitment to two weeks' paternity leave … But we … were running focus groups, essentially, with pregnant women and mothers, around the country, and the thing they wanted was to be able to share their maternity leave with their partner. And I really pushed it with my officials, because I thought that's what we ought to be doing. I got stuck. I didn't have a manifesto commitment to rely on. The unions and business groups were generally opposed, so were most of the women's organizations, and there wasn't yet a strong voice amongst men at that stage wanting to share family responsibilities. I still regret not having found a way through to the right place.[55]

As well as lack of a strong campaigning voice within civil society, Hewitt felt that the case had not been made for better parental leave rights for men owing to lack of strong evidence, in the way that survey and focus-group evidence on mothers' preferences had been gathered over more than a decade.

Meanwhile, the EOC had been steadily building research evidence on fathers' work–family preferences. The Fatherhood Institute, initially established (then as Fathers Direct) in 1999 with the support of the Home Office to inform fathers of their rights, sought to promote positive views of fatherhood. With Hewitt's support, Julie Mellor brought Duncan Fisher, CEO of the Fatherhood Institute, into the EOC as a commissioner.[56] Mellor, backed by Hewitt and other sympathetic women ministers like Beverley Hughes, Minister for Children and Families, reframed fathers in public discourse as carers, making a positive contribution to children's development and well-being.[57] This work also helped to overcome initial resistance to parental leave from some mothers' groups who feared loss of maternal rights.

Such efforts to change cultural attitudes were broadly in line with shifts in social attitudes, which from the late 1980s had shown a sharp decline in traditional views about men's breadwinner role.[58] Employers' organizations, however, took longer to persuade. Support for working mothers was in comparison well established but still met resistance from some, particularly smaller, employers. Paid paternity leave was new and initially controversial.[59]

The idea of shared parental leave was even newer, and complex to administer, as it was linked to the partner or spouse's entitlement. According to Hewitt, 'the employers were against it because they thought it would double the number of people, potentially, for whom they had to arrange cover'.[60] Lack of top-level support coupled with fear of employer resistance helps to explain Labour's timid approach to the introduction of new rights for fathers. Without the 2005 Warwick agreement, parental leave stood little chance of inclusion in the general-election manifesto, but the push by Labour-affiliated unions in 2005 meant that work–family rights now moved to centre stage, particularly as further collective rights were more difficult for the Labour leadership to accept than individual rights. Hewitt worked at the Warwick policy forum to secure agreement with unions on a package that found its way into the 2005 general-election manifesto.[61]

The Work and Families Act, adopted in 2006, introduced a new right to Additional Paternity Leave (APL), which increased fathers' leave entitlement in terms of duration, from two weeks to a maximum of twenty-six weeks, paid at the statutory paternity pay rate. It was enacted in 2010 and came into force in April 2011. However, campaigners expressed concern about the legislation, which was not an individual right but dependent on mothers' maternity leave and their willingness to sacrifice part of that leave. Only fathers whose partner was in employment prior to childbirth and entitled to statutory maternity leave were therefore eligible. APL was also criticized, as leave could be taken only in blocks, rather than, for example, in Sweden, where employees are able to change the form of parental leave up to three times.[62]

At the 2010 general election, Labour proposed increasing paid paternity leave from two to four weeks and allowing mothers to allocate three of their nine months of paid maternity leave to fathers.[63] The Conservative manifesto included a commitment to allow parents to share leave between them, without specifying the duration of leave for either parent.[64] The Liberal Democrats pledged to 'seek to' extend shared parental leave to eighteen months without specifying allocation between parents.[65] Thus, while parental leave had become a subject of electoral competition, the lack of specificity in policy design indicated weak consensus for fully shared leave with a reserved portion for fathers. In the event, it was the Liberal Democrat Minister for Employment Relations Jo Swinson who introduced Shared Parental Leave (SPL) in December 2014. From April 2015, parents were able to share all but two weeks of the full fifty-two weeks available to mothers as leave, under the same conditions as maternity leave and pay.

Although hailed as a step towards fully shared parental leave, SPL falls short of this goal in several respects. It is complex, requiring both parents to have been in work for the qualifying period of twenty-six weeks, and above all it fails to take account of the low level of replacement pay, which deters the higher-earning parent from taking leave. In the absence of a dedicated portion of leave for fathers, it can also create the perception that mothers have to sacrifice their entitlement.[66] A sense of limited entitlement for fathers pervades workplace attitudes to SPL, creating further barriers to take-up by men.[67] Consequently, despite a high-profile media campaign in 2019, take-up remains very low (well under 5 per cent of eligible fathers).

The Right to Request Flexible Working

The right to request flexible working is a 'very British' solution to the problem of reconciling work and family life, according to the Trade and Industry minister then responsible for this area of policy, Alan Johnson,[68] although it has also been adopted in a number of other countries, such as Australia (in 2009).[69] By British, Johnson meant a preference for relatively light-touch regulation, so the right, as introduced in the Employment Act 2002 and implemented in 2003, was framed as a right to request rather than a right to choose.

While the manifesto had referred only to mothers returning from leave, the new right was available to all parents of children up to the age of 5, and this constituted a new right for fathers.[70] However, as has been argued for similar types of right that are embedded in employer discretion and subjected to strong eligibility constraints, policy design can limit take-up and result in unintended consequences such as stigmatization of those who make requests.[71] The 'trailblazing companies', such as Lloyds TSB, which in 1999 had introduced policies on flexible working, opened them up to all employees (regardless of family situation), and gave employees choices about how they would like to organize their working time,[72] whereas the 2003 legislation limited employee choice by giving broad authority to reject requests on 'business' grounds, strictly limited eligibility, and imposed relatively weak sanctions for failure to deal with requests fairly.[73]

The restrictions were justified by government ministers on the grounds that it would take time for the right to become part of the workplace regulatory culture. While the flexible working agenda was pioneered by large companies in the finance sector, the trailblazers represented only a minority of employers, and the bulk of employers would need to adjust their practice. In response to backbenchers' criticism, Johnson argued that 'a completely new and fairly radical right is being proposed and people have to get used to it'.[74]

The right to request flexible working was a novel solution between 'hard' law enforceable through legal redress and voluntary action by employers. The Confedaration of British Industry (CBI) director general Digby Jones wrote to the prime minister in March 2001 stating that the organization could not support an automatic right for employees returning from maternity leave to switch from full-time to part-time hours,[75] which was the demand of the TUC, the EOC, equality and family-rights groups, and many backbenchers.

The select committee on Education and Employment, which examined part-time work in 1999, recommended among other things stronger rights for women returning from maternity leave:

> There should be a presumption that women will be allowed to return to work after maternity leave on a part-time basis, with pay and benefits no less favourable, mutatis mutandis, than those which they were receiving before they took maternity leave. We recommend that the Government introduce legislation guaranteeing women the right to return to work after maternity leave on a part-time basis, while retaining their right to transfer to full-time work, unless the employer is able to demonstrate that it would be to the detriment of the operation of the employer's business.[76]

Consequently, the Labour Party manifesto in 2001 included a commitment to a right to part-time working for women returning from maternity leave. The idea of an automatic right to part-time working was problematic for the government, however, because of the opposing positions of trade unions and employer organizations. Hewitt did not support an automatic right for mothers, on grounds that it reinforced maternalization of domestic care and the 'mommy track' in the workplace. Hewitt's long-standing interest in flexible working led her to prefer policy solutions aimed at changing organizational cultures through flexible working time arrangements.[77] Her approach was that the law could change only through consensus, and this could be achieved only by focusing on flexible working for parents, rather than mothers.

To identify a way between the opposing employer and union positions, and find alternative solutions, a task force was established in May 2001, following a DTI review and consultation process. The Work and Parents Task Force on Flexible Working was chaired by Professor Sir George Bain, then chair of the Low Pay Commission, and its eight other members represented business (with four representatives plus the CBI, making an overall majority), trade unions (with Kay Carberry representing the TUC alongside Maureen Rooney), the EOC, and Sue Monk, the chief executive of the campaign group Parents at Work.[78]

From the outset the group was divided between the employer approach and that of the trade-union representatives and equality and family campaigners, who emphasized rights for mothers to request part-time working.

Bain later emphasized the difficulty of reaching agreement in the task force and his conviction that consensus was needed for government to accept any recommendations.[79] By adopting a softer approach to regulation, policymakers shifted the organized business position of outright opposition. A key actor in this shift was the CBI's deputy director, John Cridland (another member of the Low Pay Commission), who by 2001 had acquired extensive experience of negotiations with the Labour government and the TUC, and who took a personal interest in the question of part-time work (see Chapter 7).

However, having succeeded in bringing the employer and trade-union positions together on the principle of a right to request changes in working hours, the task force failed to reach agreement on the issue of enforceability, and talks broke down. The President of the CBI (Sir Iain Vallance) wrote to the prime minister arguing that the organization had moved its stance to accept a right to request changes to working hours but could not accept the TUC position that employment tribunals should be able to overturn employer rejections of requests. Whereas the DTI had worked behind the scenes to persuade the CBI to accept the principle of a right to request and participation in the task force, it (and the task force chair) now had to spend 'a great deal of time twisting arms'[80] to convince the TUC to return to negotiations and accept a soft-law approach relying on individual requests and employer discretion (on the grounds defined by law, relating to operational needs).

The outcome of the task force deliberations was a compromise that sought to ensure engagement with requests by as many employers as possible, including small businesses. Although the right to request flexible working, as adopted in the Employment Act 2002, fell short of trade union and campaigners' demands in several respects, it was widely supported as a first step in changing workplace attitudes to the needs of employees (particularly those with caring responsibilities) for flexibility in working hours. The campaign group Maternity Alliance welcomed the move, although 'the proposal isn't perfect', admitting that 'it opens the door to flexibility'.[81]

In broad terms, the right to request flexible working has undoubtedly contributed to a shift in workplace regulatory cultures concerning changes to working hours. The campaign group Working Families has identified in its annual surveys a growing number of employees who report having access to flexible working arrangements, many of them through a request to change to flexible hours.[82] However, Working Families also highlights the inequalities in access to flexible working among different groups of employees, which could be addressed through policy design. The Chartered Institute of Personnel and Development (CIPD) also lobbied for more extensive employee access to the right to request, based on its regular surveys of members, which found that the pace of change in flexible working was 'glacial': between 2005 and 2017, the proportion of employees with access to such arrangements rose from 23 per cent to 27 per cent, with most of the (small) increase due to increased use of zero-hours contracts, which have been criticized for giving individuals (particularly those with caring responsibilities) insufficient control over working hours.[83]

Much of the initial criticism of the right to request flexible working focused on eligibility criteria based on the age of the child. The new right was available to parents of children aged under 6 (other than for parents of disabled children), and campaigners pushed for its extension, first to all parents, then to all employees, on the grounds that universal availability would normalize expectations of flexible working, as well as on equality grounds. The right was extended in the Work and Families Act 2006 to include all carers of children under the age of 18 (and in some cases over the age of 18), in line with the Warwick agreement, andsubsequently under the Coalition government to cover all employees (in the Children and Families Act 2014). These extensions helped to spread awareness of the right and embed it in organizational practice.[84]

Later criticism focused on the qualifying service period (of twenty-six weeks), which excludes the growing number of employees on short-term contracts. The CIPD and several campaign organizations lobbied for 'day one' rights, alongside the idea that flexible working should be the default arrangement for all jobs, unless specific service requirements require otherwise. Following the establishment of a task force on flexible working in 2018, and its re-establishment in 2020 in the wake of the Covid-19 pandemic and the consequent shift to remote working for many jobs,[85] this pressure grew. After a further consultation, in December 2022 the government announced that it would support a private member's bill (tabled by Labour MP Yasmin Qureshi) extending the right to all employees, allowing employees to make two requests per year, and requiring employers to consult with employees if they decide to refuse requests.[86]

Qureshi's bill addresses another of the criticisms of the right to request flexible working, which is the large degree of latitude given to employers in justifying their decision, on broadly defined business grounds. The DTI's evaluation of the measure showed that, according to employers, around 80 per cent of requests were granted in the first years of the new right's existence.[87] A TUC survey of working mothers and expectant mothers found that around half of those who had made requests for flexible working had seen their requests rejected. Moreover, fear of rejection discouraged other women from applying for changes to hours.[88]

The TUC survey also found evidence of stigmatization of mothers returning from maternity leave having requested flexible working arrangements, and fear of stigmatization among women who felt unable to make such requests. An earlier study by Maternity Alliance had found that 27 per cent of people making successful requests experienced a worsening of their pay or conditions because of the change.[89] By strengthening employees' rights to request changes to working hours, Qureshi's bill aimed to make it harder for employers to reject them out of hand. It remains to be seen how this change will work in practice, and whether in future further changes will be needed to tighten the grounds on which employers can refuse requests, as campaign organizations advocate.

Finally, the question of enforceability that proved a key sticking point in the task force deliberations has to some extent been answered by case law. Whereas critics of the soft-law approach embodied in the right to request flexible working argued that it represented a weakening of sex-discrimination protection,[90] individual women have been able to contest rejection of their request to change working hours on the grounds of indirect discrimination, using existing sex-discrimination legislation.[91] Given that the right was designed to avoid litigation, such cases suggest that employers may need to be able to demonstrate engagement with requests, even if the law does not require it. Again, the most recent extensions of employee rights may help to reinforce entitlement through the requirement for consultation, which formalizes the process to a greater degree than hitherto.

Conclusion

In our initial meeting in January 2020, Baroness Prosser acknowledged that 'there was a lot that was swept away' in the government's response to the Commission's 2006 report, 'especially around family-friendly rights'.[92] The Commission's own intervention in this area was relatively limited, reflecting the constraints of its remit as well as its own expertise in this area, and, no doubt, a tactical recognition that it needed to focus on the areas where it was likely to have leverage over policy. Yet, in the areas where it made recommendations, it had highlighted weaknesses in existing provision and planned interventions, in relation to the right to request flexible working and the childcare strategy. The disappointment expressed in the 2009 report reflected a sense that the hopes for a relaunch of work–family policy in Labour's third term following the 2004 Warwick agreement, had been put to one side in the context of economic downturn.

This chapter has outlined the work–family policy strategy followed by the DTI in the period 2001–5, when its secretary of state, Hewitt, was also minister for women and equalities. Rights for mothers on maternity leave were strengthened, and an innovative right to request flexible working was adopted, while rights for working fathers were brought squarely into the policy field with the introduction of paid paternity leave, which quickly became established in men's expectations and organizational practice. However, while Hewitt had wanted to strengthen paternity rights further with the introduction of paid parental leave (with a specific non-transferable quota for fathers), it proved difficult to establish the basis for this innovation straight away. This imbalance in policy meant that organizational assumptions about the gendered nature of care continued to prevail, and that the right to request flexible working was therefore largely taken up by women.

On childcare provision, Labour introduced a new policy that required sustained investment and coordination. As this chapter has shown, further structural changes and a more ambitious policy on care from the outset would have made it harder for subsequent governments to erode the policy under austerity while ostensibly retaining continuity. The UK continues to have exceptionally high childcare costs, and private provision makes it unaffordable for many, particularly those on low wages.[93] Failure to establish good childcare infrastructure cannot be explained by opposition by organized business. As outlined in this chapter, the lack of a coherent childcare strategy, despite promising beginnings under Labour, reflects rather a rigidly orthodox Treasury view of what constitutes productive investment, which has never been challenged because childcare competes with traditional priorities.

Today, a major initiative on policy on families and care is long overdue, to strengthen rights, parents' capacity to make meaningful choices, and public investment. The ILO's 2019 overview showed that the UK has one of the highest rates of women with care responsibilities in paid employment, and yet a mediocre ranking (seventeenth our of forty countries) for public expenditure on early years education, maternity benefits, and long-term care.[94] Meanwhile, the flexible working agenda has begun to take root in British working practices, but, eighteen years after the introduction of the right to request flexible working, it has not had the full impact its initiators hoped to see. In this sense, the right can rightly be seen as a catalyst for long-term change but one whose potential has so far been underused by employers.

Notes

1. Prime minister's speech to Congress, 15 September 2009. TUC congress report, https://www.tuc.org.uk/speeches/prime-ministers-speech-congress-2009 (accessed 3 November 2020).
2. HM Treasury, Department for Education and Skills, Department for Work and Pensions, and Department of Trade and Industry, *Choice for Parents: The Best Start for Children: A Ten-Year Strategy for Childcare* (London, HMSO, 2004).
3. K. J. Morgan, 'Promoting Social Investment through Work–Family Policies: Which Nations Do it and why?' in N. Morel et al., *Towards a Social Investment Welfare State? Ideas, Policies and Challenges* (Bristol: Policy Press, 2011), 153–79.
4. See S. Childs, *Women and British Party Politics: Descriptive, Substantive and Symbolic Representation* (London: Routledge, 2008).
5. The first in the OECD series, based on the experience of Australia, Denmark, and the Netherlands, was OECD, *Babies and Bosses: Reconciling Work and Family Life*, i (Paris: OECD, 2002).
6. S. J. Ball and C. Vincent, 'The "Childcare Champion"? New Labour, Social Justice and the Childcare Market', *British Educational Research Journal* (2005), https://doi.10.1080/01411920500240700, p. 560. The Daycare Trust was formed in 1986, in the wake of the closure of the Greater London Council, and the subsequent shift from radical community childcare (supported by left-wing London councils) to a more uncertain political climate: see S. E. Stoller, *Inventing the Working Parent: Work, Gender, and Feminism in Neoliberal Britain* (Cambridge, MA: MIT Press, 2023), 26–53. In 2013, it merged with the Family and Parenting Institute to form the Family and Childcare Trust, linked to the Coram Centre. The Coram Centre in Bloomsbury, London, is supported by Camden borough council, which pioneered local authority daycare in the UK.
7. D. Coates and S. Oettinger, 'Two Steps Forward, One Step Back: The Gender Dimensions of Treasury Policy under New Labour', in C. Annesley, F. Gains, and K. Rummery (eds), *Women and New Labour. Engendering Politics and Policy?* (Bristol: Policy Press, 2007), 117–31.
8. T. Fleckenstein and M. Seeleib-Kaiser, 'Business, Skills and the Welfare State: The Political Economy of Employment-Oriented Family Policy in Britain and Germany', *Journal of European Social Policy*, 21 (2011), https://doi.org/10.1177/0958928710380483.
9. See also J. Chanfreau, 'The Persistence in Gendering: Work–Family Policy in Britain since Beveridge', *Journal of Social Policy*, online (2022), 1–18.
10. This chapter focuses on families and childcare, omitting discussion of elder care. The Labour years are associated with fragmentation of social-care provision through contracting-out, accompanied by regulatory oversight: see J. C. Humphrey, 'New Labour and the Regulatory Reform of Social Care', *Critical Social Policy*, 23 (2003), https://doi.org/10.1177/026101830302300101; K. Rummery, 'Caring, Citizenship and New Labour: Dilemmas and Contradictions for Disabled and Older Women', In Annesley et al., *Women and New Labour*, 175–92.
11. S. Himmelweit and H. Land, *Supporting Parents and Carers* (Manchester: EOC, 2007).
12. See B. Featherstone, 'Why Gender Matters in Child Welfare Protection', *Critical Social Policy* (2006), https://doi.org/10.1177/0261018306062587; R. Lister, 'Children (but not

Women) First: New Labour, Child Welfare, and Gender’, *Critical Social Policy* (2006), https://doi.org/10.1177/0261018306062588.

13. M. Daly, ‘Shifts in Family Policy in the UK under New Labour’, *Journal of European Social Policy*, 20 (2010), https://doi.org/10.1177/0958928710380480.
14. Interview, Patricia Hewitt.
15. K. Rummery, C. McAngus, and A. Edwards, *What Works in Improving Gender Equality. International Best Practice in Childcare and Long-Term Care Policy* (Bristol: Bristol University Press, 2021).
16. C. Engeman, ‘Making Parental Leave Accessible to Fathers: Political Actors and New Social Rights, 1965–2016’, *Social Politics* (2022), https://doi.org/10.1093/sp/jxac038.
17. On the electoral politics of work–family policy, see T. Fleckenstein, ‘Party Politics and Childcare: Comparing the Expansion of Service Provision in England and Germany’, *Social Policy and Administration*, 44 (2010), https://doi.org/10.1111/j.1467-9515.2010.00744.x; K. J. Morgan, ‘Path Shifting of The Welfare State: Electoral Competition and the Expansion of Work–Family Policies in Western Europe’, *World Politics*, 65 (2013), https://doi.org/10.1017/S0043887112000251.
18. V. Randall, ‘The Politics of Childcare Policy’, in J. Lovenduski and P. Norris (eds), *Women in Politics* (London: Routledge, 1996), 178–92, at178.
19. Randall, ‘The Politics of Childcare Policy’, 182.
20. D. Wincott, ‘Reshaping Public Policy? Devolution and Policy Change in British Early Childhood Education and Care’, *Regional & Federal Studies*, 15 (2005), https://doi.org/10.1080/13597560500230573.
21. J. Lewis, ‘The Failure to Expand Childcare Provision and to Develop a Comprehensive Childcare Policy in Britain in the 1960s and 1970s’, *Twentieth Century British History*, 24 (2013), 274.
22. Randall, ‘The Politics of Childcare Policy’, 188–9. Pressure led to only a limited response from the Major government, in the form of vouchers for parents of 4-year-olds, which campaigners feared would not be matched by adequate numbers of places.
23. Daly, ‘Shifts in Family Policy in the UK under New Labour’; J. Lewis and M. Campbell, ‘Work/Family Balance Policies in the UK since 1997’, *Journal of Social Policy*, 36 (2007), https://doi.org/10.1017/S0047279407001067.
24. R. Phillips, O. Norden, S. McGinigal, E. Garnett, and D. Oseman, *2009 Childcare and Early Years Providers Survey* (London: Department for Education, 2009), 1.
25. Himmelweit and Land, *Supporting Parents and Carers.*
26. Phillips et al., *2009 Childcare and Early Years Providers Survey*, 3.
27. E. Lloyd and E. Hallet, ‘Professionalising the Early Childhood Workforce in England: Work in Progress or Missed Opportunity?’, *Contemporary Issues in Early Childhood*, 11 (2010), https://doi.org/10.2304/ciec.2010.11.1.75, pp. 77–8.
28. Himmelweit and Land, *Supporting Parents and Carers.*
29. The DSCF replaced the Department for Education and Skills in 2007, and in 2010 was succeeded by the Department for Education.
30. WWC, *Shaping a Fairer Future: A Review of the Recommendations of the Women and Work Commission Three Years on* (London: GEO, 2009), 32.
31. See S. Himmelweit, ‘Transforming Care’, in L. Macfarlane (ed.), *New Thinking for the British Economy* (London: Open Democracy, 2018), 68–76.

32. See M. Evans, 'National Childcare Strategy: Ministerial Moves', *Nursery World*, 16 October 2001, https://www.nurseryworld.co.uk/news/article/national-childcare-strategy-ministerial-moves (accessed 10 November 2020).
33. M. Hodge, 'Where Next for Childcare Policy? Reflections On The 2004 Childcare Strategy' (Resolution Foundation, 2014).
34. See Daly, 'Shifts in Family Policy'.
35. Fleckenstein and Seeleib-Kaiser, 'Business, Skills and the Welfare State'.
36. Daly, 'Shifts in Family Policy', 441.
37. K. Stewart and M. Reader, 'The Conservatives' Record on Early Childhood: Policies, Spending and Outcomes from May 2015 to Pre-COVID 2020', Research Paper no. 8 (London School of Economics, 2020).
38. J. Lewis and A. West, 'Early Childhood Education and Care in England under Austerity: Continuity of Change in Policy Ideas, Goals, Availability, Affordability and Quality in a Childcare Market?', *Journal of Social Policy* (2017), https://doi.org/10.1017/S0047279416000647.
39. L. Coleman, S. Shorto, and D. Ben-Galim, 'Childcare Survey 2022' (University College London, 2022), 5–6.
40. Coleman et al., 'Childcare Survey 2022', 6.
41. J. Lourie, 'Fairness at Work. Cm 3968', House of Commons Research Paper, 17 November 1998, p. 61.
42. Directive on the Protection at Work of Pregnant Women or Women who Have Recently Given Birth, Dir 92/85/EEC. The directive required transposition, as it was introduced under the health and safety provisions of the Single Act.
43. J. Earnshaw, 'Maternity rights in the UK: Light at the End of the Tunnel?', *Economic and Labour Relations Review*, 10 (1999), https://doi.org/10.1177/103530469901000202; P. Lewis, 'Pregnancy and Maternity Leave: Employment Law as a Family Friend?', *Industrial Relations Journal*, 31 (2000), https://doi.org/10.1111/1468-2338.00152.
44. Lewis and Campbell, 'Work/Family Balance Policies', 374. The number of mothers receiving the higher rate (maternity allowance) for six weeks similarly rose, but from a lower starting point: from 12,000 in 1997 to 34,000 in 2005. Government expenditure on maternity pay and allowance accordingly tripled.
45. Lewis and Campbell, 'Work/Family Balance Policies', 368–9.
46. S. Himmelweit, 'The Right to Request Flexible Working: A "Very British" Approach to Gender (In)Equality?' *Australian Bulletin of Labour*, 33 (2007), 246–63, at 249.
47. EOC, *Greater Expectations: Final Report of the EOC's Investigation into Discrimination against New and Expectant Mothers in the Workplace* (Manchester: EOC, 2005).
48. G. James, 'The Work and Families Act 2006: Legislation to Improve Choice and Flexibility?', *Industrial Law Journal*, 35 (2006), 272–8.
49. See E. Caracciolo di Torella, 'New Labour, New Dads. The Impact of Family Friendly Legislation on Fathers', *Industrial Law Journal*, 3 (2007), 318–28.
50. V. Keter, 'The Work and Families Bill: Bill 60 of 2005–2006', Research Paper 05-82, 24 November (House of Commons Library, 2005), 33. This paper refers to evidence gathered by the EOC, reported in *Dads and their Babies: Leave Arrangements and the First Year* (Manchester: EOC, 2005), which indicated that 19% of those classed as eligible by the DTI took leave at the statutory rate in 2004.

51. D. Smeaton and A. Marsh, *Maternity Rights and Benefits: Survey of Parents 2005* (London: DTI, 2006), 5.
52. James, 'The Work and Families Act 2006', 275.
53. Keter, 'The Work and Families Bill', 33–4.
54. See R. Kelly, 'Equal Partners in the Family? Views, Preferences and Policy Dilemmas', in A. Coote (ed.) *New Gender Agenda* (London: Institute for Public Policy Research, 2002), 128–38.
55. Interview, Hewitt.
56. A. Burgess, *Advocating for Involved Fatherhood in the UK (1999—-2012)* (London: Fatherhood Institute, 2012), 29–30.
57. Burgess, *Advocating for Involved Fatherhood*, 31.
58. See J. Scott and E. Clery, 'Gender Roles: A Complete Revolution?', in A. Park, C. Bryson, E. Clery, J. Curtice, and M. Phillips (eds), *British Social Attitudes: The 30th Report* (London: NatCen Social Research, 2013), 115–38.
59. Organizations representing small businesses (such as national and regional chambers of commerce) were particularly vocal in opposing the DTI plans, and consequently the cabinet was reportedly split on the proposals: see D. Orr, 'Why the Fuss about Paternity Leave?', *Independent*, 20 February 2001, p. 5. Hewitt (interview) recalls being 'roundly abused by the tabloids' for proposing two weeks' paid paternity leave.
60. Interview, Hewitt.
61. Interview, Hewitt. See also A Brady, *Unions and Employment in a Market Economy: Strategy, Influence and Power in Contemporary Britain* (London: Taylor & Francis, 2021), 155.
62. M. Weldon-Johns, 'The Additional Paternity Leave Regulations 2010: A New Dawn or "Sound-Bite" Legislation?', *Journal of Social Welfare & Family Law*, 33 (2011), 25–38, at 34–5.
63. Labour Party, *A Future Fair for All*, manifesto (2010), 45.
64. Conservative Party, *Invitation to Join the Government of Britain*, manifesto (2010), 52.
65. Liberal Democrat *Manifesto 2010*, manifesto (2010), p. 26.
66. J. L. Atkinson, 'Shared Parental Leave in the UK: Can it Advance Gender Equality by Changing Fathers into Co-Parents?', *International Journal of Law in Context* (2017), https://doi.org/10.1017/S1744552317000209; H. Birkett and S. Forbes, 'Where's Dad? Exploring the Low Take-up of Inclusive Parenting Policies in the UK', *Policy Studies* (2019), https://doi.org/10.1080/01442872.2019.1581160; G. Kaufman, *Fixing Parental Leave: The Six Month Solution* (New York: New York University Press, 2020), https://doi.org/10.18574/nyu/9781479820146.001.0001; A. Koslowski, 'Capturing the Gender Gap in the Scope Of Parenting Related Leave Policies across Nations', Social Inclusion (2021), https://doi.org.10.17645/si.v9i2.3852.
67. E. G. Ndzi, 'The Devastating Impact of Gender Discrimination on Shared Parental Leave in the UK', *International Journal of Law and Society* (2021), https://doi.org.10.11648/j.ijls.20210404.13.
68. Himmelweit, 'The Right to Request Flexible Working', 247.
69. See A. Heron and S. Charlesworth, 'Working Time and Managing Care under Labor: Whose Flexibility?' *Australian Bulletin of Labour*, 38 (2012), 214–33.
70. E. Aarons, 'New Plans to Help Parents Balance Home and Work Must Not Be Rushed through', *Financial Times*, 16 April 2001.

71. E. Kelly and A. Kalev, 'Managing Flexible Work Arrangements in US Organizations: Formalized Discretion or "a Right to Ask"', *Socio-Economic Review*, 4 (2006), https://doi.org/10.1093/ser/mwl001, p. 407.
72. Sarah Jackson (former CEO of Working Families), interviewed on BBC Radio 4 Woman's Hour, 13 April 2021.
73. R. Croucher and C. Kelliher, 'The Right to Request Flexible Working in Britain: The Law and Organisational Realities', *International Journal of Comparative Labour Law and Industrial Relations*, 21 (2005), https://doi.org/10.54648/ijcl2005023.
74. Hansard, HC, Ninth Standing Committee on Delegated Legislation, Draft Flexible Working (Procedural Requirements) Regulations 2002, col. 019 (5 December 2002).
75. Letter from Digby Jones to the prime minister, 15 March 2001: John Cridland papers, CBI archive, MSS 200/C/2014 Box 218, Modern Records Centre, University of Warwick.
76. House of Commons, Education and Employment, 'Part-Time Working', Second Report of Session 1998–1999 (1999), para. 77.
77. Interview, Hewitt.
78. Hansard, HC, vol. 370, col. 1707 (28 June 2001). Like the Daycare Trust (see n. 6), Parents at Work (formed in 1996) grew out of an earlier charity with feminist roots, the Working Mothers' Association: see Stoller, *Inventing the Working Parent*, 9–6. In 2003, Parents at Work merged with New Ways to Work to form Working Families, and its emphasis shifted towards advocacy of flexible working arrangements.
79. G. S. Bain, 'The Bullock Committee and the Low Pay Commission: Some Reflections by Sir George Bain', Advisory Board Lecture, 29 November 2001 (University of Warwick, 2001).
80. Personal communication, Hewitt, 7 June 2023.
81. 'Election 2001: Parents' Right to Flexible Work Hours', *Birmingham Post*, 31 May 2001.
82. Working Families, *Working Families Index 2022: Families and Flexible Working Post-Covid-19* (London: Working Families, 2022), 6–8.
83. CIPD, *Flexible Working in the UK* (London: CIPD, 2019), 3.
84. See J. Atkinson, 'Letters Aren't Good: The Operation of the Right to Request Flexible Working Post-Maternity Leave in UK Small and Medium-Sized Companies', *Journal of Social Welfare and Family Law*, 38 (2016), https://doi.org/10.1080/09649069.2016.1239346.
85. See T. Dobbins, 'Flexible Working: Remote and Hybrid Working', House of Commons Library no. 9391 (London: HM Parliament, 2021).
86. Employment Relations (Flexible Working Bill), HL Bill 107 (as brought from the Commons to the House of Lords, 27 February 2023). The bill was tabled by Labour MP Yasmin Qureshi.
87. DTI, *The Third Employee Work–Life Balance Survey: Main Findings* (London: DTI/HMSO).
88. TUC, *Denied and Discriminated Against: The Reality of Flexible Working for Working Mums* (London: TUC, 2021).
89. Maternity Alliance, *Happy Anniversary? The Right to Request Flexible Working One Year on* (London: Maternity Alliance, 2004).
90. Croucher and Kelliher, 'The Right to Request Flexible Working', 505.
91. On 12 September 2021, the Right to Request Flexible Working hit the headlines when estate agent Alice Thompson was awarded over £184,000 in compensation by an

employment tribunal under the Sex Discrimination Act. Her employer was found to have breached sex-discrimination law by refusing her request to work four days a week after the birth of her daughter, and finish work at 5 p.m. so as to be able to pick her up from nursery. The tribunal found that requiring Ms Thompson to work until or after 6 p.m., when most nurseries close, placed her at a disadvantage in relation to male colleagues and that the company had failed to consider her request seriously (for example, by allowing her to reduce her hours on a trial basis): https://assets.publishing.service.gov.uk/media/61323241e90e070442fbdd27/Ms_A_Thompson__vs_Scancrown_Ltd_-_Trading_as_Manors.pdf.

92. Interview, Margaret Prosser.
93. See M. A. Yerkes and J. Javornik, 'Creating Capabilities: Childcare Policies in Comparative Perspective', *Journal of European Social Policy*, 29 (2019), https://doi.org/10.1177/0958928718808421.
94. ILO, *A Quantum Leap for Gender Equality: For a Better Future of Work for All* (Paris: ILO), 80.

12

Training and Skills

A Long-Standing Policy Gap

Introduction

The third of the UN's seven principles for empowering women in the workplace states the need to 'promote education, training and professional development for women'.[1] In fact, British women's educational attainment relative to men's has steadily increased since the start of the millennium, and this trend helps to explain why the gender pay gap has narrowed.[2] The proportion of women who have no qualifications is now well below that of men.[3] However, a sizeable gender pay gap remains, despite better educational outcomes for women at the top and bottom of the pay scale.

Occupational segregation is estimated to account for around 20 per cent of the total gender pay gap,[4] and since the 1990s the situation has changed little at the extremes—that is, the occupational groups where women or men form the great majority of those employed. Based on figures for 2021, the most male-dominated occupations at professional level are in information technology (IT), where 21.6 per cent are women, and engineering, where 12.5 per cent are women, while in health 74 per cent are women (87.3 per cent in nursing), and in education 67.5 per cent (82.5 per cent in primary and nursery education). Professions thus exhibit an asymmetrical pattern, whereby men dominate technical and women caring occupations.

At intermediate (associate and skilled) level, the most striking imbalance is evident in women's over-representation in administrative and secretarial occupations, where they represent 72.4 per cent and 91.2 per cent respectively of those employed, and men's over-representation in skilled trades, where they represent 88.2 per cent of the workforce. At lower skill levels, women dominate care occupations, where 81.2 per cent are female (91.5 per cent in childcare), while men dominate transport occupations, where they represent 94.1 per cent of the workforce, and process, plant, and machine operatives, where 86.6 per cent are men.[5] In all cases, the female-dominated

Women and Employment in Public Policy. Susan Milner, Oxford University Press. © Susan Milner (2024).
DOI: 10.1093/9780191987359.003.0012

occupations are paid less than those that are male dominated, reflecting historical undervaluation of women's skills.[6]

Investment in education and training is seen as a way of boosting women's economic empowerment, but training systems are themselves factors of occupational segregation by class, gender, and race. Women's initial choices at school are constrained by a mixture of gender stereotypes within the educational setting and within wider society, and of practical barriers such as unavailability of high-value courses (for example, computer science or engineering). Once in the labour market, women in low-paid employment have poor access to training opportunities that could help to lift them into higher-paying jobs.

Because vocational training systems develop within culturally shaped (gendered) divisions of labour, feminists challenge the cultural assumptions underpinning training systems and argue that simply seeking to create a 'level playing field' by widening access to training is likely to reproduce existing gender inequalities.[7] At the very least, attempts to rebalance labour markets through skills training need to take account of how stereotyping restricts choice and how women's situation as carers affects their capacity to choose. Such attempts also need to recognize that additional support is required for people training in a non-traditional area or retraining after parenting-related leave or following long periods with no skills development.

Moreover, training policy must address employers' labour-market behaviour, particularly in systems such as the British, which is occupation based (rather than education based), driven by employers' needs, and institutionally weighted towards decision-making by employer representatives. The British system of vocational training has, according to experts, relied too heavily on persuading employers to take skills seriously, resulting in a 'low skills equilibrium', which successive English governments—from the launch in 1981 of the Manpower Services Commission (MSC) to the introduction of an employer levy to fund apprenticeships in 2017[8]—sought but failed to address.[9]

Ewart Keep's analysis of vocational training policy highlights three main causes of this failure: lack of government intervention in poor workplace skills usage, which requires a different set of policies; lack of clarification in public policy about expectations regarding the rights, responsibilities, and roles of employers in skills training; and the absence of a strong collective mechanism for organizing employers on the question of skills.[10] Its consequences are an imbalance between relatively high numbers of young people in higher education and relatively low numbers of employed people (of all ages) at intermediate skill levels, despite the latter being the target of successive reviews and reforms since 1981.[11] Over-qualification (or under-valuation) of employees has been a consistent feature of the British labour market: for example, the 2001 Skills Survey showed that 'the overall supply of qualifications outstrips demand by a comfortable margin'.[12]

Under such circumstances of employer underinvestment and policy failures, it is hardly surprising that, although equality and diversity have been stipulated objectives of policy on initial training throughout the period from 1981 to the present, in practice they have struggled to make headway against other priorities.

The Women and Work Commission (WWC), in focusing on the role of education and training in shaping the choices available to girls and women (as outlined in Chapter 7), was in line with the broader thrust of Labour policy since 1997, which famously prioritized 'education, education, education', in Tony Blair's words, to equalize life chances.[13] This meant that the commission could feed recommendations into an existing policy framework, and its members included training experts Chris Banks (chair of the Learning and Skills Council) and Ruth Silver, a lifelong further-education practitioner and leader.[14] Strong expertise and good fit with government preferences combined with conditions for consensus, as discussed in Chapter 7, and led to the most strongly worded recommendations in the 2006 report, and indeed the only recommendations with significant budget implications.

However, despite these auspicious conditions, when the commission was reconvened in 2009, it found that insufficient progress had been made on its recommendations concerning education and training. This chapter considers why it has proved so difficult for successive governments to invest in skills training for women. As a European network of experts commented in 2009, the UK had put in place a series of initiatives on vocational training since the 1970s, but they lacked coordination, risked reinforcement of gender stereotyping, and failed to address long-standing employer labour-market behaviours, which led to undervaluation of women's skills.[15] Without a systematic consideration of the needs of women and use of evidence to monitor, and without attention to wider structural disadvantage constraining women's access to training, training initiatives were unlikely to have much impact on women's labour-market position.

As discussed in this chapter's conclusion, skills training has returned to the agenda in the context of concerns about productivity, discussions about the challenges and opportunities provided by digitalization, and the need for a balanced economic recovery after the Covid-19 pandemic. Focusing on these questions, the All-Parliamentary Group on Women and Work reported in 2021 that women remain disproportionately located in low-paid, insecure sectors and under-represented in high-value jobs.[16] Jobs in care and catering will still be needed in the labour market of tomorrow, but low pay and poor conditions have led to high staff turnover and labour shortages, while women's exclusion from many high-value jobs in engineering and technology is a drain on productivity; yet there is no strategy in place to support women's entry and progression into economically and socially strategic occupations.

Labour and the Skills Agenda

Before considering the role of vocational training in relation to gender equality, it is useful to set out the institutional framework governing policy in the Labour years. In 1997, the incoming administration faced a fragmented system that it sought to rationalize and strengthen through the creation of a new structure, based on regional, subregional, and sectoral skills bodies coordinated by the Learning and Skills Council (LSC), established in 2001 to 'bring together, for the first time into a single learning and skills sector, a wide range of learning opportunities in further education, community and adult learning, work-based training for young people and workforce development for adults'.[17] Labour was 'almost hyperactive' in introducing reforms and initiatives in the field of education, particularly in respect of targets for educational attainment in secondary schools and expansion of numbers in higher education.[18] Spending rose from an average of 1.5 per cent of national income under Conservative governments between 1979 and 1997 to an average of 4.2 per cent annually (peaking at 6.4 per cent in 2009–10) under Labour, with most of this expenditure growth in schools and further education.[19] Education and training policy had both efficiency and distributional aims: the improvement of productivity and the narrowing of socio-economic inequality.[20] Overall, the result of this investment was to decrease socio-economic inequality,[21] largely as a result of the reduction in class sizes in secondary school and investment in early years education.

However, vocational training remained a 'Cinderella' policy area. Work-based training was the subject of 'frantic activity', much of it in the form of subsidies to employers, with little evidence of significant impacts on productivity or distributional effects.[22] Part of the problem lay in the modernization agenda driven by Labour, which encompassed often contradictory objectives and perverse incentives for practitioners (such as target-chasing and the constant quest for funding). The 'super complexity'[23] and 'constant flux' that characterized policy on training in the UK provided opportunities to raise concerns about equality of opportunity, but also in practice crowded out such concerns and made it difficult to pursue systematic reform.[24] Reliance on employer leadership also posed problems, and government lacked policy levers to bridge the gap between aspirations and what employers were willing to accept and pay for.[25] In practice, sectoral skills councils varied significantly in resources and capacity, and employers were found to have little awareness of their role.[26] Weak employer engagement characterized interventions in initial and continued training, particularly the flagship Train to Gain initiative established to subsidize employers through matched funding to encourage them to train their employees to Level 2 qualifications (a basic level of skills higher than entry level).[27]

Train to Gain was designed in response to Lord Leitch's government-commissioned review of skills in 2006. Like the Foster review of further education conducted the previous year,[28] the Leitch review argued that, beyond upskilling individuals (investing in supply), training of young and older people should follow employer demand. However, employer demand was constrained by government's decisions concerning which courses it wished to fund, in line with national skills policy.[29] This meant that in practice training provision was caught between competing priorities, creating a disequilibrium in which the content of training was under-regulated and often of poor quality.[30]

In 2009, the dissolution of the LSC was announced, and two successor organizations established: the Young People's Learning Agency, for 16–19-year-olds, a non-departmental body under the responsibility of the Department for Education, and the Skills Funding Agency for adult learners, an agency of the Department of Business, Industry, and Skills. The creation of two separate funding strands meant the end of Labour's attempt to bring together initial and continued training within an overarching rationale and institutional framework. Train to Gain was closed by the Conservative-led Coalition government in 2010, having faced criticism on grounds of value for money, at a cost of nearly £1.5 billion by 2009 for around 500,000 trainees. Take-up was initially lower than expected, and the National Audit Office found that much of this low-level training would have taken place anyway.[31] Despite Train to Gain, the number of people receiving workplace training fell during the millennial decade, bottoming out after 2015.[32]

Perhaps unsurprisingly in this rapidly changing (and often under-resourced) policy environment, there was little attention to the role of education and training in empowering women and girls, despite formal commitment to embed equality of opportunity into the curriculum. From the outset, the LSC was tasked with meeting national standards for post-16 learning and the promotion of equal opportunities, yet it lacked a strategy for doing so, or any monitoring mechanisms to judge effectiveness. As the following sections show, there has been some limited progress in apprenticeships, but real problems persist in the use of skills in low-pay sectors and weak prospects for career progression, which indicate structural features of the British economy as well as institutional and policy failures.

Apprenticeships and Initial Vocational Training

From the 1990s, when education and training became a major policy concern in the UK, equality campaigners focused on the way in which initial vocational training, particularly apprenticeships, embedded gender segregation in the labour market. As policymakers sought to integrate 'key' skills into the national curriculum and to strengthen vocational training pathways, the Equal Opportunities Commission (EOC) expressed concerns that the education system restricted choices by gender, channelling boys into technical and craft subjects and girls into 'domestic' subjects. Under its chair Joanna Foster, the EOC launched a formal investigation into vocational training in 1993, but sixteen of the eighty-two employer-led local Training and Enterprise Councils (TECs) failed to respond to its investigation, and, of those that did, very few could provide gender-disaggregated statistics, let alone describe actions to address equality of opportunity. The EOC's investigating officer, John Sharman, found that TECs lacked mechanisms for responding to any complaints of discrimination, and showed little understanding of discrimination law.[33] The EOC recommended that take-up of training opportunities should be monitored by gender, race, and occupation, and published nationally. It also called on the Department for Education to issue statutory guidance to careers advisers on equal opportunities, which the Conservative government pledged to do.[34]

The EOC's interest in vocational training reflected a growing number of requests from individuals. In 1994, an employment tribunal ruled that Karen Bishop, a trainee motor mechanic studying at college, had suffered sex discrimination when her application for an apprenticeship with a BMW franchise in Surrey (Cooper Thames Ditton) was rejected in favour of male applicants. Bishop had initially been given verbal acceptance, but the tribunal heard that the employer felt that the male applicants would 'fit in' better with the all-male environment of the company.[35] The Bishop case was the first to be judged after the tribunal decision, which rejected the government's limit on sex-discrimination cases (see Chapter 4): Bishop was awarded £24,000 compensation, more than double the existing limit of £11,000. The clear lesson of the Marshall ruling, the EOC argued, was that 'discrimination is costly and must be avoided'.[36]

Apprenticeships increasingly became the focus of attention as governments sought to modernize and expand provision. Apprenticeships—that is, training schemes (of at least twelve months' duration) combining formal skills education and on-the-job learning—form the route into many intermediate occupations. However, in the British context they form only a small part of the training and employment system (attracting 6 per cent of 16–18-year-olds in 2018, compared to 50 per cent of that age group in Germany),[37] and they have often been undervalued and under-specified. While the expanded range of subjects available in Modern Apprenticeships, launched in 1994, served to encourage wider participation by moving away from traditional crafts and manufacturing to include, for example, retail and care, under-specification has in practice meant wide variation in quality, particularly when compared to countries with well-established systems of dual training such as Germany, Netherlands, or Switzerland, where apprenticeships result in higher levels of skills.[38] Poor skills training is more likely in the newer sectors with no previous history of apprenticeships, such as retail, while higher-level apprenticeships (sometimes to university level) have increased in male-dominated occupations such as engineering and construction.[39]

Although the number of apprenticeships rose from 76,000 in 1997 to 256,000 in 2005,[40] the Leitch review argued that investment in intermediate skills remained low by international standards, and recommended a target of one million apprenticeships by 2020.[41] In 2015, the Conservative government announced that it would increase the target to three million starts by 2020.[42] However, although successive governments increased investment to meet this target, numbers fell short, with new apprenticeships at around 800,000 per year after 2010.[43] Moreover, policy was criticized for undue emphasis on numbers at the expense of the quality of apprenticeships,[44] and little progress had been made on widening participation. Although almost half of apprentices are female,[45] strong patterns of gender segregation exist, limiting women's access to higher-paying skilled intermediate and advanced-level jobs.

In June 2003, the EOC launched a formal investigation (supported by the European Social Fund) into Modern Apprenticeships, in five occupational areas marked by a high degree of segregation: 98 per cent of apprenticeships in early years care and education were filled by young women, while men formed the vast majority of trainees in construction (98 per cent), engineering (97 per cent), plumbing (93 per cent), and ICT (85.5 per cent).[46] Pay in childcare was less than half of that in the other sectors. This stark imbalance did not reflect evidence on girls' interest in possible careers—for example, in construction or skilled trades. Overall, the EOC concluded, 'our findings show that the current "education to training to work" system is failing the young women who need it most by channelling them into generally lower paid jobs than young men and not opening up genuine opportunity and choice'.[47] Noting that these male-dominated occupations all had severe labour shortages,[48] the EOC called on government to develop a comprehensive strategy, with targets for more gender-balanced recruitment to apprenticeships. As well as identifying gender imbalance as a drain on national productivity, the EOC drew a direct link between poor training policy and sex discrimination, with its chair Julie Mellor arguing that, 'until there are many more women plumbers—and fund managers', the EOC would need to continue 'opening its chequebook' to back discrimination claims.[49]

In 2018, the Equality and Human Rights Commission (EHRC) again investigated apprenticeships and found strikingly similar levels of gender segregation. In England, women made up only 5 per cent of new apprentices in construction in 2017–18.[50] More recent data show the same pattern, with women representing 7 per cent of starters in 2021–2.[51] Gender balance in construction apprenticeships has increased by five percentage points over nearly two decades: the pace of change could hardly be slower. The construction sector presents especially adverse conditions for gender desegregation, owing to entrenched cultures of embodied (hegemonic) masculinity and a high degree of informality of working practices.[52]

Progress was slightly faster in engineering (the sector with the largest share of apprenticeships), where women made up 9.5 per cent of new apprentices in 2021–2. In information technology, the proportion of women apprentices has grown steadily to reach nearly a third (32.1 per cent) in 2021–2. These figures show that occupational segregation is still perpetuated through initial vocational training. Although there are signs that initiatives in some sectors have resulted in greater numbers of female apprentices in information technology, those numbers are still low both in absolute terms and in comparison with much bigger take-up of engineering and construction apprenticeships.

The Role of Careers Guidance

In its 2005 report on segregation in apprenticeships, the EOC identified failures in careers guidance in schools. It called on government to make careers education a formal part of the school curriculum, subject to inspection on the extent to which it integrated gender equality. Every school student, it urged, should be entitled to a personal careers interview with a teacher or adviser 'who has been trained to open up choices, challenge gender stereotyping and promote non-traditional work opportunities'.[53] The Trade and Industry select committee echoed the EOC's recommendations, as did the WWC, whose 2006 report set out an agenda for better training for advisers and teachers in the world of work and in ways to challenge stereotypes about occupations and sectors dominated by one gender.[54]

However, the policy agenda of making careers guidance a tool of gender equality has been unfulfilled. Writing in 2014, Baroness Howe (founder of Opportunity Now and a former deputy chair of the EOC) singled this out as a matter of particular concern: 'Women's career choices still depend on the kind of careers advice young women receive. This was a problem when I was at the EOC and it still is.'[55] In line with Labour's broader emphasis on upskilling and employability, the Connexions service (launched in 2001) represented a £450 million investment in support for young people, creating a network of personal advisers working in schools. Arising from research conducted by the Social Exclusion unit, its principal focus was on young people most at risk of leaving school with no qualifications and no employment, who were more likely to come from disadvantaged family backgrounds. From the beginning, the service was concerned to improve career choices of young people, such as those from Black and ethnic minority backgrounds, who were at higher risk of becoming NEETs (young people not in education, employment, or training).[56] Given that the EOC's inquiry into apprenticeships had highlighted the poor range of choices open to young women from lower socio-economic groups in particular, the professionalization and expansion of careers guidance professionals provided an opportunity systematically to address constraints on girls' educational choices.

However, despite this broad commitment to tackling social exclusion, the service lacked a strategy for tackling gender-based disadvantage. Although Connexions advisers were given 'clear and explicit guidance' on the need to challenge gender stereotypes, the EOC found that in practice they often reacted to students' initial choices without raising questions about wider options or addressing unfounded fears about non traditional choices. Government had not set a sufficiently robust agenda for careers advice, the EOC argued in its submission to the Trade and Industry select committee's inquiry into occupational segregation.[57]

More broadly, the Connexions service was based on sound evidence and good intentions, but from the outset it lacked the resources to have much impact on young people's choices or the capacity to follow them.[58] Its remit encouraged a target-chasing culture, and advisers reportedly often found themselves torn between a need to meet targets and a desire to provide wide-ranging support to young people making their way through difficult circumstances.[59]

The Women and Work commissioners found evidence of poor careers guidance when they visited Quintin Kynaston secondary school in Westminster in 2005. Female students there reported that the quality of guidance of the Connexions advisers was poor, and that teachers and events organized by the school, such as 'taster days' presented by visitors employed in a range of occupations, provided a better source of information and ideas.[60] Although the commission's 2006 report emphasized the need to improve the quality of careers advice and information, it advocated doing this by embedding guidance into the schools curriculum, alongside well-planned work experience placements and visits.[61]

Responsibility for the Connexions service was transferred from central government to local authorities in 2008, and, in the context of local-government cuts, the service was subsequently fragmented, with some local authorities choosing to retain the label for teams of career advisers. The Coalition government in 2012 established the National Careers Service, which took over responsibility for guidance, but removed any duty for local authorities to provide services. Instead, the National Careers Service provides information and resources within a voluntary framework. Effectively, responsibility for careers information and guidance was placed in schools and colleges, at a time when funding for state schools was being steadily reduced.

In 2007, Lord Sainsbury (former chair of Sainsburys plc and Minister of Science and Innovation during 1998–2006) was commissioned to conduct a review of science and education policy, concluding with a call for a major expansion of STEM (science, technology, engineering, and mathematics) teaching in schools. Highly critical of the existing Connexions service, he recommended a new programme of career guidance on these subjects, coordinated by the then Department of Innovation, Universities, and Skills with support by sectoral skills councils and a network of industry ambassadors.[62] In 2013, Sainsbury's Gatsby Foundation commissioned a report that, starting from the premise of the poor quality careers advice in British state schools, looked to best practice in other European countries (Finland, Netherlands, Germany, Hong Kong, Canada, and Ireland), and drew up a list of eight principles giving priority to an embedded careers programme, personalized advice taking into account equality and diversity considerations, a full range of work experience options, and multiple opportunities to encounter the world of work and higher education. The report estimated that it would cost around 1 per cent of schools' budget to implement in full.[63]

The Gatsby recommendations were incorporated as statutory guidance to schools in a new government strategy in 2017,[64] with government oversight of annual monitoring of progress on the benchmarks. The Careers & Enterprise Company, which publishes annual reports on implementation of the Gatsby principles, found evidence of slow but steady progress, particularly in the most disadvantaged schools, although, as actions are voluntary, these reviews are based on self-reporting and likely to include only those schools that engage with the Gatsby process.[65] However, whereas the most recent reports have shown a majority of participating schools recording visits from employers and organizing encounters with further and higher education, they have little to say about equality of opportunity for boys and girls.

Silver expressed regret that careers guidance had 'gone to hell' since the WWC sat. She contrasted the fragmented and competitive English system with Scotland, where careers advisers

> still are properly professionally trained, researching, careers officers, they go into schools and employers, and they've still got a labour market information set-up. ... So you can see that because we didn't do that seam, that holding seam, when we went into the world with it, it didn't hold.[66]

Schools, Work Experience, and Actions to Tackle Gender Stereotyping

The idea that schools should be preparing students for the world of work through 'work experience' programmes was promoted during Margaret Thatcher's years of government, with the launch of a new Technical and Vocational Education Initiative (TVEI) run by the MSC. TVEI had a specific mission to promote equality of opportunity for boys and girls. However, dependence on employers' willingness to host students created a double bind for schools, which, on the one hand, had to exploit all available placements and, on the other, face employers' gender-traditional attitudes. A pioneering initiative, TVEI undoubtedly contributed both to the spread of work experience in schools and to broader awareness of equal opportunities in education and training, but it lacked the capacity to challenge embedded gender stereotyping and therefore perpetuated it, in many cases.[67]

In 2004, the Department for Education and Skills (DfES) introduced a requirement for all schools to include an element of work-related learning at

Key Stage 4 (for ages 14–19), including work experience as well as taster visits. The EOC in its evidence to the parliamentary Trade and Industry committee in 2005 argued that schools often lacked resources to put in place effective work experience programmes, and the committee agreed with this view.[68] It recommended that, rather than leaving the organization of work-experience placements to schools, sectoral skills councils should coordinate taster events across regions, 'to share responsibility more widely'.[69]

The WWC also paid attention to the EOC's evidence on work experience. It called on the DfES (and relevant Scottish, Welsh, and Northern Ireland departments) to create and implement a national World of Work programme coordinating schools' careers guidance and employers local bodies to organize work experience for girls across a range of occupations, including non-traditional jobs, within a coherent framework for vocational training.[70] The government's response to the WWC recommendation stated only that the DfES 'may' review DfES guidance to schools to avoid gender stereotyping in 2007.[71] Given that the Minister for Women Ruth Kelly had praised the commission's recommendations on gender stereotyping, this policy response was remarkably weak not only in its scope but even in its wording, and the call for a national strategy was simply ignored, as was the recommendation for government to run a communications campaign showing women in non-traditional occupations.

Failure to establish a comprehensive strategy for work-experience programmes and careers guidance has left an unfinished agenda, as Women and Work commissioner Sally Hopson (who went on to lead two large retail companies) reflected:

> Careers advice while it's Ofsted-listed it's not Ofsted inspected, so there's no standard, so it's [a question of]: is career advice offered, yes, tick the box, as opposed to having properly trained people to advise young people at a younger age. Work experience is left to parents to organize largely, so if you do it at all you do what your parents have always done. If your mum works in an office, she gets you work experience in an office. ... I've always believed that businesses could help, but there isn't that coordination that you need.[72]

In 2019, the Fawcett Society published the results of a year-long commission on gender stereotyping, which demonstrated that stereotyping in education from early years onwards reflected widespread gendering of products for children in the commercial world, including toys and clothes. Not only does gender stereotyping negatively affect girls' employment chances; it has adverse impacts on mental health for boys as well as girls. The report emphasized that a 'gender-neutral' approach is not enough but rather that stereotypes must be actively countered.[73]

Echoing the WWC's report thirteen years earlier, the Fawcett Society called for guidance to be integrated into the content of teacher training, as well as guidance to schools and early years providers, and for practice to be assessed by Ofsted in its inspection framework. It also called on government to fund pilot projects tackling gender stereotypes in early years education and to scale up successful initiatives. The Fawcett Society's recommendation on assessment of actions to tackle gender stereotyping in early years education was taken up by Ofsted: it is now a requirement that settings demonstrate engagement with stereotyping in order to be classed as 'good'. This move, described by Fawcett's policy and research manager Alison Henderson as a 'small but mighty step', goes some way towards redressing policy neglect of the issue.[74]

Sectoral initiatives

Sectors where women are significantly under-represented have seen a proliferation of initiatives aimed specifically at increasing female recruitment, particularly through training programmes. Organizations include Women in Engineering and Science (WES) and Women in Science and Engineering (WISE), Women into Construction, and Women in IT, all of which provide resources to employers and schools and colleges and may offer bursaries to encourage young women to take up training places.[75] Given the evidence presented above, such initiatives have had mixed success. As the Trade and Industry select committee found in 2005, they also lack coordination and mechanisms for exchange of good practice across sectors.[76]

The Labour government's first Gender Action Plan, drawn up in 2000 by the Women's Unit (then at the Department for Education and Employment), focused heavily on education and training. It aimed to challenge gender stereotypes 'through better advice on careers choice, innovative approaches to work experience and a major initiative to ensure women have the skills and opportunity to benefit from expected employment growth in ICT',[77] as well as investment to ensure better access for women to lifelong learning opportunities.[78] Among the initiatives in ICT, the Computer Clubs for Girls (CC4G) scheme was rolled out nationwide in 2005, having first been piloted in the south-east region, where it was funded by the south-east regional development agency. Run by the IT sector skills council (E-Skills), it took the form of an after-school club exclusively for girls aged between 10 and 14, based on a common curriculum that aimed to make computer-based activities fun and relevant for teenagers. The CC4G approach has continued, alongside several other similar initiatives such as Girls who Code, aimed at providing early opportunities for young women to learn coding, which can open up lucrative careers in IT or help career progression as an additional skill in other chosen occupations.

Evaluation of the pilot CC4G initiative found little or no impact on girls' career choices, although it also observed that girls who had taken part showed little difference in attitudes towards or competence in IT than boys of the same age.[79] The authors of this evaluation study argued that isolated, voluntary initiatives would have little impact on socially embedded stereotypes, particularly in the absence of supporting measures across schools, integrating IT skills into the curriculum and challenging gender stereotyping.[80] Later evaluation of the nationwide project, however, reported high proportions of participants saying they would consider a career in IT: 64 per cent in 2006 and 84 per cent in 2011.

Skills, Career Progression, and Workplace Training

The WWC devoted much of its time to the situation of older women workers who may have been trapped in low-paid work, and the training gap experienced by women later in their working life, because of time out of the labour market, or because of part-time workers' unequal access to training. It also saw training as a means by which women could access non-traditional jobs, such as technical occupations that are typically relatively high-earning and where employers reported skills shortages. Based on visits to women studying IT and plumbing at Bradford College, and reports from LSC pilot projects,[81] it argued that older women could benefit from training opportunities in non-traditional sectors because of increased confidence and experience.[82]

The commission's 2006 report recommended a £20 million package aimed at supporting women's career progression through skills training, aimed particularly at women not in work and those working in sectors characterized by low-level jobs, with free Level 3 training (funded by government and employers) piloted for women working in the 'five C' sectors, especially those working part-time. Training should ensure that the needs of women from ethnic minority backgrounds were met, and that it was organized flexibly to suit women's work and non-work time constraints. For example, following evidence from Unison, it was recommended that women working in low-paid sectors who wished to retain as nurses or teachers should be able to follow flexible, modular courses rather than be expected to give up work to train full-time.[83] Training centres with on-site creche facilities were recommended, and the commission urged the government inspection agencies to include consideration of whether training providers met the needs of women through provision of childcare facilities and flexible study arrangements.[84]

However, when the commission reconvened in 2009, it flagged the area of skills training as 'amber', meaning that more work needed to be done. Overall, a £40 million package of training support had been put in place to support women's skills, through the Train to Gain programme as well as apprenticeships. In the context of economic downturn, the commission urged government to take further measures to build women workers' skills and expressed concern that organizational changes (leading to the disbanding of the Learning and Skills Councils by 2010 and the creation of the new Skills Funding Agency) could result in a loss of focus on those most in need of support. The 2009 report therefore included a new recommendation that the Skills Funding Agency include gender equality objectives in its annual reporting.[85] The department for Business, Innovation, and Skills (BIS, which had replaced the DTI) should be more proactive in evaluating the Train to Gain programme and learning from its successes and failures.[86] BIS also needed to be more proactive in ensuring that it took account of gender, and in particular the specific needs of women working part-time, in assessing apprenticeships through robust reporting and monitoring mechanisms.[87] This included dissemination of good practice as well as identifying areas where gender segregation still existed in training provision and access. A clear message in the 2009 recommendations on training was that BIS was failing in its public-sector equality duty (PSED) by giving insufficient attention to women's unequal access to training opportunities.

Train to Gain did not directly target women, and it suffered from a major drawback in that it depended on employers taking the initiative: if women wanted to retrain in high-skill occupations, they were likely to need to change employer to do so; it did little to address the problem of 'low-road' employers who did not wish to upskill their workforce.[88] As Silver argued, reliance on employers tended to mean quick and easy gains that left aside employee needs in many cases: a strategy of 'low hanging fruit'.[89] Only in London was there a deliberate strategy to work with employers to identify the skill needs of women. In fact, women outnumbered men in the early years of the initiative, showing the strong demand for upskilling among female employees. In all waves of the programme, evaluation showed that women particularly appreciated (more than male participants) the 'soft' skills-building and increased confidence provided through mentor support.[90] Training was also found to be of particular benefit forwomen returning from periods of maternity leave.[91]

Successive skills strategies did not fully integrate the needs of women as a specific group of workers, other than through the Women and Work Sectoral Pathway Initiative, which provided training to relatively small numbers of women (fewer than 5,000 each year).[92] This initiative was explicitly established to respond to the WWC's 2006 recommendations, and its objectives related to gender equality, under the remit of BIS. Managed by the Sector Skills Development Agency, it was funded jointly by the government (to the tune of £10 million initially, and a further £5 million in 2009) and employers and invited bids from sector skills councils for specific projects aimed at encouraging women to enter sectors such as automotive, logistics, and construction. The initiative was found to have increased positive attitudes towards training among participating employers, although these remained predominantly larger and medium-sized companies, and a high level of satisfaction among women trainees. The initiative focused on recruitment in most cases, but also had a modest impact on women's chances of progression within their existing job following training.[93]

Research investigating women's experience of such initiatives could have been used to develop policy and practice. But, when skills policies were assessed, women's needs were never taken into account in the evaluation criteria, as the WWC had pointed out in its 2009 follow-up report. When Train to Gain was evaluated by the House of Commons Public Accounts Committee at the end of the same year, no mention was made of women's needs, or indeed of the objectives set by the WWC.

Conclusion

As this chapter has shown, training policy in the UK performs poorly compared to many European countries. Problems are structural, related to the wider political economy, institutional, and political, resulting in a lack of effective policy levers. For too long, policy outputs have taken the form of pilot initiatives that were evaluated but not adequately followed up, remedied, or scaled up. Policy failed to follow evidence. As Hopson reflected, from the point of view of remedies for structural inequalities, 'that whole area [of training policy] for me is still pretty untapped'.[94]

The UK has a long-term, structural weakness caused by underinvestment of a significant number of employers in skills, and a preference in some sectors for 'low-road' competitive strategies where costs are kept low by squeezing wages.[95] These sectors tend to employ large numbers of women, and employers' (including public-sector employers') reliance on cheap, expendable female labour has never been challenged. Institutionally, attempts to coordinate policy while paying attention to regional imbalances and sectoral specificities have proved ineffective, resulting in a high degree of instability in the system. While a succession of high-level expert reviews gave guidance on strategic objectives and suitable frameworks, in practice training policy fell foul of competing priorities (such as the drive to boost numbers in higher education). According to Silver, vocational training is seen by policy-makers as the 'adaptive layer' rather than a sector where strategic investment is central to economic policy objectives, and successive initiatives have lacked a 'strong holding seam'.[96]

Overall, training policy since the 1980s has largely failed to meet stated policy aims of boosting skills and productivity. Since 2008, the situation has worsened, with lower funding than in the 1980s. Although the creation of an employer levy for apprenticeships in 2017 raised hopes of improved quality of training, the government's review of apprenticeships found that training is poor in many cases, particularly in sectors such as retail and catering, and the drop-out rate is high.[97] Industrial policy focuses increasingly on high-paid jobs in finance and technology while neglecting skills improvement at lower and intermediate levels.[98]

These fundamental weaknesses form a large part of the reason why there has been so little investment in the progression of low-paid women. But another significant explanation is the lack of attention to structural inequality and the intersection of gender, race, and class, which requires actions to address the reasons for under-representation of marginalized groups in high-value occupations, and undervaluation of the work performed in low-paid jobs.

Institutionalist analysis helps to explain this public policy absence by highlighting the lack of influence of women's policy agency in the specific sector of education and skills. In their comparative overview of public policy, Dorothy McBride and Amy Mazur found little relationship between the development of national women's policy machinery and training policy for women. They observed that, although women's movements lobbied strongly for initiatives to challenge occupational segregation in education and training, they had strikingly little influence over policy, and that education and training in any case had a 'low profile' in public policy debates.[99] The analysis in this book highlights the lack of gender mainstreaming in a policy area that might in some respects be thought favourable for the promotion of women's policy interests (for example, because it is one of the government departments where a woman minister is most likely to be appointed), and the low priority given to vocational training overall, which can be explained with reference to regime theory as well as the lack of institutional policy coordination.

These gaps and absences point to lessons that could be learnt from the experience of the last few decades of training policy and that could potentially feed into a more effective national strategy. The first lesson concerns the starting point advocated by the EOC in the 1990s: the need for statistics that are disaggregated by gender and race (and ideally also region and other characteristics such as disability), and regular monitoring with the authority to make recommendations to the government department with responsibility for education and skills. These exist for apprenticeships but should be extended to cover all forms of training. The second lesson concerns the need for more effective monitoring of equality of opportunity by regulatory bodies such as Ofsted and the Skills Funding Agency, with publication and monitoring, based on reliable, disaggregated statistics.

The third lesson is that the aim of encouraging greater investment by employers will not happen without specific mechanisms such as the levy to fund apprenticeships, which could be extended to cover workplace training.[100] This long-standing recommendation of training experts was considered by Labour policy researchers in the 1990s but never implemented.

The final lesson relates to the need for a sectoral framework for skills and career development, covering both initial and continued (workplace) training. For highly paid jobs in growing sectors, this entails a comprehensive multi-employer programme of work with schools and training providers to embed vocational skills within the wider curriculum, encourage wide participation, and tackle gender and other stereotypes. All sectors should monitor career progression for all groups. For female-dominated low-pay sectors, sectoral bodies should work to support employers in creating progression ladders. Intensive work on both supply and demand sides requires regulatory oversight by central government and statutory agencies (such as the EHRC) as well as appropriate fundings streams and mechanisms, with equality of opportunity built into the funding process, including via an employer levy, and mainstreamed with support for intensive support as needed to redress the balance. Such actions have the potential to make a serious impact on the gender pay gap,[101] and to address the British problem of low productivity.

Notes

1. United Nations, 'Endorse the Women's Empowerment Principles', https://www.unglobalcompact.org/take-action/action/womens-principles.
2. M. Costa Dias, R. Joyce, and F. Parodi, *Wage Progression and the Gender Wage Gap: The Causal Impact of Hours of Work*, Briefing Note BN223 (London: Institute for Fiscal Studies, 2018), 7–8.
3. T. Schuller, *Gender and Skills in a Changing Economy* (London: UK Commission for Employment and Skills, 2011), 9.
4. W. Olsen, V. Gash, S. Kim, and M. Zhang, *The Gender Pay Gap in the UK: Evidence from the UKHLS* (London: GEO, 2018).
5. ONS, *Employment by Occupation (SOC2010) by Sex*, Nomis database (London: ONS, 2021).
6. D. Grimshaw and J. Rubery, *Undervaluing Women's Work* (Manchester: EOC, 2007).
7. See B. Niemeyer and H. Colley, 'Why Do We Need (Another) Special Issue on Gender and VET?', *Journal of Vocational Education and Training*, 67 (2015), https://doi.org/10.1080/13636820.2014.971498.
8. The levy applies to employers with a wage bill of more than £3 million and amounts to 0.5% of the wage bill, whether they employ any apprentices or not.
9. E. Keep, 'Employers, the Ghost at the Feast', *Journal of Education and Work*, 33 (2020), https://doi.org/10.1080/13639080.2020.1852501.
10. Keep, 'Employers, the Ghost at the Feast', 503–4.
11. G. Mason, 'Higher Education, Initial Education and Vocational Training, and Continuing Education and Training: Where Should the Balance Lie?', *Journal of Education and Work*, 33 (2020), https://doi.org/10.1080/13639080.2020.1755428.
12. D. N. Ashton and J. Sung, *Supporting Workplace Learning for High Performance Working* (Geneva: ILO), 63. See also E. Keep, 'The Limits of the Possible: Shaping the Learning and Skills Landscape through a Shared Policy Narrative', SKOPE Research Paper no. 86 (Cardiff University, 2009).
13. 'Full Text of Tony Blair's Speech on Education', *Guardian*, 23 May 2001.
14. See K. Parker, 'Meet Ruth Silver, the Grande Dame of Further Education', *TES Magazine*, 30 April 2021.
15. European Commission's Expert Group on Gender and Employment, *Gender Segregation in the Labour Market: Root Causes, Implications and Policy Responses in the EU* (Brussels: European Commission, 2009).
16. Women and Work All-Party Parliamentary Group, *Building Back Better: Securing the Future of Women's Employment* (Women and Work APPG/House of Commons, 2021).
17. F. Coffield, R. Steer, A. Hodgson, K. Spours, S. Edward, and I. Finlay, 'A New Learning and Skills Landscape? The Central Role of the Learning and Skills Council', *Journal of Education Policy*, 20 (2005), 631–56.
18. A. Heath, A. Sullivan, V. Boliver, and A. Zimdars, 'Education under New Labour, 1997–2010', *Oxford Review of Economic Policy*, 29 (2013), https://doi.org/10.1093/oxrep/grt003, p.228.
19. H. Chowdry and L. Sibieta, 'Trends in Education and Schools Spending', Briefing Note BN121 (Institute for Fiscal Studies, 2011).

20. D. Cobham, C. Adam, and K. Mayhew, 'The Economic Record of the 1997–2010 Labour Government: An Assessment', *Oxford Review of Economic Policy*, 29 (2013), https://doi.org/10.1093/oxrep/grt014, p. 11.
21. Heath et al., 'Education under New Labour', 240.
22. Cobham et al., 'The Economic Record of the 1997–2010 Labour Government', 13.
23. Coffield et al., 'A New Learning and Skills Landscape?', 640.
24. E. Keep, T. Richmond, and R. Silver, *Honourable Histories: From the Local Management of Colleges via Incorporation to the Present Day: 30 Years of Reform in Further Education 1991–2021* (Manchester: Further Education Trust for Leadership, 2021), 11.
25. J. Payne, 'Sector Skills Councils and Employer Engagemen—Delivering The "Employer-Led" Skills Agenda in England', *Journal of Education and Work*, 21 (2008), https://doi.org/10.1080/13639080802090260, p. 94.
26. Payne, 'Sector Skills Councils', 98.
27. J. Payne and E. Keep, 'One Step Forward, Two Steps Back? Skills Policy in England under the Coalition Government', SKOPE Research Paper no. 102 (Cardiff University, 2011).
28. A. Foster, *Realising the Potential: A Review of the Future Role of Further Education Colleges* (London: DfES, 2005).
29. S. Leitch, *Prosperity for All in the Global Economy: World Class Skills* (London: HMSO, 2006).
30. N. Panchamia, *Choice and Competition in Further Education* (London: Institute for Public Policy Research, 2012), 5.
31. National Audit Office, *Train to Gain: Developing the Skills of the Workforce* (London: NAO, 2009).
32. J. Dromey and C. McNeil, *Skills 2030: Why the Adult Skills System is Failing to Build an Economy that Works for Everyone* (London: Institute for Public Policy Research, 2017), 45.
33. D. Summers, 'EOC says Women Overlooked by TECs', *Financial Times*, 31 March 1993.
34. EOC, *Annual Report 1993* (Manchester: EOC, 1993), 21–2.
35. *Bishop* v. *the Cooper Group plc* [1994] IT/60,910/92.
36. EOC, *Annual Report 1993*, 4.
37. M. Brockmann, '"It Doesn't Take Much Force": The Negotiation of Gender by Two Women Motor Mechanic Apprentices through the Biographical Lens', *Journal of Vocational Education and Training*, 73 (2021), https://doi.org/10.1080/13636820.2020.1734061, p. 436.
38. M. Brockmann, L. Clarke, and C. Winch, 'The Apprenticeship Framework in England: A New Beginning or a Continuing Sham?', *Journal of Education and Work*, 23 (2010), https://doi.org/10.1080/13639081003627439; T. Hogarth, L. Gambin, and C. Hasluck, 'Apprenticeships in England: What Next?', *Journal of Vocational Education & Training*, 64 (2012), https://doi.org/10.1080/13636820.2011.590221; P. Ryan, 'Apprenticeship: Between Theory and Practice, School and the Workplace', Working Paper 64 (University of Zurich, 2011).
39. A. Fuller and L. Unwin, 'Creating a "Modern Apprenticeship": A Critique of the UK's Multi-Sector, Social Inclusion Approach', *Journal of Education and Work*, 23 (2010), https://doi.org/10.1080/1363908022000032867.
40. Leitch, *Prosperity for All in the Global Economy*, 10.
41. Leitch, *Prosperity for All in the Global Economy*, 14.

42. HM Government, *English Apprenticeships: Our 2020 Vision* (London: HMSO, 2015).
43. ONS, *Apprenticeships and Traineeships*, dataset (ONS, 2022). Data are for England, as training is a devolved responsibility.
44. In 2022, Ofsted data showed that apprenticeships provide the poorest quality of learning of all further-education types, with one-third of provision rated as inadequate or requiring improvement: see B. Staton, 'Apprenticeships in England Deliver Lowest Quality of Further Education, Analysis Finds', *Financial Times*, 6 November 2022.
45. 48.8% of starters in 2021–2 were female: Staton, 'Apprenticeships in England'. In 2000, young women accounted for only 40% of apprentices.
46. EOC, *Free to Choose: Tackling Gender Barriers to Better Jobs: Great Britain Summary Report* (Manchester: EOC, 2005); L. Miller, F. Neathey, E. Pollard, and D. Hill, *Occupational Segregation, Gender Gaps, and Skill Gaps* (Manchester: EOC, 2004).
47. EOC, *Free to Choose*, 4.
48. EOC, *Talking about Sex: Annual Report 2003-2004* (Manchester: EOC, 2004), 12–13.
49. H. Stewart, 'Counting the Cost of Sexism', *Guardian*, 9 January 2005.
50. C. Davies, 'Exploring Positive Action as a Tool to Address Under-Representation in Apprenticeships', Research Report 123 (EHRC, 2019), 6.
51. ONS, *Apprenticeships and Traineeships.*
52. D. Bridges, E. Wulff, L. Bamberry, B. Krivokapik-Skoko, and S. Jenkins, 'Negotiating Gender in the Male-Dominated Skilled Trades: A Systematic Literature Review', *Construction Management and Economics*, 38 (2020), https://doi.org/10.1080/01446193.2020.1762906.
53. EOC, *Free to Choose*, 16.
54. WWC, *Shaping a Fairer Future* (London: DTI, 2006), 13.
55. E. Howe, 'Women and the State: Regendering our Institutions', in R. Campbell and S. Childs (eds), *Deeds and Words: Gendering Politics after Joni Lovenduski* (Colchester: ECPR Press, 2014), 133–5, at 135.
56. See K. Sheehy, R. Kumrai, and M. Woodhead, 'Young People's Experiences of Personal Advisors and the Connexions Service', *Equality, Diversity and Inclusion: An International Journal*, 30 (2011), https://doi.org/10.1108/02610151111124923.
57. House of Commons, *Jobs for the girls*, 9. See also A. Fuller, V. Beck, and L. Unwin, 'The Gendered Nature of Apprenticeship: Employers' and Young People's Perspectives', *Education + Training*, 47 (2005), 298–311.
58. Learning and Skills Improvement Service, *Career Learning for the 21st Century: A Leadership Issue for the FE Sector* (London: Department for Children, Schools and Families, 2009), 10.
59. See L. Russell, R. Simmons, and R. Thompson, 'Playing the Numbers Game: Connexions Personal Advisers Working with Learners on Entry to Employment Programmes', *Journal of Vocational Education & Training*, 62 (2010), https://doi.org/10.1080/13636820903127561.
60. WWC, *Shaping a Fairer Future*, 13.
61. WWC, *Shaping a Fairer Future*, 20–2.
62. Lord Sainsbury of Turville, *The Race to the Top: A Review of Government's Science and Technology Programmes* (London: HMSO, 2007).
63. J. Holman, *Good Careers Guidance* (London: Gatsby Foundation, 2013).

64. Department for Education, *Careers Strategy: Making the Most of Everyone's Skills and Talents* (London: HMSO, 2017).
65. Careers & Enterprise Company, *Gatsby Benchmark Results for 2021–2022* (London: Careers & Enterprise Company, 2022).
66. Interview, Ruth Silver.
67. S. Heath, 'One Step Forward, Two Steps Back? Work Experience, Equal Opportunities and TVEI', *British Journal of Education and Work*, 8 (1995), https://doi.org/10.1080/026900095008030.
68. House of Commons, Business, Enterprise and Regulatory Reform Committee, 'Jobs for the Girls: The Effect of Occupational Segregation on the Gender Pay Gap', Sixteenth Report of Session 2004–2005, HC 300, p. 10.
69. House of Commons, 'Jobs for the Girls', 11.
70. WWC, *Shaping a Fairer Future*, 16–17.
71. Department for Communities and Local Government, *Government Action Plan Implementing the Women and Work Commission Recommendations* (London: DCLG, 2006).
72. Interview, Sally Hopson.
73. Fawcett Society, *Unlimited Potential: Report of the Commission on Gender Stereotypes in Early Childhood* (London: Fawcett Society 2020). See also N. Chambers, E. Kashefpakdel, J. Rehill, and C. Percy, *Drawing the Future* (London: Education and Employers, 2018).
74. A. Henderson, 'Small but Mighty Steps to Tackle Gender Stereotypes' (London: Fawcett Society, 2021), https://www.fawcettsociety.org.uk/blog/small-but-mighty-steps-to-tackle-gender-stereotypes (accessed 6 December 2022).
75. C. Davies, *Equality at Work? Positive Action in Gender Segregated Apprenticeships* (London: Young Women's Trust, 2018), 13.
76. House of Commons, 'Jobs for the Girls', 24.
77. DfEE, 'Draft Gender Action Plan', 1. The draft document was included confidentially in a letter from Jenny Eastabrook to the EOC Equal Pay Taskforce, 13 April 2000: EOC Equal Pay Task Force 595/Box 1/2 Report/Background material, Modern Records Centre, University of Warwick.
78. DfEE, 'Draft Gender Action Plan', 2.
79. A. Fuller, H. Connor, B. Johnston, and J. Turbin, 'The Evaluation of Computer Clubs for Girls: Final Report to SEEDA' (University of Southampton, 2009).
80. A. Fuller, J. Turbin, and B. Johnston, 'Computer Clubs for Girls: The Problem with Seeing Girls as the Problem', *Gender and Education*, 25 (2013), 494–514.
81. WWC, *Shaping a Fairer Future*, 57.
82. WWC, *Shaping a Fairer Future*, 53.
83. WWC, *Shaping a Fairer Future*, 65.
84. WWC, *Shaping a Fairer Future*, 67.
85. WWC, *Shaping a Fairer Future: Review of the Recommendations of the Women and Work Commission Three Years on* (London: GEO, 2009), 8.
86. WWC, *Shaping a Fairer Future: Review*, 21.
87. WWC, *Shaping a Fairer Future: Review*, 23.
88. L. Miller, 'Women Work-Based Learners: Factors Affecting Lifelong Learning and Career Opportunities', in S. Jackson, I. Malcolm, and K. Thomas (eds), *Gendered Choices: Learning, Work, Identities in Lifelong Learning* (London: Springer, 2011), 95–111.

89. Interview, Silver.
90. S. Hyde, 'Where is Gender within the Workplace Learning Agenda?' in Jackson et al, *Gendered Choices*, 112-28.
91. LSC, *Train to Gain Learner Evaluation: Wave 3 Research Report* (Coventry: LSC, 2009).
92. See, e.g., BIS, *The National Skills Strategy* (London: HMSO, 2009), 48. The 2009 national skills strategy did not mention the WWC.
93. J. Wiseman, E. Parry, and D. Devins, 'Evaluation of Women and Work Sector Pathways Initiative—Phase 2' (Leeds Metropolitan University/Boston Marketing Group, 2012).
94. Interview, Hopson.
95. T. Lanning and K. Lawton, *No Train, No Gain: Beyond the Free Market and State-Led Skills Policy* (London: Institute for Public Policy Research, 2012).
96. Interview, Silver.
97. EDSK, *No Train, No Gain. An Investigation into the Quality of Apprenticeships in England* (EDSK, 2022).
98. N. Lee, A. Green, and P. Sissons, 'Low-Pay Sectors, Earnings Mobility and Economic Policy in the UK', *Policy & Politics*, 46 (2017), https://doi.org/10.1332/030557317X15072086455899.
99. D. E. McBride and A. G. Mazur, *The Politics of State Feminism: Innovation in Comparative Research* (Philadelphia: Temple University Press, 2010), 253. The 'low profile' of the policy area was in contrast to 'hot issues' largely related to doctrinal debates such as abortion, but also to women's political representation and violence against women and girls.
100. Dromey and McNeil, *Skills 2030*.
101. Costa Dias et al., *Wage Progression and the Gender Wage Gap*.

13
Setting the Standard?
The Public Sector's Role in Promoting Gender Equality

Introduction

During the Labour years, the public sector was a site of policy innovation, particularly in the field of equality. Part of the reason for this policy attention was historic: long-standing demands for equal pay had focused on the public sector in the mid-twentieth century because this was where women were employed in increasing numbers, and it was relatively easy to compare their pay with male employees. This left a legacy of equal-pay claims that could not be ignored.

Another part of the reason was that inequalities resulting from the delivery of public services became a pressing social problem that was highlighted by the media and required policy solutions. The 1993 murder of Black teenager Stephen Lawrence and the subsequent McPherson inquiry (1999), which uncovered institutional racism within the police force,[1] led to the first public-sector equality duty (PSED), introduced in 2001 and related to race, with duties relating to disability and to gender adopted in 2006 (coming into force in 2007).[2] In the Equality Act 2010, duties were placed on public-sector employers to collect data and demonstrate actions not just to ensure non-discrimination but actively to promote equality. The duties applied both to service delivery and to employment within public services.

Beyond these duties enshrined in law, there are two main reasons why the public sector has a particular role to play in equalizing opportunities at work. The first is that it is a major employer of women: in 2000, it employed 26 per cent of the total workforce, two-thirds of these women (and this proportion has remained roughly constant: it was 65 per cent in 2018).[3] Over 30 per cent of employed women worked in the public sector in 2000, compared to 20 per cent of male employees.[4]

Second, the public sector is subject to stricter regulation of employment conditions, which in principle ensures consistency of grading and job content across a given sector such as education, healthcare, government departments

Women and Employment in Public Policy. Susan Milner, Oxford University Press. © Susan Milner (2024).
DOI: 10.1093/9780191987359.003.0013

or local government, and therefore also greater transparency around pay and conditions. 'Single status' agreements introduced after 1997 (placing manual and administrative staff in a single national pay system) ushered in systematic job evaluation. The public sector is more highly unionized, giving employees stronger leverage in upholding formal rights. Pensions are also higher in the public sector, helping to narrow the gender pensions gap overall.[5]

Transparency about pay is higher in the public than the private sector, because government is involved in pay-setting both directly (through public spending reviews) and indirectly (through independent review bodies, which are publicly accountable), and local councillors and government ministers are held to account. Trade unions are also involved in pay-setting and have an interest in ensuring transparency.[6] All of this, as well as the development of 'family-friendly' work schedules such as flexitime, mean that there has long been a 'public-sector wage premium' such that women's pay was higher in the public than the private sector, and it provides better continuous career progression for higher-paid women.

However, although more consistent and transparent job grading means that the gender pay gap is narrower in the public than in the private sector, significant inequalities remain. Across the public sector, and within each employing body, there is strong vertical and horizontal segregation, 'with all of the attendant problems for women employed in this sector, not least from the standpoint of pay'.[7] Women represented over 60 per cent of public-sector employees in 2010, but occupied only 30 per cent of senior posts.[8] The 2001 Kingsmill review found that public-sector managers gave low priority to equality and diversity in practice, and lagged behind larger private-sector employers in this respect.[9]

One of the reasons the gender pay gap is smaller in the public than the private sector is the higher proportion of women working full-time. This is because of the greater possibility for flexible working options such as flexitime and time banking (Time Off in Lieu), as well as job-share arrangements, allowing women to avoid having to switch to part-time work after childbirth. Nevertheless, the public sector employs large numbers of women on part-time contracts, and pay is likely to be relatively low for such employment. Part-time working in the public sector is overwhelmingly female: in 2019 they outnumbered male part-timers by a ratio of 6.5 to one, whereas in the private sector there are just over twice as many female part-timers as men.[10] Consequently, the part-time gender pay gap in the public sector (the difference between full-time male pay and female part-time pay) has grown steadily.[11]

The public sector's role as a standard-setter in employment relations and the promotion of equality was also weakened by marketization trends, which negatively affected lower-paid women, whose jobs were more likely to be contracted out.[12] After 2010, public-sector employment as a proportion of total employment fell, with women particularly affected by job losses in local government.[13] Pay freezes in the public sector after 2010 resulted in slower wage growth each year than in the private sector.[14] Although performance pay is less widespread in the public than the private sector, its use has increased and is found to result in worse outcomes for women than men.[15] Moreover, organizational cultures in the public sector have been found to disadvantage Black women and those from other minoritized backgrounds, on whom the sector relies, even as equality and diversity programmes have become more visible.[16] The gap between strong regulation and unequal outcomes suggests that the policies designed to prevent the latter suffer from design and implementation weaknesses.

This chapter discusses the tensions evident in the role played by the public sector in setting standards for equal treatment of men and women in employment and considers the impact of successive policy interventions to strengthen its role, particularly the PSED. The PSED raises important questions about the extent to which statutory intervention can change the behaviour of employers and challenge problematic organizational cultures, and whether (and if so, how) policy design can increase its chances of effective impact.

As in other chapters in this book, the Women and Work Commission (WWC, 2004–9) provides a useful starting point for examining the public sector as a site of tensions in the regulation of employment and equalities. The commission's terms of reference specified that, 'as a substantial employer of women, the public sector warrants particular attention'. The WWC devoted a significant amount of its time to the public sector, partly as a way of trialling proposed actions, which could later be transferred to the private sector, and partly in recognition of the specific role played by public services as essential social and economic infrastructure. It focused in particular on the PSED and on public procurement.

Pay and Job Evaluation in Local Government and Health

Between 1976 and 1998, the vast majority of equal-pay claims were lodged by public-sector employees, notably in the Coal Board (then publicly owned) and the National Health Service.[17] Subsequently, in the 2000s, most claims still involved public-sector organizations, particularly in local government and health, peaking in 2007–8,[18] with the potential to result in millions of pounds in reparatory pay if successful. Public-sector unions were involved in most of the large equal-pay claims of the 1990s, with Unison sponsoring some 40,000 claims and the GMB (a union with members in both the public and private sectors) over 25,000.[19] Although these developments did not feature in Labour's 1997 manifesto, the new government very quickly had to deal with them.

In 1997, agreement was reached by the largest bargaining unit in the UK, the National Joint Council, bringing together local-government employers and three recognized unions (Unison, Unite and GMB), on the introduction of Single Status in local government. The agreement introduced a single pay spine for all employees, bringing together staff previously whose terms and conditions were governed by the 'white book' (manual workers), the 'purple book' (administrative, professional, technical, and clerical workers) and the 'red book' (skilled craft workers), based on local job evaluation. The catalyst for the agreement was the 1996 case of 150 canteen workers in Cleveland, supported by the lawyer Stefan Cross for GMB union (who became the leading 'no-win-no-fee' lawyer in equal-pay cases), which resulted in an award of £4 million on grounds of equal pay, following an earlier £1 million award on grounds of sex discrimination. At issue was the payment of bonuses to male workers, whom the tribunal agreed could be viewed as doing comparative work (such as gardeners and refuse collectors), which had been negotiated in earlier decades as compensation for wage freezes in the sector, but did not apply to the female canteen staff. The 1996 case therefore opened the way for widespread challenges in the public sector, particularly in local government, where male manual staff had been able to negotiate bonuses not available to female workers.[20]

The Single Status agreement represented a 'significant achievement' for the public-sector union Unison,[21] but soon became dogged by problems of inertia and uneven implementation.[22] Therefore, further waves of litigation were encouraged by the failure of Single Status to resolve inequalities rapidly. Moreover, settlement of decades-old inequalities would be costly to local authorities under pressure from the Labour government to reduce spending and restructure service delivery. A study in 2006 found that in the 'early implementers', which moved quickly to establish job evaluation, the pay bill rose by an average permanent increase of 3.7 per cent.[23]

Stella Manzie, one of the Women and Work Commissioners, had handled the implementation of Single Status at Labour-controlled Coventry council (graded as 'one of the eleven worst councils in the country' in the comprehensive assessment exercise before she took over its management):

> There were some very, very knotty problems, like the fact that our refuse operatives had massive bonus schemes, which gave some but not all of them very high salaries for what they were doing, compared to say female admin assistants in an office. But it was even more complicated than that, because you were taking down the salaries of the bin men, never a good thing to do in industrial relations, and on the other hand when you looked across the female workforce at the lower to middle end, while some of those people went up, because of the job evaluation process some of them went down. So some of the female staff were saying, well hang on a minute, this was supposed to be about driving us up and my wage is going down, how can that be? And of course when you do a big exercise, some of it does go up and some of it does go down. So it was very, very fraught.[24]

Similar processes occurred in the National Health Service. Although the question of NHS staff pay was absent from Labour's 1997 manifesto, reform of health service management featured heavily; indeed, the party promised to do no less than 'rebuild the NHS'. The White Paper introduced as early as 1997 included reference to the need for a single national pay system, while retaining local flexibility. In 1999, the proposed new pay structure was published under the heading 'Agenda for Change', but negotiations with the main unions proved difficult, and it was not until January 2003 that a framework was published and not until December 2004 that implementation began. The new pay structure, based on a pay spine for nurses and other health professionals, and a separate pay spine for other directly employed staff, was underpinned by a job evaluation scheme based on sixteen factors.[25] Agenda for Change proved even more complex to implement than Single Status, because the aim was not to evaluate existing jobs but to embark on a programme of job redesign. Like Single Status, it was implemented differently across different trusts and in addition across clinical specialisms, with consequently varying impacts. Also like Single Status, implementation costs were estimated in the region of 3–4 per cent of the total wage bill.

Political tensions around public-sector management increased in Labour's second term with the encouragement of contracting-out of services from local government and the marketization of health provision (in particular the creation of foundation hospitals). The stage was set for confrontation between unions and government over the 'two-tier workforce' resulting from such changes, as savings usually entailed poorer pay and conditions for contracted-out workers. The three leading unions with public-sector presence made the 'two-tier workforce' a priority in Labour's second term. Across the trade-union movement, the Blair leadership's increasing discourse of public-sector reform led to widespread discontent, expressed in critical resolutions at annual conferences. After 2003, the leaders of the big four unions, which included three large unions involved in the public sector, began to coordinate their activities informally and formally, resulting in successful pressure on the Labour leadership, which culminated in the Warwick agreement of July 2004 (see Chapter 5).[26]

The long and difficult process of national job evaluation programmes meant that the question of mandatory pay audits, which met determined opposition from employer representatives when discussed in the context of the private sector, had already been aired for the public sector and could be accepted more easily:

> Because this whole single status issue was going on in local government ... there was more of an acceptance, or a recognition let's say ... that even then, in the early 2000s, there was a hell of a lot more transparency about employment than there was in the private sector, and the kind of arrangements for maternity leave and that kind of thing were not perfect ... but better ordered, let's put it that way. And there was kind of a sense that the public sector could be the opener-upper, if you like, of the ground which other people then needed to fall in with.[27]

Crucially, public-sector employers supported the idea of mandatory gender pay reviews, the NHS employers body arguing that 'equal pay reviews should form an integral part of all organizations' equality and diversity and pay policies.'[28] The same logic applied across a range of WWC recommendations, where it was felt the public sector either already led the way, or could comfortably accommodate greater scrutiny: time off and facilities for a network of equality representatives, initiatives on quality part-time work and senior role models, training for all line managers on flexibility and diversity, and outreach programmes to introduce girls to non-traditional occupations.

The WWC's recommendations therefore gave a strong steer on public-sector practice: 'We believe that the public sector should lead the way, learn from this report and adopt our recommendations. Public sector employers should carry out equal pay reviews.'[29] The commission's 2006 report proposed the establishment of a ministerial committee, reporting to the Cabinet Office, to monitor reports from public-sector employers on the implementation of equal-pay reviews and other recommended actions.[30] However, despite consensus on the role of the public sector as standard-setter, the

WWC's recommendation on pay reviews was not accepted by government. It was toned down in discussions with the government departments: 'the one about mandatory pay reviews in the public sector was never accepted.'[31] Instead, the government's action plan stated an intention to 'continue to encourage Departments and Agencies to review their pay systems on an annual basis ... and to carry out full equality proofing of their reward systems every three years,'[32] the latter being a condition of pay delegation to civil-service departments. The action plan wrapped the question of setting objectives for actions to address pay disparities into the expectations of the forthcoming PSED.

The Public-Sector Equality Duty

The public-sector equality duty (PSED) introduced in the Equality Act 2010 has the potential to effect transformative change—that is, change that addresses structural causes of inequality, because it challenges all public bodies to ensure the promotion of equality of opportunity, rather than relying on individual litigation to pursue claims of discrimination. This approach is not only proactive but comprehensive, pointing the way towards full mainstreaming of equality into all aspects of delivery of public services.[33] However, its implementation has largely failed to live up to this potential.

Equality checks on policy were practised by government departments by the end of the 1980s. The inter-ministerial committee on women's issues, located in the Cabinet Office, drew up model guidelines in 1998 for departments to 'equal opportunities proof' policies to avoid sex discrimination,[34] but departmental practices 'remained a closely guarded secret', with no coordination across departments and no publication of documents.[35] Following the promotion of gender mainstreaming by the United Nations in the 1990s (particularly the 1995 Beijing conference), its influence peaked in the late 1990s, when the devolution acts were passed. In the case of Northern Ireland, where equality mainstreaming was seen as an instrument for overcoming sectarian discrimination as part of the peace settlement, guidelines (named Policy Appraisal and Fair Treatment or PAFT) were circulated in 1993 to 'ensure that issues of equality and equity inform policymaking and action in all spheres and at all levels of Government activity'.[36] The Belfast (Good Friday) agreement brought equality considerations into the mainstream of political negotiations, moving beyond impact assessments to commitments to proactive attention to social inclusion.[37] As discussed further below, the three devolution acts of 1997–8 embedded equality of opportunity into new constitutional arrangements and democratic processes, with an emphasis on positive duties, although to differing degrees. In theory, these constitutional innovations should have led to policy experimentation and learning across the territory of the UK. In practice, however, mechanisms for learning have been weak and underused, and opportunities for review have focused on negative aspects of mainstreaming duties rather than leading to initiatives to strengthen them.

The gender equality duty (GED) was introduced in 2006, following the race discrimination duty in 2001, and the disability equality duty in 2005. When the WWC was convened in 2004, the GED was being prepared, but 'people were quite uncertain about how it was going to be delivered, and what form it was going to take'.[38] This uncertainty meant that the WWC could make strong recommendations to be included in the statutory duty, with emphasis on the need for pay reporting to form a central part of it, but there was no direct mechanism for recommendations to be taken up. The new gender duty, stated the 2006 report, should go beyond reporting on pay differentials and action taken to address them: it should 'specifically ensure that action is taken on all causes of the gender pay gap including occupational segregation, the impact of family responsibilities and unequal pay'.[39] More generally, the WWC, in its 2006 recommendations, emphasized the need for coordination of policy, including the government's pay policy for the public sector, and for an overarching governmental structure to oversee the implementation of the duty. In the 2005 pre-budget report, the government had announced that all decisions on pay in the public sector would be subject to a new committee reporting directly to the chief secretary to the treasury, to establish a common set of objectives and monitor pay according to these objectives. The aim of this policy move, termed a single 'gateway', was to control wage increases in the public sector. No explicit public-sector pay policy existed in the period 1997–2008, although ministers had called for a 'responsible' approach, and in practice increases fell slightly below those in the private sector.[40] The WWC insisted that the new gateway should be a means of integrating equality objectives into pay policy.

The GED was widely expected to give an impetus to efforts that had been under way in public services for over twenty years but that were under-resourced and weakly institutionalized.[41] It required public bodies to pay 'due regard' to the need to eliminate discrimination on grounds of sex (in line with the Sex Discrimination Act 1975 and the Equal Pay Act 1970).[42] This formulation is intentionally vague: it allows public bodies to determine the means of ensuring equality objectives through consultation with internal and external stakeholders (employees and service users, respectively) through processes of reflexive and responsive deliberation. Reflexive regulation denotes internal discussion and scrutiny, while responsive regulation is based on engagement with external stakeholders.[43] In practice, the means by which reflexive and responsive forms of regulation are practised can be tricky to pin down.

Gender mainstreaming, too, is a contested concept that has proved difficult to implement in a meaningful way. The GED stipulated the use of gender impact assessment tools, which central and local government adopted as an integral part of their practice.[44] They present a dilemma: in rigidly prescriptive forms, they can be overly bureaucratic and divert attention away from the underlying inequalities they are meant to address; in looser forms, they can lose focus and prevent robust monitoring of outcomes. Repeated consultation of internal and external stakeholders can lead to 'engagement fatigue', resulting in disillusionment and a sense of 'going through the motions'.[45] Indeed, when the Equality and Human Rights Commission (EHRC) investigated the implementation of the three equality duties in health authorities and trusts in England, it found little evidence of improved outcomes for the groups covered, and a tendency towards bureaucratic compliance over meaningful action in relation to impact assessments.[46]

When the WWC was reconvened in 2009 to review progress on its recommendations, it warned that 'the proper implementation of the Gender Equality Duty' was crucial to preserve and extend the progress made to date, particularly 'during the economic downturn when budgets are being cut'.[47] One of the commission's biggest concerns in reviewing the 2006 recommendations was 'that in some areas the Government does not have in place clear arrangements, reporting mechanisms or accountability processes, particularly on gender equality issues'.[48] Campaigners hoped that the overarching equality duty enshrined in the Equality Act 2010 would strengthen the existing duties and establish robust monitoring mechanisms. However, the core of the duty remained the same: to have 'due regard' to equality aims, rather than to take steps to achieve them or achieve results.[49] In clarifying the objectives to which public authorities should pay due regard, Section 149 specified the need to 'advance equality of opportunity between people with a protected characteristic and those who do not share it', but the requirement to take steps was limited to the broad formulation of 'meeting the needs of' people with a protected characteristic. In relation to equal pay, the recommendations of the WWC were not taken up. Unlike the 2007 gender equality duty, the Equality Act 2010 did not mention pay equality. It did not include mandatory pay reviews in the public sector, nor did it specify that reporting under the gender equality duty should include full information on pay, occupations, working time, and contract type.[50]

Contrary to the hopes of more robust enforcement, the existing reliance on individual litigation (see Chapter 4) remained in place. As advocates of reflexive and responsive regulation pointed out, effective implementation required a regulatory 'pyramid' in which actions would move up from internal evidence-gathering and scrutiny, through deliberation and monitoring with stakeholders, to enforcement by an external agency (such as the EHRC) with powers to impose deterrent (that is, sufficiently weighty) sanctions, as a back-up if suitable action was not taken.[51] However, the Equality Act 2010 failed to require inclusion of internal and external stakeholders in the reporting process, and kept the enforcement powers of the EHRC, as before, reliant on individual or collective complaints (through judicial review),[52] based on evidence of insufficient engagement with the reporting duties. Altogether this meant over-reliance on voluntary self-regulation and lack of attention to the middle and higher tiers of the enforcement pyramid.

Even with these limitations, the PSED was not fully implemented in England. The Conservative-led coalition government decided in 2011 to retain only two specific duties on public authorities: to publish information demonstrating compliance, and to specify at least one objective under the Act, without any duty to show what steps had been or would be taken to meet the objective.[53] The combination of lack of specificity about actions, wide latitude in interpreting definition of objectives and assessment of outcomes, and weak monitoring of outcomes, means that the English PSED falls short of all the recommendations that had fed into it, even the relatively limited proposals of the Discrimination Law Review (see Chapter 9).

The future of the PSED was thrown even further into question with a government review conducted in 2013, which framed the duty as a set of 'useless bureaucratic practices',[54] echoing Prime Minister David Cameron's 2012 description of equality impact assessments as 'bureaucratic nonsense'.[55] The steering group charged with the review recommended reducing reporting requirements even further and gave explicit guidance to public authorities not to 'gold-plate' their attention to equality objectives.[56] The chair of the EHRC, Professor Onora O'Neill, expressed disappointment with the review and argued that over-bureaucratization of compliance could be resolved with better guidance in a statutory code, rather than dilution of expectations.[57] The discourse of 'gold-plating' risked undermining genuine efforts by some employers to achieve good practice in achieving fair outcomes for their employees.[58]

The PSED has undoubtedly helped many public authorities to address disadvantage facing specific problems, particularly on the grounds of race and ethnicity or disability.[59] Progressive practice has been developed in bodies where a combination of strong leadership and vigorous championing by local equality officers brought equality issues into the mainstream of decision-making.[60] However, in the absence of any statutory code or consistent monitoring, it is not surprising that the few studies of the implementation of the PSED have found a high degree of variation between public authorities, and relatively little sense of good practice being identified and shared.[61]

Public Procurement as a Tool for Equality and Diversity

The use of social-justice clauses in public contracts has a long history in the UK and the USA, and was promoted by international organizations in the late twentieth century. However, after the European Economic Community (EEC) had relaxed its non-discrimination rules to allow preferential contracts on grounds of gender equality, the possibility was not taken up by national governments, although some local authorities in Germany, Netherlands, and the UK did so.[62] In these cases, local councils controlled by left-of-centre parties used local government as a laboratory for equality promotion.

In the New Labour years, local government increasingly adopted social clauses committing contractors and providers to employment of disabled people and long-term unemployed, and the NHS sought to integrate environmental considerations into purchasing decisions, although cost concerns and existing organizational cultures mitigated the impact of such moves.[63] Public procurement conditionality therefore provided a potentially significant tool for those wishing not just to ensure a level playing field between terms and conditions for staff employed in public services and contracted-out services, but also to encourage minimum standards of equality on gender and other grounds. The enactment in 2001 of the public-sector race equality duty renewed this discussion.[64] The Kingsmill review in 2001 raised the question of the use of public contracts to ensure equal terms and conditions for 'contracted-out' workforces.[65]

In the context of the 'litigious background' within the public sector,[66] the WWC found in submissions from employers and in its business round tables that a strong preference existed for policy mechanisms that avoided the risk of litigation, such as the use of procurement clauses. Examples of existing practice were set out in its 2006 report, notably the Greater London Authority's fair employment clause, and the Welsh Assembly's criteria for securing public contracts: 'including practical, measurable demonstrations of commitment to equality in working practices, recruitment policy, equal-opportunity plans and contractual arrangements with others.'[67] The WWC urged that the PSED, still to be enacted, should cover procurement and ensure alignment of procurement practices with a need to ensure proactive decision-making that went beyond anti-discrimination to promote equality of opportunity: 'Public authorities should ensure that their contractors promote gender equality in line with the public sector Gender Duty, and equal pay in line with current legislation. This intention should be flagged up in contract documents to ensure that it is built into contractors' plans and bids.'[68] The GED introduced in the Equality Act 2006 included a provision that, where public authorities entered into a contract with private suppliers of goods or services, the duty encompassed the full range of goods and services covered by the contract, with legal liability resting with the public authority.

In 2009, the Local Government Association and the EHRC found in their research on local authorities that a large majority had equality policies covering procurement, but most policies were developed locally (albeit with reference to external guidelines), and the equality officers interviewed expressed a strong demand for a single guidance document.[69] The study also found that around half of local-authority equality officers felt that procurement practice did not always take account of equality policies. The EHRC therefore recommended the adoption in the Equality Bill of stronger guidance mechanisms.

When it reconvened in 2009, the WWC assigned a leading role to the public sector in the context of recession: 'If we are to support women during the economic downturn and help them come through stronger in a new economy, the public sector needs to lead the way on issues such as procurement, women on boards and in implementing flexible working policies.'[70] Its report welcomed the government's acceptance of its 2006 recommendation on procurement policy but noted a lack of oversight and coordination of practice. In its new recommendation, however, it stopped short of calling for a guidance code, as the EHRC had done, proposing instead a best practice guide to be made available by March 2010 on the Regional Development Agencies network.[71]

The Equality Act 2010 set out public authorities' duty to ensure that all services and goods procured comply with equality objectives, by ensuring that such goods and services are fit for the purposes of users (including where the needs of people with protected characteristics are different from those of other users), and that all groups have equal access to them. The Public Services (Social Value) Act 2012 further required public authorities to consider how the services they propose to procure might improve the social and economic wellbeing of the population concerned.[72] These provisions respond to the idea of responsive regulation, because they encourage public authorities to consult the populations concerned at an early stage, before contracts are issued.

In their analysis of the impact of social value in procurement contracts relating to the 2012 Olympics in London, Hazel Conley and Tessa Wright found that targets for employment of under-represented groups were not enforced, but nevertheless had an impact on organizations supplying construction services, by making them aware of equality and diversity, and by encouraging their engagement with local communities. However, they also observed a relatively weak compliance culture, compared to health and safety compliance, where enforcement bodies and mechanisms are robust and sanctions for non-compliance prohibitive. They recommended adoption of a statutory duty to consult stakeholders, as well as a stronger regulatory framework overall, incorporating more specific duties and monitoring requirements.[73]

Even in Scotland, where the PSED includes a specific duty on public authorities to have due regard as 'to whether award criteria should include considerations to enable it to better perform the equality duty', equality considerations are widely seen, including by potential contractors, as having less importance than other factors such as cost.[74]

Procurement has been demonstrated to be a potentially effective policy instrument: 'It's a fantastic strong tool, money talks.'[75] However, the lack of a coherent framework to ensure consistency and provide monitoring and enforcement, combined with the lack of specific statutory duties to consult relevant stakeholders, has led to a sense that equality objectives, although valuable, can be achieved with little attention to outcomes. This, in turn, can encourage cynicism about processes and the efforts required to move beyond 'tick-box' compliance.

Policy design can mitigate these weaknesses, but it is also important to understand procurement as a process that reflects business practices in an environment where competitive pressures are not only inherent to economic activity but actively encouraged by the budgetary constraints of public-service provision. Market-driven pressures are particularly acute in services that employ a majority of women, often already on low pay and poor working conditions.[76] Taking equality and diversity seriously in public procurement is therefore difficult, but has the potential to make a big difference if it is practised carefully.[77] However, Westminster government practice actively downplays equality objectives: the Procurement Act adopted in 2023[78] makes no reference to equality, which is likely to make it more difficult for public authorities to integrate it into procurement decisions.

Devolution and Public-Sector Equality Duties

Devolution provided an opportunity to 'constitutionalize' the promotion of equality of opportunity, alongside preparations for the Equality Act 2010 and its subsequent enactment.[79] The 1998 Acts creating new constitutional arrangements for Northern Ireland, Scotland, and Wales devolved responsibility for equality (to different degrees, and with powers subsequently transferred in stages) to the new elected assemblies. New equality agencies were created in the devolved territories. Following the adoption of the Equality Act 2010, Scotland and Wales developed distinct approaches to PSEDs, which in several respects go beyond the English provisions and seek to establish a proactive duty that the 2010 Act established in principle but (as discussed in Chapter 9) left largely unfulfilled.[80]

Research found in 2018 that public bodies in Scotland and Wales were more likely than in England to provide publicly available data on people with protected characteristics, and to report publicly on policies and actions undertaken to promote equality of opportunity.[81] Stronger duties therefore appear to result in more robust promotion of equality. However, implementation gaps were also found across all three territories. This section focuses on Wales, as a way of reviewing the questions posed above about policy design and its effectiveness in promoting equality.

Thanks to women's activism (within and outside the Welsh Labour Party), a commitment to gender equality in both descriptive and substantive terms was included in the party's campaign documents and made its way into the discussion documents that prepared the basis for devolution. Consequently, the Welsh devolution settlement was exceptional in including a formal objective to ensure that the Assembly should in its work pay 'due regard to the principle that there should be equality of opportunity for all people'.[82] This broad framing of a socio-economic duty led to the adoption in 2015 of the Future Generations Act,[83] which placed equality within a set of principles for sustainable economic and social development. In a deliberative process involving widespread consultation, forty-six indicators of national progress were drawn up, including a reduction in the gender pay gap (national indicator 17) alongside indicators of job satisfaction.[84]

However, this radical approach to equality has been fraught with difficulty from the start, not least because equality is a reserved area, meaning that all primary legislation rests with the Westminster parliament. Nevertheless, within the limits of its powers, the Welsh parliament and the government were able to adopt significant innovations. The devolved parliament has the authority to adopt secondary legislation—for example, in implementing the Equality Act 2010. Following the Equality Act 2010, Wales adopted a more robust PSED than England, giving ministers responsibility for reporting every four years on compliance. Devolved public authorities have a duty to set strategic equality objectives, undertake equality impact assessments, provide employment information, and monitor equality impacts of procurement. The EHRC found evidence that the Welsh duty raised awareness of equality and diversity, encouraged the publication of measurable equality objectives and policies to support them, and strengthened the resources of local equality and diversity champions.[85]

In 2011, the Welsh government took the opportunity presented in the Equality Act 2010 to require public bodies with 150 or more employees to report pay differences amongst all protected characteristics. The new Welsh reporting duty followed a government-backed campaign ('Close the gap'), launched in 2001, based on the Welsh Assembly's partnership work with trade unions and equality campaign groups. The Assembly's proactive approach to gender equality resulted from the work of female 'equality champions' within the newly created parliament.[86] Recognizing that the Single Status and Agenda for Change initiatives had promoted equal pay in the public sector, but resolved gender disparities only partially, 'Close the gap' provided resources to local negotiators to encourage local authorities to settle all outstanding equal-pay claims by 2007.[87]

Under the employer reporting duty, public authorities must report on pay differences by job grade but also by working pattern and contracted hours.[88] As well as taking a more comprehensive approach to reporting than the British gender pay gap reporting requirements introduced in 2017 (applicable to all organizations with 250 or more employees in England, Scotland, and Wales), the Welsh reporting duty requires an action plan to address any disparities found in the data, to be updated in line with annual reports.

However, ten years after the adoption of the reporting duty, Alison Parken (an academic equal-pay expert who had contributed to the development of Welsh gender equality policy) argued that it required renewal; it was 'not clearly drafted, obfuscating its unique aim—to address the gendered labour market inequalities that create gender pay gaps (occupational, contract and working pattern segregation and segmentation)'.[89] In addition, Parken stated, the Welsh reporting duty was undermined by the weaker form of reporting mandated in Britain.

The Welsh government also decided to adopt social-justice clauses in public procurement. Initially it did so through a voluntary code, with responsibility for scrutiny lying with service providers.[90] A new bill, adopted in 2023, was presented by the Minister for Social Partnership and requires public contractors to ensure that 'socially responsible outcomes are pursued through supply chains' and that consultation with trade unions takes place.[91] The use of public procurement as a tool for social justice was widely welcomed by campaign groups, although the EHRC pointed out that the definition of 'fair work' in the bill is broad and argued that it should be refined to refer to protected characteristics. It drew attention to problems faced by low-paid workers, many of them women, who often do not benefit from trade-union presence and coverage by collective bargaining. In recognition of the problems faced by many young people with protected characteristics (especially young women and disabled people) since the Covid-19 pandemic, the EHRC identified a further need to refer specifically to apprenticeships and collect and report on disaggregated monitoring data. The EHRC also urged the Welsh government to ensure that monitoring and enforcement will be carried out rigorously and integrated into the requirements of the general public-sector equality duty.[92] Echoing the EHRC's response, Chwarae Teg (the leading Welsh charity promoting women in the workplace) highlighted the need to align new public procurement requirements with existing equality protections and processes, in particular the PSED.

Equality campaigners' response to Welsh procurement policy highlights the risks as well as the opportunities in the shift away from a focus on equality for disadvantaged groups to a broader concern with 'fairness', seen also in the Scottish Fair Work Convention, adopted in 2015. By linking fairness with socio-economic status, the approach allows for a locally contextualized understanding of social disadvantage, including on multiple grounds, and it opens the possibility of more transparent processes through involvement of social partners. At the same time, the Scottish and Welsh policy frameworks based on 'fairness' are vague on the barriers to opportunity that exist for particular minoritized groups, and fail to establish mechanisms for dealing with them.[93]

Overall, the Welsh experience indicates both the potential for innovation and the weaknesses in implementation that limit this potential in practice. A tension exists between consistent reporting and monitoring, on the one hand, and a desire to tailor data collection and objective-setting to local organizations, which can lead to lack of confusion and disengagement. A focus on process compliance can obscure the wider objectives and result in stunted ambition.[94] The implementation gap may also reflect the place of equality objectives in the hierarchy of political priorities, particularly in difficult times such as the Covid-19 pandemic, but more broadly in the context of the dominant neoliberal economic paradigm.[95] The extent of dependence on public services in a relatively weak economy also puts a high degree of budgetary pressure on authorities, particularly as funding depends on the Westminster parliament and British government, and EU funding has disappeared.[96] At the very least, however, the constitutionalization of equality of opportunity in Wales provides a space for networked civil-society actors to continue to push for transformative change.

Conclusion

The public sector occupies a special place in the regulatory space governing gender equality, relating to its dual role as an employer of women and as a provider of services (again, disproportionately to women). Coupled with the relative ease of regulatory adoption and implementation, compared to the private sector, this situation led to the adoption of potentially transformative equality duties in the Labour period of government. However, as outlined in this chapter, the transformative potential of statutory duties has not been realized.

Two sets of reasons have been put forward in this chapter. The first relates to policy design. Adopted late in the Labour period and subject to a series of political trade-offs in its passage through parliament, the Equality Act 2010 marked a shift towards more proactive and comprehensive duties, but translated the template set out by human-rights lawyers (see Chapter 9) only partially. The duty to pay 'due regard' to the impact of service provision meant that it would be possible to fulfil objectives without demonstrating outcomes. The opportunity to enact responsive regulation was not taken up, as the duty did not specify consultation with internal or external stakeholders. The Act paid little attention to mechanisms for coordination, monitoring, or oversight. As discussed in Chapter 9, the enforcement agency responsible for overseeing compliance and promoting equality was under-resourced and ill-equipped to deal with the scale of the task.

Relatively weak enforcement not only encourages a sense that the legislation can be easily bypassed, as former Minister for Women and Equalities Meg Munn acknowledged:

> The equality duty doesn't really work. It's supposed to be enforceable, but yet we've had budget after budget which has been disadvantageous to women. Yes, you've got the Women's Budget Group who are raising it constantly, but there's no enforcement mechanism, so you can question it, but. . . . And if you've got civil servants and people in local authorities who are committed to these things, then it makes a difference, but . . . it's not enforceable.[97]

The relative weakness of the duty exposed it to criticism from the Conservative Party, which never supported positive duties. Consequently, the duty was diluted further after 2010, and there has been a lack of leadership from central government: the parliamentary Women and Equalities select committee has repeatedly criticized successive governments for failing to publish equality statements and impact assessments.

The second set of reasons relates to the way in which gender equality is viewed within the British policy context, and its relative place in the policy hierarchy. Attention to equality requires more than the publication of disaggregated data, although numbers draw attention to disparities. Gender analysis procedures need to 'provide scope for putting into question strategic policy goals and for attending to the ways in which policy produces gender'.[98] This broader point relates to the public sector both as employer and as provider of services.

Action to tackle gender pay inequality in public-sector occupations requires attention to wage determination systems and to the undervaluation of female-dominated work.[99] Job evaluation in the public sector started a process of challenging both, but went only so far, because it could not address public-sector budgets, which since 2010 have resulted in lower wage progression than the private sector[100] and the deterioration of service provision. With women bearing the brunt of austerity after 2010,[101] the public sector has struggled to maintain its role in setting the standard for equality of opportunity, and the progress of previous decades appears to be under threat, particularly in health and education.

Notes

1. *The Stephen Lawrence Inquiry: Report of an Inquiry by Sir William McPherson of Cluny*, Cm 4262-I (HMSO, 1999).
2. See B. Bagilhole, *Understanding Equal Opportunity and Diversity: The Social Differentiations* (Bristol: Policy Press, 2009); H. Conley, 'Gender Equality in the UK Public Sector: Is Reflexive Legislation the Way Forward?', in I. Jungwirth and C. Bauschke-Urban (eds), *Gender and Diversity Studies: European Perspectives* (Opladen: Barbara Budrich, 2019), 71–87; G. Healy, H. Bradley, and C. Forson, 'Intersectional Sensibilities in Analysing Inequality Regimes in Public Sector Organizations', *Gender Work and Organization*, 18 (2011), https://doi.org/10.1111/j.1468-0432.2011.00557.x; E. McLaughlin, 'From Negative to Positive Equality Duties: The Development and Constitutionalisation of Equality Provisions in the UK', *Social Policy and Politics* (2007), https://doi.org/10.1017/S147474640600337X.
3. Office for National Statistics (ONS), *Who works in the Public Sector?* (London: ONS, 2019).

4. D. Kingsmill, *Review of Women's Employment and Pay* (London: DTI, 2002), 43.
5. Trades Union Congress, *Women's Pay and Employment Update: A Public/Private Sector Comparison. Report for Women's Conference, 2012* (TUC, 2012), 5.
6. I would like to thank Dame Stella Manzie for highlighting this point: personal communication, 13 June 2023.
7. C. Thornley, 'Unequal and Low Pay in the Public Sector', *Industrial Relations Journal*, 37 (2006), 344–58. See also C. Thornley and D. Coffey, 'Model Employment? The Challenges Ahead for Public Sector Employers and Trade Unions in Tackling the Gender Pay Gap', in T. Wright and H. Conley (eds), *The Gower Handbook of Discrimination at Work* (London: Routledge, 2016), 59–68.
8. Organization for Economic Cooperation and Development, *Government at a Glance 2017* (Geneva: OECD, 2017), 97.
9. Kingsmill, *Review*, 50.
10. ONS dataset, Earnings and Hours Worked: Public and Private Sector, ASHE Table 13, https://www.ons.gov.uk/employmentandlabourmarket/peopleinwork/earningsandworkinghours/datasets/publicandprivatesectorashetable13 (accessed 16 March 2021).
11. ONS, Gender Pay Gap, https://www.ons.gov.uk/employmentandlabourmarket/peopleinwork/earningsandworkinghours/datasets/annualsurveyofhoursandearningsashegenderpaygaptables (accessed 16 March 2021).
12. See, e.g., P. Kahn, 'Gender and Employment Restructuring in British National Health Service Manual Work', *Gender, Work & Organization* (2002), https://doi.org/10.1111/1468-0432.00083; G. Kirton and C. Guillaume, 'When Welfare Professionals Encounter Restructuring and Privatisation: The Inside Story of the Probation Service of England \nd Wales', *Work, Employment and Society* (2019), https://doi.org/10.1177/0950017019855229.
13. J. Rubery, 'Public Sector Adjustment and the Threat to Gender Equality', in D. Vaughan-Whitehead (ed.), *Public Sector Shock: The Impact of Policy Retrenchment in Europe* (Cheltenham: Edward Elgar, 2013), 43–83.
14. J. Cribb, C. Emerson, and L. Sibieta, *Public Sector Pay in the UK*, IFS Report R97 (London: Institute for Fiscal Studies, 2011). A two-year pay freeze was announced in November 2010, followed by a below-inflation cap of 1% for 2013–17; although the cap was lifted in 2018, increases remained below inflation, as pay review bodies were instructed to keep pay recommendations within 'reasonable' limits: see P. Bione and B. Francis-Devine, *Public Sector Pay*, House of Commons Library Briefing no. 8037 (London: HM Parliament, 2022).
15. M. Jones and E. Kaya, *Understanding the Gender Pay Gap within the UK Public Sector* (London: Office of Manpower Economics, 2019).
16. Healy et al., 'Intersectional Sensibilities in Analysing Inequality Regimes in Public Sector Organizations'.
17. B. Hepple, M. Coussey, and T. Choudhury, *Equality: A New Framework: Report of the Independent Review of the Enforcement of UK Anti-Discrimination Legislation* (London: Bloomsbury Press, 2000), 98.
18. S. Deakin, S. F. Butlin, C. McLaughlin, and A. Polanska, 'Are Litigation and Collective Bargaining Complements or Substitutes for Achieving Gender Equality? A Study of the British Equal Pay Act', *Cambridge Journal of Economics*, 39 (2015), 381–403, at 385.

19. Deakin et al., 'Are Litigation and Collective Bargaining Complements or Substitutes for Achieving Gender Equality?'.
20. See C. Guillaume, 'Understanding the Variations of Unions' Litigation Strategies to Promote Equal Pay: Reflections on the British Case', *Cambridge Journal of Economics*, 39 (2015), 363–79.
21. C. Laughlin, 'Equal Pay, Litigation and Reflexive Regulation: The Case of the UK Local Authority Sector', *Industrial Law Journal*, 43 (2014), 1–28, at 10.
22. See A. Wright, '"Modernising" away Gender Pay Inequality? Some Evidence from the Local Government Sector on Using Job Evaluation', *Employee Relations*, 33 (2011), 159–78.
23. L. Oliver, M. Stuart, and J. Tomlinson, 'Equal Pay Bargaining in the UK Local Government Sector', *Journal of Industrial Relations*, 56 (2014), 228–45, at 237.
24. Interview, Stella Manzie.
25. See J. Buchan and D. Evans, 'Assessing the Impact of a New Health Sector Pay System upon NHS Staff in England', *Human Resources for Health*, 6 (2008), 1–12.
26. See A. Brady, *Unions and Employment in a Market Economy* (London: Routledge, 2019); L. Minkin, *The Blair Supremacy* (Manchester: Manchester University Press, 2014).
27. Interview, Manzie.
28. WWC, *Shaping a Fairer Future: Executive Summary* (London: Government Equalities Office, 2006), 92.
29. WWC, *Shaping a Fairer Future*, 3.
30. WWC, *Shaping a Fairer Future*, 9.
31. Interview, Matilda Quiney.
32. Department for Communities and Local Government, Government Action Plan Implementing the Women and Work Commission Recommendations (London: DCLG, 2006), p.26.
33. H. Conley and M. Page, *Gender Equality in Public Services: Chasing the Dream* (London: Routledge, 2014), 1–2; B. Hepple, 'The New Single Equality Act in Britain', *Equal Rights Review*, 5 (2010), 11–24, at 18.
34. C. McCrudden, 'Mainstreaming Equality in the Governance of Northern Ireland', *Fordham International Law Journal*, 22 (1998), 1696–73, at 1711.
35. T. Gallagher, B. Osborne, and B. Cormack, 'The Operation of Policy Appraisal and Fair Treatment in Northern Ireland', Briefing Paper (University of Ulster, 1996), cited by J. Gregory, 'Revisiting the Sex Equality Laws', in S. Walby (ed.), *New Agendas for Women* (London: Palgrave Macmillan, 1999), 98–118.
36. McCrudden, 'Mainstreaming Equality', 1712.
37. McCrudden, 'Mainstreaming Equality', 1733–5.
38. Interview, Manzie.
39. WWC, *Shaping a Fairer Future*, 92.
40. D. Ferguson and B. Francis-Devine, *Public Sector Pay*, House of Commons Briefing Paper no. CBP8037 (10 March 2021), 15–17.
41. H. Conley and M. Page, 'The Gender Equality Duty in Local Government: The Prospects for Integration', *Industrial Law Journal* (2010), https://doi.org/10.1093/indlaw/dwq017, p. 322.
42. Equality Act 2006.

43. S. Fredman, 'The Public Sector Equality Duty', *Industrial Law Journal* (2011), https://doi.org/10.1093/indlaw/dwr019; Hepple, 'The new single equality act in Britain'. See also M. A. Stephenson, 'Mainstreaming Equality in an Age of Austerity: What Impact has the Public Sector Equality Duty Had on Work to Promote Gender Equality by English Local Authorities?', Ph.D. thesis (University of Warwick, 2016).
44. Conley and Page, 'The Gender Equality Duty in Local Government', 324.
45. See M. Daly, 'Gender Mainstreaming in Theory and Practice', *Social Politics* (2005), https://doi.org/10.1093/sp/jxi023; T. Rees, 'Reflections on the Uneven Development of Gender Mainstreaming in Europe', *International Feminist Journal of Politics* (2005), https://doi.org/10.1080/14616740500284532; J. Squires, 'Is Mainstreaming Transformative? Theorising Mainstreaming in the Context of Diversity and Deliberation', *Social Politics* (2005), https://doi.org/10.1093/sp/jxi020.
46. EHRC, *The Performance of the Health Sector in Meeting the Public Sector Equality Duties: Moving towards Effective Equality Outcomes* (London: ESRC, 2011). Cited by Fredman, 'The Public Sector Equality Duty', 407.
47. WWC, *Review*, 40.
48. WWC, *Review*, 41.
49. Fredman, 'The Public Sector Equality Duty', 411–12.
50. Fredman, 'The Public Sector Equality Duty', 417.
51. B. Hepple, 'Enforcing Equality Law: Two Steps Forward and Two Steps Backwards for Reflexive Regulation', *Industrial Law Journal* (2011), https://doi10.1093/indlaw/dwr020.
52. See H. Conley, 'Using Equality to Challenge Austerity: New Actors, Old Problems', *Work, Employment & Society* (2012), https://doi.org/10.1177/0950017011432906.
53. Hepple, 'Enforcing Equality Law'.
54. GEO, *Review of the Public Sector Equality Duty by the Independent Steering Group* (London: GEO, 2013), 6.
55. D. Pyper, *The Public Sector Equality Duty and Equality Impact Assessments*, House of Commons Library Briefing Paper no. 06591 (London: HM Parliament, 2020), 23.
56. GEO, *Review of the Public Sector Equality Duty*, 16.
57. Cited by Pyper, *The Public Sector Equality Duty and Equality Impact Assessments*, 21.
58. See T. Wright and H. Conley, 'It Is Better to "Gold-Plate" Equality Law than Protect Institutional Prejudice', *Guardian*, 16 September 2013.
59. See EHRC, 'Public Sector Equality Duty Case Studies' (updated October 2020), https://www.equalityhumanrights.com/en/advice-and-guidance/public-sector-equality-duty-case-studies (accessed 24 March 2023).
60. H. Conley and M. Page, 'Revisiting Jewson and Mason: The Politics of Gender Equality in UK Local Government in a Cold Climate', *Gender, Work & Organization* (2017), https://doi.org/10.1111/gwao.12135. See also Stephenson, 'Mainstreaming Equality in an Age of Austerity'.
61. See H. Conley and S. Warren, *A Review of Action Plans Developed by Public Authorities in Relation to their Statutory Equality and Good Relations Duties* (Equality Commission for Northern Ireland, 2017).
62. See C. McCrudden, 'Using Public Procurement to Achieve Social Outcomes', *Natural Resources Forum*, 28 (2004), 257–67.
63. H. Walker and S. Brammer, 'Sustainable Procurement in the United Kingdom Public Sector', *Supply Chain Management*, 14 (2009), 127–38.

64. T. Wright and H. Conley, 'Advancing Gender Equality in the Construction Sector through Public Procurement: Making Effective Use of Responsive Regulation', *Economic and Industrial Democracy* (2020), https://doi.org/10.1177/0143831X17745979.
65. Kingsmill, *Review*, 58.
66. Thornley, 'Unequal and Low Pay in the Public Sector', 354.
67. WWC, *Shaping a Fairer Future*, 94.
68. WWC, *Shaping a Fairer Future*, 95.
69. EHRC, *Equalities and Procurement Research: Summary* (London: EHRC/LGA, 2009).
70. WWC, *Review of Progress*, 37.
71. WWC, *Review of Progress*, 40.
72. EHRC, *Buying Better Outcomes: Mainstreaming Equality Considerations in Procurement: A Guide for Public Authorities in England* (EHRC, 2022), 8–9. See also T. Wright, 'Can "Social Value" Requirements on Public Authorities Be Used in Procurement to Increase Women's Participation in the Construction Industry?', *Public Money & Management* (2015), https://doi.org/10.1080/09540962.2015.1007708.
73. Wright and Conley, 'Advancing Gender Equality in the Construction Sector through Public Procurement'.
74. E. K. Sarter and E. Thomson, 'Fulfilling its Promise? Strategic Public Procurement and the Impact of Equality Considerations on Employers' Behaviour in Scotland', *Public Money & Management* (2020), https://doi.org/10.1080/09540962.2019.1684615.
75. Interview, Veale.
76. See E. Herman, J. Rubery, and G. Hebson, 'A Case of Employers Never Letting a Good Crisis Go to Waste? An Investigation of how Work Becomes Even More Precarious for Hourly Paid Workers under Covid', *Industrial Relations Journal* (2021), https://doi.org/10.1111/irj.12344; J. Rubery, D. Grimshaw, G. Hebson, and S. M. Ugarte, 'It's All about Time: Time as Contested Terrain in the Management and Experience of Domicilary Care Work in England', *Human Resource Management* (2015), https://doi.org/10.1002/hrm.21685.
77. E. K. Sarter, 'Marketization, Regulation, and Equality: Towards an Analytical Framework for Understanding the Equality Impact of Public Procurement', *Social Politics* (2022), https://doi.org/10.1093/sp/jxac034.
78. Procurement Act 2023 C54.
79. McLaughlin, 'From Negative to Positive Equality Duties'.
80. Northern Ireland already had in place specific protections against discrimination, although it has proved difficult in practice to build on this legacy: see P. Devine, G. Kelly, and M. McAuley, 'Equality and Diversity in the UK: A Story in Three Acts and a Sequel', *Social Policy and Society* (2021), https://doi.org/1017/S1474746421000191.
81. M. Kotecha, J. Bury, J. Lakey, and M. Barnard, *Reviewing the Aims and Effectiveness of the Public Sector Equality Duty (PSED)*, Research Report 116 (Manchester: EHRC, 2018).
82. P. Chaney, 'The Post-Devolution Equality Agenda: The Case of the Welsh Assembly's Statutory Duty to Promote Equality of Opportunity', *Policy and Politics* (2004), https://doi.org/10.1332/030557304772860058, p.66.
83. Well-Being of Future Generations Act 2015 (anaw 2) (London: HMSO, 2015).
84. R. Jones, 'Governing the Future and the Search for Spatial Justice: Wales's Well-Being of Future Generations Act', *Fennia: International Journal of Geography* (2019), https://doi.org/10.11143/fennia.77781, p. 15.

85. M. Mitchell, K. Beninger, N. Rahim, and G. Morrell, *Review of the Public Sector Equality Duty (PSED) in Wales* (Cardiff: EHRC Wales, 2014).
86. P. Chaney, 'Critical Mass, Deliberation and the Substantive Representation of Women: Evidence from the UK's Devolution Programme', *Political Studies* (2006), https://doi.org/10.1111/j.1467-9248.2006.00633.x.
87. P. Chaney, *A Preliminary Evaluation of the Close the Gap Campaign in Wales* (Cardiff: Welsh Assembly/EHRC Wales/TUC Wales, 2003). See also P. Chaney, *Equal Opportunities and Human Rights: The First Decade of Revolution* (Manchester: EHRC, 2009).
88. A. Parken, *The WAVE Employer Case Studies: From Evidence to Action on Gender Pay Gaps: Project Overview Report for the Women Adding Value to the Economy (WAVE) programme* (Cardiff University, 2015). See also A. Parken and R. Ashworth, 'From Evidence to Action: Applying Gender Mainstreaming to Pay Gaps in the Welsh Public Sector', *Gender, Work & Organization* (2018), https://doi.org/10.1111/gwao.12239.
89. A. Parken, *Addressing Pay Inequalities in Wales: Past, Present and Future* (Cardiff Business School, 2022), 4.
90. Chaney, 'The Post-Devolution Equality Agenda', 71.
91. Social Partnership and Public Procurement (Wales) Act 2023 asc1.
92. EHRC, Consultation Response, General Principles of the Social Partnership and Procurement (Wales) Bill (response 7 July 2022).
93. See J. Mamode, 'From Good Work to Fair Work: How Scotland and Wales May Be Leading the Way in Equality', blog for Buying Social Justice, 30 March 2023, https://buyingsocialjustice.org.uk/blog-items/from-good-work-to-fair-work-how-scotland-and-wales-may-be-leading-the-way-in-equality/ (accessed 14 July 2023).
94. A. Parken, *Improving Well-Being and Equality Outcomes: Aligning Processes, Supporting Implementation and Creating New Opportunities: Report of the Well-Being and Equality Working Group* (Cardiff, 2019), https://chwaraeteg.com/news/wales-equality-and-well-being-duties-working-together/ (accessed 12 April 2022).
95. See D. Evans, K. Smith, and H. Williams (eds), *The Welsh Way: Essays on Neoliberalism and Devolution* (Cardigan: Parthan, 2021).
96. A. Parken, *Equality and Devolution in Wales: A Distinct Approach?* (Cardiff Business School, 2022), 11.
97. Interview, Munn.
98. C. Bacchi, 'Gender*ing* Impact Assessment: Can It Be Done?', in C. Bacchi and J. Eveline (eds), *Mainstreaming Politics: Gendering Practices and Feminist Theory* (Adelaide: University of Adelaide Press, 2010), 17–38, at 21.
99. J. Eveline and P. Todd, 'Gender Mainstreaming: The Answer to the Gender Pay Gap?', in Bacchi and Eveline, *Mainstreaming Politics*, 163–90.
100. D. Fitzpatrick and D. Richards, 'The Civil Service's Gender Diversity Agenda under the Coalition: Where Have the Critical Actors Gone?' *British Politics*, 14 (2019), 198–222; P. Murphy, D. Blackaby, N. O'Leary, and A. Staneva, 'Understanding what has been Happening to the Public Sector Pay Premium in Great Britain: A Distributional Approach Based on the Labour Force Survey', *British Journal of Industrial Relations*, 58 (2020), 273–300.
101. A. Rafferty, 'Gender Equality and the Impact of Austerity and Recession in the UK', *Revue de l'OFCE*, 133 (2014), 335–61.

14
Conclusion

Introduction

Women's participation in the labour market is in many ways a remarkable success story, and yet it has long constituted a political problem. Policy on women and employment is a complex problem, and one requiring action at multiple levels. But it is not a 'wicked' problem, usually defined as one that appears ill-structured or boundaryless, where demands are potentially limitless, and where it is difficult to see a clear role for the state.[1] Moreover, policy on women and employment is informed by over thirty decades of reliable statistical and qualitative analysis identifying causes of gender disparities, and evidence from work organizations, employer organizations, and human-resource professional associations on the efficacy of interventions in workplace settings.

Understanding why actions to address women's position in the labour market are still on the policy agenda is therefore important, and it requires deep analysis of policy definition, design, and implementation. How women and employment have been defined and addressed in public policy, in the British context, has been the theme of this book. By 'how', I mean not just the substantive content of policy, but also what this content revealed and what it left aside, and who set the agenda. The 'how' question also related to the mechanisms by which policy addressed the problem of women in employment—that is, how policy was formulated and implemented, and which instruments were chosen to effect the desired outcome.

From the late nineteenth century, women demanded equality of pay and conditions with men, but paid employment was largely conceived of as a male preserve. Thus, although women were employed in growing numbers as first industrial then administrative–clerical and other occupations expanded, they were treated as a marginal or reserve workforce. The two major wars of the twentieth century saw women directly replace men, but on a temporary basis only. This dual labour market, segregated on sex grounds, left a cultural and institutional legacy that dominated later discussions on equal pay and is still seen in the distinctive use of female part-time labour in the UK. It has also left

Women and Employment in Public Policy. Susan Milner, Oxford University Press. © Susan Milner (2024).
DOI: 10.1093/9780191987359.003.0014

a lasting impact on social policy, which still frames care as a predominantly female activity, whether paid or unpaid.

Two high-level bodies of inquiry were convened at the end of each of the two major twentieth-century wars, in response to women's demands for equal pay and conditions. These bodies constituted a focal point for women's rights activists, but they examined the question of equal pay in conservative terms, both socioculturally (in their concern for possible negative effects of maternal employment and for male breadwinning identity) and financially, as the Treasury's aim to limit the costs of equal pay was written into the terms of reference).[2] The policy problem was thus defined as both unaffordable[3] and difficult, owing to a perceived clash between men's and women's economic interests and incongruence with traditional gender roles.

Pressure from the European Economic Community (EEC) and the International Labour Organization (ILO) made policy change inevitable, but it was initially resisted under a Labour government, owing both to employer opposition and to a habitual adherence to a 'myth of voluntarism', which baked in the employer veto, with the collusion of male-dominated trade unions. Therefore, as discussed in Chapter 4, when equal-pay legislation was finally adopted in 1970, the pragmatic policy design had a strong initial impact but left many aspects of labour-market practice untouched, and the regulatory design contained significant enforcement gaps. Crucially, the gendered dual labour market was left to successive generations of women to challenge through their presence and through their activism. The process of change was long and uneven, and it largely followed the path set by previous policy choices.

Women and Employment in Public Policy: Agenda-Setting in the Labour Years

As discussed in Chapter 2, policy to further women's rights at work is widely (although not exclusively) associated with left-of-centre government. The period of Labour government (1997–2010) provided a favourable context for decisive change in policy, for three main, interrelated reasons. First, during the long years of opposition (1979–97), Labour women had networked inside the party to mobilize for a change in policy direction, focusing on representation in the party, the institutionalization of women's rights in government, and a policy programme covering workplace rights for parents, investment in public childcare provision, and measures to support low-paid workers including the introduction of a national minimum wage. Second, pressure for change came from the outside as Labour ended the British veto on European social and employment policy. This helped to create a 'pincer' movement of external adaptational pressure and domestic activism.[4] Third, change within the party was supported not only by women's increased presence in parliament (due to the measures adopted in opposition, notably all-women shortlists) but also a stronger and denser network of experts and activists in civil society and in the wider policy environment.

In addition, the devolution settlement introduced by Labour in 1998 provided a space for policy innovation, within the limits of devolved powers. As has been discussed in this book, Scottish and Welsh executives introduced measures to expand women-friendly policy on political representation, public-sector equality duties (PSEDs), and childcare. However, while there is evidence of organizational learning within the devolved nations, there has been little UK-wide coordination or attention to mechanisms for policy exchange and learning across the four nations.

Despite their limitations, together these drivers of change kept the policy problem of women and employment alive during the Labour years, by feeding into the process of policy formulation within the party through manifesto commitments in 2001 and in 2005. In this book I have shown how activism within the party, in parliament, in women's MPs' wider networks, and in the wider policy space, particularly in the equality machinery (then the Equal Opportunities Commission (EOC)) at the time of the anniversary of the Equal Pay Act, combined to sustain pressure on party leadership, resulting in the 2001 manifesto commitment to tackle the gender pay gap. The period 2001–5 was one of relative stability and coherence, as well as strong informational and relational (networking) resources, in the women's policy machinery. Nevertheless, the policy agenda remained constrained by leaders' competing priorities, which lay elsewhere, with public-sector management and foreign policy.

Demands for a new 'gender agenda' were strengthened as Labour prepared for its third term and became more dependent on trade unions, while rifts within the party leadership also opened an opportunity for agenda-setting. However, policy in the third term failed to make the substantive advance activists hoped to see, as the struggle to compete with other priorities resumed. The shift to an overarching equalities structure resulted in a new, proactive approach (seen in the public-sector duty and the eventual introduction of a gender pay gap reporting duty), but its adoption late in the Labour administration, in the context of economic downturn, weakened the regulatory impact, and many strengthening mechanisms that had been discussed and promoted in the preparation of the Equality Act 2010 did not make it through parliament.

Still Path Dependency in the Conservative Years?

As traced in this book, policy in the five main areas identified by the 2006 report of the Women and Work Commission (WWC) followed the path set out in the Labour years to varying degrees. Continuity is seen in the area of work–family policy, where the two main initiatives of the Labour period, parental leave and the right to request flexible working, were both extended in 2014, under the Conservative-led coalition government, but policy development subsequently stalled. Promises to extend parental leave and the right to request flexible working featured in both the Conservative and Liberal Democrat manifestos in 2010 and in the coalition agreement signed after the general election. The measures were introduced by ministers in the Liberal Democrat-led Department for Business, Innovation, and Skills, led by the Minister for Small Businesses, Jo Swinson, and closely associated with the Liberal Democrat leader (then deputy prime minister) Nick Clegg. Although they may be attributed to the political compromises of coalition government, they also reflect the modernization of the Conservative Party under David Cameron, which included measures to feminize the parliamentary party.

Yet these extensions of policy remained highly circumscribed. A scheduled review of shared parental leave in 2019 led to no new policy initiatives, despite signs of demand for a stronger policy in civil society and among business groups.[5] The extension of the right to request flexible working received even more high-level support. The 2017 Taylor review of 'modern' working practices recommended moving from a right to request to a right to access flexible working, and a government-sponsored and government-chaired (together with the Chartered Institute for Personnel and Development (CIPD)) task force on flexible working recommended that all jobs should be advertised as flexible from the first day of employment. However, the government response was slow, relying on Labour parliamentary initiative to take forward a proposal to make it easier for individuals to request flexible working.

In areas of redistributive policy, most obviously childcare, provision has failed to keep pace with demand. While elements of policy show continuity and have been extended, such as the provision of free nursery places for certain age groups, expenditure was reined in after 2010, and fell after 2015,[6] leaving the childcare and early-years sector extremely vulnerable. Reliance on the private sector under such conditions means that childcare costs are the highest of all OECD nations, in relation to women's average earnings.[7] Evidence of a stalled revolution is seen first and foremost in this policy area, where the policy reflex of problem definition as unaffordable seems to outweigh other strong drivers of policy change, such as consensus among social actors, including business groups, of the need for state intervention, and evidence of favourable cost–benefit outcomes.

In areas of regulatory policy, the pattern of policy adoption after 2010 is mixed. Regulatory divergence is most clearly seen on PSEDs, where, although the policy was not abandoned, it was substantially weakened and downgraded. Here, it is also possible to identify the clearest difference between England and the devolved nations of Scotland and Wales, where continued policy innovation has taken place.

Continuity, on the other hand, is most obviously seen in the gender pay-gap reporting regulations enacted in 2016. The regulations, which followed a failed attempt at voluntary self-regulation by business, illustrate a wider trend towards experiments in new forms of regulation between statutory and voluntary. Similarly, in relation to women's representation on corporate boards, an intensive type of voluntary target-setting and monitoring (building on an initial report commissioned at the end of the Labour years) was developed by business leaders in response to external pressure[8] and to domestic changes in corporate practice in large multinational organizations.[9] This type of regulation appears suited to a policy context like the UK, where a preference exists for market solutions over state-mandated action, regardless of ideological positioning of governments. As discussed below, it represents an attempt to influence business practice, beyond purely formal compliance, but it remains highly reliant on corporate engagement and may, depending on policy design, be subject to capture or manipulation by employers if they do not perceive either intrinsic benefits or disincentives to inaction.

Attempts to extend and deepen gender pay-gap reporting, or to strengthen equal-pay legislation to make individual claims easier to pursue, subsequently failed: for example, Labour MP Stella Creasy's bill (introduced simultaneously by Baroness Prosser in the House of Lords) to give employees the right to request salary information, and to extend pay reporting to cover ethnicity, fell at second reading in 2021. Labour's draft manifesto published unofficially in May 2023 includes a proposal to enact ethnicity pay-gap reporting, to require larger firms to publish action plans as well as pay gap data, and to allow comparison of men's and women's pay across employers.[10]

Continuity is also seen to some extent in policy relating to representation of women in public life, although again policy is viewed in largely capacity-building terms rather than authoritative action. Since 2019, when the Conservative Party in government moved sharply to the right, policy divergence has been more pronounced, as the Government Equalities Office (GEO) moved into an equalities hub within the Cabinet Office, and successive ministers for women and equalities employed a discourse that sought to deny structural inequalities and contested key aspects of existing equalities legislation.

This summary overview of the last five chapters indicates that path dependency remains strong, but that party positioning matters a great deal for policy relating to women and employment. Policy can be changed not only by programmatic divergence or innovation, but by erosion by loss of funding, in the case of government agencies, civil society organizations, or distributive policies, or erosion by means of discursive divergence and priority-setting.

At the same time, the policy agenda may be reshaped by civil-society pressure and networked lobbying. In the Conservative years, two new items came onto the agenda. The first—sexual harassment in the workplace—was not strictly a new policy measure, as it had been raised in the Equality Act 2010.[11] Section 40 of the Equality Act 2010 places duties on employers not to harass employees or job applicants. Section 109 of the Act placed legal responsibility on employers to 'take all reasonable steps' to avoid sexual harassment by an employee of another employee; however, only two tribunal cases were found to have used this provision when the Act was reviewed in 2013, and it was therefore repealed, on the grounds that Section provided sufficient protection without it.[12] In 2018, following a Court of Appeal ruling that employers could no longer be held liable for third-party harassment,[13] the parliamentary Women and Equalities Committee (WEC) ran an inquiry into sexual harassment at work, and recommended in its report that government should introduce a legal duty on employers to protect their employees from sexual harassment.[14] After a consultation in 2019, government announced in July 2021 its intention to legislate to require employers to take steps to prevent sexual harassment at work.[15] In June 2022, Liberal Democrat MP Wera Hobhouse introduced a private member's bill (with Liberal Democrat peer Baroness Burt leading in the Lords), which the government stated it would support.

However, after the Worker Protection Bill's second reading, Maria Caulfield, the Minister for Women, moved an amendment protecting employers from liability in cases where employees were overheard making remarks on 'political, moral, religious or social' matters. The amendment, which Caulfield justified on grounds of free speech, was seen by campaigners as weakening employees' legal protections.[16]

The second innovation concerns policy on support for women experiencing menopause. Agenda-setting in this case resulted from a combination of attention in women's business networks within government, and pressure from women's organizations, led by the Fawcett Society, and parliament, notably the WEC, within the policy frame established by business groups. It was developed under the Coalition government, in the Department for Work and Pensions, led by the Liberal Democrat Minister of State for Pensions, Steve Webb, and the Conservative Minister of State for Employment, Esther McVey.[17] In 2014, Dr Ros Altman (a pensions expert and campaigner, who had been director general of Saga, a company specializing in financial and leisure products for older people), was appointed as the first Business Champion for Older Workers, followed by Andy Briggs (chief executive of Phoenix Group insurance company) in October 2016.[18] Briggs championed a self-regulation approach by business, calling on employers to sign up to a pledge to recruit more workers aged over 50. As well as working with its own Round Table of employers, the Department for Employment also collaborated closely with Business in the Community on voluntary initiatives to increase retention of older workers.

In 2021, the WEC ran an inquiry into older workers, calling on government in its report to formulate a long-term strategy for workforce recruitment and retention. The WEC's report was highly critical of government and of the Equality and Human Rights Commission for failing to take action against discrimination against older workers. It also drew attention to a lack of flexible working arrangements that would benefit older and younger workers and women.[19] In July 2021, the Minister for Employment asked its employer Round Table to examine menopause and older workers, leading to the publication of an independent report in November 2021. The independent report recommended government action to appoint a menopause employment champion, allow claims of intersectional discrimination under the Equality Act, and promote a series of workplace measures including flexible working and line manager training.[20]

The WEC published a report in July 2022 that echoed the recommendations of the independent report, calling on government to appoint a menopause employment champion, publish model workplace policies, run pilots to test the value of leave for women suffering from menopause symptoms, and establish a consultation on whether to make menopause a protected characteristic under the Equality Act, thus placing a duty on employers to make reasonable adjustments.[21] The government in its response acknowledged the importance of the subject both from the perspective of health policy and on economic grounds: 'Women over the age of 50 represent the fastest-growing segment of the workforce and it is crucial that we, and business, work to retain this talent.'[22] However, it rejected most of the committee's recommendations, on the grounds that men suffering from medical conditions did not receive similar support, but it agreed to appoint a menopause employment champion, to work closely with the Women's Health Ambassador, Dame Lesley Regan. It also agreed to consider drawing up information for women, to be distributed through the National Health Service, and to work through the national health strategy to ensure that training for general practice doctors should include awareness of menopause treatment. In February 2022, the government announced the creation of a Menopause Taskforce to work with the Department of Health, co-chaired by Maria Caulfield (Minister for Women and Minister for Patient Safety and Primary Care) and Labour MP Caroline Harris (chair of the All-Party Parliamentary Group on the Menopause). Rather than establishing a new post of menopause champion, it appointed Regan to this task force.

Feminization of politics matters, but its impact is mediated by the political priorities defined by government. This is particularly true where women form a minority in the parliamentary party. Following the large increase in the number of MPs in 1997, women's parliamentary presence continued to grow slowly but steadily, to reach an all-time high of 223 (or 35 per cent of the total seats in the House of Commons).[23] Unlike the situation for their male counterparts, the majority of women MPs sat on the opposition benches after 2010, as most belonged to the Labour Party.

At the same time, feminization of parliament has led, via the concerns raised by parliamentarians (see Chapter 2), to the creation of new institutions that have both raised the visibility of women's rights and contributed to agenda-setting. In particular, as noted above, the WEC has used its power to hold inquiries to make recommendations for government action. Its recommendations are subject to government decision as to whether to accept them, but reports of parliamentary committees nevertheless constitute authoritative points of reference in public life, which may have a lasting influence beyond the immediate government response.

These observations raise further questions about the relationship between party positioning and structural regulatory choices, or path dependency. They also raise questions about the relationship between policy agenda-setting and formulation, in a context of increased but still circumscribed feminization of representation.

In their 2015 analysis of lack of progress on actions to tackle the gender pay gap, Jill Rubery and Damian Grimshaw suggested that equality was 'unlikely to be achievable while gender inequality and misogyny still pervade public and private life.'[24]

Agenda-Setting: Women Representing Women

In Chapter 2 of this book, I looked at feminist scholarship on the question of the representation of women's interests in public policy. This is really two different questions, but they are related to each other. First, how do women who take on representative functions contribute to policy: do they see themselves as representatives of women's interests, or does this depend on ideology and other factors? Second, where women purposively take on an agenda of women's rights, how do they go about achieving their aims, particularly in contexts where they are likely to be in a minority (in legislatures, and more especially in the core executive)?

Feminist scholarship sees women's agency as a prerequisite for the adoption of women-friendly policy. Women's agency in this context does not necessarily entail top-level representation, but in the absence of the latter it would mean, for example, sufficient pressure on policymakers through civil-society organizations and/or through organized political forums (most obviously, elections) and the wider public space (for example, mainstream and social media).

One of the tensions identified in this book has been between women MPs who identify as feminists and those who do not, particularly in a context where women are in a minority overall. This tension means that women who wish to promote a feminist policy agenda need to find allies across multiple, sometimes competing, dividing lines: it may sometimes mean a focus on status-based measures (aimed at promoting the interests of women as women), allowing cooperation between women across party lines; and at other times it may mean reframing women's rights as family rights, or as class-based rights. Depending on the opportunities available at any given time, networks outside parliament provide further resources for women MPs.

Another thread running through the book has been the creation of a space for feminist agency in the interface between the policy and corporate worlds. Institutionally, this interface has been most visible in employer networks close to the equality and women's policy machineries, in formal initiatives such as task forces, committees, and commissions of inquiry, and less formally in ad hoc policy initiatives. It reflects a twin process of change over three decades, which has had a significant impact on the British regulatory space. First, the corporate world has not only become aware of the need to promote women-friendly policies, such as flexible working arrangements, targets for representation of women, or measures to improve women's health, because of concerns around workforce recruitment and retention; it has also actively championed related policies through voluntary codes, information-gathering, and awareness-raising activities, and sought to set government agendas correspondingly. Second, government has established formal and informal relationships with employers through task forces, round tables, and reference groups, and sought partnerships with these bodies and with individual large employers, particularly those in the finance and information technologies sectors. This policy–business interface has created a space for feminist agency and agenda-setting, as exemplified above in initiatives on older workers and the menopause, but, even where it has resulted in recommendations for legislative action, government in recent years has usually responded with a preference for further voluntary actions such as information-gathering, awareness-raising, and further partnership bodies.

Reflections on Gender Mainstreaming

One of the most challenging concepts referred to in this book is gender mainstreaming. Both words in this term raise important questions and are subject to multiple, contested meanings. The semantic shift from 'women' to 'gender' in public discourse marks, beyond a rejection of essentialism that is fundamental to feminism, an understanding of gender identity as fluid—that is, 'living, unfinished and uncertain processes'.[25] Gendering as a process occurs in and through social relations: in households, in work organizations, and in public policy. The use of the term varies across different contexts, and changes through social processes of claims and counterclaims. Gender is constructed socially, in societies in which men continue to hold power over women, but social constructions can be challenged through public policy, although they are often reproduced in policy.

Mainstreaming (also a process, as the gerund implies) can be used to denote a broad approach that seeks to integrate women's perspectives into everyday policymaking, or as a set of instruments designed to identify, measure, and address the ways in which policies can reshape relations between sexes—that is, to assess not just the impact on men and women, but the impact on gendering of roles and practices. For example, a policy that seeks to remedy gender imbalance in early-years education staff by recruiting more men is likely to result in greater gender inequality unless it recognizes and addresses the root causes of low pay and undervaluation of skills traditionally associated with women.[26]

Advocated by the United Nations (UN) and the European Union (EU), gender mainstreaming has often in practice been implemented in ways that restrict this transformative agenda, leading to a restricted focus on policy outcomes for specific groups, or a focus on instruments such as gender impact assessments or gender budgets as an end in themselves. Keeping in mind the wider awareness of gendering as a process, and of the need for inclusive governance, rather than mainstreaming as 'a piece of machinery',[27] is a difficult process that does not easily fit with long-established practices of government departments and an overriding concern with Treasury spending reduction targets.

In the British (Westminster) context, gender mainstreaming was accepted as part of domestic commitments to the UN, but unevenly understood and implemented, and always politically contested. At times, it appeared to feminist activists to be used by policymakers not to challenge gendered power relations but rather to challenge or downgrade any representation by women of women's demands—in other words, to delegitimize and exclude women's voices. Thus, when the GEO was relocated to the Cabinet Office in 2018, the announcement was welcomed by equality campaigners on the understanding that it would be accompanied by a full-time ministerial post, as the WEC had recommended.[28]

However, the ministerial post continued to be appointed on a part-time basis. Moreover, the Minister for Women and Equalities appointed in 2022, Kemi Badenoch, argued in evidence to the WEC that equalities work within government was conducted not through policy leadership but through the provision of data:

> We have a hub and spoke model, which is a model about providing data. It is not for me to carry out health policy because it is for women. Women are 50% of the population. There is no single Minister who can do everything. What we do is support other Departments that hold the levers, whether it is on women's health, women's employment, women's education, and so on.[29]

As shown in this book, particularly in Chapters 6 and Chapter 13, the often instrumental logic thathas been applied to the use of gender mainstreaming has fuelled a backlash against it, although in Scotland and Wales efforts continue to develop its use. In the absence of a comprehensive strategy for the promotion of equality of opportunity, the policy shift away from a recognition of women's needs as women has generated fears that, as the Fawcett

Society said in evidence to a WEC inquiry on the role of the GEO in 2021, efforts to promote gender and race equality could be sacrificed.[30]

More generally, the mainstreaming of women-friendly policy is seen in initiatives that do not target women workers but have a disproportionately beneficial impact on them. The most obvious example is the introduction of the national minimum wage, which is based on consensus across political parties, and has had a measurable impact on the women's pay at the bottom of the pay scale.[31] The success of the national minimum wage has also increased support at local and national levels for the introduction of the living wage, and it has drawn attention to living standards of the lowest-paid workers. However, more remains to be done, and the wage distribution in the UK continues to widen. Only when the pay of the lowest groups of workers is substantially increased has the gender pay distribution altered, and such uprating has happened unevenly, against a backdrop of long-term growth of low-paid work.[32]

This kind of mainstreaming has disadvantages if the barriers facing women as women are overlooked in policy. This book has shown that feminists' fears of a dilution of women's rights as policy became mainstreamed have been confirmed in some respects. Janet Veitch, cited in Chapter 6, spoke of policy women's rights being '[swept] up along with everything else' in the shift from separate equality strands to an overarching equalities framework.[33] Institutionally, a lesser focus on women's rights can be seen in reduced funding for the equality agency and for women's civil-society organizations, which also has the effect of muting women's voice in the policy process.

In the policy process, particularly at the agenda-setting phase, this book has demonstrated that in the struggle for policy attention it can be difficult for women's rights to compete against other priorities: policy advisers interviewed for this book referred to the problem of limited 'bandwidth', with party leaders focused on 'big' wins in foreign policy or constitutional reform. At times, demands for women's rights have risked being viewed as sectional. Consequently, reframing women's rights as family rights, or as economic advantage (in the form of increased labour power, productivity, and employee engagement), has often been the main way to achieve policy attention. Such process of reframing is a necessary response of social movements to changes in political opportunity structures, but there are inevitably losses and omissions, which usually affect most negatively those women with the least labour-market power, and which often mean that traditionalist views of gender roles are left unchallenged.[34] In these conditions of limited legitimacy, women's voice and women's rights are contingent, and can therefore be particularly vulnerable to attack when authoritarian-right governments come to power. Social-movement theory emphasizes the need for strong civil-society networks to sustain the capacity for agenda-setting voice and resistance to attack.

What Kind of Policy?

This book (see Chapter 3) has drawn on regime theory to show how path dependency occurs, as a result of long-standing preferences for business self-regulation over statutory intervention and for commodification of family policy, resulting in a policy space characterized by weak or male-dominated regulatory institutions. Broadly, regime theory would lead to an expectation of continued preference, albeit mitigated by periods of left-of-centre government, for voluntary rather than statutory policy instruments, and limited support for redistributive policies such as investment in decommodified (publicly provided or subsidized) care. Periods of Labour government have modified but not profoundly disrupted the UK's classification as a liberal welfare state.

Labour governments have grappled with the question of how to achieve social-justice objectives while remaining within the parameters of a liberal welfare state, where benefits are kept at residual levels and incentives remain market based. Moreover, as acknowledged in Chapter 1, Labour in power has faced the legacy of long periods of right-of-centre government that took time to reset. In such conditions, the New Labour period engaged in a sustained way with business organizations to draw them into new regulatory solutions that would have an impact on corporate practice while minimizing the risk of outright opposition or backlash.

This approach was followed by the Department of Trade and Industry (DTI) during the period 2001–5, when it was also the host department for the minister and civil service unit responsible for women and equalities. As George Bain, who, as outlined in Chapter 11, was appointed by the prime minister to chair the Low Pay Commission and later the Work and Parents Task Force, argued at a press conference in November 2001 that good employers needed no incentive to act in employees' best interests, and bad employers would ignore any legislation passed anyway (in which case, the only remedy was individual litigation to remedy the worst abuses). The key to effective intervention was to work cooperatively and persuasively with those employers who lacked awareness but could gradually be induced to change their behaviour. The DTI's 'gentler' approach was intended to stimulate long-term attitudinal change within organizations.[35]

The right to request flexible working, as discussed in Chapter 11, constituted a key example of this approach. As campaigners highlighted at the time of its adoption, an important requirement of such innovative forms of regulation was effective monitoring, to gauge impact and the need for further reform or fine-tuning. However, policy innovation has not always been robustly monitored in the UK, and, when monitoring takes place, it often occurs ad hoc rather than systematically following an established process, although standard cost–benefit impact assessments of legislation are conducted. A lesson from examination of policy on women and employment is that monitoring matters.

In the case of the right to request flexible working, policymakers' concern to reduce administrative burdens on employers meant that the legislation was expressly designed to avoid enforcement by legal means. Subsequent surveys relied on statements by employers about the number and proportion of requests submitted and accepted or refused, with no means of independent verification.

Another example discussed in the book is the frequent use of pilot projects to test initiatives. Pilot projects offer a cost-effective way of verifying the usefulness of regulatory approaches that are likely to be expensive—for example, investment in training or childcare. Evidence-gathering as a basis for policy was emphasized during the New Labour years.[36] However, if pilot projects are not evaluated and lessons (of failure as well as success) fed into policy proposals in a feedback loop, they are likely to be wasteful in themselves and may generate perverse outcomes in the form of low stakeholder engagement or backlash.[37] Moreover, robust evaluation requires the definition of clear criteria for success to be included in the formulation of pilot projects from the outset. Viewed in this light, the two main capacity-building instruments arising from the WWC, sectoral training programmes under Train to Gain and support for organizations to promote 'quality' part-time jobs, were weak instruments, not only because funding allocation had not been earmarked but rather had to be negotiated, but also because they did not specify how evaluation lessons would be fed into future policy. Similarly, missing links in policy evaluation and feedback loops characterize policy development on PSEDs, although experimentation in the devolved nations continues.

Policy experimentation raises questions not just about the process of evaluation and response, but also about how to achieve effective outcomes where the intended outcome depends on influence over social and economic actors. The literature on 'new governance' from the 1990s charted the shifting relationship between state and non-state forms of regulation of business activities. The rationale for 'smarter' forms of regulation is that coercive state regulation needs to be used sparingly, as it is a blunt instrument that fails to take account of differences between businesses and is liable to lead to formal or lip-service compliance, whereas softer forms of regulation, starting with voluntary self-regulation, can more effectively mobilize actors. Smart regulation thus forms a spectrum of regulatory behaviours whereby the state intervenes with more coercive methods only when softer modes fail to achieve objectives.[38]

One aspect of this governance literature that received widespread attention was the idea of an enforcement pyramid: policymakers could gradually increase the coerciveness of instruments to achieve the desired outcome.[39] A strategy of regulatory escalation can be seen in several policy initiatives discussed in this book, most obviously in the case of gender pay-gap reporting. As outlined in this book, the threat of statutory intervention was deployed repeatedly to encourage employers to adopt voluntary pay reviews and action plans, from the Kingsmill review in 2001 to parliamentary discussions on the Equality Act 2010. After it had conspicuously failed to change employer behaviour in 2011, with the poor response to the 2011 voluntary initiative 'Think, Act, Report', statutory action was finally announced in 2015 and adopted in 2017. However, regulatory escalation has rarely been used in the policy area of women and employment.

Failure to use regulatory escalation effectively may be one factor contributing to the sense of a stalled revolution explored in this book. Scholars have also questioned the 'pyramid of enforcement' approach, on the grounds that employer behaviour is not solely motivated by fear of enforcement action.[40] Rather than a linear approach moving up the regulatory pyramid to strengthen compliance, they emphasize the idea of a policy mix in which different types of instrument may be used both experimentally and incrementally. The policy initiatives examined in this book suggest that an approach combining escalation and a responsive policy mix could be used more effectively in the British context.

Finally, policy was marked in the New Labour years by a tension between regulatory action for larger organizations and small firms. As discussed in Chapter 7, the WWC saw different approaches towards regulatory action among business representatives, with small-business representatives seeing managers from larger organizations as 'corporate'. Indeed, this difference appeared larger than that between large private- and public-sector organizations.

The compliance costs of adjustment to new regulation are significantly higher for small businesses, leading regulators to examine ways of reducing the administrative or financial burden, or to prefer a self-regulation approach. In the UK, this concern led to the adoption of a deregulatory approach whereby regulations increasingly became framed in public policy as 'red tape'.[41] It has also been suggested that the British way of dealing with regulatory burdens on small and medium-sized enterprises (SMEs) relies too heavily on SMEs' perceptions of burdens, which can be overestimated and wrongly attributed.

Without ignoring SMEs' legitimate concerns about administrative costs, it is worth asking whether alternative approaches could allow policymakers to support small businesses while at the same time adopting forward-looking regulation that could help to disseminate good practice more widely. Three possible sets of solutions have been put forward by researchers: first, network-building support, since small businesses that are well networked—for example, through sectoral employer associations—find it easier to comply with regulation than others; second, financial support through differential taxation or targeted support; and, third, differential regulatory requirements based on company size.[42] The latter approach is noticeable in the policy experimentation that has marked several European states' approaches to gender pay reporting, and is sometimes combined with a phased approach in which the lessons of regulation of larger companies are fed into a later stage of application of regulations to smaller organizations.[43]

These observations indicate the need for a more thoroughgoing approach both to responsive regulation as a process within the machinery of government, and to the state's relations with socio-economic actors and civil society in the policy process. Longer-term thinking about the machinery of government and regulatory actors has long been difficult in the Westminster system but could in principle be aided by the still-unfolding and as yet poorly coordinated process of devolution. A more systematic approach would not exclude the capacity to experiment but on the contrary could enhance it by increasing the effectiveness of experimentation through stronger feedback loops.

Gender and Institutions: Revisiting the Women and Work Commission

In this book, I started with the deliberations of the WWC as a way of understanding conflicts over the substance of policy and over policy instruments. Within the commission, there was very little disagreement on the causes of the gender pay gap, at least in part because the evidence base was strong. However, differences in direct experience of the gender pay gap as a problem to be addressed at organizational or societal level differed between commissioners. Differences in standpoint in relation to regulatory strategies differed sharply.

Independent commissions are a particular form of deliberative governance, and their mode of operation varies as a result of their status, remit, composition, resources, agreed working methods, and the steering capacity of their chair. In practice, their composition is limited and carefully chosen by government to strike a balance between wide representation and likelihood of being able to reach agreement. The scope of their recommendations is also usually circumscribed at the outset. Nevertheless, commissions can provide a focal point for civil society to seek to influence recommendations for action, and indeed the way policy problems are defined and addressed. This is particularly true for social-policy problems that respond to new or changing social norms that are being considered for the first time—for example, as family responsibilities are brought from the private into the public sphere.

During the New Labour years, the policy space widened, creating new opportunities for the expression of women's organizations' demands through an intentionally pluralist approach to policy formation, partly because of changes in the way Labour leaders sought to manage the party, and partly because of the need to achieve consensus on new areas of policy in a context where traditional modes of tripartite (neocorporatist) deliberation were being reshaped.[44] However, as discussed in this book (Chapter 6), feminists complained early in Labour's first term that their voice was not being heard. The WWC provided an opportunity to amplify women's voice, through the evidence-gathering phase of deliberations and visits to schools and workplaces, and through the media and other public discussions opened by publication of its interim and full reports and the follow-up report.

As discussed in Chapter 6, many women's organizations express concerns that the space available to women's voice has shrunk since 2010. Although the parliamentary space for expression of women's interests has grown, and provides an opportunity for voice through public inquiries, gatekeeping by parliament presents some risks for civil-society organizations, in particular the risk that agenda-setting follows government priorities. Campaign groups have responded to the loss of coordinating mechanisms (such as the Women's National Commission (WNC)) with informal alliances that have proved effective in exploiting opportunities for agenda-setting, such as general elections.

As discussed in Chapter 8, the WWC's recommendations set out a programme for incremental change across several areas, with coordinated oversight by government departments. Lack of top-level leadership meant that the programme of recommendations remained largely unfulfilled, although the commission's influence can still be seen in the areas of policy continuity highlighted above. A substantial policy agenda remains incomplete. A question therefore arises about how best to relaunch policy in women and employment. Based on the analysis presented in this book, I argue that a combination of approaches is needed: stronger labour-market protections for the most vulnerable groups of workers, where women are over-represented; stronger wage-setting mechanisms, such as sectoral wages councils and support for collective bargaining, as well as better enforcement of minimum wages; stronger and more clearly defined duties on providers of public services; and a stronger institutional voice for women in government and in civil society, based on as wide a range of women's voices as possible and the lessons of social-movements activism in the early twenty-first century.

Notes

1. G. Peters, *Policy Problems and Policy Design* (Cheltenham: Edward Elgar, 2018), 63.
2. See K. M. Fraser, *Same or Different: Gender Politics in the Workplace* (London: Routledge, 1999; reissued 2018); P. Scott, 'From "Pin Money" to Careers: Britain's Late Move to Equal Pay, its Consequences, and Broader Implications', *Enterprise & Society* (2023), https://doi.org/10.1017/eso.2022.44.
3. See Peters, *Policy Problems and Policy Design*, 41.
4. This pincer effect has been seen in other European member states where adaptational pressure was applied owing to regulatory gaps: see A. van der Vleuten, *The Price of Gender Equality* (Farnham: Ashgate, 2007).
5. The government consultation that took place in 2019 was shelved.
6. According to the social-expenditure database of the Organization for Economic Cooperation and Development OECD), expenditure rose steadily between 2000 and 2010, then remained stable until 2015, when it decreased. This pattern can be contrasted with expenditure in the UK's close neighbours France and Germany, where it rose significantly after 2010, and now stands at more than double that of the UK in both cases: see https://www.oecd.org/social/expenditure.htm (accessed 5 October 2023).
7. OECD, 'Is Childcare Affordable?', Policy Brief, June 2020.
8. The EU proposed mandatory quotas in 2012: see House of Lords, *Women on Boards*, Fifth Report of Session 2012–13 (House of Lords, 2012).
9. See S. Milner, 'Self-Regulation Comes at a Cost: Closing off Authoritative Policy for Gender Equality on Corporate Boards in the UK', in I. Engeli and A. G. Mazur (eds), *Gender Equality and Policy Implementation in the Corporate World: Making Democracy Work in Business* (Oxford: Oxford University Press, 2022), 59–85.

10. By early 2024, the draft manifesto had still to be published, although the 2023 party conference set out the main items: see K. Neame, 'Revealed: Full Final Policy Platform Set to Shape Next Labour Manifesto', Labour List, 5 October 2023, https://labourlist.org/2023/10/labour-national-policy-forum-final-document-summary-policy-manifesto-party-conference/ (accessed 21 February 2024).
11. Sexual harassment in the workplace was not considered by the WWC, because the existing evidence base had not raised it as a cause of the gender pay gap: decomposition of the gender pay gap does not allow analysis of sexual harassment as a factor of economic disadvantage.
12. *Worker Protection (Amendment of Equality Act 2010) Bill: Explanatory Notes* (House of Lords, 2023).
13. *Unite the Union* v. *Sally Nailard* [2018] EWCA Civ 12-3. This was a Court of Appeal ruling overturning an industrial tribunal judgment in favour of Nailard.
14. House of Commons Women and Equalities Committee, *Sexual Harassment in the Workplace*, Fifth Report of Session 2017–2019, HC 725 (House of Commons, 2018).
15. See Fawcett Society, *Tackling Sexual Harassment in the Workplace: Report on Employer Actions to Prevent and Respond to Workplace Sexual Harassment* (London: Fawcett Society, 2020).
16. J. Godard, *Worker Protection (Amendment of Equality Act 2010) Bill: HL Bill 101 of 2022–2023*, House of Lords Briefing (House of Lords, 2023). The bill was enacted on 26 October 2023 as the Worker Protection (Amendment of Equality Act 2010) Act 2023 Chapter 51.
17. See Department for Work and Pensions, *Fuller Working Lives: A Framework for Action* (London: DWP, 2014).
18. Altman was made Minister for Pensions under the Conservative government in 2015 and made a life peer.
19. WEC, *Older People and Employment*, Fourth Report of Session 2017–2019, HC 359 (London: House of Commons, 2019).
20. 50+ Employer Taskforce, *Menopause and the Workforce: How to Enable Fulfilling Working Lives* (London: Phoenix Group/50+ Employer Taskforce, 2021).
21. WEC, *Menopause and the workplace*, First Report of Session 2022–2023, HC 91 (London: House of Commons, 2022).
22. WEC, *Menopause and the Workplace: Government Response to the Committee's First Report of Session 2022–2023*, HC 1060 (London: House of Commons, 2023), 2.
23. E. Uberoi and Z. Mansfield, *Women in Politics and Public Life*, Research Briefing 01250 (London: House of Commons Library, 2023), 8. This is low in international comparison, with the UK in 48th place among United Nations countries, as discussed in Ch. 2.
24. J. Rubery and D. Grimshaw, 'The 40-Year Pursuit of Equal Pay: A Case of Constantly Moving Goalposts', *Cambridge Journal of Economics*, 39 (2015), 319–43, https://doi.org/10.1093/cje/beu053.
25. J. Eveline and C. Bacchi, 'What Are we Mainstreaming when we Mainstream Gender?', in C. Bacchi and J. Eveline, *Mainstreaming Politics: Gendering Practices and Feminist Theory* (Adelaide: University of Adelaide Press, 2010), 87–110, at 95.
26. See the examples discussed in C. Bacchi and J. Eveline, 'Approaches to Gender Mainstreaming: What's the Problem Represented to Be?', in Bacchi and Eveline, *Mainstreaming Politics*, 111–61.

27. K. Staudt, 'Gender Mainstreaming: Conceptual Links to Institutional Machinery', in S. M. Rai (ed.), *Mainstreaming Gender, Democratizing the State: Institutional Mechanisms for the Advancement of Women* (Manchester: Manchester University Press, 2003), 4–65, at 63.
28. WEC, *Women and Equalities and the Place of GEO in Government*, Second Report of Session 2017–2019, HC356 (London: House of Commons, 2018).
29. Badenoch further upset members of the WEC by saying that she left policy on the menopause to the Department of Health and disputed the idea of leave for women suffering from menopause symptoms; and she left childcare policy to the Treasury and the Department for Education and Employment. Instead, she could use only such 'levers' as were available in her capacity as Secretary of State for Business, Energy, and Industrial Strategy: see WEC, *Oral Evidence: The Work of the Women and Equalities Committee*, HC1068, 1 March 2023.
30. Fawcett Society, 'The Role of the Government Equalities Office (GEO): Embedding Equalities across Government', Written Evidence GEO0032, February 2021.
31. See H. Joshi, A. Bryson, D. Wilkinson, and K. Ward, 'The Gender Gap in Wages over the Lifecourse: Evidence from a British Cohort Born in 1958', *Gender, Work & Organization*, 28 (2020), https://doi.org/10.1111/gwao.12580.
32. Rubery and Grimshaw, 'The 40-Year Pursuit of Equal Pay'.
33. Interview, Janet Veitch.
34. For further discussion, particularly in the context of changed opportunity structures in the devolved nations, see N. Charles and C. A. Davies (eds), *Gender and Social Justice* (Cardiff: University of Wales Press, 2010); N. Charles and F. Mackay, 'Feminist Politics and Framing Contests: Domestic Violence Policy in Scotland and Wales', *Critical Social Policy*, 33 (2013), https://doi.org/10.1177/0261018313483488; K. Grosser and L. McCarthy, 'Imagining New Feminist Futures: How Feminist Social Movements Contest the Neoliberalization of Feminism in an Increasingly Corporate-Dominated World', *Gender, Work & Organization*, 26 (2019), https://doi.org/10.1111/gwao.12267.
35. M. White, 'DTI Backs Flexitime for 3.8m Parents', *Guardian*, 21 November 2001.
36. See, e.g., I. Sanderson, 'Evaluation, Policy Learning and Evidence-Based Policy-Making', *Public Administration*, 80 (2002), https://doi.org/10.1111/1467-9299.00292.
37. B. W. Head, 'Towards More "Evidence-Informed" Policy Making?', *Public Administration Review*, 76 (2015), https://doi.org/10.1111/puar.12475.
38. I. Ayres and J. Braithwaite, *Responsive Regulation: Transcending the Deregulation Debate* (Oxford: Oxford University Press, 1992).
39. J. Braithwaite, 'The Essence of Responsive Regulation', *University of British Columbia Law Review*, 44 (2011), 475–535.
40. See discussions in P. Drahos (ed.), *Regulatory Theory: Foundations and Applications* (Australian National University Press, 2017), especially N. Gunningham and D. Sinclair, 'Smart Regulation', 133–48.
41. F. Chittenden, S. Kauser, and P. Poutziouris, *Regulatory Burdens of small Business: A Literature Review* (Small Business Service Research Directorate, 2002).
42. See O. Mallett, R. Wapshott, and T. Vorley, 'How Do Regulations Affect SMEs? A Review of the Qualitative Evidence and a Research Agenda', *International Journal of Management Reviews*, 21 (2019), https://doi.org/10.1111/ijmr.12191.

43. See A. Veldman, *Pay Transparency in the EU: A Legal Analysis of the Situation in the EU Member States, Iceland, Liechtenstein and Norway* (European Commission, 2017).
44. See S. Milner, 'Gender Equality and Employment Regulation in the New Labour Years, 1997–2010: The Problem of the Gender Pay Gap', *Historical Studies in Industrial Relations*, 43 (2022), https://doi.org/10.3828/hsir.2022.43.5.

Index